THE NEW EXILES

THE NEW EXILES

American War Resisters
in Canada

ROGER NEVILLE WILLIAMS

FOREWORD BY
WILLIAM SLOANE COFFIN, JR.

LIVERIGHT PUBLISHERS
NEW YORK

1.98765432

ISBN: 0-87140-533-4 (cloth)

Library of Congress Catalog Card Number: 78-148662

Manufactured in the United States of America

FOR MY PARENTS, WITH LOVE

Contents

ACKNOWLEDGEMENTS

Thank you Phil Jones for compassionate editing,
  even on Christmas Eve.
Thank you Janice Byers and Cathy Gower
  for patiently typing the damn thing.

Foreword

The author of this book will never appear live on one of those American television shows that promote books. For the American-Canadian border is now closed to him. He is a draft dodger. He is also patriotic because he believes 1. his country should not engage in senseless slaughter and 2. his country is worth saving. So he has written for Americans a heart-warming and heart-rending book. Its essential message is this: As Ezekiel said of ancient Tyre so it can be said of the United States today: "Your heart was proud because of your beauty; you corrupted your wisdom for the sake of your splendor . . . all who know you among the peoples are appalled at you."

So the judgment of history has fallen on America, and the land to which more people came in a century than to any other country is now being deserted by its youth in huge numbers.

But how many will hear this message? There is a basic unacceptability about unpleasant truth, particularly truth of this kind, and particularly to citizens nourished in the belief that the United States is the last best hope of mankind. As one deserter in this book puts it, "Americans are raised in the belief that there is no place else to go."

So while Germans fleeing to America a hundred years ago from Prussian conscription and Prussian wars are considered the most conscientious of escapees, those Americans who today similarly choose exile over war or prison are considered unpatriotic and cowardly. So unacceptable is the unpleasant truth that some excuse must be found. Let the judgment fall on those who flee, not on what is being fled.

But Americans patriotic and courageous enough to read this book will learn a lot. For in talking about themselves these exiles tell us who we are. In words that are brutally honest—and honesty here means a healthy disrespect for respectability—the deserters describe how in Vietnam men "ball chicks" and then shoot them, how truck drivers barrel through villages "making those slant-eyed bastards jump," how children are napalmed, and refugees "enslaved for freedom." They also describe how a destructive military mentality works on American soldiers in training, and particularly, it would seem, on the marines. (Parris Island must be one of the most closed systems in all the world.) Then draft dodgers and deserters alike describe the passive acquiescence, the almost slavish obedience, that saps democratic vitality and makes of America a nation of practicing cowards. (How often is common integrity made to look like courage!) And finally, in words that are truly poignant, these exiles tell us what it means to leave America and what it costs to accept the law.

The reader will not only learn a lot; he will have many profound and painful questions forced upon him. For instance, these men are guilty as charged. They are draft dodgers, they are deserters. And so, for destroying draft files is Father Daniel Berrigan guilty as charged. And so was Jesus. In other words, when times are evil can decent men live decently only as criminals and exiles?

Further, this book forces respect for the fact that these men acted. They reached a decision about themselves and their country. Most Americans have not begun to be that decisive. They are paralysed by the fear of facing truth. So who is more courageous: the deserter or his detractor at home who calls him cowardly?

It is a terrible thing that a book of this type has to be written. It would be more terrible yet if it were not widely read. For as in personal life, so in national life, only the truth can set men free.

I am grateful to Roger Williams and his fellow exiles for being willing to share their experiences with us in the apparent hope that there are a sufficient number of Americans still capable of hearing them. I am glad some exiles still want to return to America. I hope when this war is over we shall have the decency to pass legislation that will allow them their choice. It seems only right, a very small way for a country to make amends to citizens it offered the choice only of becoming killers or criminals.

WILLIAM SLOANE COFFIN, JR.

THE NEW EXILES

More than half the men who died in Vietnam last year were infantrymen and nearly nine out of ten infantrymen were draftees. As long as this war is going on, you're not going to get volunteers for $160 more a month to go over and fight as infantrymen in those jungles.

Senator John Stennis, before the
House Armed Services Committee.

I would hope, myself, that every American of draft age came across the border here, or went to Sweden; then, they wouldn't have anybody to fight their wars.

William Kunstler, at a speech
in Toronto.

I cannot condone a government that lies, that demands my life, and says it is my highest duty to die for the state, or the majority, or for God. I choose to live or give my life in the manner that I see fit, not as the government or the army see fit for their needs, for the needs are not greater than my own need to *live*.

—a deserter.

"Washed ashore, hell!" Yossarian declared, jumping all about also and roaring in laughing exultation at the walls, the ceiling, the chaplain and Major Danby.

"He didn't *wash* ashore in Sweden. He rowed there! He *rowed* there, chaplain, he *rowed* there."

"Rowed there?"

"He *planned* it that way! He went to Sweden deliberately."

Joseph Heller, *Catch 22*

Introduction

The war in Vietnam is now six years old. It is seven years old as the reader reads this, and we may yet see the tenth anniversary of the Gulf of Tonkin incident before the bombing ends and the last combat infantryman is brought home from the shattered country- side of Vietnam. Older still than this long war is the system of enforced conscription, now in its twenty-third year, that *enabled* the United States to become involved in an endless conflict on the mainland of Asia. Undeclared and unpopular wars can never be fought 10,000 miles from a nation's borders without a means of forcing men to go, a system of enslavement whereby young men are forced to serve the state and do its dirty work, and therefore it is an important story—in this case a story as long as this war—when such a war is proved so wrong that for every man who has been forced to give his life in it, another, perhaps two, have refused to bear arms at all or have laid them down. This book is part of that story—about the young men who refused arms and then left the country that had offered them the terrible choice of becoming killers or criminals.

More than an important story, there is a history here. It is

American history made in Canada, where this book was written. It is about men who left the United States five years ago when both they and the war were young, and it is about men who were boys of twelve when the war started who arrived in Canada yesterday. It is a history of many organizations, many active young exiles, and many helpful Canadians that aided and encouraged the exodus of America's first refugees.

The United States of America, once the acceptor of the world's exiles, is now a major producer of them, and this is not altogether pleasant to read about for it reflects tragically not so much on the exiles themselves and whatever hardships they have faced but on the country that made them leave. One hundred thousand young men and women do not choose exile—never to return again—from the Land of the Free, the Last Best Hope on Earth, without very good reasons. Some of those reasons are recorded here.

Hopefully, however, this book is more than a chronicle of an exodus and a catalog of reasons and answers. It is intended as a testament from the living, the people who by some lucky fate were able, in the end, to choose life over killing and death. A testament for America from this generation's war dead would be more fitting, but they are forever silenced, and so we speak in their place as they died in ours.

I was drafted while living in Europe following four and a half years of study in the U.S. and Switzerland and four years of protesting the Vietnam War. As a journalist I had intended to go to Vietnam and write, despite the draft, which I eventually did while under indictment for draft evasions. They never thought to look for me there. In Vietnam I watched young men of my generation come into the field evacuation hospitals wrecked and torn and dead on the Medevac choppers, and I will never forget it. They and the men like them whom I visited in the field had not had the same opportunities I had enjoyed, that most draft resisters enjoyed: understanding parents, moderate affluence, an education, the advantage of being twenty-four and not eighteen or nineteen when the call came and the decision had to be made whether or not to go. In the case of those soldiers who were a little older, college educated, middle-class, they had not, thanks in most cases to unenlightened parents, geographic isolation, and the great American brainwash, been able to see through the duplicity of this war in time, though they saw it now. They had grown up in a country whose foreign policy was posited on anticommunism. They had been taught that presidents don't lie, and so they believed in the Gulf of Tonkin incident and every other cynical duplicity by which the war was begun and enlarged: they believed the reasons for Vietnam because they had no way of knowing otherwise. Now they knew, but it was too late. There is no way out of the war if you're a combat infantryman. What struck me in Vietnam was that, in all of the infantry companies I went out with, I had the distinct feeling that I would have been regarded as somewhat of a hero had I said I was a draft dodger, not because I was out there suffering with them anyway—I suffered little by comparison—but because they all knew by then what this war was all about. They would have gladly dodged it themselves a second time around and therefore felt an affinity for anyone who actually had said no to this insanity. But I didn't feel like a hero for having said no; there is nothing heroic in saying no to this war; it is common sense. I could only feel sadness that propaganda had destroyed common sense in so many, that so many had been deceived by the United States of America into saying yes.

Another fact hit me in Vietnam. Ninety-nine percent of every combat infantry unit in Vietnam had been for several years, and was now, made up of draftees—not volunteers, as was the case when the war began, but conscripted men because the war was so unpopular that no one else would fight it. One commander, himself assigned to the field for only a six-month tour, bragged to me that his entire company, including sergeants and field-commissioned lieutenants, were draftees. In other companies, what few enlisted men could be found were teenagers who had been conned by some recruitment officer into joining up *in order to avoid serving in the infantry.* "You get a choice if you enlist, boy!"

When I got to Montreal and settled into the exile community and began writing, I wanted more than ever to do what I could to help end the draft. Very little was being done however in Montreal by draft resisters toward that end. But much to my surprise I found that U.S. Army deserters, including a number of Vietnam veterans, were doing what they could to end the war, the killing, the draft. They were encouraging GI resistance by making it known that Canada was open to deserters as a refuge from war and militarism. And having seen the same young faces on the Medevac litters in Vietnam that I was now seeing on the young deserters coming into Montreal at the rate of fifteen or twenty a week and being quite pleased to see them whole in Canada rather than broken and bloody in Vietnam where I had seen too many, I offered what support I could and became involved in their politics and their protest. The result of that involvement is this book.

However, the book is not an angry polemic meant to join the long shelf of antiwar books. As I became involved with American exiles, deserters in particular, it became apparent that although their protest against the United States, their politics of anger and frustration, fit into the *anti* category, the story here was very *pro—* optimistic, good, promising. It was clear that the whole story of young Americans coming to Canada, if it were told in its entirety, would be essentially a *positive statement.* There is nothing nega-tive, nothing sad, nothing tragic about young men and women consciously choosing freedom over enslavement, a new country over prison, and life over death; and, even though many Cana-dians, American reporters, and even older exiles feel a genuine sadness when they encounter an eighteen-year-old deserter or draft resister, at the root of this grief is the knowledge that the state of affairs in the United States today is such that men this young have had to flee—that the tragedy lies not with the fleeing but with what is being fled. And while this book has a lot to do with the country that these men have left, it has even more to do with the new awareness that caused them to refuse or to remove the military uniform and to set themselves on a positive course. It is not so much about running away from war and killing and death as it is about running *toward* peace and freedom and life. *That* is a story.

The first three chapters deal with the collective history of the exodus, including a brief outline of draft resistance and the GI movement in the United States in order to establish a context through which one can more clearly view the exiles. The body of the book comprises a number of individual histories—thirteen in all—which I feel are representative of nearly all the "types" of people who have come here. While the people are representative, they are not entirely typical as they are quite extraordinary in many ways, some of the best of this generation. Being extraordinary may set them apart, yet their personal experiences and their thoughts are shared by hundreds of thousands of young Americans, not only in exile in Canada but in exile in their own country. At the same time, they are not cynosures of the antiwar movement, but simply everyday people who said no to war. They have more to say than I have, and so I have chosen to let them say it without interruption or comment. Together, *they* really tell the history, the *whole story*, while I merely edit and chronicle the events which they and thousands like them created in their northward trek. The final chapters of the book offer a first-hand look at the exile community and what it had become by 1970—and where it might be going.

Of the thirteen exiles, one is a woman, nine are deserters from the U.S. Armed Forces, and only three are draft resisters. Because actual events are approximately two years ahead of book publishing, when it came time for a book to be written on the "draft dodgers in Canada," the draft resisters themselves had already become relatively well adjusted to their new life and new country, and the phenomenon of their coming had been eclipsed by the arrival during 1969 and 1970 of two deserters for every dodger. Therefore, the story now—perhaps the greater story in the end—is that by 1971 there was well over half an American division in Canada with more ex-soldiers on the way.

Deserters are more obvious, more visible, and for the most part have more to say. They have kept their identity as deserters and are proud to say it. They have not been as quick as their predecessors to forget what forced them to leave their homeland. For this reason, almost by natural selection, it is largely deserters who tell their stories here. I would stress to the reader, however, that it was not a prejudicial choice on my part—I did not *choose* deserters over draft resisters for the interviews. Rather, in an attempt to find the people I needed, I ended up by pure chance with nine deserters and three draft dodgers. It would be best when reading the individual stories which collectively complete this history to forget the words "deserter" and "draft resister" and call them exiles.

The "interviews"—really *personal narratives*—were tape recorded and usually involved two to four hours of casual conversation. Several of the subjects were friends and others were acquaintances, and in these cases response was easy and thorough. With the rest it was usually necessary to meet several times with the person, explain myself and the purpose of the book, see if he or she had anything to contribute or wanted to contribute anything, establish a degree of trust, and then arrange for a meeting. In every case there was complete cooperation, and I never felt that anyone was holding back. That I am also an exile was an added advantage; I could be trusted for if I edited anyone's remarks badly I couldn't escape their wrath by returning to the U.S.

For the many quotes and myriad generalizations which appear in the last three chapters, I've drawn on conversations with the several hundred exiles I've met during the past two years and in the course of writing this book. They include war resisters as diverse as twenty-nine-year-old university professors and eighteen-year-old high school dropouts.

If this book seems to contain a bias, I would point out to the conservative reader who may feel that the subject has not been treated "objectively" that I will be criticized by my peers and by radicals to the left of me for not writing a truly revolutionary phillipic, for attempting a detached objectivity in a polarized time. And should the nonexile reader feel that this book and the people contained therein are not "representative" it is only because a good many writers, journalists, and TV reporters, consciously or not, have done a successful job for the past five years of *mis*-representing the war resisters in Canada.

As for the contention that the only people qualified to do such a "study" as this are psychiatrists and psychologists, I would say that if there are any spare researchers around who wish to employ the psychoanalytic method in order to determine why these men came to Canada, let them stay in the U.S. and begin by analyzing Richard Milhous Nixon, Lyndon Baines Johnson, Spiro T. Agnew, and any number of senators and generals and policy makers. The answers are there.

A note on terminology: Draft resister and draft dodger are interchangeable as far as I am concerned, draft dodger being a completely acceptable term in Canada without negative connotation. War resister and exile, of course, can apply to both resisters and deserters.

It is with deep gratitude and a sense of awe that I thank the people whose story this book is.

ONE

War, Conscription, and Resistance

The United States government has had a difficult time these past years convincing America's young men that their nation's freedom and way of life were threatened by several hundred thousand guerrilla insurgents in a small peasant country in East Asia. The government has had an easier time convincing America's young men that their own freedom and way of life were threatened if they didn't go and fight those distant rebels anyway, even if they weren't convinced that America's national defense required it. Men willingly go to war to defend their homeland. Men *un*willingly go to war if faced with jail or exile, and thousands have gone to this war under those threats. But from the beginning, there have been those who refused to go unwillingly to war or be convinced that they should.

The beginning was August 3, 1964, when two U.S. destroyers entered the territorial waters of North Vietnam and were harassed by several North Vietnamese PT boats. We were told that the PT boats torpedoed the American ships and missed and that they also opened fire on the two destroyers. Later testimony, buried in the irreversible onslaught of history, revealed that the PT boats had fired no ordnance at all. At any rate, even if the North Vietnamese PT boats had fired on U.S. ships in the Gulf of Tonkin, it was hardly enough to start a war about. But apart from the destroyers in the Gulf of Tonkin and 25,000 U.S. advisors in South Vietnam where the National Liberation Front was gaining ground, there was a consummate politician in the White House who cajoled Congress into passing the Gulf of Tonkin Resolution to give the commander in chief the authority he needed to stop "the tides of Communist aggression." (This was Vice President Humphrey's phrase.) And there were professional warriors waiting to be unleashed. The incident *was* enough to start a war about. The White House and the air force had been drawing up plans to bomb North Vietnam since the spring of 1964—and so the war began.

There were marines, too, and they wanted a piece of the action. The commander in chief landed them on the beaches of Vietnam in March 1965, several weeks after systematic bombing of the North had begun. Honest Americans asked why, and Dean Rusk answered before the House Armed Services Committee in April that there had been an armed invasion of South Vietnam by the North Vietnamese 325th Division "as a division," though Pentagon intelligence figures released later in the spring showed only a "suspected" four to five hundred North Vietnamese regulars acting as advisors in the South. There were 50,000 U.S. troops there by then. Further proof of communist aggression was outlined in the government's white paper which stated that, of a total of 7,500 weapons captured in South Vietnam during the previous eighteen months, 179 of them were of communist manufacture.

And President Johnson came on national television on April 11, 1965, quoting Deuteronomy and proclaiming, "We will not be defeated. We will not grow tired. We will not withdraw, either openly or under the cloak of a meaningless agreement." The protest began and the antidraft movement was born.

Up until this time, only tiny groups of radicals had refused to be convinced of the righteousness of the Vietnam crusade. As early as the spring of 1964, a few perspicacious intellectuals, members of the May Second Movement (the group that originated the slogan, "Hell No, We Won't Go") could see where we were heading in Vietnam and signed a pledge not to serve there. Members of the Student Peace Union also spoke out against the draft. Except for a few pacifist groups—the War Resisters League, the Quakers, Arlo Tatum's Central Committee for Conscientious Objectors—outright draft resistance was propounded by only small radical-left groups, and these people were often viewed with suspicion by the vast majority of draft-age men for they ran around spouting phrases like "U.S. imperialist aggressor," "a criminal war," "war of genocide," which very few people could accept though they could several years later: Lieutenant Colonel William Corson of the U.S. Marine Corps would write in 1968 in discussing a Marine operation, "This was not and is not war—it is genocide." Open draft resistance gained wider credibility however when David Miller burned his draft card at the army induction center in New York in January of 1965. Here was a believably concerned and honest young man doing a very radical thing. It gave many men courage.

Opposition to the war was loudest on the university campuses and for the first few years was almost exclusively a student issue. Students were not getting drafted—there were volunteers in Vietnam and they were being replaced by conscripts from the non-student, working-class population—yet they felt the threat of the draft. Moreover, America's seven million university students had more access to information about the new American involvement than people outside of the universities and the majority of students quickly saw that the war in Vietnam was not really in America's interests. A whole generation of university students had the leisure to read reports, articles, books, by such men as former Green Beret Donald Duncan, Vietnam expert Bernard Fall, and professor of history Marvin Gettleman, and to examine what this war meant and would mean, and they didn't like what they discovered. And so their reaction became the vanguard of opposition, though the students would in many cases be the last to feel the war's effect. Although it was the sons of the working class who were dying and the workingman whose taxes paid for the war, it ironically became the task of the least affected to protest the sacrifices necessary for waging war.

The spring of 1965 saw the first antiwar march on Washington in April and the beginning of the university-centered teach-in movement where the ludicrous white paper was flouted and the government was strongly criticized by leading academicians. Hans Morgenthau, whose textbook, *Politics Among Nations*, had been read by a generation of political science students, wrote in the *New York Times Magazine* that we were deluding ourselves in Vietnam—the article, by that name, was circulated widely on most campuses. Student support of what the government was doing was diminishing quickly, and young men began to think twice about the draft. In March the government had gained time with the Supreme Court's Seeger decision which broadened the application of "religious training and belief" to include beliefs that were not traditional and not theistic, and thereby provided a legal option for those men who felt the war was wrong but who might not have qualified for CO (Conscientious Objector) status under the earlier definition. But in May the United States invaded the Dominican Republic.

It was now clear to more and more male students across the country that to wear the uniform of the U.S. Armed Forces was no longer merely a duty to be fulfilled or legally gotten out of, but a moral dilemma: to give or not give oneself to a military machine that was being wrongfully used to intervene in the internal affairs of a sovereign nation and to support corrupt and fascistic military regimes. The Dominican invasion confirmed that misuse in the minds of those students who had already begun to doubt their government's action in Vietnam.

On May 6 a number of University of California students burned their draft cards to protest the invasion. In July, nine pacifists attempted to block the Whitehall induction center in New York. A week later President Johnson announced that draft calls were to be increased to 35,000 a month from the usual prewar quota of 6,000. In August a live homemade bomb was discovered outside the draft board office in St. Ann, Missouri. President Johnson announced that exemptions for married men would end on August 26 and on August 25, 171 couples got married in Las Vegas to beat the draft. General Hershey, the Selective Service System director, said men who married hastily to escape the draft would face call-up the following year because of rising quotas.

Also that summer Congress managed to pass Strom Thurmond's bill providing up to five years' imprisonment and a $10,000 fine for burning draft cards. Senator Dirkson defended the bill and querulously intoned on TV, "It wouldn't be so bad if these people didn't make a public protest with their cards but just went out behind the barn and burned them." Many did.

By early September there were 75,000 U.S. troops in Vietnam with more on the way and Robert McNamara saying they would all be home by Christmas. Students knew that that couldn't be true. Why would the government lie to them, they asked. Did the policy makers really believe 75,000 American soldiers in six months could end a war that 150,000 determined guerrillas had been fighting and winning for the past five years? Did the men in Washington think American air power could defeat a force that fought with the tenacity and will that the National Liberation Front exhibited, and did they think that bombing the North would weaken the struggle in the South? Some prescient youth began to doubt the sanity of their government, and the first fissure was opened in what was to be the Johnson Administration's most unique contribution to U.S. politics—the credibility gap.

●

Draft resistance was now a major issue. It was not so important that only a handful of people had actually refused induction, gone to jail, or left the country, but rather that many young men were talking about doing these things. Through the media, information about particular acts of draft resistance became widely known, and every act was celebrated silently or in concert by tens of thousands of young men who were thinking about what they would do when called. As the war expanded and the Washington rhetoric became more inane, individual acts of draft resistance erupted spontaneously all over the country. In September, SDS, replacing the Student Peace Union, printed a small flyer outlining ways to "beat the draft," but it had little effect on young men everywhere who were having to make their own decisions based on individual conscience and common sense. (The first SDS draft advice was not even radical advice. It merely told of several tricky ways of dodging the draft and explained the CO option as provided by the Seeger decision—few people then had realized that for every middle-class college student who managed to escape the draft, a working-class white, black, or Mexican-American went in his place.) At the time, simply to become a CO was a radical act when most men had never previously thought of doing so.

In October Senator Kuchel said the SDS flyer was a "dirty little sheet." Attorney General Katzenbach announced that the Justice Department had launched a probe of groups behind the antidraft movement, and at a news conference he reported that "some Communists are involved." President Johnson backed the probe for possible "Communist involvement." Every young male faced with the draft who had been considering evasion simply laughed at this remark for he knew his decision was purely his own. He knew he wasn't a communist; he also knew the government was getting more ridiculous than he would have ever believed. One young man who had become so angry while watching U.S. Marines burn a village on the evening news that he had written the president stating his refusal to serve in "your war" received from the White House three weeks later an envelope enclosing both a letter which urged him to reconsider and a copy of the white paper.

That fall many young people for the first time seriously questioned the quality of leadership in the United States after the Senate Internal Security Subcommittee issued its report, endorsed by eight prominent senators, entitled *The Anti-Vietnam Agitation and the Teach-In Movement* which stated, "The control of the anti-Vietnam movement has clearly passed into the hands of Communists and extremist elements." The subcommittee had clearly passed into the hands of fools: the teach-ins had been simply a manifestation of student concern over the direction of the conflict in Southeast Asia, but the government was telling the nation that essentially anyone who had attended a Vietnam teach-in that spring and summer of 1965 was an unwitting dupe of communism. A lot of students had attended teach-ins.

More troops went to Vietnam that fall and more young men burned their draft cards. For every publicly announced decision not to serve in the armed forces, dozens were made privately. The press began to report many cases of student deferments being withdrawn. In November five pacifists burned their cards before a crowd of 1,500 at a Union Square rally in New York. That gave more men courage, but it was also announced that month that the December draft quota would be 45,000, the highest since the Korean War. By the end of the year there were 200,000 troops in Vietnam and none of them were coming home for Christmas.

In December the country witnessed a sit-in by thirty-five University of Michigan students at the Ann Arbor draft board office. SSS director Hershey quickly reacted with a recommendation that the dissident students be drafted. By the end of the month nine of them had been declared either delinquent or 1-A by their local boards. That made a lot of students very angry. And some people asked why military service, if that service is such an honorable duty, was being used by General Hershey as a punishment?

By the end of 1965 most of the initial outrage over the beginning of an American land war in Asia had been expanded, and 1966 was marked by a feeling of disbelief, a sense of frustration, and a lot of watching, waiting, and talking. The war and the draft were nearly talked to death, but no great national mobilization of dissent was formed. There was much vociferous appeal for an end to the draft, or at best, draft reform—middle-class college students, who had protested the war, realized that they would also be asked to fight it one day so the draft as well as the war became a target for protest action. In March Hershey sent down his college deferment tests which one was free to take or not take—few bothered. The tests were one more indication of the inherent unfairness of the Selective Services Act. The educated could study; the ignorant could die. Many students began to feel guilty in having a deferment at all, and in May 250 University of Chicago students protested the existence of all deferments. It was felt that if there must be a draft, then students and those with technical deferments should be as eligible as anyone else. It was thought that the end of deferments would not only make the draft fair but would end the war because the colleges would explode and there would be massive draft resistance—that as long as college students could hide in college, their dissent would be cooled.

Other students felt that the university, in cooperating with the Selective Service System, was being used as a government tool, and protests were directed against that cooperation. In May one hundred Hunter College students had a sleep-in and blocked the administration office; while at the University of Wisconsin, six hundred students seized the administration building to protest complicity with the draft. A number of university presidents said their institutions would no longer forward grades or class standings to local boards. Several professors stated they would give all A's in their courses, since a B or C might mean death in Vietnam for a student.

The inequities of the Selective Service System had become painfully clear and many newspapers and magazines editorialized for "draft reform." The new mood of concern over the operation of the draft cooled the protest movement for awhile, and much energy was directed toward discussion and writing rather than organizing for direct resistance. People listened to concerned liberals and honestly hoped for reform. Many optimists discussed a possible end to the draft by the following spring. Belief in liberal reforms, however, was somewhat reduced when the greatest liberal reform of all was announced by Robert McNamara. He, and several presidential advisors, suggested all youths, male and female, serve two years in either a civilian or military capacity—of course,

they would have their choice. This, ironically, when even conservative clubs, the Young Americans for Freedom, and Ayn Rand
were denouncing the draft as "involuntary servitude." The most
preposterous liberal plan of all was McNamara's proposal to "salvage" 40,000 draft rejects and substandard volunteers. He hailed
the ability of the armed services' vast education system to eventually prepare an estimated 100,000 men a year, classified as substandard, for productive military careers and later for productive
roles in society. To left-wing, right-wing, and even middle-of-the-
road college students McNamara's plans smacked of the Hitler
Youth. "If that's liberalism," many were quoted as saying, "then I
guess I'm now a radical." So it went.

Those who already had a radical perception were analyzing the
draft in another light. They saw the Selective Service Act as a
device used not only to procure manpower for the armed forces
but to suppress and manipulate American youth. They had only to
quote the Selective Service System's own report entitled *Channeling*, relased in mid-1965, as evidence. One essayist called it a
"classic totalitarian document":

> The meaning of the word "service" with its former restricted application
> to the Armed Forces, is certain to become widened much more in the
> future. This brings with it the ever increasing problem of how to control
> effectively the service of individuals who are not in the Armed Forces.
> ... The young man registers at 18 and pressure begins to force his
> choice. ... The psychology of granting wide choice under pressure to
> take action is the American, or indirect way of achieving what is done by
> direction in foreign countries where choice is not permitted. Here, choice
> is limited but not denied, and it is fundamental that an individual
> generally applies himself better to something he has decided to do rather
> than something he has been told to do. ... The process of channeling
> manpower is entitled to much credit for the fact that there is not a
> greater shortage of teachers, engineers, and other scientists working in
> activities which are essential to the national interest . . . .Throughout his
> career as a student the pressure—the threat of loss of deferment—
> continues. It continues with equal intensity after graduation. His local
> board requires periodic reports to find out what he is up to. He is
> impelled to pursue his skill rather than to embark upon some less
> important enterprise and is encouraged to apply his skill in an essential
> activity in the national interest. The loss of deferred status is the
> consequence for the individual who has acquired the skill and either does
> not use it, or uses it in a non-essential activity.

(One SSS administrator was quoted as saying, "Those students in engineering, chemistry, and math will naturally get consideration when seeking deferrals over those just taking things like English and history.") Two exile writers later summed it up this way: "Under this compulsion, grades become literally deadly, and the multiversity is clearly revealed: more than a factory, it is in fact a macabre iron-clad prison controlling the lives of captive students with the dictum, 'conform or die'!"* As for CO status, it was difficult to get and reserved for only a few middle- and upper-class youths. For every youth granted CO, a poor boy would go in his place. The SSS worked hardest on the poor. Though many were exempted in the lower classes for failing to qualify, the draft, in essence, took the very best male youth that the poor had; or else the threat of the draft induced the unemployed or the badly employed to enlist as a means of upward mobility.

More and more young men began to take this radical view of the draft (the report *Channeling* was withdrawn, but the SSS continued to operate exactly as the document described) and, in doing so, saw applying for CO, feigning homosexuality, faking medical deferrals, and otherwise beating the draft with student deferments as immoral and no different from entering the service itself. Moreover, many students were getting tired of being channeled, which they had been for most of their lives; they wanted freedom to move about, to travel, to work, to study how and when they pleased, and this, as much as objection to the Vietnam War, is the reason that a very great many young men resisted the draft (especially in the case of those who chose Canada). Seeing the draft as an oppressive instrument and understanding exactly how it worked induced many young men to adopt the tactic of noncooperation, and the first noncooperators conference was held in September 1966. They would not appeal classification, nor apply for CO, nor inform the local board of anything and would simply take the consequences and refuse to fight induction in the

*Rick Ayers and Melody Killian, "The Exploitation of Youth," *Our Generation*, Montreal, May 1970.

courts. Noncooperation had the distinct disadvantage of bringing to a head the young man's battle with the draft and there was a tinge of martyrdom to it, however moral a tactic it was. Nevertheless, it was total draft resistance and it took courage, for the ultimate decision then had to be made: jail, underground, or exile? In 1966 only a handful did any of the three (seventy-five in prison, perhaps a thousand in Canada), but again they provided a model to follow as more men pondered their decisions.

There was a preference at this time to consider jail over any other course, and a number of noncooperators ended up there. Many people, however, saw this as actually complying with the system; after all, they argued, a clause providing imprisonment for enforcement purposes was written into the Selective Service Act. Certain radicals said the system was not impeded by men going to jail, that the system allowed for dissent, that the only way to stop it was to beat the system entirely by going underground or to Canada. Meanwhile, a number of pacifists trooped off to prison with the belief that they would "fill the jails." They went so silently that few people ever heard of their going. It could be generally stated that the pacifists, though very brave and the first people to actually resist the draft, offered less and less inspiration to the many tens of thousands who were planning to resist but who were not themselves pacifists.

The great draft debate continued. Politicians, editors, academicians all urged draft reform as soon as possible. Martin Luther King pointed out that the draft is highly descriminatory toward blacks—that nearly twenty-two percent of the men in Vietnam were black though blacks made up only ten percent of the population at home. A long article in the *New York Times*, headlined "Pressures For Change In Draft System Mount," said that "thorough revision seems likely," and that "the Defense Department may recommend long range overhaul." Later, the House Armed Services Committee opened hearings on the Selective Service System. Mendel Rivers indicated that liability could be cut substantially below age twenty-six. Meanwhile, responding to these pressures, President Johnson named a twenty-member National Advisory Commission to the Selective Service System which was asked to make recommendations for reform.

At the same time, the escalation continued. Men were being drafted and men were dying. The National Student Association in November demanded abolition of the SSS and opposed forced service to government while Stokely Carmichael traveled around the country and urged blacks to defy the draft boards. Individually, men were making decisions. Draft resister Jeff Segal was sentenced November 1, 1966 to four years' imprisonment, twice the normal term, and the judge cited the need to "halt the willful evasion." More than anything, he unintentionally helped to halt the need to go to prison. The *New York Times* reported that fall that 50 to 400 draft evaders had found a "haven" in Canada—a more reasonable estimate would have been two thousand—and the SSS admitted to the 400 figure in a press release which stated that these men faced prosecution if they should decide to return. And by January 1, 1967, the United States had 360,000 men in Vietnam.

In his 1967 State of the Union address, President Johnson said that the SSS must be modernized. In February, Robert Kennedy offered a resolution to the Senate urging a major overhaul of the draft by executive order rather than legislation. The President's Advisory Commission on draft reform proposed a "radical reorganization" of the SSS, but the report was scored by the National Student Association for not dealing with ways to end the draft. In March, seventy-two clerics, educators, writers, and civil rights leaders called a press conference to appeal for a volunteer army to replace the draft, and New York attorney Richard Nixon made the first of his famous statements favoring abolition of the draft and creation of an all-volunteer army. Conservative economist Milton Friedman spoke in favor of an all-volunteer force, and the *New York Times*, quoting him, observed that the right and the left were united on the issue of draft abolition. So was the middle; later that spring, Mark Hatfield proposed a bill to end the draft entirely.

Students weren't waiting, however. In April, sixty-six Princeton University students placed an ad in the *Daily Princetonian* announcing their refusal to fight in Vietnam if drafted. At the same time, 200 Cornell students similarly advertised their commitment to resist the draft if called. Many such draft refusal statements were signed and printed in campus newspapers in the spring of 1967, continuing a very effective form of war protest that had begun at the University of Michigan a year earlier. Thousands of young men were committing themselves totally against the war in Vietnam. For the Spring Mobilization, the first of the massive nationwide protests, the newly formed Resistance passed out their "We Refuse To Go" statement in Berkeley which announced that the purpose of the organization was "to organize and encourage resistance to, disruption of, and noncooperation with all the warmaking machinery of the United States." In New York 200,000 people marched in the streets, and at the same time, despite having been disowned by the Spring Mobilization Committee, a splinter group numbering several thousand and carrying signs reading "Burn Draft Cards; Not People" gathered at Central Park's Sheep Meadow and 175 young men publicly burned their draft cards (the *New York Times* reported seventy). Many of them were later imprisoned; many were never found, having either gone underground or to Canada, but their public witness lived on as an inspiration to thousands of others to do likewise.

In June, with a House vote of 377 to 29 and a handsome Senate majority, the bill to renew the draft in the same form without changes or reform was passed by the Congress of the United States with little more than a total of fifteen minutes of debate. This raised even the choler of the *New York Times* which called it a "small but regrettable victory for Representative Rivers of South Carolina and the know-nothing sentiment prevailing in the House Armed Services Committee . . . nothing can undo the pettiness of Congress in yielding to the ugly spirit of some of its least enlightened members."

Any hopes of Congress ending the war or the draft which draftable men still held were quickly dissolved. School was out;

many men received their induction notices, and thousands ignored them, for one could plainly see that there was no other way. There were now several hundred silent martyrs in prison, an undetermined number of resisters underground, and perhaps five thousand in Canada; *Newsweek* insisted there were at least 1,500 "hiding out" there. News of Canada as the most desirable option was spreading quickly. By January the Student Union for Peace Action in Toronto had already sent out 1,000 of its pamphlets on how to "dodge the draft by emigrating to Canada," and the *New York Times* helped to spread the word by dutifully reporting it. In March Canada's Secretary of State, then Miss Judy LaMarsh, had said in a speech in Philadelphia that Canada "welcomed draft dodgers." "We already have several thousand," she said proudly. In May Oliver Clausen, a journalist with the Toronto *Globe and Mail* and "a fascist if there ever was one" according to one exile leader in Toronto, wrote a wholly unsympathetic though very comprehensive article in the *New York Times Magazine* entitled, "Boys Without a Country." Its insensitive and critical tone did not detract from its effectiveness as a recruitment tract for exiles. Today one can literally encounter hundreds of men in exile who were convinced by that article to come to Canada. In August 1967, Gail Cameron wrote a mildly sympathetic though somewhat maudlin piece for the *Ladies' Home Journal* in which she stated, "The novelty of American boys abandoning their country in time of war—and, indeed, arguing that their criminal violation of the draft law is a greater virtue than old fashioned patriotism—has made their flight one of the most publicized happenings of the decade." And so it was to the degree that the publicity aired in the popular press and the mass media had far more to do with helping men decide to leave the country than any antiwar organization ever did. For every potential draft resister that The Resistance reached directly, *Time* or *Life* reached a thousand.

●

The support of draft resistance had become a popular cause by the summer and fall of 1967. Berkeley's Resistance became a nationwide organization when the Committee of Draft Resistance was formed in July by Quakers, clergy, professors, and student radicals. Joan Baez, one of the committee's founders, urged men everywhere to resist. In September 320 professors, writers, ministers, and other professionals signed a statement pledging to raise money to aid youths who resisted the draft; signers included Linus Pauling, Bishop Pike, and Russell Lowell. During the same month the National Conference on New Politics, a hastily formed national group organized for the purpose of mobilizing and channeling antiwar dissent, attended by 3,200 delegates, adopted a resolution demanding abolition of the draft and ROTC. The resolution also committed conference members to "help protect draft resisters and conscientious deserters from the armed forces." They stated, "Since it is not in our power at present to abolish the draft, we are for open resistance." In plain sight, an underground was being born. In October, under the aegis of Clergy and Laymen Concerned about Vietnam, eighteen clergymen pledged to risk imprisonment to aid those resisting the draft on grounds of conscience, and Yale's chaplain William Sloan Coffin urged Yale students to turn in their cards. What had been deemed a radical act by leaders of the antiwar movement eighteen months earlier—destroying, burning, returning draft cards and openly advocating draft resistance—was now commonplace accepted action.

In conjunction with ad hoc committees in Berkeley that organized the famous march on the Oakland induction center, The Resistance coordinated a national draft-card-turn-in and collected and returned to the Justice Department 1,158 cards on October 16. The Oakland demonstration itself, where 119 people were arrested including Joan Baez who later served a thirty-one-day jail term for participating, along with the march on the Pentagon that same month, ended the era of exclusively nonviolent demonstrations when girls had put flowers in the ends of rifles. The peace and love aura that until now had suffused the antiwar movement and especially the antidraft movement was shattered by the events at Oakland and the Pentagon. Peace and love and nonviolence and goodness and going-to-jail were becoming untenable virtues to many people, and The Resistance had to vehemently defend its commitment to these things. The situation was reversed. The antiwar movement had now become militant, if fractured, while organized draft resistance lay firmly in the hands of radical pacifists, clergymen, professors, and concerned young women.

This, in fact, permitted The Resistance to gain needed support across the country, and Resistance chapters and draft counseling centers blossomed by the hundreds out of nowhere and remained quite outside the domain of the more radical groups. Professors, ministers, and students spent long hours counseling men on the draft, explaining the options, discussing the consequences of whatever path a young man chose. The Resistance centers' important function was providing a place where draftable men could turn for advice, information, support, and not feel alone in their struggle. Tens of thousands of youths felt a camaraderie in what they were doing, tens of thousands resisting when they may not have otherwise. What was unfortunate, however, was that the camaraderie was often lost as soon as someone chose a different path from that which Resistance nationally, through the Joan Baez group, was recommending: prison. Hundreds of nondraftable sympathizers would rush to the support of someone who chose prison and encourage him even if he had doubts.

But when a man chose exile, it was usually with little fanfare and a man would feel alone again. Nevertheless, many did choose exile because Resistance made information on Canada readily available as did every local chapter of SDS which, more often than not, was also engaged heavily in draft counseling. For a short period most local SDS groups considered going to Canada a radical act, though they would also recommend staying in the country by harassing the draft board in whatever way one could for as long as one could and then, if possible, going underground. Late in 1967 many local SDS chapters were stressing the tactic of joining the army for the purpose of organizing within the ranks. Many did that too, although a lot of those people ended up in exile in the end—after a good fight.

The national resistance movement's initial tactic failed, however. Never did tens of thousands of young men return their cards and publicly bear witness to their stand. If thousands *had*, the tactic would have been valid for the draft and, hence, the war-making machinery *would* have been disrupted by concerted non-compliance on the scale envisioned by The Resistance—the laws of the land cannot stand massive public flouting. The tactic failed because the consequences of the act it demanded were never dealt with realistically. It was not difficult to convince a young man who intended to resist the draft to publicly resist the draft—in every case he was proud to do so—but it was difficult to convince him that he should spend two years of his young life in a prison cell. To quote from The Resistance manifesto: "As the resistance grows, the government will either have to allow the draft non-cooperators to go free and thereby swell our ranks, or fill the jails." Not one draft age male in a hundred thought the government could be intimidated nor did many believe in filling the jails. People countered Resistance naiveté by pointing out that the entire German left once filled the jails of the Reich, and the government never ran out of room. But partially because The Resistance in most cases did make information about Canada available (while trying to dissuade people from going), there were by 1970 at least 40,000 draft resisters in Canada plus 800 in jail, and therefore The Resistance had succeeded. It seemed that Resistance organizers, however, would not consider the creation of an American exile community a success for it revealed the failure of their own position: "going to jail for what you believe in." They failed to see that few people believed in being jailed by a system that would put them in jail for refusing to fight its criminal war.

In other words it was fine, many men thought, to have gone to jail in World War II such as Ralph DiGia of the War Resisters' League had or Dave Dellinger had, as a universal human protest against killing one's fellow man for it was a protest not so much against the U.S. government doing the killing as against killing in general, man's human folly. The World War II war objector was quite obviously not blaming America for the killing for America was trying to stop the killing that another country was enormously engaged in. The protest in 1967, however, was not only against killing; it was mainly against America doing the killing, making a profession of it, counting bodies, paying heed to no one, and planning for more. By 1967, America had already done so much killing in Vietnam with no intention of stopping it that not a few war resisters were actually thinking that it might take a little more killing on the home front to stop it. That extreme attitude and less extreme variations of it, an intense outrage over what the system in the United States was doing, did not always readily accord with the Gandhian metaphysics of nonviolent resistance, be they however noble.

The Resistance might have survived had it made a public announcement everytime it got word of another youth who had gone to Canada, worked closely with exile groups, and encouraged men to leave, all the while stressing the concept of Canada as a temporary sanctuary. This didn't happen for Resistance believed, quite logically, that you couldn't build a political movement in the U.S. with a bunch of émigrés; it also didn't happen because, as one draft resister wrote from Canada, "America has indoctrinated its young so well that the thought of emigration is extraordinary—emigration is only considered when a better job offer, more money, is found elsewhere." This applied to antidraft organizers as well. As it was, with the nation remaining unmoved by anything antidraft forces did, with relatively few men going to prison, and with most Resistance leaders having—in the process of organizing —gotten radical to the point of believing that draft counseling alone was not a radical function, The Resistance would eventually fold. Many Resistance organizers themselves would become "prison refusers." Fortunately, local draft counseling would remain functioning, held together by a loose network of pacifist organizations refusing to complicate their operation with political ideology and silly tactics. By 1970, according to record albums, books, films and *Look* magazine, it appeared that all that existed of The Resistance was Joan Baez's husband, David Harris, in prison.

It must be pointed out, too, that even if going to jail had been considered to be indisputedly the correct tactic, not all that many more men would have had the courage to go. The leaders of civil disobedience have that courage and that is what makes them leaders; but the average young person does not. Yet there can be no massive organized struggle without enlisting the total support of average people, and it was a basic failure of the draft resistance movement that it refused to do that. Quite simply, not all young men were David Millers or David Mitchells or David Harrises and should have never been expected to follow their examples. Tens of thousands of young men, however, did choose to resist in their own way and this fact was never sufficiently recognized.

Also, by the end of 1967, reports were leaking out explaining what prison was really like. Ironically, it was the pacifist groups, which supported and remained in contact with the men in prison, that circulated through peace movement publications dismaying and depressing letters of incarcerated war resisters, effectively convincing many others not to follow that path. Antidraft organizers never managed to nullify the common belief that prison could easily break a man. Later, in a book on the imprisoned war resisters, Dr. Willard Gaylin would write, recalling his initial involvement with the subject, "I had not yet measured the brevity of time in which youth can be lost and hope abandoned."* After finding out, he would discover that nearly every war resister he interviewed had been overcome with despair, disillusionment, bitterness, and cynicism, several going so far as to say that they had made a serious mistake. One of them would be quoted: "I think our government is too insensitive to respond to anything

*Willard Gaylin, M.D., *In the Service of Their Country*, Viking, 1970.

except violence and destruction. I mean literally. Intellectually, I can now even justify murder and assassination . . . how else do you deal with a structure that has no conscience, that is beyond the normal control of men?" A black would be quoted: "As far as violence is concerned, at one time I didn't buy it. But I'm beginning to see the advantages of what the brothers mean when they talk about going out and taking off a cop." Finally, a former Catholic seminarian: "When I came in here I knew precisely where I stood. I would have called myself a Christian pacifist. Now all that has changed." This change toward cynicism, destructiveness, self doubt, an increasing distrust of one's self was what Gaylin would consider to be the most damaging impact of imprisonment. Many young men already knew that, three years before Dr. Gaylin wrote it down, and they were terrified of prison and what it would mean.

But perhaps the most basic reason that the idea of going to prison never caught on was because it demanded a total commitment to a *political* idea, a political strategy which would serve the larger community, the nation. America, unlike most Western nations, having no viable political left (out of 585 members of the federal legislatures, not one is a socialist) in behalf of which commitment can be asked, is therefore not the place to expect total commitment to a public cause outside of the nominal commitment to establishment politics that the system requires. It is the reason that 300,000 French youth will fill the streets of Paris, but only 10,000 in a country with a population four times greater will come to Chicago to engage in a protest action at which the organizers ("conspirators") expected 100,000. America does, however, have a tradition of respecting commitment to personal freedom, and it is therefore not surprising that despite what is happening politically in the U.S. millions of young people will look to themselves for their freedom, will commit themselves to being free. If that means drugs, music, new life styles and philosophies, going underground or to Canada, then they will go that way and not to prison. It is the difference between the "political revolution" and the "cultural revolution," Leninist revolutionaries and Jeffersonian anarchists, or as one deserter in Toronto put it, the "public revolution" and the "private revolution." Today is the age of the private revolution; it is millions of young people making revolution and finding liberation inside themselves. Whether the political revolutionaries like it or not and whether it is new or not, it is what is. There may be a political message in going to prison for a cause but there is nothing liberating about it.

●

As 1967 drew to a close, The Resistance was preparing for Stop the Draft Week which culminated on December 4 with 264 arrests at New York's Whitehall induction center, including Allen Ginsburg and Dr. Benjamin Spock. Draft cards were returned to the Justice Department from over thirty cities and Stop the Draft Week also garnered much publicity; at distant campuses students vicariously experienced the New York antidraft campaign. At the same time on-campus military recruiting had become an issue and students at dozens of universities would succeed in having the recruitment tables moved off campus. In November the cover of *Ramparts* showed four of the magazine's editors burning their draft cards, a bit of photo-journalism that was to get them all indicted.

In mid-November General Hershey issued his famous memorandum suggesting the reclassification of those interfering with draft procedures, and despite a strong response from the ACLU and even a statement from the Johnson Administration in mid-December rescinding the Hershey directive, the ancient general reiterated his opinion that war protesters be inducted. His opinion was taken as God's Truth by local boards. If Hershey wouldn't listen to the government, certainly no one believed any longer that his draft apparatus would be responsive to youth's CO appeals and requests for continuing student deferments, especially if the youth involved were known to be protesters; and so more young people became disillusioned with the system. Meanwhile, public reaction to the so-called "draft card burners"—nearly anyone who opposed the draft in any way was called a draft card burner—was mounting. A Louis Harris poll indicated that seventy-six percent of the U.S. public thought antiwar demonstrations "encourage the communists to fight all the harder," and fifty-three percent agreed with General Hershey that students blocking draft offices and induction centers and interfering with military recruitment should be drafted. In the Congress, Senator Thomas Kuchel called Stop the Draft Week a "terrible disservice to dissent," and Senator Mike Mansfield said that the anti-draft protests "inflamed opposition rather than attracted support," and that the antiwar activists had created a "difficult position for those who believed in an honorable negotiated settlement." Hundreds of protests and three years later, after many more thousands of young men had died, people would still be waiting for that negotiated settlement.

Nineteen sixty-seven ended with fully half a million U.S. troops in Vietnam. Not even the most radical critic in 1965 would ever have believed that. In Vietnam U.S. casualties were averaging 200 dead and over 2,000 wounded per week. The efficient technological warfare with which the United States was murderously blanketing this small strip of East Asia had produced massive "enemy kills." The enemy often included civilians—over one hundred thousand had been killed in South Vietnam by January 1968, and no one knew how many had died in the North. A blistering barrage of dispatches from the war zone unnerved the most dedicated news readers. It was too much to take. Pressed by the weight of the awful knowledge of what was going on in Vietnam, thousands more draft-age men who one year before had been only mildly concerned with Vietnam now made their decisions not to serve and commonly felt a sense of relief. For the yet unconvinced there was a whole shelf of books condemning the war and they sold briskly in every city and on every campus; nearly every draft resister in Canada would be able to trace his decision to refuse service back to one or two of those books.

Draft related events moved quickly in 1968. Yale chaplain William Coffin, former White House aide Marcus Raskin, writer

Mitchell Goodman, Harvard graduate student Michael Ferber, and Dr. Benjamin Spock were indicted in Boston for conspiracy to counsel young men to violate selective service laws. On January 18, David Harris destroyed his induction notice outside the Oakland induction center. In the wake of the Pueblo's sailing into North Korean waters was the huge reserve call-up on January 26, and by February 15, as warned, the Administration abolished graduate school deferments. The same month front page photographs of N.L.F. guerrilla fighters lying dead on the lawn of the U.S. Embassy in Saigon extinguished the tiny light at the end of the tunnel, and the following Tet offensive ultimately proved the futility and absurdity of waging a war against an Asian people's liberation struggle; General Westmoreland's words before the U.S. Senate the previous November now echoed in bathos.

More men refused to fight. One hundred former student body presidents and college editors signed a declaration to refuse to serve in Vietnam. The student body presidents of Brown, Columbia, Harvard, Yale, and Dartmouth signed a statement stating they would leave the country or go to jail rather than serve in Vietnam. At Harvard a *Crimson* poll revealed that ninety-four percent of Harvard seniors opposed U.S. policy in Vietnam while over a fourth of them said they would go to jail or leave the country before serving in the armed forces. Sixty percent said they would make a "determined effort to avoid military service." This, at the college that had provided the policy-making elite that had got us into Vietnam, the college that America traditionally drew upon for leadership in law, science, government, and medicine. Columbia's equivalent dissidence exploded during the spring strike, setting new examples of rebellion for college students everywhere; Columbia's few short hours of "liberation" was liberation ecstatically shared by hundreds of thousands of radical American students across the nation who, afterward, accepted less than ever the totalitarian arm of the military over their young lives. On May 31, David Harris was sentenced to three years in prison; summer followed the funeral of Robert Kennedy who might have conceivably ended the war and abolished the draft; and in June, Spock, Coffin, Ferber, and Goodman were convicted by the Federal District Court of Boston where U.S. Attorney Paul Markham, countering the defense, contended for the government that, "There can be no doubt that United States presence in Vietnam is in compliance with domestic law, the United Nations Charter, and international law."

Meanwhile, in Canada, the Toronto Anti-Draft Programme in February had mailed out the first 5,000 of its now-famous *Manual for Draft Age Immigrants to Canada*. According to the SSS approximately 20,000 young men so far had evaded the draft. Where were they? Only a handful were in prison. The British Union of American Exiles reported in March that they could speak for 300. One can assume that the majority were in Canada or on their way, the remainder underground. Also, the *New York Times* reported in April that a record number of American graduate students had sought admission to Canadian schools.

Nineteen sixty-eight saw the war against the draft escalate significantly. The SDS had come a long way from their "Part of the Way with LBJ" slogan in 1964 and was now a "mass radical and anti-imperialist student movement" which was attempting to urge "all young men to wage a collective struggle in resistance to the draft by refusing to serve in the military." Although SDS at their spring conference didn't resolve the numerous differences that beset resistance organizing, they did decide that many of their own members would, "when forced by threat of imprisonment or exile . . . organize within the Armed Forces, advocating desertion and other forms of resistance to U.S. foreign policy." This was an offensive against the military, the ramifications of which would not be too difficult to measure after a year or so. Immediately, SDS's renewed initiative to fight the draft had an affect on the smallest of campuses, if only through their literature. Other men, less given to cumbersome organizations, formed small action groups which they felt could initiate more effective action against the Selective Service. One group bombed the Whitehall induction center in February; another firebombed the SSS office in Berkeley; another bombed the draft board office in Lancaster, Pennsylvania; another firebombed the Madison, Wisconsin draft board office; and in Washington, D.C. a fire was set inside the National Headquarters of the Selective Service, doing minor damage. But this was terrorism, however justified, and it only bought a mood of repression. Although thousands of draft resisters may have cheered everytime a draft board office saw its fiery end, these small moments of revenge were never paid for by any positive result. The public was inevitably angered.

In May, using a nobler tactic, the Reverends Philip and Daniel Berrigan along with seven other formerly peaceful men who had been driven to act by an honest dedication to peace and humanity burned 600 draft files in Catonsville, Maryland. They gave themselves up, stating that their action was symbolic only. They became the "Catonsville 9" and were summarily tried, convicted, and sentenced to six years apiece. In September, fourteen people broke into the draft office in Milwaukee and burned the records and they also turned themselves in. The "Milwaukee 14" became a symbol of resistance throughout the Midwest. No matter what anyone said, these were brave men and they became heroes to thousands. Many radicals asked why they had given themselves up and not kept up the raids for as long as possible; that was not their intention for they knew they couldn't effectively prevent the SSS from doing its work. They merely wanted to call attention, through one small illegal and violent act, to their sincere and desperate opposition to what they knew to be an obscenely violent and criminal war and thereby inspire other people to directly oppose the war in whatever way they could. They were not interested in terrorism, and they chose instead to go to prison as a final, anguished appeal to a nation's conscience.

Looking back on the campaign of 1968, one hesitates to recall that there was no more outspoken critic of the draft among the candidates, including Eugene McCarthy, than Richard Milhous Nixon. In speech after speech he emphasized that he *understood* what divisions the draft had wrought in the nation and that the draft must go if he were to bring us together. In a nationally televised speech on October 17 he unequivocally urged replacing the draft with a volunteer force as soon as the war ended, and he said ending the war was his first consideration. Hubert Humphrey criticized Nixon's proposal to end the draft and form an all-volunteer force; he said we needed the draft. And Eugene McCarthy endorsed Humphrey's candidacy with the reservation, "Humphrey's position on the draft falls far short of what I think it should be." At any rate, Nixon's continual promising to end the draft convinced many young people that he would do it and they actually voted for him for that reason.* So Nixon got elected. It was not exactly a mandate majority, and ironically it may have been his end-the-draft speeches that tipped the balance. His election, coupled with the previous events in the city of Chicago, probably did more to send men to Canada than the Vietnam war had in the past four years.

Following the election of President Nixon, fewer and fewer people were going to prison. That act had finally come to be defined as a useless form of resistance, almost devoid of meaning. The exodus to Canada nearly doubled in the year after Nixon took office; a mood of hopelessness had settled on the young, and it immediately affected many a young man's decision about the draft (and by now, desertion). Men originally planning to go to jail now chose Canada. Men waiting underground for an amnesty, for an end to the draft, for social change, now saw that none of that was going to come, and they headed north. At the same time, the underground itself grew larger as the country had by this time managed to totally alienate several million young people who no longer accepted Nixon's America as their own; it was not their country anymore. The counter-culture sheltered a huge number of draft evaders and deserters. Even the mass media recognized this as

*See Chapter 8 for the case of deserter Jim Reihle.

exemplified by the account a young war resister wrote for *Look* magazine entitled "An Exile in My Own Country . . ."

The President's earnest pronouncements on draft reform took the wind from The Resistance sails and November 16, 1968 was the last national-draft-card-turn-in day until the spring of 1970. Except for the student body presidents of 253 universities who informed the White House that they were going to refuse service in the armed forces, 1969 passed with little organized draft opposition although a great many draft board offices were destroyed or partially destroyed by bombs or fire. Many of these were never reported in the media, but news of them spread quickly in the underground press. People waited in early 1969 to see what Nixon would do. In the fall he managed to institute a lottery system— against the wishes of Congress—and that, too, took more support away from organized resistance. Why should a man care about the draft if he received a good number? Government cynics knew what they were doing: destroying draft opposition while continuing to supply the manpower the armed services needed for Vietnam. Radical cynics knew that too, and therefore increased terrorist tactics. While Nixon cooled the draft debate for that year, he continued the war, now known as "Nixon's War." And so the quiet summer of Woodstock and the Moon Landing, during which many young people for the first time in four long years forgot about the war, ultimately gave way to a winter of renewed discontent: Moratorium one and two, the New Mobilization, the march on the Justice Department, Days of Rage in Chicago, the Trial of the Chicago Eight, and the not-so-pleasant reality of Altamont rock festival reflecting essentially the not-so-pleasant reality of the United States of America.

In May of 1969 there was one last call to conscience promulgated by a group later known as the "Chicago 15." After destroying draft records affecting some 50,000 men in a predominantly black and Spanish-American southside Chicago ghetto, the group, including three Catholic priests, was found dancing around a fire

of burning draft files singing "We Shall Overcome." They released
a signed statement which said in part:

> Today, May 25, 1969, we enter the Chicago Southside draft board
> complex to remove and burn Selective Service records. *We still have a
> dream of being able to communicate with this society* [italics mine]. But
> we can no longer confine our peace making efforts to the ordinary
> channels of polite discourse . . . The poor people of this earth are taught
> to hate and kill one another in order that the powerful can enjoy the
> freedom to increase their fortunes through exploitative foreign invest-
> ments. At the same time, the expansion of war related industries diverts
> tax dollars away from the social programs so desperately needed here
> . . . Young men from America's urban ghettos are forced to burn and kill
> poor peasants in the land of the third world . . . Our action is negative
> but also creative—for there is implied in our loud "No!" a quiet but hopeful
> "Yes!" In our elimination of part of a death-dealing and oppressive system
> is the prelude to the creation of life and freedom.

It was a very beautiful statement. It may have been the last of its
kind. When the trial opened for the "Chicago 15" in the spring of
1970—the defendants had been freed on bail—only half of them
showed up. Some were underground and several were living in
Montreal.

●

It was obvious toward the end of 1969 that during the past
three years antidraft organizing had paid off in one very definite
way: the courts could no longer handle all the draft cases that
were piling up. Three hundred new cases were being initiated each
month while the backlog grew larger. Many others were indicted in
absentia, and their cases were not opened for prosecution at all.
One U.S. District Court Judge said in an interview, "We are very
concerned about what is happening. At the present rate of progress,
persons indicted for draft evasion will have to wait at least a
year or eighteen months for a trial." As this news became wide-
spread, the steady increase in draft-resister emigration to Canada
slacked slightly since men realized they could remain safely in the
U.S. a little longer. Many resisters who later emigrated used this
period to earn money for the move. Nevertheless, the *New York*

Times was now reporting that estimates of the number of exiles in Canada ranged from thirty to sixty thousand.

The year passed into history while a world recovered from the shock of My Lai 4. The terrible revelation of American soldiers firing point blank into huddled groups of elderly men, women, children, and babies, murdering 567 of them in a morning's shooting, was the tragic denouement of the Vietnam War. Less than four months later, as if it were vindicating its war and its massacres, the U.S. invaded Cambodia and the response was so hostile among the young in America that it became necessary for American soldiers to again fire point blank into a retreating crowd of civilians, massacring two girls and two boys at Kent State University. It happened again at Jackson State; again at Kansas State; it happened in a Panther apartment in Chicago; and amongst the vast majority of the American people there was no moral outrage whatsoever. As the seventies opened it had already become an American tradition to cold-bloodedly mow down unarmed people. These events caused a lot more young men to leave the country for they either didn't care about America any longer or they cared too much. In Canada they would discover that they were the first exiles to arrive who didn't hear the question asked, "Why did you leave the U.S.?"

It was becoming increasingly difficult for many outraged young radicals to remain in the U.S. without turning into violent revolutionaries and for that reason many young radicals left—*they didn't want to become revolutionaries.* Even though they intellectually believed that perhaps violence was the only way to change things, they would not commit themselves to violence: if they were draft resisters they left for Canada; if they were not affected by the draft for one reason or another, they often left the U.S. by retreating to the hills.

Meanwhile, a whole new wave of nonradical yet antiwar youth were arriving at the decision of whether or not to be drafted— young men who were twelve or thirteen when other young men had begun refusing the draft five years before. Many of these youths were not acquainted with the older radicals' position that to apply for and to accept CO status (it was considered all right to apply for CO as a disrupting and stalling tactic only, but not to actually *accept* alternate service) was to cooperate with the system, and for them, as it had been for the others in earlier days, applying for CO classification was a radical act. And out in the small towns of America it *was* a radical act; in some places it was the nearest thing to treason. Typical of middle-American attitudes toward the CO was an editorial comment in the *Spokane Spokesman Review* which said that the term "conscience is derogated if it comes to mean avoidance rather than the grasp of unwelcome duty." Nevertheless, more young men than ever before were applying for CO classifications—most of them only eighteen or nineteen years of age—and by this time the Supreme Court had chosen to rule on a decision which would reaffirm and liberalize the earlier Seeger precedent; all of which brought the issue of conscientious objection back under the spotlight. The Welsh decision in June 1970 went further than Seeger and stated that one need only prove that objections were based on "philosophical, political, sociological beliefs, or merely a personal code." The application of the decision insisted on very well substantiated proof of having arrived at this moral code—years of study, reading, professional guidance, and so on, a process which, again, only the well-off and very well educated could ever manage. The personal moral code of a less sophisticated man would not count. A poor boy from the hills of Tennessee could not simply say, "I think killing is wrong," and get away with it, but Elliot Ashton Welsh II could, and did.

More hypocritical still was the guideline on the Welsh decision issued by the SSS emphasizing that very, very, few applicants would actually qualify under the new court precedent. The guideline, in fact, was so harsh that a newsman felt constrained to ask SSS director Curtis Tarr whether or not Welsh himself could have qualified under the stipulations of the new directive and he answered, "Mr. Welsh qualified only because the Supreme Court said he qualified." So it goes.

Decisions were left to local boards which were now having to deal with mountains of CO applications. Even *Life* magazine, five years too late, ran an eight-page article on the trials and tribulations of applying for CO status. In the happy story the board grants it, and the father embraces his son, and the son goes off to work as a hospital orderly. Oddly enough, if it were like that—or had been—there might have been fewer draft resisters, for many of them *had* applied for CO status and were turned down. They would have been faced with the dilemma of whether or not to do alternate service since up to that point the system would have worked for them; what *Life* failed to point out was that for tens of thousands the system, as corrupt as it was, didn't work. Only a tiny percentage of the total CO applicants from 1965 to 1970 were actually granted the classification. Since most local boards considered applying for a CO classification to be no better than burning one's draft card, they constantly denied CO requests and subsequent appeals. Over fifty percent of the war resisters in Canada might not have gone there had draft boards even bothered to abide by the original Seeger decision.

All this discussion of the CO retreats before the larger issue of the drafting of poor and working-class youth: in 1969, for example, out of 283,000 men drafted, only 28,500 had attended college. Even Stewart Alsop, also five years late, could correctly point out that "the radical young, especially in the prestigious Eastern Ivy League colleges, talk as though they were a lost generation, condemned by the system to be hauled away to Vietnam, and killed or wounded—this has been the theme of many a youthful valedictorian. But it is nonsense." This was chiefly a war for the working class, and college-centered draft resistance eventually took second place to GI dissent and eventually to desertion. Men who had not had the opportunity to learn about or protest the war in college now found themselves on the way to it, learning about it and protesting it from within the ranks. Although they had not been counted in it, they had not been deaf to the many years of dissent and protest across the land, and they would have their say at last. Many would want out. History might yet prove them to be the real heroes.

While thousands of young men applied to become COs, and GI dissent and desertion became the new radical issue, other young activists managed to reinvigorate draft resistance with the Union of National Draft Opposition (UNDO) headquartered at Princeton. Their national draft-card-turn-in in June 1970 collected 6,000 cards, exceeding the total collected by all previous resistance organizations combined. Draft-counseling centers were mushrooming; Los Angeles county had sixteen draft information offices. The Oakland induction center, where draft counselors were sending men who wished to help disrupt the draft and also stall their own cases for up to three years, reported that for the first six months of 1970 only fifty-two percent of those called showed up, and, of that group, another seven percent refused to be inducted by not stepping forward at the moment of swearing-in. Thousands of younger men refused to register on their eighteenth birthday as draft counselors advised them that their chances of getting caught were slim as long as they didn't remain in their home towns. The Supreme Court ruled that there was a statute of limitations on prosecution, and after five years the nonregistrant would go free. Many came to Canada to spend those five years. Since they didn't register, it follows that the total number of these draft refusers will never be known. In August the SSS said that prosecutions for draft evasion had soared to ten times their level of 1965. It had gotten so serious that if the Nixon administration needed troups to save the Lon Nol government in Cambodia and to prevent defeat in Indochina, there was the possibility that it might not get them.

In March 1970, Melvin Laird predicted that Congress would extend the draft for at least two years beyond the July 1, 1971 expiration date. In May the Presidential commission on the draft recommended an immediate fifty percent pay increase for military recruits and an elimination of the draft by July 1, 1971. In response to the commission's recommendations, Senators Mark Hatfield and Barry Goldwater, both long-time opponents of conscription, proposed a measure to do just that. It was nicknamed the "amendment to end the draft" and was of course soundly rejected by the Senate in a vote of 52 to 35. Melvin Laird, fulfilling his prediction, had dispatched dozens of Pentagon lobbyists to the halls of the Senate Office Building to convince senators to vote against the amendment. Even President Nixon's opposition to the bill had been put in writing and passed around the Senate.

The same week, the Senate also rejected a bill to end the use of herbicides in the war which, according to researchers, were causing a generation of deformed babies in Vietnam, not to mention upsetting the small country's ecological balance for perhaps a thousand years. And it came as a surprise to no one that the Senate would also vote down during that week the Hatfield-McGovern amendment which was designed to cut off funds for U.S. troops in Vietnam by the end of 1971 and which Vice President Agnew called "a blueprint for the first defeat in the history of the United States."

So, it was clear by mid-1970 that America was not going to be defeated in Vietnam; that although the U.S. ground troops might one distant day be withdrawn, the U.S. would continue the fight: the B-52s would continue to fly, the fighter-bombers would continue their missions in support of the "allies," America's sophisticated and advanced weaponry would continue slaughtering 500 enemy soldiers a day (the Department of Defense average of enemy kills per day for the past three years) plus countless civilians in a war of attrition that would go on and on and on. Using American money and American tools we prefer to have Asians fight Asians.

Should it have come as a surprise, then, that part of the fragmented New Left would go underground and engage in guerrilla warfare in the U.S.? It was not a question of it being right or wrong, it was simply a matter of it being inevitable. Most radicals deplored the bombings as a tactic but nevertheless could not help feeling a sense of satisfaction everytime one occurred; this was especially true amongst the exiles—it was good to know someone was doing *something*. Few young people felt badly each time an ROTC building was burned to the ground or when the SSS revealed that there had been 271 destructive attacks (bombing, arson, destruction of records) on draft board offices in the past two years. How many of the young men felt anything but a sense of satisfaction when a bomb did a half million dollars' worth of damage to the Minneapolis induction center in August? How many secretly rejoiced when radicals almost completely destroyed the entire Army Mathematics Research building at the University of Wisconsin? They were upset that a young graduate student had been killed there, leaving a wife and small children, but many young people were also dismayed that the concern Americans showed for this one accidental casualty was not now, nor had ever been, matched by any degree of concern for the hundreds of thousands of widows and fatherless children in North and South Vietnam and Cambodia. Unfortunately, the only result the bombings would have would be to arouse the anger of America, not against the war but against all those who by peaceful means or any other were trying to stop it.

This chapter outlining draft resistance must end here. Plainly, much of whatever is left of the struggle against this war will be carried on underground; it is a history for future chroniclers. And what is happening in the U.S. today is no longer a story having to do only with that country, but is now involving American exiles as well, for many of America's guerrillas are now exiles themselves. Their story and a part of American history may yet be told in exile. Some of it is already known but cannot yet be written.

TWO

Yankee Refugees

They usually came alone, with a suitcase or two, a little money, riding the bus from Seattle to Vancouver, from New York to Montreal, from Buffalo to Toronto, or with a knapsack they walked across the bridge from Detroit to Windsor—to freedom. Some flew in. Others had cars and drove in. If they were lucky friends would come up with them and stay a few days. Nothing was comparable in a young American's life to the sensation he experienced while approaching and crossing the border: a turmoil of anticipation deep in the gut, fear perhaps, then an almost indescribable relief as the immigration officer said, "Have a nice stay." It was more than relief, it was exultation; it was joy in discovering that one no longer needed to run, that one could stop right here and begin to make a new life. It was the unutterable contentment that is felt when a man finds for the first time that he is free: a feeling that had been reserved, so everyone had been taught, for those who *came* to the United States of America.

The arrival of the first war-resister immigrants met with little notice for Canada is an immigrant country. And even though they were Americans—America, after all, being the country one immigrated *to*, not emigrated *from*—the early draft dodgers remained well hidden so that no one remarked on their coming for well over a year. They were understandably afraid; *paranoid* is the common word. Would they be arrested and shipped home? Would they meet with hostility if it were learned that they had refused to go into the United States Army? There was no easy way to find out in those days. The first war resisters must be credited with a special courage since it took courage for a young American, with no one to follow, to take his life into his own hands and strike out to find a place where he could live it.

A desire for freedom was the first impulse which spurred most men to Canada. This was an honest motive, and in keeping with America's traditions. If a young man accepted the draft and went into the service he lost his freedom for a reason he couldn't justify; he might also lose a limb or even his life; and to stay in the U.S. and go to jail or go underground would cost him his freedom as well. In this sense then—searching for freedom, running *toward* something rather than running away—going to Canada was a positive act and should have caused little havoc in a young man's life. But there were negative factors too, and one was that the choice of army, jail, underground, or Canada was an unwilling choice which made unwilling immigrants of men who decided on Canada as the least painful way, a last option. It is difficult to be an immigrant to another country when one really doesn't want to be, and so the first years of the draft exodus were colored by this unexpected disorientation that often produced unhappy and directionless young men.

The more serious and less recognized negative aspect to going north was that most men considered it a duty to leave the country and become exiles if they couldn't abide the other alternatives. Here too, there was a tinge of martyrdom, though of a less obsessive nature than that which characterized war resisters in prison. No one who went to Canada felt it was right to completely avoid the draft legally by being dishonest with it. It was honest to refuse outright, to go to jail, to go underground, to clog the courts, to stall one's case legally until it was propitious to leave, and even to be dishonest with the Selective Service System as a tactic by which one could buy time; but ultimately, to manage to beat the draft entirely by dishonest means was simply not right. And so the men, as they came to Canada, knew that they had done one of the *right* things; they had not permitted a man to go to war in their place without due payment, which was a costly, personal, important statement in opposition to that war: becoming an exile. Yet when these men got to Canada they were not treated as exiles, as men who had put their future on the line against a war they couldn't accept; they were merely welcomed as willing immigrants who chose Canada over the United States. Even though most of them eventually would choose Canada over the United States—many other young Americans would be coming by 1970 who were neither dodgers nor deserters, people truly choosing Canada—this was simply not the case with the majority of resisters who arrived between 1965 and 1969. They had not chosen Canada; they had chosen the United States by making in its name the strongest statement for the good of that country that they felt they could make commensurate with their own well-being. They weren't getting out of making that statement, though they easily could have by dishonestly evading the draft; they weren't dying for their country or going to jail for it, but they were going into exile for it. They were not immigrants to Canada, though Canadian law said they were; they were American exiles.

Worse than not being recognized in Canada *as exiles* was being entirely misunderstood in the U.S. by the peace movement and The Resistance. Going to Canada was a "cop-out" from the struggle. Occasionally antiwar organizers, with an easily-gotten medical deferment, told those bound for Canada that they were cowards. Even more significant was that men in Canada would get letters from home, perhaps from a girl, which said, "We know so-and-so who beat the draft by faking a trick knee. He says anyone with a little brains can get out of the draft; you don't have to go to Canada. He thinks you're a fool to be up there." (Joe Namath, football hero of the sixties, had gotten out with a trick knee.) If that wasn't psychologically devastating, nothing was, and it happened in one way or another to nearly every war resister in Canada. They could see that their exile meant nothing to anyone.

There was the satisfaction within oneself, of course, that exile was the right thing, but there was little outside encouragement. Therefore, the vast majority of war resisters tended to withdraw into their personal lives, forgetting politics or why they had left, and thereby perpetuated the notion among the left that going to Canada was a selfish act. If these men had been selfish, really selfish, caring for nothing but their own lives and "making it," you would find them today living in the United States; for it *was* true: anyone with moderate intelligence *could* get out of the draft. They didn't have to go to Canada.

Most men eventually would resolve this dilemma and finally understand the reasons for their temporary dislocation and undefinable trauma. Many would dissolve back into the middle-class milieu from which they had come, seldom reflecting on the brief fling with radicalism which they had experienced. Others would rectify their disorientation by attempting to make known the reasons for their exile and to enlarge the exile movement by working with war-resister aid groups. Some, of course, needed these groups, but for the most part working in war-resister politics was the result of an intellectual commitment. These men helped to make Canadian exile a significant issue. Still others, forgetting both the U.S. and their exile, began to identify with Canada and made a great effort to become Canadian. It was not really important what one did, however, since any positive course of action usually relieved the depression and despair that at one time or another enveloped every young man who crossed the border.

The press normally found its specimens in this state of mild depression, which very often lasted a year or so, and even the most sympathetic reporters (of which there were really very few) tended to come away struck by the "sadness" they encountered. Oliver Clausen—very unsympathetic—wrote in the *New York Times*, ". . . a frustrating sadness settles upon you after talking to a dozen or so of these young men." Over the years the *New York Times* gave thorough coverage to exile affairs, but it always seemed to go out of the way to paint a picture of bewilderment and dejection. *Time* magazine mindlessly reported that the draft dodgers were childish malcontents and that their abject state was of their own making. As late as 1970 the press, prejudiced by its own misrepresentation of the story, would continue to convey this "sadness" to the point of nonsense. Mike Wallace, on the CBS show "60 Minutes" in 1969, concluded a report on the draft resisters in Canada with: "They were the saddest and most subdued group of young Americans I have ever seen." This was too much, even for Canadians. A TV reviewer for the *Toronto Telegram* pointed out in a column on the Wallace program, "And so they may have been sad, except that the camera did not show it. Instead it showed young Americans of intelligence and sensitivity whom any Canadian would, or should, be glad to have around."

Although being an American exile in Canada was difficult, and the promise of being recognized as such at home continued to be a false hope for the first few years; being an immigrant to Canada was always relatively easy. Canadians went out of their way to welcome the draft resisters. Even the Canadian left, which welcomed them as "war refugees," thought of them not as exiles but as immigrants and prospective citizens. And the draft resisters, not wishing to offend their Canadian hosts, were often completely absorbed into the Canadian life stream, most of the time quite successfully and very often making a valuable contribution to Canada. While this did have the effect of debilitating the radical exile, as has been mentioned, the degree to which the war resisters obliged Canada by assimilating themselves increased Canadian willingness to open their doors completely to as many resisters as wanted to come, having a greater political effect in the long run than if a great fuss had been made earlier about draft resisters being exiles. At any rate, Canada's tolerance, which that country seems to have more of than almost any other, allowed the exiles who so desired, to work out these contradictions for themselves.

●

To understand Canada's readiness to accept and welcome draft resisters from the very beginning of the Vietnam War, one must know a few facts. First, Canada is a country which, like the U.S., has been built and grows by immigration. It is not crowded, and its twenty-one million citizens, living in the second largest country in the world and right next door to the world's most powerful nation, feel slightly insecure. From this stems, logically, a government program of encouraging immigration so that Canada will one day have a population whose size is more in keeping with its land area and large enough for it to remain independent of its geographic neighbor. Prior to 1965, Canada lost people to the U.S., especially people with above average intelligence—the brain drain. Figures for 1965 showed for the first time that Canadian emigration was being offset significantly by American immigration. It is hard to say whether this was because of Washington's decision in 1965 to limit the number of Canadians allowed to immigrate to the U.S. or because the Vietnam War was already sending large numbers north while discouraging Canadians from going south as was clearly the case a year later. Anyway, it didn't really matter; this was good for Canada, and there was no reason to discourage it.

Second, by early 1967 it was apparent that the American war resisters were the best educated category of immigrants to a country which needed skilled manpower according to Department of Manpower and Immigration statistics. In a lengthy article in the *Toronto Star*'s Sunday magazine in 1967 five draft resisters were interviewed, among them an accountant, a doctoral student and a supermarket produce manager. It was an extraordinarily *pro* draft-resister piece, commending them for their decision to refuse the army while praising them as being among the best of Canada's immigrants.

Third, Canada has a long history of outright hostility to the mere suggestion of conscription. It was once that way in the U.S. too, and many of its immigrants were people opposed to conscription in Europe. But, unlike the U.S., Canada has not forgotten her traditions—what it means to be a civilized country—and has managed to fight in two world wars without making con-

scription a permanent institution. Conscription was briefly instituted before each war and abolished immediately afterward. Each
time it was proposed it met with strong resistance. A former
mayor of Montreal was elected from jail where he was serving a
sentence for encouraging draft resistance; a Quebec minister of
justice had formerly been a draft refuser. Pierre Elliot Trudeau was
an anticonscriptionist during the war years who once said, "Like
most Quebecers, I had been taught to keep away from imperial-
istic wars." In Toronto, faded Oppose Conscription signs can still
be seen on old buildings along the waterfront.

Fourth, the great majority of Canadians never saw any sense in
the Vietnam War. There has never been the extreme fear of
communism in Canada that exists in the United States. Canadians
simply never believed that "the Communists" were a threat to the
western world. To most Canadians Vietnam at first merely seemed
a foolish, later a disastrous, mistake.

And so, there was little concern over the arrival of the draft
resisters. At best, their coming was a humorous episode in
Canadian-U.S. relations. A cartoon in a Toronto paper in 1966
showed an American mother fretting over her son's decision to
leave for Canada and saying, "But I didn't raise my boy to be a
Canadian." In the U.S., meanwhile, General Hershey was blaming
Canada as well as the communists for the phenomenon of draft
resistance, saying things like "American conscription provides the
military strength to protect Canada. She has no right to harbor
draft dodgers." Canadians paid little attention.

In August 1966, the chief of the American World War II
Veterans organization publicly urged negotiations between Ottawa
and Washington to "halt the growing practice" of draft dodgers
"hiding out" in Canada. Later in the year, ABC news sent an
unenlightened producer, Dick Hubert, to find out, in his words,
"why such a friendly neighbor would harbor draft dodgers instead
of just packing them off home." On the program, entitled "Sanctuary," the External Affairs Minister, then Paul Martin, told him,
"No country in the world has in its domestic law any requirement

that imposes on it any obligation to enforce the military service laws of another country." A Canadian TV commentator discussing the program later said, "That Martin should even have to explain this is rather sad."

Except for a few newspaper reports—unbelieving in the U.S. press, extraordinarily sympathetic in the Canadian press—that American draft dodgers were indeed in Canada, it really wasn't an issue in 1966. Not until March 1967 did Prime Minister Lester Pearson find it necessary at a press conference to announce that the government of Canada was not planning any measures to prevent U.S. citizens dodging the draft from coming to Canada. Incredibly, two weeks later General Mark Clark told the Senate Armed Services Committee that he would like Canada to return the "one thousand or so draft dodgers hiding out there." He said he would leave no stone unturned in getting details about them, and then left for Ottawa to "try and expedite the draft dodgers' return." At the same time the State Department was examining the possibility of a treaty with Canada which would extradite draft resisters to the U.S. In May 1967, a report was released to a congressional committee indicating that such a treaty was unfeasible.

By mid-1967 there were easily five or six thousand draft dodgers in Canada. Immigration figures alone listed a total of over three thousand draft-age American males who had immigrated since 1965. Nevertheless, despite these numbers, this issue was not yet able to arouse much Canadian interest. So they were here, so what? It was an American problem.

It was not until late in October that a member of Parliament saw it as a Canadian problem. Tory M.P., J. N. Ormiston, proposed a bill that would amend the Visiting Forces (NATO) Act so that dodgers could be returned. The bill met with only scattered applause in the Commons. The argument for the bill was sound— that since Canada and the U.S. are allied countries by international treaty, to weaken the forces of one country is to weaken the forces of both. Nevertheless, the bill got nowhere. It did, however, provoke a great deal of comment and the *Toronto Star*, in one of its first editorials supporting the draft resisters, said:

> U.S. draft dodgers have broken no Canadian law by their presence here. Moreover, Canadian tradition has long made room for persons who refused to fight in wars for whatever reason. The 50,000 United Empire Loyalists who came in the 1780's are proof enough. So why this special antipathy to today's draft dodger? Is his hair too long, or his beard too wide, or his trousers too round: Perhaps the hostility toward them among some Canadians is based on a false assumption that they are all cowards. But who knows? They've broken with home and country perhaps for good, since going back means jail or a 10,000 dollar fine. This requires its own courage and is surely evidence enough to make us stop attributing motives to people we don't know.

In August 1968, Canadian ire was raised again, a little more vehemently this time. The assistant director to the SSS, Colonel Frank Kossa, spoke in Calgary at a veterans convention and, aside from doing the exiles a favor by corroborating exile aid group figures with SSS's own estimate of 15,000 dodgers in Canada, stated that the FBI and the RCMP (Royal Canadian Mounted Police) were cooperating to expose organizations in both the U.S. and Canada devoted to helping American draft dodgers. That may have been true for the U.S., but it was a patent lie that the RCMP was investigating the exile aid groups in Canada—the Mounties themselves even took offense at the implication. The *Star Weekly*, a conservative independent weekend magazine similar to America's *Parade*, said in a half-page editorial countering Colonel Kossa, ". . . we would have been willing to let it all go if he'd stuck to the usual song and dance about draft dodgers being human rubble anyway and if we want them we can have them. Kossa did say all that, of course, but he also came out with a statement that was dumb at best, and, at worst, downright malicious." The magazine explained that all the RCMP ever did in regard to draft dodgers was to politely ask any they happened to find if they planned to stay in Canada and make that information available to the FBI so the case could be closed. The RCMP had never investigated the exile organizations, nor discouraged draft dodgers from entering or staying in Canada. The editorial suggested that Colonel Kossa "shoulder arms, and bug out." Replying to the Selective Service administrator's gratuitous remarks about draft dodgers being cowards anyway, that they would make poor citizens, the staid *Globe and Mail* said:

> It is easy to convince rednecks that evasion of the draft is nothing more complicated than an act of cowardice, but the argument carries no weight among those who have talked with some of the fugitives and found them to be soberly conscious of the enormity of the step they have taken by going into voluntary exile.
>
> Canadian Authorities take no special interest in the motives which bring young Americans over the border, beyond those which normally concern them. Nor is there any defensible reason why, subsequently, they should serve as enforcers of the draft system. *In effect, political sanctuary is being extended and the principle is one Canada must not reject.* [italics mine]

Even the *Calgary Herald*, a very conservative newspaper in Canada's most Americanized city, had this comment:

> It is a matter for regret that the Army, Navy and Air Force Veterans convention saw fit at its session here to pass a resolution calling for the government to deny asylum in Canada to any U.S. citizen suspected of draft evasion . . . it would be dangerous for the nation to set up barriers to entry in the clouded areas of personal conscience and conviction. It has always been the boast of free countries that they can be a refuge for non-criminal foreign exiles.

The editorial called the Canadian veterans representative of an "extreme element."

The main issue, of course, was that draft dodgers were simply immigrants, immigrating to Canada under Canadian law, and any attempt by Americans to have that law interpreted so that it would benefit the United States Government normally met with a very hostile reception. Canada was Canada, not the United States, Canadians were saying—even if Americans never listened.

Not all was sympathy for American war resisters in Canada

however. To quote from a 1970 editorial in the *Winnipeg Tribune*: "With the regularity of tired old movie re-runs, the CBC interviews U.S. armed forces deserters and draft dodgers—treating them with reverential interest and respect. But who really wants this type of American in Canada? . . . Canada needs immigrants, but not necessarily of this sort."

The most vitriolic public attacks on draft resisters came from where it should have been least expected—the churches. A columnist in the *Toronto Star* wrote, "In spite of the traditional Christian aversion to killing in general and war in particular, the draft dodgers are not terribly popular with a lot of churchgoers. A recent survey made by the United Church Observer showed that when 2,201 laymen were asked if they felt Canadian Christian organizations were justified in aiding American draft exiles, more than 50% answered No." Dr. I. R. Hord, secretary of the board of evangelism and social service for the United Church of Canada, Canada's largest Protestant church, was nearly forced out of the church in what the *Toronto Star* called a "backlash of conservatism" directed against draft dodgers. In 1968, he had undertaken the poll of laymen and had called on the church to aid U.S. draft dodgers. The *Toronto Star* angrily noted that churchgoers had called him a communist, a traitor, and a man who should be driven from the country. "Others suspected the poll itself was designed by communists," the editorial continued, "and one even wanted draft dodgers shot."

For the most part, this too was an extremist element. The general attitude continued to be one of enforcing the law, that is, Canadian immigration law, which did not take into consideration a young man's draft status when he applied at the border to become a landed immigrant. Occasionally, an official would prejudicially turn back a young man if he could get information out of him indicating that he was a draft evader. This always brought a protest from either a member of Parliament, a radio or TV commentator or a newspaper columnist. After one such incident in 1968 the *Toronto Telegram* ran a column about these Canadian immigration officials who seemed to be aiding the Americans under the headline, "Law Breakers Who Work For The Government." In this case a nineteen-year-old draft dodger and his wife had been detained at the Canadian customs office while the officer phoned the FBI, who picked up the young couple after the Canadians returned them. Many Canadians were outraged. Another issue that invoked the media's wrath was when U.S. firms operating in Canada refused to hire a draft dodger; there was much noise made about this recurring problem, but little was ever done.

There has always been a good deal of vociferous public support for at least permitting draft dodgers to come to Canada. Most of the time couching that support in terms of Canadian tradition or immigration law was a convenient way of stating a broader sympathy with the draft resisters themselves. At the same time, the American people were learning just the opposite about this Canadian feeling. A Mr. David Jewell wrote for the *Los Angeles Times-Washington Post* news service in 1969: "Officialdom in Ontario and the city of Toronto, where most draft dodgers live, has let it be known it doesn't think much of having such people as immigrants. Public sentiment in Ontario, to the extent it is possible to assess it, seems to be against the draft dodgers." If that's what the establishment press wanted the American people to read, then that's what they read.

Perhaps the best defense of draft resisters ever uttered by a Canadian was the summary sentence to a piece on the resisters in the winter of 1968 by Harry Bruce in the *Toronto Daily Star*: "I've talked with a number of these American kids and, for what it's worth, I've never met a draft dodger I didn't like."

●

It was in Vancouver in 1966 that a University of British Columbia professor, Benson Brown, first saw the need for Canadians to provide information and friendly assistance to American war objectors. Brown brought together a group of university professors, their wives, and an attorney who shared these views and formed the Vancouver Committee to Aid American War

Objectors which opened an office in October of 1966. The group thoroughly researched the matter of immigration and published a fact sheet which was sent to student organizations across Canada and the U.S. Margaret Brown and Myra Riddel, wives of UBC faculty, operated the new office and organized a list of Canadian families who were willing to take in a draft resister for a few weeks until he found his bearings. From the start Canadians were very generous in this respect and eventually several thousand families across Canada would be opening their doors to American war resisters. Late in 1966 Mrs. Brown expanded the immigration fact sheet into a pamphlet called *Immigration to Canada and Its Relation to The Draft* and the committee began mailing them out in answer to inquiries. Two other Canadian volunteers, Elizabeth Briemberg and Betty Tillotson, began counseling at the Vancouver office and together provided immigration and job information to newly arrived Americans for most of 1967 until the Committee had funds to pay a draft resister, John Gonzalez, for full time counseling. He was followed by Steve Strauss, a graduate of the University of Colorado and a very able counselor, who worked long hours and with a quiet intensity to help solve the manifold problems that every new arrival faced. Strauss was one of the few resisters employed by the aid organizations who didn't eventually suffer a total breakdown—known among the groups as "burn-out"—from the excruciating burden of responsibility which the job of exile counseling and coordinating entailed. He later moved east where he took a job as youth counselor for the Montreal Youth Clinic. After Steve Strauss left, the Committee hired Peter Maly, a Canadian-born U.S. military deserter who with his experience in the American army and his soft-spoken and casual yet serious demeanor was able to put at ease many of the deserters that were beginning to arrive by early 1969. A second worker was hired at the usual $35 per week in mid-1969: Peter Burton, a burly, young Torontonian who in 1967, when he worked at Expo '67 as superintendent of ticket sales, had the image and appearance of an all-Canadian hockey star. By the time he came to work for the Vancouver aid group he was competing with Allen Ginsberg for hirsute magnificence. Burton, a likeable and dedicated counselor who as a Canadian never had to worry about the draft, made the draft and the war refugees his problem too. His undivided attention to the cause of American exiles through 1969 and 1970 was such that people were calling the Vancouver operation the Burton Committee to Aid American War Objectors. It was hardly that, however, for by then the Committee had a full-time paid staff of nine permanent employees.

The Vancouver Committee served as a model for the Montreal Council to Aid War Resisters which was formed in the summer of 1966 in the living room of a dodger from Connecticut, John Callender. Doug Sanders, a young Canadian attorney who had handled a number of dodger immigration cases in Vancouver for the Committee, visited Montreal several times and aided in organizing the Montreal Council before becoming a professor of law at the University of Windsor. These groups had little radical foundation and were merely intended to be of assistance to young men who were in desperate need of help, but Ed Miller brought a little more radical consciousness to the Montreal Council when he arrived early in 1967. Miller had come from New York where he had worked with the group of early resisters that had supported David Mitchell, the CO whose appeal and court defense were based on the Nuremberg principle (the Nuremberg defense was ruled out and Mitchell went to prison). These men, along with Vance Gardner, a dodger and child care worker at a Montreal hospital, and draft resister Bruce Garside, a tall quiet professor of philosophy at McGill, opened an office in Montreal in 1967, later expanding to a bigger one in Old Montreal's St. Paul Street in 1968. Unlike Vancouver, the Montreal group was made up largely of Americans, but they shared similar concepts with their western counterparts. The main motivation for this kind of work came simply, according to Vance Gardner, "from the desire to help other guys like us who'd just come up. We'd gone through the same thing and we wanted to make it easier for the new people."

Gardner explained, "In 1967 there weren't such overwhelming numbers and you didn't so easily tire of it. By 1968 it became much more serious business and we had to hire several dodgers to work full time. Peter Benning joined us then, and later Tim Anderson. The National Lawyers Guild in the U.S. sent up two workers to help us during the summer of 1968 and paid their salaries and expenses." In 1969 the Montreal Council hired Bill Mullen, a very thorough and hard working army deserter who managed to counsel from five to fifteen draft resisters per day plus mail out thirty or forty copies of the Council's detailed immigration pamphlet in answer to the queries of prospective resisters in the U.S.

Montreal was becoming increasingly popular with the new immigrants. Here was a city second to none in beauty, charm, grace, congeniality. Its bilingual and bi-cultural character offered an attraction that no other city in North America could. If one wanted to get away from North American civilization, this was the place to do it. Charles Lazarus, a *Montreal Star* columnist, wrote in 1968: "One of the effects of Expo '67 is the manner in which Montreal has caught on as a place to immigrate. No question that thousands of Americans, overwhelmed by the general turbulence created by such issues as Vietnam, racial equality and the clash between old right and new left, visited here last year and experienced a different kind of society." Looking ahead, Lazarus asked anxiously, ". . . and who knows what will happen if Richard Nixon becomes President of the United States?"

The Montreal Council eventually drew a deeper political awareness from their heavy involvement with the new exiles, but very little ever came of it except a continued determination to keep the gates open for the northward flow—that, of course, was a political act in itself and one not always sufficiently appreciated. The Montreal exile activists were characterized by a pronounced lack of political rhetoric and an uncompromising acceptance of serious responsibility: a mature politics as it were, a willingness to deal with the complex realities of being American exiles and immigrants to Canada at the same time. Canadian hospitality and the resister's legal eligibility for immigrant status should not be jeopardized in favor of radical action as exiles it was felt. In Montreal it would later be deserters, having less to lose and arriving in an angrier state, who picked up the revolutionary torch. Aside from helping many thousands of young men gain legal admission to Canada, the Montreal Council's one important effort was the continuous publication of its thorough leaflet on immigration which was printed in lots of five thousand and which seemed to disappear as fast as copies arrived from the printers. Thousands of them were carried south to eastern campuses by visiting radicals.

The council did its share of experimenting with hostels. Because the housing lists of sympathetic Canadians couldn't always handle the flow, hostels were opened by most of the groups by the summer of 1967. Also, there was the problem of those few dodgers, no more than ten percent of the total arrivals, who actually fit the image of draft dodgers fostered by the American press—dirty, raggedy young people unwilling to work or to care for anything or anyone, including themselves. More a pathetic product of an alienating society than of their own shortcomings, they nevertheless held little appeal either as war resisters or as possible new citizens to the Canadian families that took in refugees, and therefore they had to be housed somewhere else. A house or large apartment would be rented—cheap—and a responsible resister would usually volunteer to become the *concierge* or housemother for the hostel. Men who had little money could usually stay for several weeks, or until they were able to find a room of their own. The Montreal Council opened a fifteen-bed hostel in 1967 and a twenty-bed hostel in 1968 with the idea of helping guys get settled, but it turned out each summer that the hostels would usually fill up with those people who didn't want to get settled or do anything. At the same time the hostels were necessary, for these sorry individuals, wasted on drugs, directionless, depressed, came through the city regardless and had to be looked after. Also, there was always the problem of sorting out real draft dodgers from the usual North American transient youth who would "crash" anywhere—many posed as dodgers to get free lodging and food. (From time to time hostels worked and some that did are discussed later in this book.)

•

The focus of exile activity in Canada has always been Toronto. Although Montreal is Canada's largest city (2.5 million), Toronto is the heart and soul of English Canada; it is the Queen City to the Tory Canadian, the descendents of the United Empire Loyalists who fled the American Revolutionary War; it is "hog town" in the friendly pejorative, referring to the large packing industry which colored the city at the turn of the century; to the immigrant from Europe it is a boom town, the American dream without the demeaning American melting pot, a place where everyone's language and culture are respected; to the American, visitor and exile alike, it is the liveliest city between New York and San Francisco. The American comes to Toronto and then contemplates his own cities—Chicago, Detroit, Philadelphia, Cleveland, Pittsburgh, Cincinnati, St. Louis, Kansas City, Denver—and asks what happened. Toronto is a North American city at peace with itself. It may be the only one.

In 1966 in Toronto the Student Union for Peace Action (SUPA), a group with close ties to older Canadian peace groups and the SDS in the U.S., decided that it ought to do something about the American war resisters who were beginning to arrive. In fact, it became a cause célèbre for Canadian peace activists. SUPA hired draft resister Danny Draitch to operate its program of counseling American war refugees and in midyear SUPA printed five thousand pamphlets called *Escape from Freedom* which were carried south and distributed by various SDS chapters and peace groups. In February 1967, this brochure got into the hands of former Prime Minister Diefenbaker who asked on the floor of the

House of Commons whether or not any of the $4,000 given by the Privy Council office to SUPA the previous year had gone toward printing *Escape from Freedom*. Prime Minister Pearson eventually cooled the blustering Diefenbaker by assuring him that none had, that the pamphlet was an independent enterprise. Whether or not the Canadian Government had inadvertently paid for this "subversive" effort, the job had been done, and twenty to thirty Americans were arriving at SUPA's door every week.

In January 1967 a nineteen-year-old draft resister named Mark Satin stepped off the plane into exile. Satin had grown up in the Midwest but called his home Wichita Falls, Texas, where his father had recently secured a professorship at the university. He spent a year at the University of Illinois studying city planning, and made straight A's. Disillusioned with college, he left for the South and worked on black voter registration with a civil rights group, and then later enrolled at the State University of New York's Harpur College for one semester where he was chairman of the SDS chapter. Disillusioned once more, he dropped out, received an induction notice, and left for Canada. A rebel product of the Midwest, of small-minded parents, and of small-town intolerance, Mark Satin was a very angry and very bitter young man when he arrived in Toronto, and his hostility toward all that America was doing to its young men drove him to doing something about it.

Satin met Heather Dean, an aggressive Marxist-Leninist who worked with SUPA, and she convinced him that he should join the SUPA staff. He was employed at the usual meager salary and began putting in twelve-hour days at an upstairs Spadina Avenue office as director of the Student Union for Peace Action Anti-Draft Programme. He studied immigration procedures and problems, going deeper than the Vancouver Committee's pamphlet, and professionalized SUPA's immigration counseling to the point where it could guarantee that any young man, no matter how difficult his case, could become a landed immigrant if he went through SUPA's immigration program. No one was ever turned down while Satin worked for the Anti-Draft Programme. (Draitch, his predecessor, had left to become a professor at the University of Toronto.)

Satin's reasons for going to Canada can be stated in a single quote: "As a CO I would have been serving the war machine in a non-combatant way—the only thing I wouldn't be doing was pulling the trigger. Jail was out because the U.S. makes no distinction between political prisoners and murderers, drug addicts, and rapists. As far as my friends would know, I would be in jail as a criminal." The intensity with which Satin took the entire exile movement onto his shoulders cannot be explained so easily. Not that it is necessary to discern hidden motives and psychological needs to explain a person's commitment to a cause; it normally isn't, although in the case of Satin who in the eyes of the press was the quintessential draft dodger and who later became a retired radical at twenty-two, it perhaps is. For it refutes the premise that the young radical of the sixties was a result of permissive child rearing. If anything, the opposite is true.

Satin became a rebel because there was much to rebel against and it started at home. Gail Cameron interviewed his family for the *Ladies' Home Journal* and noted, "Probably no two people understand Mark's decision less than his own parents." They refused to admit that Mark dodged the draft for they were afraid it would hurt his father's career. Mrs. Satin said to the interviewer, "I cannot condone what he's done, he may say he's right, but I know he's wrong." Then she was quoted as saying, "Oh Mark, my sweet little Mark, why don't you grow up and become a big boy." That is not permissive child rearing, but it is the sort of stuff that has produced many an angry young man. So Satin, one of the early dodgers and suffering therefrom, younger than most with only a year and a half of university education and thereby finding little identity with the establishment-oriented resisters who had degrees, and having experienced the very worst of the paternalistic rectitude that causes America to figuratively make war against its

young while sending youth away to make real war against imag-
ined enemies, became the angry young revolutionary. Small
wonder.

At any rate, it was Mark Satin who hammered the Toronto
Anti-Draft Programme (TADP) out of an ineffectual student organization. SUPA eventually folded, but by late 1967 the Toronto
Anti-Draft Programme was on its own and doing nicely. Satin and
several volunteer workers were seeing approximately thirty-five
new Americans a week. TADP now had a wide group of supporters.
One of them was Max Allen, who had helped found Support
in Action in New York—the forerunner of the New York Resistance—and later left the staff of the New York Medical College
Department of Psychiatry to help organize draft exiles in Canada.
Responding to the Clausen article in the *New York Times*, Allen
drove up to Toronto to see if Support in Action could honestly
tell young men to go to Canada—he personally was having difficulty telling men to go to prison, especially since he didn't have to
face the question himself. Allen had an honorable discharge from
the U.S. Army but nevertheless chose voluntary exile after seeing
Toronto. He felt he could contribute more through the Toronto
Anti-Draft Programme than through the antidraft groups in New
York, since TADP at least could offer a realistic alternative to the
draft whereas the American organizations could not. Allen also
says his decision to remain in Canada was sealed after the United
States entered the demilitarized zone in Vietnam. Other early
activists were Peggy Merton, John and Nancy Pocock with the
Quakers, Richard Paterak in charge of TADP's information program, and Vince Kelly, a Toronto lawyer who over the years has
handled several hundred difficult immigration cases for the exiles.
"In the early days at TADP," Allen recalls, "there was an extraordinary difference of opinion on how to run things." As could be
expected, by mid-1968 the young Satin and Heather Dean clashed
with the older people who supported TADP, and Satin finally left.
Later, Allen pulled away from the TADP and opened Toronto's
controversial Cinema 2000.

An indication of local feeling toward the new exiles and the new groups assisting them can be found in this mid-1967 editorial in the *Toronto Star* which said of the draft resisters:

> Whatever the reasons for abandoning their homes and coming to Canada, when they arrive they are frequently lonely, frightened and uncertain of the future.
> They need help, financial and psychological, to tide them over until they can find a job and a place to live.
> The United Church of Canada, through its board of evangelism and social service, is acting in the best humanitarian tradition by voting $1,000 to support the volunteer groups helping U.S. draft dodgers.
> A similar gesture of support has been offered by the student council of University College, representing 2,000 undergraduates, who voted to back a fund drive organized by 40 University of Toronto professors.
> These young men have every legal right to apply to become citizens of Canada and to be free from official harassment while they do; the Canadian government has been most careful to make that clear.
> But they also need community support at a most trying period in their lives. The church and the university are appropriate places for that support to gather.

The editorial continued with a warning against groups helping draft resisters to get involved in political action against the U.S.:

> ... But a distinction must be drawn between assistance for those Americans who have reached a personal decision to come to Canada to avoid the draft and propagandizing in the United States to promote draft dodging ... The Student Union for Peace Action (SUPA) has been actively promoting a 12-page tract in the United States [*Escape from Freedom*] which tells Americans how to disobey the law and slip into Canada.
> SUPA's job should be to confine its activities to answering requests for information about Canadian citizenship and giving draft dodgers what help they can when they arrive. But it should not seek to promote draft dodging within the United States.

This attitude on the part of Canada's liberal establishment never changed. Draft dodgers, and later even deserters, were fine; Canada was glad to have them, but they must forget whence they came. They must not be political exiles.

Although political activity was frowned upon from the beginning, it was never openly discouraged. Radicals in the U.S. tended to feel that an American in Canada would be forced to live within a political vacuum or else be deported, but this was never the case. Sensitive to liberal support, the various exile aid groups never let political action jeopardize that support, but, at the same time, they were not afraid to engage in whatever political organizing they felt was worthwhile. The liberals would either end up supporting the action or looking the other way. Also, it should be noted that never in the history of the exile movement was there any degree of police harassment whatsoever from either the Royal Canadian Mounted Police or local authorities. (In fact, in one case, the RCMP publicly contradicted a Toronto official who accused draft dodgers of selling marijuana in the high schools and said it was not true. With deserters it was a different story, but the police went out of their way to be fair to draft dodgers.) As for political action, the TADP didn't let the *Toronto Star*'s editorial dissuade them from expanding their procurement program which amounted essentially to encouraging draft resistance in the U.S. from a Canadian base.

This brings us back to Mark Satin. His most important contribution to draft resistance was editing the TADP *Manual for Draft-Age Immigrants to Canada* which he compiled from his own well-researched knowledge of Canadian immigration and from material submitted by a number of Canadian and American contributors. The ninety-page book contained every conceivable piece of information that a young American could possibly need to know about moving to Canada, including the demolition of a number of myths.* All of it was presented in a strikingly thorough and concise format. It is excellently written. The manual was first published by Toronto's House of Anansi in January 1968 in an

---

*This was important, as the American press was still printing outright lies about the exiles in Canada such as this item, in April 1968, in the *National Observer:* "The FBI, accompanied by a representative of the RCMP, tries to visit every draft dodger offering to drop all charges if he'll return home to the U.S. for immediate induction." Not once did this happen. FBI agents are not even allowed in the country except to attend conferences. Two agents were once arrested by the RCMP for questioning two deserters in Montreal.

edition of 5,000. An edition of 20,000 was printed in March and shipped across the border in bulk, somehow circumventing American publishing laws which prohibit the importation of more than 1,500 copies of a foreign work. By mid-1968 the TADP manual had become the first entirely Canadian-published best seller in the United States. Toronto papers reviewed it favorably and the *New York Times* carried a lengthy piece on it. An article in the *London Observer* was headlined, "Dodge The Draft Book Is Best Seller In U.S." There was an editorial reaction at the *Toronto Star*, however, for the manual was doing exactly what they warned against and they said that Satin's proclamation that it merely would "inform" was in their opinion a narrow definition of "encourage."

Encourage it did. If a resister had any doubts about going to Canada before he read the book, he seldom had any after finishing it. The book could be purchased for two dollars at any Resistance, SDS, or draft-counseling office in the U.S. and also at most campus bookstores. Or it would be mailed by the TADP itself upon request. Incredibly, by 1970, the manual was in its fifth edition, expanded to 105 pages including material for U.S. military deserters, with 65,000 copies in print. Both the TADP and the now not-so-fledgling House of Anansi were doing very well from it.

By the spring of 1968 estimates of the number of resisters in Canada was running from an accepted minimum of ten thousand to a maximum of twenty thousand. The TADP now had a full-time paid staff of four counselors and was receiving—especially after Tet and the Pueblo affair—as many as eighteen new people a day, a jump from the 1967 average of five a day. The TADP office moved to Yonge Street near the end of the subway line and settled down to a stable, although impecunious, respectability. Toronto's Trinity Church opened its basement to the TADP for a hostel— several other hostels had folded or had become urban communes —and the upstairs became the site of several antidraft rallies. Joan Baez sang and spoke at one Trinity Church rally and gratuitously told the audience that the draft dodgers in Canada should all return and go to jail. She was never asked back, and exiles two years later still smiled sardonically and shook their heads in disbelief when they recalled that evening. As the Programme geared for summer, the *Globe and Mail* headlined a sympathetic article, "Summer Crisis Seen, Anti-Draft Office Asks Backers For Funds."

One of those backers was William Spira, a Toronto business-man who began early in 1968 to assist the Anti-Draft Programme with considerable time and money. Formerly an American citizen, Spira came to Canada in 1953 during the McCarthy era to escape an attitude he described as "Our roses are the reddest and our cherries are the sweetest." Spira also objected to the FBI constantly questioning everybody. In Canada he founded a structural steel business that eventually employed twenty people and did a million dollars' worth of business a year including contracts for several notable Toronto civic buildings. It is difficult to say whether or not the Toronto Anti-Draft Programme would have suffered a spiritual and financial collapse without the aid of William Spira, but it is certain that he did more than any single American or Canadian to see that it didn't.

Spira was a huge help in his willingness to counsel and hide U.S. military deserters in 1968 when their legal status in Canada was still in question and exile aid groups were wary of having direct contact with them. The stocky, heavy-jowled businessman once had seventeen deserters staying at his $30,000 home in the pleasant suburb of Thornhill.* The *Toronto Telegram* commented that the deserter underground railroad ended beside Bill Spira's thirty-six-foot swimming pool. When the TADP could safely handle deserter counseling from its office, Spira gave up the presidency of three firms, including his own (while remaining a forty-five percent partner), and became an immigration counselor at the Programme's Yonge Street office where the flow of deserters—his main concern—was surpassing that of the draft re-

*See Chapter 3.

sisters. Needless to say, he played a dominant role in the TADP by mid-1969. Somehow, William Spira and hip, radical counselors like Bernard Jaffe managed to work side by side at the Programme's office, but the staff voted Spira down a lot.

In 1968 Naomi Wall, who had been operating an employment service from her living room for Mark Satin during the previous year, came to work at TADP as a full-time staff member. American, and a university graduate from Philadelphia, Mrs. Wall was the wife—later separated—of a University of Toronto psychology professor who had returned to his native Canada to avoid the draft after becoming a naturalized American citizen. At TADP she continued to be in charge of the employment service which is the most essential part of each exile aid program since many young men could not qualify for landed immigrant status without an offer of a job. Naomi Wall survived the usual male dominance and prejudice against females counseling male dodgers and deserters, and by 1971 she was the senior staff member. She turned thirty-one then, though she never looked a day over twenty. She attributed her youthfulness to radical politics.

Not so young and not so radical, William Spira worked himself as hard at immigration counseling as he had at his business, and in early 1970 his health was threatened. Concurrently, there was the feeling among the younger staff members and workers at TADP that Spira's influence over the Programme was a little too strong, that they needed room to breathe and to direct the organization as they saw fit. Spira took a holiday and crossed Canada and helped the many new antidraft programs in Thunder Bay, Winnipeg, Saskatoon, Calgary, and Edmonton get off the ground. When he returned to Toronto, he left TADP and directed his energies toward the campaign to liberate Canada from American economic control. This came as a surprise to those people who had thought that because of Spira's strong dislike of exile political action against the U.S.A. he really had been employed all along by both the CIA, to help keep the pressure valve of Canada open, and by

Canadian corporate interests to channel dissident American manpower back into the multinational industrial state of North America. But such imputations were out of order, for even though he seemed to be serving capitalism and the establishment much more than his young radical colleagues liked, Bill Spira helped to bring thousands of young American fugitives legally into Canada.

Throughout the late 1960s American refugees were coming into Canada at many points other than Montreal, Vancouver, and Toronto. As early as July 1967, students at the University of Windsor launched Information '67, a campaign to urge Americans across the border to "beat the draft and come to Canada." The group mailed out thousands of Information '67 pamphlets to adjacent Michigan high schools and then formed an aid committee to deal with new arrivals. In the Ontario towns of Kitchener and Waterloo, west of Toronto, where several universities are located, the Reverend Walter Klassen and Dr. Ron Lambert, both Canadian, began operating an assistance program for war resisters, some of whom were American students at the University of Waterloo and who chose not to return when their student visas expired. New arrivals were referred to the Kitchener-Waterloo area from the active Ann Arbor draft-counseling center, as it was known that it was easier to find work and get "landed" there (become a landed immigrant). A group of American professors, several of them draft resisters, at the University of Saskatchewan formed the Regina Committee to Aid American War Immigrants in 1967. Although life for a young American in Regina might be described as somewhat akin to Siberian exile, this middling prairie city could claim the unique distinction up until 1969 of being the capital of Canada's first socialist province. Roger Howard, a political science professor from New York who left the U.S. as a draft resister in 1965 and who later worked with the Regina Committee, found that his own Marxist politics were not entirely alien outside the walls of the university as is the case in most of North America. Howard discovered that the politics of Saskatchewan provided a fascinating model of the successes and failures of social-left government. Regina later became a channeling point for American deserters who had difficulty getting landed elsewhere.*

The most important group outside Canada's three large urban centers was, and is, Ottawa's Assistance with Immigration and the Draft (AID). Immigration counseling began in Ottawa in 1967 under the sponsorship of several Canadian peace activists, and, when the influx became too large for them to handle, a formal committee was set up in January 1968, with Jim Wilcox, a thirty-six-year-old American professor of English at Carlton University, elected as chairman. Within a year the Committee provided ten part-time counselors for war resisters: eight Americans and two Canadians.

Wilcox moved to Canada in 1967 with his wife and children from Adrian College, Michigan, where, he said, "We led a beautiful existence if you didn't bother to think." After the Detroit riots and as their friends in the peace movement educated them to the realities of Vietnam, Wilcox and his wife Joan began to think more and more. They could no longer accept the seventeenth-century atmosphere of the small liberal arts college. "Our friends made us see that we were really those despicable paper-liberals," Wilcox once said. It also occurred to him that his son was beginning to look more and more like cannon fodder, and so, as a protest against what he considered to be unacceptable and unchangeable conditions, the family left for Canada. Perhaps out of an attempt to justify self-exile or out of pure compassion or a mixture of the two, Jim Wilcox committed himself to several soul-consuming years as director of AID.

During the first half of 1968 AID was receiving roughly five Americans a week, and it gradually increased to twenty and thirty a week in 1969-70. Approximately half the resisters came directly from the U.S., having chosen to live in Ottawa, while the rest were referred to the Ottawa group from the Toronto Programme. Ottawa had the advantage of being able to "land" people in both Ottawa and Hull, Quebec, across the river from Parliment. At

*See Chapter 5.

both points there was no delay as in the larger cities where American and European immigrants faced a four- to six-month wait for internal immigration appointments. Ottawa was reserved for those young Americans who did not qualify easily for landed immigrant status or for the fugitives, especially deserters in the days preceding May 1969, who stood a good chance of being refused immigration at the border. Also, the Ottawa group had the advantage of sending men through immigration offices that were right under the noses of Parliament. If American war resisters and later deserters were having a hard time of it with a particular immigration officer or a particular office, a call to Parliament Hill from Jim Wilcox to one of the many sympathetic M.P.'s could very often clear it up. The immigration offices at Ottawa and Hull were too close to the government for individual prejudices on the part of immigration officers to be tolerated. If a war resister got turned down, Wilcox found out why and made sure that it did not happen the second time around.

Wilcox and his wife became the American exiles' experts on Canadian immigration law. All of the exile aid groups were in touch with AID to keep abreast of the latest rulings that might concern American immigrants. The crucial issue of immigration as it related to the war resisters can best be appreciated after understanding how Canadian immigration works. Neither draft dodgers nor deserters had as yet been given political or humanitarian asylum or had been officially classed as refugees such as the Czechs in 1968 and the Hungarians before them or the 250 Tibetan families in 1970 who qualified for government aid. War resisters were considered, officially, no different from any other immigrants. (The resisters did, however, have several advantages immigrants from Europe—other than those fleeing Eastern Europe during upheavals—didn't have, and that was extraordinary Canadian sympathy toward their situation which led, as explained, to the organizing of immigrant assistance groups within Canada.) The war resisters came to Canada first as tourists, visitors: Americans could simply drive across the border whereas immigrants from anywhere else had to apply for immigrant visas in their home countries. Few Americans actually became landed immigrants at the border (as the author foolishly attempted, somehow making it) when they crossed into Canada for the first time. It is at the border that most American immigrants to Canada are immigrated, reserving overburdened internal immigration (a six-month wait) for Europeans with tentative immigrant visas—but the war resister could not afford being turned back if his application was refused, which it could be for any number of reasons: insufficient funds, no job offer, no skill, no degree. And so they first entered as visitors, visited the aid groups and, wishing to avoid the six-month wait, returned to the U.S. and recrossed back into Canada. At this time they applied for landed immigrant status. Canadian officials did not make a practice of informing the Americans on the other side that they were returning a draft-age male who had attempted to immigrate—this *did* happen, though seldom. It could have been a common practice, and many Americans were surprised that it wasn't. The problem, however, was that if one's application was not accepted, regulations prevented one from continuing into Canada as a visitor. The prospective applicant had to return to the U.S. and, if he wanted to go to Canada as a visitor, cross at another point. Technically, he was supposed to return to the U.S. and reapply at a Canadian Consulate or by mail directly to Ottawa. (In several cases deserters who were refused, and knew the FBI awaited them on the other side, frantically called the nearest aid group and explained their predicament. The exile staffer called a lawyer who called immigration who called the border and the regulation was waived and the deserters were allowed in on special visitors' passes.)

The assistance programs were of utmost importance since it was always very difficult for an American to find out exactly how to immigrate and then successfully do it. Nonresisters could afford the risk of being turned back, usually had the time to go through the consulates (a more difficult procedure), or could apply directly by mail. Many Americans who worked for U.S. companies in

Canada had their immigration paper work done for them by their firms. Also, war resisters were young and hence not so well qualified, although extra points were given for being young, as Canada wanted younger immigrants. But most war resisters didn't have a lot of money, a skill, nor always a lot of education. A college degree alone could usually get one in, but it meant only squeaking by. Older people coming to Canada usually had many years' experience at a trade or type of work and normally had a job waiting. Their acceptance at the border was automatic; they had more points than they needed.

The point system, briefly, was implemented in 1967 to limit subjectiveness and provide a fairer system of determining who is or who is not a qualified immigrant. It was a great boon to the war resisters for in most cases it removed personal prejudice from the system. However, it made the system complicated to the degree that very few resisters could get in if they hadn't at least read the TADP manual. One had to have fifty points—so many for being of an optimum age, so many for a job offer, so many if one was bilingual, so many for adequate funds, so many for skills, education, and so forth. One also received ten extra points for immigrating at the border. It was important for the prospective immigrant to know which skills were worth the most points, how high a listing his education would receive, what a particular job offer was worth. It was important for each war resister to go prepared to impress the interviewing officer as best he could because he would receive ten points for a good "personal assessment." This didn't amount to much in the case of older immigrants who usually got seventy and eighty points automatically, based on years of experience and job demand (until the mid-sixties, Americans didn't immigrate to Canada unless it was for more money, meaning their job was in demand), but, in the case of the war resisters, it usually made the difference between being accepted or not being accepted. The Canadian Immigration officer could give zero points to a middle-aged businessman whom he didn't like, and the middle-aged businessman would still make it. If the immigration officer gave less than eight points on personal assessment to the war resister, more than likely the war resister would not be allowed in. That there are at least 25,000 American war resisters now *legally* in Canada testifies to the fairness of Canadian immigration officers.

Or, it might tell you that Canadian government officials at all levels generally like American war resisters. In literally hundreds of cases, young exiles-to-be told the officer they were deserters or dodgers and they received the maximum points for the interview. Many were allowed in with only forty-eight or forty-nine points when their plight as refugees was made clear.

Essentially, then, the exile aid groups had to provide responsible immigration counseling on a professional level before they could advise a young man that he was ready to return to the U.S. and enter again, this time applying at the border. They were dealing with a man's life, or at least five long years of it if he were caught. The groups all provided Canadian drivers when it was necessary to take the young man across the border. The resister and his escort would then cross into the USA at an easy point and reenter at a major crossing where there was an immigration office. This was always a frightening ordeal for every war resister, save those who applied from within. Usually a lot of sleep was lost before getting landed, and a lot of grass was smoked and wine or beer consumed immediately afterward.

Jim Wilcox's group not only could land people from within, but it had one of the best "border-running" operations going in Canada. Each of the ten part-time counselors was responsible for the war resister assigned to him, from counseling, to housing, to procuring the Canadian driver, to the crossing itself—usually at one of the St. Lawrence River bridge points in upper New York State. AID's finesse in this came from several years of running deserters through the underground to Ottawa where, if they could be, they were discreetly landed. They would show up at Wilcox's front door and introduce themselves by the code-name, Mike. Referred to Ottawa's "subprogramme" by Montreal and Toronto, deserters were from then on called Mike until they were landed. (Prior to 1969, few deserters were getting landed anywhere but Ottawa.) Wilcox writes, "One day there were so many 'Mikes' running around that one of my Carlton University colleagues, a Canadian named Mike, found himself assigned a counselor and housing before he could defend his identity."

By late 1969 the American exile community within stone-throwing distance of the Federal Parliament numbered approximately 700 people. Hundreds of other war resisters passed through Assistance with Immigration and the Draft and moved on. Jim and Joan Wilcox may not have done anything to impede the American war machine, but saving over a thousand young men from its grasp was quite enough to exonerate them of the title "despicable paper-liberals."

Exile aid groups were later founded in the Ontario towns of Kingston, Hamilton, Guelph, and Welland and usually comprised Canadian professors and local ministers. In the maritime provinces, with forty to fifty American exiles in each major city, two groups were started in early 1969: The Nova Scotia Committee to Aid American War Objectors in Halifax and the St. John Anti-Draft Programme in New Brunswick, the first operated largely by Canadians and the latter run by several exile couples. At the University of New Brunswick in Fredricton there were over forty American draft resisters taking courses by 1970. When Victoria, British Columbia, was a popular place through which to immigrate, the Victoria Committee to Aid War Resisters was normally receiving at least one American a day at the home of Phil Rogers, and he was able to see that they were all immigrated. With its temperate and lovely climate, forests and Indian reservations, and long Pacific beaches, Vancouver Island became the hippie mecca of the Northwest, and draft resisters suffered from the reaction that inevitably followed and were no longer able to immigrate through the Victoria immigration office at all. One other group that appeared in late 1968 in Kamloops, B.C., and disappeared one year later, was Us, an alternate-culture youth organization founded by draft resisters and dedicated to aiding both new resisters and Canadian transient youth. Us published several editions of *American Refugee News*, but energy was soon diverted to other things. The group received favorable comment in this Fastest Growing frontier city which looks like it was imported whole from southern California—quotes from the president of the Chamber of Commerce and the mayor of Kamloops respectively: "In many respects I sympathize with the young men who do not want to fight a war they don't believe in"; "The draft dodgers and deserters should be commended for the courage of their convictions." The warm air and warm attitude in this central B.C. town on the Trans-Canada highway continued to attract young Americans despite the disappearance of Us.*

Altogether, the 1970 *Manual for Draft-Age Immigrants to Canada* was able to list thirty-two active exile aid groups and contacts throughout Canada.

•

Exile politics began in October 1967, when several hundred draft resisters marched as a contingent in a Toronto anti-Vietnam war demonstration.** They carried placards that read simply, "We Refused To Go." There was a note of pretentiousness in that announcement, or so it seems looking back, but it did take a bit of courage to so brazenly inform Canadians at Toronto's first big peace march that exiles were in Canada in strength. The march down Yonge Street drew the curious gaze of Toronto shoppers and businessmen who had never seen a big antiwar march before— Whose war? What war?—complete with real American draft resisters. There was little public antipathy.

The exiles did not hold back from politics previous to 1968 out of fear of a negative public reaction, however, but because the aid groups could not afford to impede their immigration and employment programs by engaging in anti-American political

*See Chapter 6.
**An up-to-date and more comprehensive discussion of exile politics appears in Chapter 10.

work. Nonetheless, a separate group was founded in April 1968, apart from the TADP, called the Union of American Exiles (UAE). It immediately brought together fifty radical activists who wanted an organization through which to channel dissent. Tom Kane, the president, wrote at the time, ". . . there is a very real task ahead for the UAE, in what can be called a political sense. It can be the vehicle for learning and communicating the why of our exile." At the behest of Ronnie Nevin, one of the most active exiled women, the University of Toronto student council gave the Union of American Exiles, rent free, the entire basement of their building on St. George Street, and, for more than two years, this was the center of American exile activity in Canada. New England Resistance was pleased with this turn of events and promptly sent up two organizers to help arouse political consciousness among the exiles. They crossed Canada on this mission and wrote in *Infinite Eye*, the UAE's first publication, "The establishment of a collective identity in a nation that would like nothing more than to absorb these exiles into her middle class quietly will be a difficult and perhaps dangerous task. The establishment of an exile politics is altogether likely to result in repression—it is a risk that exiles must decide if they are willing to take."

The UAE was willing to take the risk, but the task was far too difficult for this unwieldly 150-member group, beleaguered from the start by fractionalization. It was a bunch of anarchists attempting to elect officers and write a constitution. Nevertheless, the UAE worked closely with Canadian student groups and together pulled off some large peace demonstrations at which the exile voice was raised more loudly each time. Draft resisters also burned their draft cards and induction notices in front of the American consulate to protest the sentencing of Dr. Spock and demonstrated again in August to protest the Chicago convention, splattering the consulate with paint and ink and getting two of their number arrested. In November 1968, 150 exiles voted for a president-in-exile and elected Eldridge Cleaver. Ernesto Fusco, Jr., a draft resister whose revolutionary rhetoric always outshone the most revolutionary action the UAE could possibly come up with, wrote, "The election of Cleaver as the first president-in-exile marks the beginning of exile politics." This kind of hyperbole almost marked the end of the UAE.

Apart from protest, the UAE managed to operate a number of social services for newly arrived refugees such as the weekly New Arrivals Night, organized by Graham Northcott, several Christmas dinners, and various social gatherings including speeches and films. It began its aid work where the TADP left off, and also ran a housing program and employment office. There was a coffee room at the UAE office stocked with fresh coffee and records and reading matter where, the advertisements read, exiles could "drop in for inimitable conversation." For a nervous young resister to find such an organization at the end of his trek north did a great deal for his morale; friendships were made, and people quickly learned they were not alone.

An exile Kiwanis Club was not what the radicals had in mind, however, and splits soon developed. Tom Kane felt political work was important, but insisted "The union is performing a political function simply through its existence and its aid work." This, of course, was true but it was not an acceptable revolutionary defini- tion to the Marxist-Leninists who saw their work as "educating" the new immigrants to a political consciousness. Mere political consciousness as exiles was not enough; the only "correct" politi- cal consciousness was Marxist-Leninist. It is the story of most of the Left. Does the Left purge itself of the nonbelievers, the impure ones, or does it collectively fight the oppressor? Since the UAE couldn't resolve this, it broke up, its active members drifting into the Internationalists, the Trotskyites, the Canadian Party of Labour, and the Canadian National Liberation Front; others going to work for the underground press; and still others, mainly a group of southerners who had worked together in civil rights before coming to Canada, abandoning politics altogether in favor of the cultural revolution.

It must be noted, however, that the Union of American Exiles did have an enthusiastic though terrible baseball team. One reporter wrote in a Philadelphia paper, "They have the only baseball games in the world where both teams are the dodgers."

The one enduring success of the Union of American Exiles was its publishing enterprise which began with a news sheet and eventually became a magazine that took the title, *The American Exile in Canada*. It was originally intended as a voice of the UAE, but, as it had to present all sides of the many arguments, it became more of a forum and ultimately a news magazine reporting on exile affairs. In the fall of 1969 when the UAE folded, *The American Exile* had an active volunteer staff of approximately ten people. Among them were Dee Knight, a former McCarthy campaign worker and assistant manager of Canada's "Canair Relief" for Biafra; Tom Needham, a radical journalist; Charles Campbell, an exile at work on a Ph.D. in English, and his wife, Maryanne; and Stan Pietlock, editor, a graduate of Fordham with a masters from the University of Pennsylvania who had worked for several years in the research and photo department of *Newsweek*. Strangely enough, *The American Exile* began to look very much like an amateur *Newsweek*—so much so that eventually it didn't even look amateur anymore.

In the spring of 1969, with issue number 17, *The American Exile* was changed to *AMEX: The American Expatriate in Canada* and the magazine was expanded to thirty pages, later issues going to forty and more. A long debate went into changing *exile* to *expatriate* and it was decided, to the displeasure of many, that the latter word more accurately reflected the staff's orientation and the direction of the magazine, especially since the publication dealt mostly with American war immigrants' affairs in Canada and not with the American political scene as one would expect an *exile* publication to do. *Expatriate* implies choosing to remain outside the U.S., even if one didn't originally want to leave—most of the staff of *AMEX* would not have returned to the U.S. were it possible. *Exile*, on the other hand, implies going back or at least a desire to do so; *exile* reminds people that the resisters were forced to leave and cannot return, while *expatriate* accepts that fact—having to remain outside the U.S. perhaps forever. Both words can apply; it's a matter of emphasis. Nevertheless, the magazine continued to refer to resisters as *exiles*, not expatriates, even coining the term, *amexiles*. Essentially, then, *AMEX* adopted a dual character reflecting the reality of the situation, and became the expatriate publication of American exiles. *AMEX* accomplished what the UAE couldn't: bringing the exiles together. By 1970 *AMEX* had a paid-subscriber list of nearly four thousand with another one thousand issues going out to newsstands in Montreal, Toronto, and Vancouver.

Although the publication of *AMEX* is a collective enterprise and encourages contributions from exiles across Canada, much of its content is a reflection of its editor, twenty-seven-year-old Stan Pietlock. Pietlock, from Wilmington, Delaware, and the first draft resister from that state, had never so much as even participated in a peace march during college or graduate school. The war meant nothing to him. He preferred, if he had to choose national service, to go into the Peace Corps, and so he applied and was accepted. He had stalled his draft board with a CO application which was refused and then appealed. The appeal rejection plus an induction notice came through on the same day—one day before Peace Corps training was to begin. Not being a radical, Pietlock had no second thoughts about going to Canada; it only made sense to leave for a country where he could live his life as he saw fit, since he couldn't do that in the United States. Pietlock, however, like many other draft resisters, became a radical *because* he went to Canada. As he explained it, he had heard about American imperialism but had never seen it. Only a blind man can't see it in Canada, and Pietlock saw it quickly. America owned Canada! He began to identify with the Canadian antiimperialist groups which usually had a few American members and found friends in the Union of American Exiles. In Toronto he marched in his first antiwar demonstration. Before long he was dedicated to antiimperialism and a free Canada. At the same time, he continued as a high school teacher for the Toronto

Public School Board and devoted much of his spare time to putting *AMEX* together.

Issues of *AMEX* carried articles on everything from burning draft boards to "Eating Out" in metropolitan Toronto. The expatriate-exile controversy was thrashed out in print between advertisements for UAE charter flights to Europe and notices of dodger-deserter softball on Sunday afternoons in High Park. Charles Campbell contributed thoughtful and well-written book and movie reviews while Vladimir Sutherland Brown (an alias), a doctoral candidate at the University of Toronto and a member of the Canadian Party of Labour, castigated the drug culture in one essay and wrote frequently on revolutionary purity and the imminent rising of the working class. Brown occasionally contributed pieces demanding "the eviction of Yanqui exploitation and the assertion of Canadian independence." *AMEX* availed itself very little of Liberation News Service and instead concentrated on material that was not being aired elsewhere. Much space was devoted to educating Americans about Canadian life and reminding Canadians of the American threat. Since exiles were experts on the American threat, they did not feel out of place as part of the vanguard of the Canadian independence movement. Although editor Pietlock soon became one of the most "Canadianized" of all American war resisters, he never forgot he was an American exile as well. He could easily have blended into the Canadian woodwork like so many others have done, identifying entirely with Canada to the point of convincing himself he was Canadian, but he chose not to and has little respect for those who have. (One Canadianized resister who became an executive in a Toronto advertising agency stated that he faced the reality of his exile for the first time when he had to refuse to go on a business trip to the home office in New York.) Pietlock felt that Americans, for their own benefit and Canada's, should stay recognizable as a subgroup, stating, "There are certain things we can do together—there are a lot of things we know that Canadians don't; there is a role for a publication."

AMEX was well received by Torontonians. Reviewers called it a veritable Baedeker's for Toronto. Ron Haggart, a daily columnist for the *Toronto Telegram*, devoted a column to the "trade paper for exiles" with a detailed discussion of its contents and commented, "The magazine is surprisingly nonpolitical (which drew a critical letter recently from a puzzled Canadian). It is also surprisingly free of antiwar tirades (they've been through all that, I suppose) and just beneath the surface seems to lurk a rather vague disappointment that Canadians are not more chauvinistic about their own country." If Pietlock, his staff, and *AMEX* have contributed in any way to an awareness that Canada must liberate itself from the American cultural and economic empire, then together they have made a revolutionary contribution, as it is nothing less than revolutionary for a country to oppose American imperialism.

●

In April 1969, on the CBC national television show "Public Eye," Bill Spira announced that there were now 60,000 draft resisters and deserters living in Canada. The figure left many people stunned; they had no idea so many had come. Since there was no way to prove how many exiles there were, the figure 60,000 occasionally met with skepticism, but a close examination of the exodus revealed that Spira could not have been too far off. There may not have been 60,000 exiles in Canada in April of 1969, but there certainly were by early 1970. By then immigration figures showed that approximately 20,000 draft-age American males had immigrated to Canada since 1965. These figures did not include the thousands who had applied for landed immigrant status in 1969 but had not received it at the time of the tally, nor did it include those who came in the first half of 1970, *the heaviest period of the entire exodus.* An extrapolation of official statistics, then, would show that there were approximately 25,000 *legal* male war-immigrants in Canada by the end of 1970. At the same time, most people who have worked with the exile aid groups admit that perhaps no more than half the exiles actually become landed, accounting for another 10,000-15,000 Americans living underground—living openly in Canada but not as legal immigrants. Some people felt that there were even more unlanded Americans in Canada than that, largely because of the huge influx of armed forces deserters into Canada, many of whom would never qualify for legal status. Exile spokesmen were reluctant to admit, however, that so many could be coming up and staying illegally. Very important, and usually forgotten, are the many thousands of young women who went to Canada with their husbands and boyfriends. Approximately one in four male exiles came with a girlfriend or wife which, by 1971, brought the exile total up to somewhere between fifty and sixty thousand. Finally, one must include a large number of the three thousand American students studying at Canadian universities who were eventually drafted but who remained in Canada on student visas. (It is interesting to recall the Chinese Inclusion Act passed several years ago for the purpose of legally immigrating any Chinese who were in Canada illegally, living and working in the Chinese communities. Many more thousands than anyone had expected came forward to register as immigrants. Similarly, there may be more young Americans illegally in Canada than current estimates reveal. Americans are much less conspicuous than Chinese.)

In the fall of 1969 the *New York Times* reported that there were 60,000 exiles in Canada while the Canadian Press (the Canadian wire service) was quoting a figure of 80,000. Congressman Edward Koch visited Toronto, Ottawa, and Montreal briefly at the end of the year to speak with exiles about his proposed amnesty bill and was informed that 60,000 might even be a conservative figure.* He presented the 60,000 figure at his press conference the following week in New York. Meanwhile, several members of Parliament were being quoted as saying there were 100,000 American exiles in Canada and that they would eventually have a big effect on voting patterns. One M.P. said they were expecting 200,000 to come. At the same time two Canadian psychologists

*See Chapter 12.

who have worked closely with exile organizations addressed a convention in San Francisco in the spring of 1970 and reported that there were 100,000 American war immigrants in Canada. Whatever the figures, for the first time since 1932 more people immigrated to Canada from the States in 1969 than went to the U.S. from Canada.*

An indication of the flow into the Toronto area alone in late 1969 was an article in *AMEX* reporting that in September 162 people were housed by the Union of American Exiles and the Toronto Anti-Draft Programme; for every person requiring housing at least three exiles arrived and found their own. The winter and spring of 1970 saw the greatest number of monthly arrivals. Just as the flow was easing, giving the aid groups a chance to catch their breath, the United States invaded Cambodia, and U.S. troops and police fired on students at Kent and Jackson State Universities. The onslaught which followed these events was greater than any group could handle. The Toronto Anti-Draft Programme was seeing between fifty and eighty new men per day and was able to give only the most cursory counseling. CBC news announced that mail inquiries to the Montreal Council were running sixty a day and that over a thousand war resisters per month were coming into Montreal. In May Canadian Secretary of State Gerard Pelletier predicted in a speech in Los Angeles that Canada would have a greater influx of young men from the U.S. because of the Cambodian war. He told reporters at a news conference, "This increase is coming at the same time that antidraft factions in Canada have begun a drive to bring more draft dodgers and deserters into this country."

In December of 1969 the New York based Clergy and Laymen Concerned About Vietnam (CALCAV) decided that it was time to lend assistance to the Americans in Canada. For the past six months they had helped finance the American Deserters Com-

---

**Since these figures can be regarded as roughly accurate, it is interesting to note an article appearing in the *New York Times* on February 5, 1970: "Figures on the number of draft dodgers vary greatly, but a State Department official said his most reliable estimate was about 2,000."

mittee in Stockholm and had provided a minister, Reverend Tom Hayes, to act as a counselor in residence for the 300 American deserters there. As an adjunct to the General Assembly of the National Council of Churches (NCC) in Detroit in December, CALCAV convinced a number of religious leaders to cross over to Windsor for several days to meet with spokesmen for the Toronto, Ottawa, and Montreal exile organizations. A report of the Windsor consultation was issued at the Detroit convocation and the National Council of Churches adopted guidelines for action. From this evolved a fund-raising campaign which brought in $10,000 by January 1970. In ceremonies at the Canadian border and in the large cities, $5,000 of it was turned over to the various groups with the rest going into a fund that was administered by Canon Maurice Wilkenson of the Canadian Council of Churches and a former combat officer in World War II. The Canadian Council also held a fund drive, and money collected from churches in both countries was thereupon channeled to aid groups through Wilkenson's special committee. If it had not been for this last-minute interest of the churches, several of the aid groups might have folded or been forced to cut back staff and services. To coordinate and analyze the funding of the exile programs, an American Mennonite with a CO deferment, Jim Wert, was assigned to Reverend Wilkenson as his assistant. The assignment to the National Council of Churches constituted alternate service and the irony of it evoked much laughter among those who knew the story. Wert, of course, could not let it be known until his service was completed—lest his local board find out that the NCC had assigned him to Canada to help bring draft resisters north.

At the same time the NCC in New York set up an Emergency Ministry Concerning U.S. Draft-Age Emigrants In Canada headed by Reverend Richard Killmer. This group continued to send funds north but more importantly instituted a program of contacting local ministers to visit parents of dodgers and deserters in an attempt to secure parental support when necessary and to acquire the documents that the son needed for immigration. Parents refusing to send records, especially birth certificates in the case of

GIs who came to Canada directly without stopping at home to pick them up, was a serious problem, and the Emergency Ministry helped alleviate it to the gratitude of many. Killmer's group also published *Contact*, a newsletter for parents in the U.S. whose sons were in Canada.

Canadian churches by this time had managed to pass resolutions in support of the war resisters, often against the wishes of local congregations. The Synod of the Anglican Diocese of Huron officially encouraged Anglicans to open their doors to exiles from the United States. The Anglican church also assigned retired brigadier general, the venerable E. S. Light, archdeacon of Saskatchewan and general secretary of the Anglican Church of Canada to Canon Wilkenson's Canadian committee on exiles. The former Canadian army chaplain thereafter spent much of his time counseling U.S. Army deserters. The Lutheran Church in America, Canada Section, decided by a vote of their executive council in May 1970 to "support the Canadian Council of Churches exile aid program not on the basis of whether it is proper or not for these young men to evade the U.S. draft laws: rather, on the ground of compassion in that it is a fact that these men are in Canada and are in need." In Vancouver the Unitarians set up Immigration Aid to Refugees of Conscience, feeling that the stance of the Vancouver Committee to Aid War Objectors had become too radical. The Unitarians seemed to have an endless supply of money and paid several full-time staff members to counsel Americans. In early 1970 the two Vancouver groups amalgamated and the Unitarians shared their money. Liberal and church support in Vancouver was then administered through a new group called the Co-Ordinating Council to Aid American War Refugees.

No doubt the most helpful Canadian church was the Mennonite. The Mennonites' own history was one of fleeing conscription in Eastern Europe en masse in the late 1800s and coming in several large groups to the United States and Canada. The American Mennonites, for the most part, have completely forgotten their traditions and would as soon turn a draft dodger over to the police as give him assistance. But the Canadian church, based in

Winnipeg, was driven by its astute leadership to do something about the problem of American refugees. To explain the situation to the laymen and local ministers, the Mennonites published *I would like to dodge the draft dodgers but . . .*, a ninety-six-page book in which several dodgers and deserters tell their stories and exile writers explain the needs and problems of the draft-age immigrants. The editor, Reverend Frank Epp, had been personally involved with war refugees through his church in Ottawa which had provided AID with a free office. One of the best things the Mennonites did, aside from opening an exile coffee house in Ottawa operated by a young Canadian folk singer and his wife, was to encourage Mennonite farmers in Ontario to hire draft resisters at $200 a month plus room and board for as long as they needed work. (Farming counts high on immigration job points.)

In the U.S. there was little public comment regarding the National Council of Churches' decision to aid draft exiles and deserters. The NCC is far removed from small-town congregations whose members think that the National Council is run by communists or whatever and therefore ignore whatever it says. The FBI did announce, however, that it was concerned about Clergy and Laymen Concerned About Vietnam and would begin investigating to what extent that group had aided the exiles. In Canada, the American exiles being a very public issue, there was a certain amount of expected reaction against all the discussion of church support. A "Religion Today" column in the *Vancouver Sun* was titled, "Churches Aid Dodgers, Ignore Canadian Youth—draft resisters get welcome, our own youngsters on breadlines" (which, unfortunately, was true). In the *Montreal Star*'s "Faith in Action" column, one Francis Allen commented on the Anglicans' decision to welcome dodgers and reported that that resolution was "hotly received, drawing remarks from some clergymen that draft dodgers are 'rats' and 'traitors' to their country. These clergymen may be expressing themselves rather strongly," Allen wrote, "but their opinions are certainly closer to the reality of the situation than that expressed by the woolly-minded do-gooders who passed the resolution." In another column Allen said, ". . . helping and encouraging youngsters who have deserted their own country is contrary to basic morality and the ethics of international law." Less hypocritical but equally representative of such attitudes was an address before the Royal Canadian Legion Convention by a Legion secretary who said, "Comrades, these antidraft organizations in Canada contain every shade of red from pinko to Trotskyite to Maoist."

Even if this antiexile reaction had been the majority opinion, which it wasn't, Canadian leaders in the government, the media, the universities, and the churches would continue to support the exiles in every way they could. And even if the support and assistance emanating from Canadian church leadership was, at best, paternalistic, and the clergy's attitudes clashed with the young radicals who operated the aid groups, their aid, nevertheless, was invaluable. And, again, it was the Mennonites who went all the way, going so far as to send a delegation of Mennonite leaders to meet with Prime Minister Trudeau in March 1970, presenting him with a brief calling on the government to encourage U.S. draft dodgers and deserters to come to Canada.

Trudeau had never publicly commented on these new exiles, and the Mennonites awaited his reply. After reading the appeal, the prime minister said that he had never before received "such a beautiful brief . . . with views close to my heart," and noted that "draft dodgers may not be consciously Christian but doesn't what they are doing have to do with ideas of brotherhood, a kind of religious conviction?" He told the Mennonites, "Your motivation is like mine. It stems from a belief in a transcendent God. The young radicals are looking for the same thing too, whatever existentialist and nihilist elements there may be in their thinking." Trudeau said to the press at the same time, "The government is welcoming U.S. draft dodgers and deserters to Canada," and, pleased with the Mennonites' concern, he remarked, "I, too, hope Canada will become a refuge from militarism."

So it is.

THREE

The Deserters

A man who refuses the army after he's already been inducted, instead of before, is called a deserter and he remains saddled forever with an appellation that traditionally conjures images of a shirker, a coward, an almost subhuman entity. It is therefore difficult to write about deserters without rectifying the term. But then perhaps no amount of amending can remove the prejudicial connotations aroused by this word and, if so, it would be good to use another name like *conscientious escapee* for example as coined by *Avant Garde* magazine to replace the pejorative *deserter*. But that is gimmickry; and it also defers to popular prejudice instead of trying to change it. So *deserter* will have to be the word used here—it doesn't even have the advantage of being acceptable in Canada as is draft dodger—and the reader is only asked to reconsider the meaning of the word in the light of the massacre at My Lai 4.

There have always been deserters, to be sure. During great wars there are a great many deserters. And during peacetime, too, no army can boast a record of zero desertions. In the United States, even in the fifties and early sixties, the AWOL and desertion rate was surprisingly high. But in those years, desertion was usually attributable to a clash with a particular officer, an inability to get along with others, marital problems, a chronic dislike of authority, or the logical act of a pathological misfit. Others left the army because they were petty criminals and their innate lawlessness was suppressed by military service—they could do better in the underworld. These were the deserters prior to Vietnam. And even though the army was nearly as brutal and dehumanizing in the fifties and early sixties as it is today, soldiers put up with it, for it was a ticket back to the good life; it was normal for a GI to "take it" as his father before him had taken it; and it was also out of a respect for his country that he tolerated the indecencies and incivility of the military. It would not have been normal to run away from military oppression during times of severe normality. Deserters in those days were abnormal.

But in those days the air was not yet suffused with the spirit of rebellion, with the popular idea of not taking it. When it happened that young people in America (and it's young people who fight wars—old people only make them) no longer held much, or any, respect for traditional authority and leadership, it was bound to happen that young men in the armed services would question military leadership and no longer feel compelled to obey all the rules. Rebellion against authority was no longer abnormal; it was regarded as heroic. This would take its toll in any army, not to mention one currently engaged in fighting a criminal war and one in which only young recruits regularly saw combat and death.

The same kind of men as in the past continued to desert as Vietnam progressed, but the desertion rate for the U.S. Armed Forces by 1967 had increased 300 percent over the normal peacetime rate of the fifties and sixties. Who were these other men? According to the army they were misfits too—America was simply producing more social misfits and men of weak character—but in the eyes of their peer group, young America, these new deserters were heroes of a sort, newly aware young men who obviously were eminently sane.

Not many ran at first, however. Dissent preceded desertion. Before many people knew what the inside of a stockade looked like and before it had become common knowledge that there is precious little military justice, a few brave individuals stood up to the army one at a time or in small groups and said that they were refusing to fight in Vietnam. A Private Oval went on a hunger strike in July 1965 until he was released as a CO. In September, two soldiers whom no one remembers refused to go to Vietnam and were sentenced to five years each while another antiwar soldier received three years. In 1966 a Private Brown refused to draw combat equipment and was immediately sent to the stockade until he was discharged. The most publicized early case of GIs opposing the war in Vietnam was that of the Fort Hood Three: James Johnson, a black, David Samas, of European immigrant parents, and Dennis Mora, Puerto Rican—a genuine cross section of the army and America. They refused to board ship for Vietnam on the grounds that this was an illegal war, and cited international treaty obligations and provisions in the *Army Field Manual* holding that the individual soldier is responsible if he commits war crimes. The military courts sentenced all three to three years apiece, stating that the U.S. Army was not committing war crimes in Vietnam. The Supreme Court refused to hear the case, wishing to avoid a ruling on the legality of the war. Justices Stewart and Douglas dissented and wrote, "We cannot make these problems go away simply by refusing to hear the case of three obscure army privates."

The year 1967 opened on the military bases with a number of GIs at Fort Bliss, Fort Benning, and Fort Dix refusing to wear their uniforms on grounds of conscience, and all were sooner or later sentenced to the stockade or Leavenworth. A Private Bratcher at Fort Lewis applied for a CO discharge and was denied. He refused a direct order to board the plane for Vietnam and was sentenced to four years in prison. Few of these cases received very much publicity, however, and these quietly courageous soldiers went silently off to jail.

It was the case of Captain Howard Levy who refused to train

Special Forces troops for Vietnam which caught the attention of the peace movement in the spring of 1967. His trial received national coverage. His counsel argued that the Green Beret medical aid men that Dr. Levy was being asked to train were "liars and thieves and killers of peasants and murderers of women and children" and that, moreover, they were "killers first, healers second." The defense, surprisingly enough, was allowed to prove that Green Berets were guilty of war crimes but the evidence presented by Levy's attorney—prisoner torture and the ten-dollar bounty paid to Montagnard tribesmen on each set of VC ears turned in were two examples—was said not to constitute "a general pattern of practice." Although the judge accepted the Nuremburg principle in his court, he would not accept that the American military could possibly make a general practice of committing war crimes in Vietnam. In Sweden the Russell Tribunal was deciding differently, but it had no effect and so, two years before the revelations of the Colonel Rheault case and the My Lai massacre, Captain Howard Levy went to prison.

At the same time Captain Dale Noyd, a fighter pilot and Air Force Academy psychology instructor, was seeking to be classified as a conscientious objector to a particular war. As a pilot, Captain Noyd had a special knowledge of what the United States was doing in Vietnam, and he asked the air force to allow him to resign or to assign him only to duties unrelated to combat—he refused to fly a training mission with a student pilot. His answer was a two-year prison sentence and a Supreme Court refusal to review his case. Although Captain Noyd is the only fighter pilot during the Vietnam war who refused to be counted among the air force pilots who systematically bomb, strafe, and napalm Asian peasants, it is doubtful that more than one American in a thousand remembers, or ever heard of, his name. Noyd served his time and came out two years later only to find that air force bombers were still pulverizing Asian villages as a daily, standard practice. So much for going to prison.

In 1968 there were more dissenters in the services who were careful not to break rules that would get them put away, rendering themselves ineffective. One such soldier was Lieutenant Henry Howe, Jr. who, while not one of those that believed in going to prison, ended up serving one year's hard labor anyway. Lieutenant Howe had marched in an El Paso anti-Johnson march with a sign which read, "Let's have more than a choice between petty ignorant fascists in 1968." Here the army made a mistake, however, for until they decided to prosecute Howe, few GIs had ever heard of him; and though the example the army made of him did, perhaps, keep a few GIs from engaging in outside or on-base political activities, more soldiers than ever before had been presented with a challenge. Soldiers who had not planned to speak out although they thought the war was unjust were now told, in effect, that they couldn't. And so they did.

Among the first organizers of GI dissent was Private Andy Stapp, a former draft resister who wrote his draft board that he had changed his mind and had decided he wanted to serve. Backed up by the radical New York group, Youth Against War and Fascism (YAWF), Stapp arrived at Fort Sill, Oklahoma, with piles of antiwar literature and immediately began passing it out and placing it under pillows and in dayroom book racks. He talked with as many soldiers as possible and began getting them together for discussions and told them about books they should read.* The army harassed Stapp but could find no way to prosecute him until the authorities moved to seize his books and pamphlets and he refused to open his footlocker, claiming a violation of his First Amendment rights. He was court-martialed for refusing a direct order and served forty-five days in the stockade. The brass warned everyone on the base to keep away from "Communists" like Stapp, and the more they berated him to the troops the more he became a hero. After his sentence was served he continued organizing, and the army ordered constant surveillance. Once more, he was arrested, along with two of his fellow organizers, Specialist Paul Gaedkte and Private Richard Perrin, for minor pass violations.

*See Chapter 5; deserter Richard Perrin was one of the first to join Stapp's Fort Sill group in 1967.

Gaedtke was cleared, but Perrin received thirty days. An Emergency Civil Liberties Committee lawyer succeeded in having the charges against Stapp dismissed for lack of evidence. At the same time, the New York organizers from YAWF who had attended Stapp's first trial were arrested for trespassing on government property, found guilty in a civil court in Lawton, Oklahoma, and sentenced to six months in prison. The judge said, "Although this is a petty offense, acts lowering the morale of the troops at Fort Sill are a serious matter."

By the end of 1968 troop morale as defined by the brass had never been lower in the history of the United States Armed Forces, while morale among the organizers had never been higher. GIs, along with everyone else, had by now witnessed several years of demonstrations, and tens of thousands of soldiers had returned from Vietnam duty teaching stateside GIs the truth about the war. In New York, Jan Crumb had already founded Vietnam Veterans Against the War, and Andy Stapp had started the American Servicemen's Union and had taken over publication of *The Bond*, one of the first GI papers. A Vietnam veteran, Jeff Sharlet (who died of cancer at 27), started a paper called *Vietnam GI* which was circulated widely in the peace movement, on army bases, and in Vietnam. Independent GI papers began springing up at Fort Dix (*Shakedown*), Fort Hood (*The Fatigue Press*), Fort Gordon (*Last Harass*); all of which were filled with local news of GI activities against the army and the war. There was coverage of busts, demonstrations, stockade riots, and news of atrocities, suppression of rights, and general army stupidities. More and more GIs were beginning to see that there was something happening here and that the brass didn't know what it was. Although previously many soldiers had been only peripherally aware of army injustices and the criminality of Vietnam, they began to become aware of these things in the same way that most college students had. At the same time, many more college students were entering the ranks. It was a potent brew.

The most important ingredient here was peace movement

interest in the GI, and it had been a long time coming. It meant support for the GI papers, the formation of the GI Press Service in Washington, and most important, the opening of the GI coffee-houses. The army felt threatened by these coffeehouses existing quite inconspicuously just off bases in a number of army towns and said that they were responsible for creating GI dissent. It was the army and the war, rather, that had created the dissent, and the coffeehouses merely provided a vehicle by which that dissent could be organized into a movement and coherent politics. The army eventually saw that the fostering of dissent was far more important than creating it and repeatedly had the various coffee-houses placed off limits or convinced local authorities to shut them down completely (each time a coffeehouse was placed off limits, countless GIs who had never heard about it went to see what was going on there). By that time, however, they had done their job in that the GI movement was too big to be easily crushed, and many thousands of GIs had already decided, after contact with a coffeehouse project, that they would make the supreme antiwar statement, refusing to fight. Many applied for CO status and noncombatant positions, for CO discharges, or refused orders to Vietnam. Others refused to have anything at all to do with the army and went over the hill, having learned of the underground and Canada through their coffeehouse visits.

Harvard graduate and radical journalist, Fred Gardner, along with a young San Franciscan, Donna Michaelson, were largely responsible for setting up an organization which opened and supported the coffeehouses. They were revolutionaries to the core, though the coffeehouse project was criticized by other radicals as being liberal and even bourgeois. Gardner and his group knew what they were about, however, and Gardner would find several years later that, partially as a result of his organizing, there were several divisions of U.S. Armed Forces deserters both under-ground in the U.S. and living openly in Canada.* Other peace

---

*At no time did members of the coffeehouse projects ever advocate desertion.

movement radicals continued to look upon GIs as something to organize, not people who would organize themselves if given a chance and a little help. Here both the liberal-left with its legions of pacifists, attorneys, and concerned young civilians, and the extreme left, comprising hard-core Marxist-Leninist organizers, had something in common: neither respected the GIs as people. The left-liberals seemed to feel that someone who had allowed himself to be drafted would remain forever a little tainted while the enlisted man was completely beyond the pale—they wanted to help the poor young unsophisticated soldier see the light. To the left-liberals the GI was always a GI, unless of course he was a deserter and then he was always a deserter. To the extreme left radicals, GIs represented an untapped working-class force of potential revolutionaries, and any soldier whom they couldn't convince of this truth wasn't worth talking to anyway. The extreme radical Left disliked the man who talked of deserting since he was quitting the working-class struggle. It seemed that one side would have the GI go to jail rather than Vietnam, and the other would have him die in the revolution rather than go to Canada. In any case, despite these tactical implausibilities, in part rectified by the more flexible position of the coffeehouses, GIs, one by one, numbering thousands, heard all the arguments, squinted out a mental vision of killing and being killed in a far-off Asian rice field, and chose freedom and life in the underground or Canada. They created their own political reality.

Nineteen sixty-eight saw GI resistance become an important force. A number of reservists, 256 in all, filed suits with Federal Courts to prevent their shipment to Vietnam, and Justice Douglas signed the restraining order while 170 Wisconsin guardsmen protested the Pueblo-initiated call-up. Forty-two GIs, mostly black, refused riot duty at the Chicago convention, and in July, nine servicemen "resigned" in San Francisco and chained themselves to some clergymen and took refuge in a church. The *New York Times* called it "the newest form of protest in the antidraft movement." All were arrested and subsequently court-martialed.

A Private O'Conner was granted sanctuary at MIT by students while a Private Chase took sanctuary in a Boston church. A Private Brakefield was given sanctuary at the City College of New York student center by the executive council of the student government and police eventually broke into the building and arrested Brakefield and 125 students who had refused to vacate the area. In August several draft resisters and one deserter took sanctuary in a Quaker meeting house in Boston and a Private Kroll, a deserter, was removed by police and the FBI from the Boston University chapel where he had taken sanctuary. In Hawaii, Marine AWOLs periodically took sanctuary in the small Congregational church near the Kanehoe Marine Base, eventually escaping or getting arrested. The largest sanctuary of all came a year later in Honolulu at the Church of the Crossroads near the University of Hawaii. It was led by Airman Buffy Parry* who was joined by thirty-three military deserters for six weeks before the military police smashed their way into the church. These sanctuaries were all widely publicized, and news of them spread through the underground and GI press. Most GIs could sense that they represented only a dilettantish interest by the peace movement in GI resistance, creating temporary heroes and many martyrs, but they were at least one method of confrontation, and the GI now knew he could count on civilian support should he decide to desert. Deserters en masse began showing up on every university campus and at every draft- counseling office in the country. Draft counselors spent as much time shipping deserters off to Canada as they did talking with draft resisters. In the case of the sanctuaries, there was usually an attempt to use a willing soldier for peace movement interests. It made a great show for a radical group to say they had a serviceman in a church somewhere who was saying no to the military. Unfortunately, it usually didn't serve the GI's interest when his ultimate arrest and court-martial brought him two or three years in Leavenworth—or worse, six months in an army

---

*See Chapter 5 for Parry's account of this.

stockade. Meanwhile the peace movement's "GI organizers" went free and searched for another willing "example of GI resistance."

Solidarity on a more meaningful level was sought in San Francisco where on October 11, 1968, organizers—mostly servicemen—led an antiwar march of seven thousand people from Golden Gate Park to the City Hall. One thousand marchers were active GIs, airmen, navy personnel and marines. A navy nurse, Lieutenant Susan Schnall, was later charged with "conduct unbecoming an officer," having appeared at the march in uniform. Many servicemen who had participated were charged or harassed upon returning to their bases and peace movement organizing on their behalf expanded GI resistance even further. A day before the march at the Presidio Army Base in San Francisco, Private Richard Bunch was shot in the back while walking away from a work detail near the stockade. News of this did not get out in time to be received by the marchers, but the world heard about it several days later when twenty-seven stockade prisoners sat in a circle, chanted Om, sang *We Shall Overcome*, and flashed the 'V' sign to protest the killing of their fellow prisoner. The army read them mutiny charges with a maximum penalty of death.*

Few servicemen remained isolated from news of these events, and many subsequently began to examine their personal role in the military. Would they continue their duties without protest? Would they resist? Desert? Both? More servicemen came forward with a decision. They would refuse to fight, apply for CO discharges, refuse orders to Vietnam. Literally thousands of men engaged in concerted acts of resistance against the military, but their cases were too numerous to be publicized.

Most acts of resistance, including repeatedly filing for CO classification (a perfectly legal option in the military) and repeatedly having it refused, eventually led to a court-martial and the stockade, and, once a man had seen the inside of a military stockade, he would never again care about service to his country.

*See Chapter 6 for Lindy Blake's eyewitness of these events.

Thousands of men faced with the stockade for their resistance activities deserted to Canada while hundreds of others deserted immediately after release from the army's dungeons. Through the Presidio trials, the huge revolt in the Long Binh Jail, and the Fort Dix stockade rebellion, news of the conditions in these infamous military prisons began to emerge and the public—or at least the peace movement—was outraged. In the largest march ever for solidarity with GI resistance, ten thousand civilians demonstrated outside the stockade at Fort Dix, New Jersey, in October 1969. They demonstrated against "the military dictatorship" and the trials of thirty-eight men, including Terry Klug, who were charged on some count or another with fomenting the famous Fort Dix riot. As the often-told story goes, the Fort Dix MPs could not be trusted with maintaining order, and a military police battalion from Fort Meade, Maryland was flown in to deal with the demonstrators.

GI resistance continued apace through 1969 with the appearance of approximately forty new GI papers (among them: *OM*, U.S. Navy; *Above Ground*, Fort Carson; *Short Times*, Fort Jackson), the founding of the Movement for a Democratic Military in San Diego, and the opening of several new coffeehouses. But for whatever victories the peace movement, civilian and within the ranks, could claim, the overwhelming reality that every young soldier faced was still an unmitigated oppression. This was made very clear when the army originally handed down fifteen-year sentences to the Presidio "Mutineers." Any GI who organized resistance was eventually confronted with something the peace movement, enjoying its civil freedom, could never understand: a choice between a brutal stockade, the infantry in Vietnam, or desertion. For the average soldier who chose to resist in the army, the ultimate act of resistance was to refuse to be a soldier anymore.

●

During the autumn of 1967, four seamen from the aircraft carrier *Intrepid* deserted ship in Japan, and with the help of Beheiren (Japan Peace for Vietnam Committee) were taken to the

Russian coast by a small boat and flown to Moscow and then Sweden. The "Intrepid Four," Richard Baily, John Barilla, Michael Lindner, and Craig Anderson, were the first American servicemen to protest the war by deserting and asking for asylum in Sweden. The Swedish government granted them "humanitarian asylum" and the four made world-wide headlines. That four American servicemen would desert the armed forces in protest against the war in Vietnam was so fantastic to the press that for several months the young sailors were front page news. *Pageant* magazine, for example, ran seventeen full pages on the "four Navy traitors" including a "touching visit with their shocked families." It was big news, and every serviceman at America's three thousand military installations around the world heard about it and knew that Sweden was safe for U.S. deserters. Desertion from U.S. bases in Europe continued to make headlines during 1968 as many men emerged from the underground in Paris and others continued to go to Sweden. Exile groups were formed in Paris: the French Union of American Deserters and Draft Resisters, the far-left American Deserters' Committee (an independent group which shared the same name, ADC, as a previously formed organization of deserters in Sweden) and Richard Perrin's and Terry Klug's Resistance Inside The Army (RITA) organization which began publishing *ACT*, a newsletter published by deserters and mailed regularly to over ten thousand GIs in Europe and the U.S. *ACT* was one of the first GI papers and was an inspirational force in getting others started in the United States. Deserters kept arriving in Paris and Stockholm, and by the end of 1968 there were several hundred in both cities—those in Sweden being quite conspicuous since the Swedish government officially announced the arrival of each. In Paris, they formed a small community but then gradually dispersed to other parts of France or flew to Sweden and later to Canada. Meanwhile, Japan's Beheiren and its subgroup called JATEC (Japan Technical Committee for Assisting Deserters) kept funneling deserters from Japanese bases and Vietnam to Sweden where the deserter community eventually had a population of four hundred. That was no longer news to the U.S. press, however, for it was getting too embarrassing. One of the few reminders Americans had that there were still American deserters in Sweden came when U.S. longshoremen refused to unload ships full of Swedish Volvos.

The Paris group must be credited with formulating and propagating the first realistic resistance tactic for GIs. From outside the army, RITA's *ACT* appealed to men to resist within the army and to "harass the brass by acts of political sabotage (such as peace stickers, posters, etc.),'' but the RITA organizers, being exiles themselves, were aware that most resisters would eventually have to desert. *ACT* published lists of contacts in many countries, including Canada, though at the time deserters were still underground there. As for detailed information on what a deserter should do, the American Deserters' Committee in Sweden published its own pamphlet mailed on request and printed in large numbers for distribution in the U.S. and Europe. It was also published in the U.S. Most of the Swedish ADC pamphlets were designed to look like an official army document with army insignia and official type. Printed on the front was Army Regulation 381-135: "All GIs have the right to receive any written matter they desire in the mail and have the right to keep any books, newspapers, or pamphlets they want." There was also a notice which stated, "This pamphlet is your personal property. It cannot be taken from you for any reason. This information may be very valuable to you. Hold on to it."

Valuable it was, especially to stateside servicemen who were having difficulty getting information through peace movement contacts. GI organizers were sometimes reluctant to give soldiers information about desertion either because of tactical reasons or for fear of arrest. (Federal marshals arrested Jim Hayes in Boston in 1968 for aiding desertion, but he was acquitted after nearly two years' delay. The government, for one reason or another, chose to prosecute very few people on this count.) The peace movement had not yet faced the fact of desertion as a very real issue in the lives of many American servicemen and was hotly debating the merits of staying in the army over those of leaving it. As mentioned, this problem was squarely faced by exiled deserters themselves in Paris and Stockholm, and they founded the dual tactic of advocating resistance first, desertion last, feeling that with a group like the ADC keeping the final option of desertion open, GI dissenters could be induced to resist that much harder. The peace movement, however, choking on its ideology and the endless discussion of tactics, could never grasp this, and such appeals seldom went out to servicemen in the U.S.

In any case, oppressed people form a *de facto* political force not by talking and thinking but by acting, and that is exactly what U.S servicemen were doing. In 1968 it was revealed by a Defense Department official under questioning by a Senate committee that in 1967, 40,227 men had deserted the American armed forces. Approximately a third had returned to their units and only three hundred had been prosecuted for desertion. In 1968 Pentagon spokesmen said 53,352 men had deserted, and they blamed this on propaganda emanating from Sweden and on Sweden's granting of asylum to deserters. Again, scarcely more than a third had returned to their posts and only a handful were charged with desertion; most were court-martialed for being AWOL. It suddenly occurred to a great many people at once that there were an awful lot of deserters running around somewhere. Pete Hamill wrote in the *New York Post* in November 1969 that the deserters ". . . are gone, moving around America, hiding out, worried about pursuit, assuming new identities, cutting themselves off from everything that made them in the first years of their lives. Some are in Sweden, some wandering around the edges of the Orient, some in Canada." Hamill commented, "It is a terrible thing to be young in a bad time."

Despite the occasional brief recognition this new phenomenon of mass desertion received, before mid-1970 little mention was ever made in the press of the thousands of U.S. military deserters who had surfaced to the north in Canada, forming aid groups and churning out information and propaganda. Perhaps this was just too close to the U.S. for comfort; perhaps the government put pressure on segments of the media not to cover desertion on this continent as eagerly as it had covered desertion in Europe two years before. Or perhaps it was as Pete Hamill had said, that the government and the people of America had "decided that it has lost a generation," and therefore the innocent shock displayed in 1967 when four Navy sailors went over the hill in protest had been lost to the tumult of the times so that when America learned that at least fifty thousand armed forces deserters were living underground in the U.S. and that there were another five to ten thousand in exile in Canada, it didn't matter at all.

In 1970 the Department of Defense announced that 73,121 desertions had taken place in fiscal 1969.

●

Canada has been a refuge for deserters from many armies for many years. One can meet Americans in Canada who deserted the army during the Korean War. And since the beginning of the Vietnam War, servicemen have quietly slipped in and become immigrated. But it was not a phenomenon of any significance. There were probably more Canadians enlisting in the American armed services than there were American deserters taking up residence in Canada. By early 1968 it was a different story however. In Montreal, Toronto, and Vancouver there were small underground deserter communities. They were underground because if immigration officials learned that these men were deserters, it severely prejudiced their chances of receiving immigration papers. What is more, the resister aid groups didn't want to have anything to do with them.

In April 1968, the *Globe and Mail* reported that there were approximately three hundred American military deserters in Canada and that the government had granted immigration permits to ten openly-declared deserters which proved that in some cases, at least, the immigration officials were not taking into consideration an applicant's military status in his home country. Nevertheless, the aid organizations were fearful that too much contact with deserters would impair their established function of aiding draft dodgers while keeping themselves and everyone they aided clean. The *New York Times* also reported in April that approximately fifty to one hundred deserters a year were leaving for the north, quoting David Harris as saying that The Resistance had helped two or three deserters a week get to Canada. The *New York Times* reporter interviewed Ed Miller of the Montreal Council who said, "These organizations officially shun deserters." Asked what they did when a deserter showed up anyway, he replied, "We've never seen one.".

They had seen plenty of them actually, but it was true that the assistance groups shunned them. Middle-class, college-educated draft dodgers simply could not understand the generally younger, not-so-well educated, working-class deserter. If the deserter happened to be middle-class, as many were, and had an education, the draft resisters still could not fathom why he hadn't dodged the draft instead of going in the army and later deserting, and they tended to regard him as something less than a true war resister—a confused kid maybe, nothing more. In Toronto Bill Spira was discreetly handling the deserters so as not to compromise the Anti-Draft Programme, but in Montreal the Council actually felt threatened by these newcomers who it seemed might interfere with the pure, noble, and steadfastly righteous cause of the draft resisters. The draft resisters were concerned with staying legal, stating that one day all would be forgiven and they would be allowed back into the U.S. and they didn't want to decrease the chances of that happening by having been judged dangerous revolutionaries which they felt they would be if they aided desertion.

At the same time deserters in Montreal, with no Bill Spira to help them get immigrated and find work, realized that deserters were being aided by the American Deserters' Committee in Sweden and the deserter groups in Paris, yet in Canada they were told they were too hot to handle. To counter the pusillanimous liberalism and insensate paranoia that infected the Montreal

Council at the time, several deserters along with a draft resister
and one non-exile, both with previous political experience in the
U.S., formed the Montreal American Deserters' Committee
modeled on the ADC in Sweden. These were radicals with close
ties to New Left Marxist revolutionists in the U.S. and all the
appropriate contacts among the Old Left in the U.S. and Canada.
They saw deserters as working-class people whose aspirations were
only hampered by the pacifist-resistance groups in the U.S. and
the antidraft forces in Canada. They said that desertion was a
much more radical—braver—act than resisting the draft. Until they
fell into disfavor with Marxist GI organizers in the U.S. who didn't
support desertion, the Montreal Deserters' Committee claimed
that desertion was the only way to stop the war. In deference to
the American GI movement, they eventually adopted a policy of
making it known that Canada was safe for deserters, but that it
wasn't easy to make it in Canada, and that one should only come
if there was nothing else to do—resist to the limit, knowing that
desertion is a final option if necessary. This remained the strategy
of the Montreal ADC. To publicize Canada as an option, the ADC
published several issues of an intelligently written yet jargon-filled
magazine called *The Rebel: Published in Exile.* It was circulated
widely and clandestinely in movement circles in the United States
and was the first published report that Canada was safe—to a
degree—for deserters. Some people said *The Rebel* was several years
ahead of its time, while others maintained it was merely a trans-
planted organ of one or another stateside group like the Socialist
Workers Party, Progressive Labor, or the Communists. At any rate,
it published articles by Robert Williams from Peking, discussed
sabotage and terrorism, talked about the Quebecois struggle, and
attempted to build a political consciousness among exiles. Deserters were arriving in larger numbers than ever before, and by
late summer 1968 the ideological romanticism of *The Rebel* con-
signed it to collectors' files when it, and several of its staff, seemed
more interested in talking about revolution than helping to do
something for the hundreds of deserters who were making their

own revolution by coming to Canada. Several of the early organizers fortunately turned their energy toward the problems these new arrivals faced, mainly immigration, and got down to the realities of working with the liberals, the "bourgeois press," and the government.

Montreal was the only place in North America where such a group as the American Deserters' Committee could have been organized in 1968. In Vancouver the police would have quickly seen that any such group was quickly disbanded. In Toronto the Union of American Exiles and the Toronto Anti-Draft Programme had preempted the scene. In Quebec, on the other hand, were the only revolutionary and far-left groups in Canada. The French radicals had little use for the Montreal Council and its supporters and were quick to give assistance to the radical ADC. The Union Général des Etudiants de Québec, whose 70,000 students as early as 1965 had issued a manifesto that offered to hide U.S. deserters and resisters in the woods of Quebec, gave the ADC its first office free. From the beginning the ADC identified with the people of Quebec and not the English "colonials" (there are 800,000 English-speaking people in Quebec), but because of language difficulties the solidarity was largely ideological. The ADC later drew its practical support from the English community, although retaining strong ties to the Confédération des Syndicats Nationaux (trade unions). To quote from the ADC "Declaration of Purpose": "We do specifically condemn and actively oppose . . . the cultural corruption and economic exploitation of the people and natural resources of Quebec, of Canada, and of all countries into which the U.S. system extends." That was more than any other American exile group in Canada had said.

In July 1968, Minister of Immigration Allen MacEachen—perhaps at the behest of U.S. officials, perhaps after merely reading the newspaper accounts of the deserters in Canada—issued a departmental memorandum to immigration officials leaving it to their discretion whether or not to admit deserters to Canada as either visitors or immigrants. This was taken by border officials to mean that they should deny entrance to a proclaimed deserter and that men who were subsequently found to be deserters were to be deported. Suddenly, deserters could no longer get immigrated if it was discovered that they were deserters, and anyone who was caught with military ID at the border was turned back. Canada was no longer safe for deserters, although they continued to arrive. It was at this point that the ADC took Lenin's one step back and approached liberals whom they thought would be receptive to their problem. The ADC even talked to the Montreal Council to Aid War Resisters which was beginning to grasp the plight of deserters.

For the next ten months, deserters faced a serious problem. *Esquire* magazine ran an article on the "Magical Mystery Great Lakes Express" which had "smuggled" fifty deserters and resisters to Canada. Very romantic, indeed. Actually, things were not that bad. Anyone could get into Canada as a visitor; the problem was staying there legally. As the *Globe and Mail*, reporting on the crisis, pointed out six months later when the situation had been made public, "Deserters are still entering the country as visitors. An average of five a day are reaching Bill Spira through the Toronto Anti-Draft Organization." Quoting Spira, the *Globe and Mail* wrote, "I can't stop the deserters coming up. And they're not going back to the States to be put in the stockade. They should be processed just like other immigrants. If the immigration officials would stick to the immigration law we would have no trouble." Spira reported at the time that he had already seen six hundred deserters, that half of them were from the Marine Corps, and that ninety percent were on orders for, or about to be sent to, Vietnam. Since December 1968 only two had got landed as opposed to nearly one hundred in the several months before the Mac-Eachen memo had taken effect. Vincent Kelly, the TADP lawyer, spent weeks landing one deserter. Discussing Ottawa's hard line on American deserters, Ron Haggart wrote in the *Toronto Telegram* about one deserter at the Toronto immigration office who was asked to swear on a bible whether he was a U.S. deserter. Haggart quoted immigration officers as saying to the young man, "Why are you scum up here?" and was clearly outraged at the whole state of affairs. Rhetorically, he asked in his column, "Speaking of scum, I wonder if Canada's immigration department intends to apply that term to the highly-placed official of a Toronto hospital who deserted in disgust after two years as a U.S. Navy medic?" And he, too, quoted Bill Spira who said, "To me, as a Canadian citizen, the usurpation of the rights of Parliament to pass immigration laws by some third-rate bureaucrat is simply impermissible. On how many other issues will Canadian officials buckle under to American pressure?"

Many Canadians soon began to realize that the deserter question was a far more important issue than the draft dodgers ever were. As people learned of the astounding desertion rate announced by the Pentagon they could finally understand the magnitude of the problem. Here were literally tens of thousands of young fugitives running scared on the North American continent with no place to go—those who came to Canada should at least be made welcome. If the veracity of the reported huge number of deserters was in question in the minds of some Canadians, it no longer remained questionable when the Canadian press reported that an American couple who had worked in the Pentagon as civilian accountants had moved to Canada and then had helped their son to desert. From this couple it was learned that 65,000 servicemen had not cashed pay checks for the past three months.

During the spring of 1969 the aid groups including the Montreal ADC launched a campaign to have the immigration policy changed. The problem was discussed on literally dozens of Canadian television shows. The press was approached, found to be sympathetic, and asked to run frequent articles on discrimination against deserters, which it did. In May the *Globe and Mail* ran a cartoon showing immigration officers at the border holding a book entitled, "Quotations from Chairman MacEachen." An editorial in the *Toronto Star* was titled, "Remove The Barrier To U.S. Refugees" and said,

> ...some are unsavory and unpleasant young men who quit the army ...but many deserters are not running away from wives or debt or reveille. They are *political refugees* [italics mine] who have rightly or wrongly been expelled by the American military and the war it is fighting. It makes little sense to penalize them because they didn't make their run for Canada before their induction was called. There is every indication that a true public hue and cry is in the making. The public is not going to shut up and the question is not going to go away.

The paper also devoted half the editorial page to an article by Professor Stephen Clarkson of the University of Toronto entitled, "Wanted: a Liberal Policy on Political Immigrants from the U.S." (The American exiles never tire of commenting with amazement on the editorial outspokenness of the Canadian press as compared with the editorial timidity of the American media.)

The campaign included sending five York University students across the border who returned to Canada and declared at the border that they were deserting from the U.S. Army. The Canadian border officials turned them back, notified U.S. authorities on the other side, and all five were arrested by the FBI. Then they proved that they were Canadians, returned to Toronto, and told their story to the newspapers and television which carried it Canada-wide, further incensing the public against these petty bureaucrats who were enforcing American laws while ignoring their own. Meanwhile, the *Washington Post* reported that spring that "Prime Minister Trudeau recently estimated there were about fifty deserters now resident in Canada and he hinted that if American officials were to ask for them they would be handed over."

In reality, even before the *Washington Post* article appeared, Trudeau had indicated privately to a young Liberal Party M.P. from Montreal, Marcel Prud'homme, that he wouldn't be against Parliament bringing pressure to bear against the immigration department's recent antideserter policies. Trudeau apparently preferred to have nothing to do with it himself, however, though he was once reported to have said he would step in if Parliament did not. Prud'homme had awaited just such a signal from his party's leader (the prime minister), and thereupon brought together twenty-five Liberal M.P.s who met with Minister MacEachen and urged him to change his policy. He admitted to the anomaly in the law which allowed draft dodgers citizenship and not deserters and promised a review and a clear statement of government policy.

Marcel Prud'homme previously had been in touch with the Montreal American Deserters' Committee and the Toronto Anti-Draft Programme and had learned of the seriousness of the situation. (Representatives from the TADP, the Montreal Council, and ADC had together drawn up a brief and had presented it to the Immigration Minister and Members of Parliament.) The young radicals and the Liberal Party M.P. became allies. Prud'homme had been interested in immigration to Canada since his college days when he had organized a group that welcomed the Hungarian refugees in 1957. He also had an interest in the Canadian program to aid the Czechs who left Prague in 1968. As for deserters, he had seen them on the streets of Montreal, had talked with many, had met them at parties (believe it or not, in Canada people as diverse as members of Parliament and U.S. military deserters can often be found attending the same social gatherings), and had spoken before college radical groups in the U.S. who questioned him on Canadian policy toward American deserters. Also, during a trip to Sweden he had met with members of the ADC there. During his campaign to gather support behind a change in policy, he was quoted in the press as saying, "If I have to work underground to help deserters in this country, then I will. I think this country is big enough to accept military deserters. And I also think it is liberal enough to accept them." He said at the time that he would be very unhappy to remain a member of the party if the policy were not changed. Meanwhile, he had seriously split the Liberals.

Oddly enough, Marcel Prud'homme could never be called anti-American. His motives for aiding the deserters were purely humanitarian and libertarian. More radical support for deserters came from the New Democratic Party (democratic-socialist—almost) which the previous summer in Winnipeg had produced a policy committee vote in favor of helping U.S. deserters obtain landed immigrant status. New Democratic Party M.P. Ed Broadbent, who spoke for the party on the deserter issue on the floor of the Commons, explained the party's reasons for supporting deserters: 1. profound opposition to the war in Vietnam, an abhorrence of the war to the degree of desiring to do whatever was possible to help young men fleeing from it; and 2. as a traditional human rights issue. Dr. Broadbent, formerly a political science professor at York University who had been involved with draft dodgers there (a number of whom were on the faculty), met with cabinet minister MacEachen to appeal for a change in policy.

Also pressuring the immigration department for a return to basic policy was the Conservative Party, and a Tory M.P. said in the Commons, "The Immigration Act and regulations are plain and straightforward, and any change in policy by departmental decree is unacceptable." After several more Liberal Party caucuses sponsored by Prud'homme and fellow M.P. David Weatherhead, at which a party majority declared itself in favor of change, MacEachen finally announced on May 22, 1969, that "If a serviceman from another country meets our immigration criteria, he will not be turned down because he is still in the active service of his country." The argument that won the minister over was that the United States did not take military desertion into account when accepting Canadian deserters as immigrants between 1939 and 1941.

As for opposition in the government, there was little. When MacEachen announced his decision in the Commons it met with enthusiastic applause. Conservative M.P. Robert Thompson made a critical speech, however, and said that "any friendly nation would have consulted the U.S. in advance of such a policy statement." The *Montreal Star* reported that Thompson had "thundered about the breakdown of law and order throughout the world and accused the Liberals of inciting Americans to 'flout the law of their country,' " and said that "throughout Mr. Thompson's harangue, his own party leader Robert Stanfield listened in stony silence and visibly cringed at some of the more right-wing remarks."

The gates were open. The American Deserters' Committee in Montreal held a "victory rally" in a McGill University auditorium on May 19, and Yale Professor Staughton Lynd, Reverend Dick Fernandez of Clergy and Laymen, Quebec union leader Michel Chartrand, and McGill professor, and former television commentator Laurier LaPierre welcomed the deserters to Canada. The ADC's recent newsletter, *The Second Front*, which had been distributed to troops in the U.S., was beginning to bring men north as were advertisements in the *Guardian* and stories sent out by Liberation News Service. During the summer the ADC, operating on a large grant from the McGill Student Society plus money raised with a benefit performance by Tom Paxton, ran an office on Wolfe Street in Montreal which was receiving from fifteen to twenty-five men a week. Deserters with duffle bags and knapsacks could be seen all that summer on the McGill lawn, smoking grass, talking with friends, sleeping. In Toronto, a "test case" deserter was sent through border immigration by the TADP the day after the Immigration Minister's policy statement and he was landed immediately, even receiving extra points for U.S. Army training as a helicopter repairman. In June 1969, the *Toronto Telegram* ran a headline over an "Exiles" page which said, "New Wave of U.S. Army Deserters Hitting Toronto" and estimated that there were approximately three thousand deserters in Canada already. The piece included interviews with several deserters including a teacher in a Toronto high school who said, "The principal found I'm a deserter but he's never said anything to me about it. In fact, I've never had any static from the people here about it. Men who were veterans of World War II have said to me, 'I don't blame you a bit: I'd have done the same thing.' Literally everyone thinks the U.S. is wrong about Vietnam and about its militarism."

By October the *New York Times* saw fit to print a front page, six-column story titled "Underground Railroad Aids Deserters To Canada" which detailed the arrival of this latest group of exiles. The *New York Times* reporter crossed the border with a deserter who said as the car pulled away from the Canadian customs booth, "It's beautiful. I'm not gonna stop smiling for weeks."

•

The word *deserter* tends to encompass and thereby misleads. That the term *GI* can represent the myriad types of young Americans who end up in the service is as erroneous a notion as believing that deserters are all of a kind. There is a common bond to desertion and subsequent exile to be sure, but the term serves little use beyond that of forming a necessary association. Although facile categorizations are sometimes not much better than an all-embracing descriptive term like deserter, it might nevertheless be helpful to separate the deserters that went to Canada into four groups:

First, there are the organizers, those whose experiences in the military turned them radical so that they attempted to politicize their fellows by openly discussing Vietnam in small groups, passing out literature, working at GI coffeehouses, working on GI papers, organizing Conscientious Objectors.* In every case active GI dissenters who went to Canada had been charged with an offense and often faced severe prison sentences or an infantry assignment in Vietnam. By late 1969 dozens of such GI activists had arrived at the Montreal ADC office, including Vietnam Moratorium coordinators and men who had helped put out *Shakedown*, *Fatigue Press*, *Last Harass*, *Gig-Line*, and *Head-on*, all well-known GI papers. Perhaps half of this group—"the organizers"—were college educated. Most were draftees.

The second group, and by far the largest, are the nonactivists who simply object to war, to being forced in peacetime to fight wars and who, through a common intelligence, knew that the war in Vietnam was wrong. Theirs is a gut reaction to fighting and

*See Chapter 5.

killing: a feeling that one has to draw the line against the curtailment of freedom, and a knowledge that they could not take the brutality of the U.S. Army, the dehumanization, the loss of identity and what Dr. Peter Bourne, an orthopsychiatrist and decorated Vietnam combat veteran, calls the "mortification of the self." Their decision to come to Canada was not political, nor were they fleeing persecution for dissenting; their choice was merely human. They are sensitive, intelligent, aware, and not necessarily angry at anyone. They have accepted their fate, unlike their activist brethren, and they are content with the freedom they've found in Canada. This group is the most variegated, including drop-out hippies and men with post-graduate degrees, workers and artists, technicians and poets. Youth's alternate-culture is well represented. Perhaps half have been to or graduated from college, while a great many hold skills in one profession or another. Again, a seasoned guess would be that half are draftees and half are enlisted men. Many have families; a number of them had homes and even businesses in the U.S. which they sold before leaving. The most poignant quality which marks these men is that they are much closer to being, or having been, all-American boys than most draft-resisters who were usually rebellious, dissident, and intellectually detached. After all, these young men had not chosen to resist the draft; they preferred to serve their country as they were expected to do and only wanted to avoid that which they felt was wrong—Vietnam. However, they either found more wrong with the armed services and the United States than just Vietnam, or they were ordered to Vietnam when they might have gladly served in Germany, Korea, Japan, or the U.S. Essentially, they became "radicalized" by the army experience to the degree of wanting out, but not to the point of committing themselves to changing anything beyond the direction of their own lives. If everyone did that much it would be enough.

The third category, perhaps thirty percent of the deserters in Canada, can be defined as being very young, very frightened, very sad. They are the real American refugees who at seventeen, eighteen, or nineteen have been forced to run for their lives and begin a new life in a foreign country. Unlike the aforementioned group of men who seem to have consciously taken control of their lives and who will quite obviously make it, these young refugees have lost control of theirs. The world they once knew was collapsing around them. The army which they had been taught was the noble defender of goodness and freedom turned out to be ugly, brutal, and evil. They don't understand what went wrong, what is happening to themselves, or anything about Vietnam unless they've been there and then they know too much but still don't understand. They ended up in the army because they were too young to choose otherwise, because of parental pressure, or because they either weren't worthy of college admittance or couldn't afford it. However, they quickly realized Vietnam was not a good place to go, although they knew nothing of the political arguments against the war but only that men were dying there and they could not see the reason why. They all shared the new consciousness of youth which sets those under twenty-five apart from anyone older. It is a different kind of consciousness from that which a twenty-seven-year-old draft resister usually knows; the consciousness of an eighteen-year-old American today is not intellectual; it has not come from books, from travel, or from manifold experiences; it simply *is*, a wholly natural and universal feeling that they unconsciously constructed as they observed the mad world around them. This new consciousness emanates from within and says to these young people that killing is wrong, that hating your brother is wrong, that acting ugly to one's fellow man is wrong. And then they meet the U.S. Army.

Naturally they cannot adjust to the military life, least of all to Vietnam. Terence Hallinan, the civilian defense attorney for the Presidio 27, said of these men:

> Of course, you've got to understand that inability to adjust in terms of the society they come from and the nature of the Army and the war in Vietnam. These are the children of America's poor whites, a hidden class of people. They are uneducated but not at all stupid. They may have

come from loveless homes, but they can love. In peacetime they would never have been held in the Army, but because of the war—because the Army needs every body it can get—they couldn't be discharged. The war is really so unpopular among the GIs that the Army senses that if it started giving these discharges—CO, psychiatric—the floodgates would open and thousands of men would try to get out. Since they can't let them out, yet they can't use them in the fields, they fill the stockades with them.

. . . Or the army finds that they have deserted.

But for this group desertion is little better than what they knew before. Perhaps some will make it eventually and one day be glad they left the army, but many face a gravely difficult period. They cannot become landed immigrants in many cases so must continue to live in the underground.* Many have not graduated from high school. They are a part of the youth culture in every respect, but are more likely to know the perverse aspects of youth's anticulture: speed, coke, heroin, bad acid, nihilism, intense loneliness, petty crime, and dealing drugs as a way to stay alive. In many ways this is the most important and least understood group of American refugees in Canada. If older war resisters don't understand them nor the terrible stories they tell after crossing the border about being young in America, then who does?

And finally, there are those dull young men, perhaps mentally deficient or emotionally disturbed who end up in the army for lack of anywhere else to go, often sent there by civil courts instead of to youth correction centers. In America the military becomes the catch-all for those people who in any other society would get help from the state (one recalls McNamara's "Salvage" program). They need help and they don't get it in the army. The army either drives them to the stockade, to suicide, or to Canada if they happen to find out they can go there. Nor does the army ever discharge these men; they discharge themselves. In Canada they become wards of the exile aid groups which usually are ill-

*See Chapter 12 for a discussion of North American channeling and the asylum question.

equipped to handle such cases—approximately five percent of the deserters. Unlandable, they are destined to be fugitives for the rest of their lives. (Among this group are of course the incorrigible criminals with records of serious offenses in the U.S. A number of these deserters are presently serving sentences in Canadian jails for armed robbery, assault, and rape. So far, Canada has accepted them as an inevitable part of the new influx.) In Canada, without family, friends or relatives, they stand small chance of going anywhere other than to a Canadian correctional institution or psychiatric hospital which, in any case, is better than being destroyed completely by the American military or American penal—as opposed to correctional—systems which is what happens to them if they return to the U.S. (Some do return out of desperation.) Canada isn't easy for them but it isn't the stockade either.

With its limited resources, the Montreal ADC attempted to help as many of these men as it could, finding psychiatrists for them, assigning them a social worker, finding work for them if possible, but, for the most part, little can be done. They, and the tens of thousands like them in the U.S. where they are less visible than here, are truly lost, a whole mass of children driven to real or near madness, called insane while they attempt to choose sanity in the face of an insane reality. They represent the real American tragedy.

●

In 1969 the American Deserters' Committee in Montreal provided immigration counseling for approximately 650 deserters, successfully landing more than half of them. Several hundred visited the ADC office merely for information but did not avail themselves of the counselor's services. (One young American, a Loyola College professor, along with his English wife, together must receive credit for two years of arduous immigration counseling—hundreds of men were indebted to them. However their names cannot be used.) During 1969 and for half of 1970 the deserters' committee held open Wednesday night meetings at a Montreal community center and weekly attendance averaged thirty to fifty deserters through the winter, always including a large turnover. The meetings served as a clearinghouse for information, as a welcoming committee, and as a means by which political action could be formulated. In Quaker fashion, chaired by a steering committee, men who perhaps had never taken part in a political discussion in their lives, had never spoken before a group—had never even been included in a group of any kind—sat in a large circle and talked about Vietnam, about Marxism, about Cuba, about the struggle in the U.S., and so on. Practical problems with immigration, the ADC hostel, and drugs were also hashed out, and new arrivals were told where to find warm clothing, cheap food, part-time work, and whatever else they needed. The activists who regularly attended the meetings—among them Paul Petrie, Ken Treusdell, Dr. Don Burke, Laurence Svirchev, Dave Beauschene, Steve Argo—usually refrained from dominating the discussions, giving new men a chance to speak. For the most part, these meetings helped to ease the pain of sudden exile and restored a certain dignity to the individual, and they provided a transition for the new arrival who otherwise would have been out on the street wondering if he were the only American deserter in Canada, wondering what he had done and why, and if it was the right thing. They were therapy sessions, a congregation of fellow aliens with similar problems, and men came to as many as they needed.

Stemming from these meetings were various political activities: newsletter mailings to the stateside peace groups and the underground press; several Vietnam Moratorium rallies at McGill University in October and November of 1969; an incredible Christmas dinner attended by 150 deserters plus 100 wives and friends and girlfriends with food provided by the ADC and sympathetic Montrealers; producing and editing a film for distribution through the underground in the U.S.; a march on the American Embassy in Ottawa; speaking engagements by deserters at women's clubs, Montreal high schools, and before several trade union groups (where one deserter was received with cheers); a May Day march in solidarity with Montreal workers; the production of a number of radio and television programs, several of which were broadcast in the U.S.; and a huge march on the American consulate in conjunction with the Vietnamese Patriots Association and the McGill Student Society to protest the Kent State Massacre. In this last march, sixty deserters formed a contingent which carried four black coffins to the consulate steps—huge plate windows in the consulate were shattered one by one as the Montreal police stood by.

As of November 1969, the ADC was paying a full-time office manager and provided salaries to a succession of people to operate their eighteen-bed hostel. Local supermarkets and welfare agencies provided food for the hostel where meals and lodging were free for deserters. The committee had arranged for free medical and dental care to be provided by local doctors and had several attorneys who handled touchy immigration cases without charge. There was, of course, a housing list of families willing to take in deserters plus a number of contacts for part-time employment and job offers.

By the end of 1969 Old Left and revolutionary New Left association with the ADC had pretty well dissolved. The group had become peace-movement oriented, and amateurishly run, though still effective. It would, however, turn back to the radical Left for support in mid-1970. As for communist support of the ADC, the degree to which that was forthcoming can best be explained by the following incident: One of the original ADC organizers represented the committee at an international meeting on war crimes in Stockholm. His way over was partially paid by the ADC, but he expected to return to Montreal on Aeroflot (Soviet Airlines) via Moscow, arranged by a local CP member. The Communist officials in Sweden who arranged the international transportation for delegates would not provide a seat on Aeroflot for him, apparently wishing to have nothing to do with American deserters in Canada. He paid his own way back.

Meanwhile, in Toronto, where the Montreal ADC was being castigated as a bunch of dangerous wild-eyed revolutionaries, a group of deserters and concerned resisters formed their own ADC to deal with practical needs only and not political doctrine. The Toronto situation was getting serious as deserters continued to pour in and found only condescending draft-resister groups and little helpful assistance outside of immigration counseling. In December 1969, the ADC staff—Bill Debra, Tony Wagner, Ann Ross, Jerry Samuels, Harvey Maurer, Dan Zayre and his wife Mona—rented a house for $200 per month which became the staff collective, a twenty-four-hour office, coffeehouse, and drop-in center. A licensed psychologist spent twenty hours a week at the center; a Canadian woman helped with office correspondence; and a YMCA social worker donated his services as an employment counselor. Through a group of helpful Torontonians (Friends of the ADC—a similar group existed in Montreal) including Rabbi Feinberg, a well-known Canadian peace activist, the committee was soon operating a housing program that could find accommodation for every young American who came to their office. By the spring of 1970 they were able to relieve the Toronto Anti-Draft Programme of this function when they opened two hostels with twelve rooms each in downtown Toronto. Deserters cooked communally and paid one dollar per night for lodging. Not long after the Toronto ADC had publicized its existence, it was receiving during the spring twenty to thirty new deserters a week plus referrals from the TADP. It goes without saying that the staff wore itself out. Eventually they had to concentrate on merely operating the three cooperative hostels—which formed a remarkable exile community in themselves.* The Toronto deserters felt it was necessary to forego outright political action in favor of building a community, reducing alienation, aiding integration into Canadian life, and keeping Canadian exile a "good trip."

As the decade closed, deserters were everywhere, becoming more visible every day. They were not only visible in the sense that the Canadian media gorged itself on stories about them and thus

*See Chapter 11.

produced a public consciousness on the subject, but they were physically visible in the downtown section of every Canadian city. Americans, be they businessmen, tourists, or hippies, are extraordinarily obvious in Canada, but even easier to identify is a young man with ridiculously short hair, the stubble of a new moustache, and black, bulbous-toed army boots—or easier still, green canvas Vietnam jungle boots and a field-issue fatigue jacket with a First Cavalry shoulder patch. *AMEX* commented, "Canada is presently so flooded with deserters that an ordinary draft dodger causes one to sit up and take notice. This is a sharp reversal of the situation less than a year ago when very few deserters even knew Canada was open to them."

Public acceptance of their coming was such that editors at the *Montreal Star*'s Sunday magazine *Weekend*, a supplement included in thirty-nine Canadian papers every week, felt confident in running a cover story on the Montreal ADC in early 1970. The six-page article with color photos and eight interviews was actually biased *in favor* of the ADC and made a subtle appeal for public support. The only reaction to the story was several angry letters to *Weekend*'s editor, Frank Lowe, who responded with an angry comment of his own in a *Weekend* editorial in which he defended the deserters, drawing a parallel between them and the United Empire Loyalists who settled Ontario during the American Revolution. He asked rhetorically how these Canadians, who had denounced the deserters as "creeps," "cowards," and so on, would have regarded their own forebears, and then he asked Canadians to recall "one of the most memorable quotes of the decade: 'I had to obey the rules of war and my flag. I am ready.' Those were the last words of Adolph Eichmann." Young men denounced by Vice President Agnew as common criminals were receiving almost a hero's welcome in Canada.

The government and the media had another opportunity to defend deserters in the first months of 1970, getting the issue off to a good start in the new decade. First, in Ottawa the *Montreal Star*'s bureau chief, W. A. Wilson, who had housed an American deserter for AID, found that the Royal Canadian Mounted Police had been questioning his fourteen-year-old daughter about the deserter when Wilson wasn't home. Wilson made a great noise about it on Parliament Hill, claiming that the police were deliberately harassing deserters—not to mention those that aided them—and trying to solicit information from minors to do it. As it turned out, the deserter who had stayed with Wilson had apparently been wanted on a criminal charge, not because he was a deserter. But even the major Canadian newspapers refused to believe the police spokesman until the solicitor-general (corresponding to the attorney general in the U.S.) explained the situation and the RCMP apologized to Wilson for not approaching him directly. The solicitor-general observed, "Persons trying to help deserters have innocently in their over-enthusiasm drawn false conclusions when they learn of deserters being questioned." He calmly and correctly pointed out, "Those who desert from an army as large as the American army are bound to include among their number a certain proportion of criminals." For several days the story appeared on the front page across Canada and then was soon replaced by another one. This time the solicitor-general was up against the wall and could not honestly defend the RCMP.

In British Columbia, three deserters, John Kreeger, Charles Leonard, and Earle Hockette asked a Mountie about local hitchhiking laws and were told to get in the car and were subsequently delivered to the Huntingdon-Sumas border station when they admitted to being deserters. They were turned over to the U.S. Shore Patrol and driven to Fort Lewis, Washington in a military van. John Kreeger escaped, however, returned to Canada, and called the Vancouver Committee to Aid War Resisters. Don Rosenbloom, the committee lawyer, called Ottawa and spoke with David Lewis, the leader of the New Democratic Party. Lewis brought up the illegal deportation in the House of Commons and told Solicitor-General McIlraith that the three Americans had been "kidnapped and shoved across the border." The solicitor-general disagreed and initially supported the police, but then John Kreeger appeared on national television and told his story. McIlraith then launched a full judicial inquiry.

In June the report of Judge E. J. Stewart, the commissioner for the inquiry, was presented to the House of Commons by the Minister of Justice. Leonard and Hockette had by this time escaped and returned to Canada and had testified before the judicial commission. The report blamed the RCMP for the "unlawful" deportation, while criticizing the customs officer for "failing to appreciate the significance of the return of the three deserters" whom the Mounties had brought to the border. The customs officer had actually phoned the U.S. Shore Patrol. Before Judge Stewart's report was completed, the RCMP had apparently been warned by "higher authorities" to refrain from interfering with the rights of deserters and draft dodgers. An especially large headline across the front page of the *Montreal Star* read, "RCMP Told To Stop Probing U.S. Deserters."

Unfortunately, newspaper headlines don't always carry influence proportionate to the size of their type face. As the Toronto magazine *Saturday Night* pointed out in a cover article bearing the title, "How Did the Canadian Mounties Develop their Unfortunate Habit of Deporting People They Don't Happen to Like?": "The Kreeger incident is not an isolated phenomenon. It is merely the latest episode in a story of periodically unjust and even apparently illegal behavior on the part of the RCMP and immigration officers." Elsewhere in Canada, deserters had occasionally reported the Shanghaiing of their friends. An ex-marine and important war-crimes witness who knew too much about President Johnson's son-in-law, Marine Captain Charles Robb, and his alleged participation in one of the Bantangaan Peninsula massacres in Vietnam, one day disappeared from Ottawa and was traced by a UPI reporter a week later to the Camp Pendleton brig. (No one would touch the story.) It may be unfair, in this case, to attribute the kidnapping to the RCMP for it could well have been the work of undercover agents who pop up from time to time among the deserters.

In yet another incident in the spring of 1970, the immigration department was finally brought into line by the government and the media and it was made very clear that no discrimination on any level against deserters would ever again be tolerated. A U.S. deserter, married, with two small children, with a good factory job, was caught on a technical slip in his immigration application and ordered deported for giving false information to the Department of Immigration. Again, the *Montreal Star* championed his cause, spreading deserter Jerry Mihm's and his family's picture across the front page over a long article which began, "Is young Jerry Mihm being railroaded out of Canada because he is a deserter from the American army and the FBI is after him? This reporter says he is." At his final deportation hearing, the decision stood, and Mihm was told to leave or be deported. He disappeared, and his family returned to the U.S. Under government pressure, the immigration appeals board reopened the Mihm case several months later and, in an unprecedented step, held a second hearing. Meanwhile, there were rallies and several demonstrations in Toronto for Mihm, and the exile aid groups and the media together appealed to the public on his behalf. Mentioning both the Kreeger incident and the Mihm case, the *Montreal Star* editorialized on immigration law and the "spirit of its enforcement" and commented that "the deserters' welcome had been tarnished." In May, the appeals board reversed its original decision and allowed Jerry Mihm to remain in Canada as a landed immigrant. Mihm returned from Jamaica where he had been awaiting the outcome of the appeal and his wife joined him in Toronto. The press happily pointed out that Mihm's wife arrived in time to have their third child in Canada: "Cindy Ann Mihm arrived the day after Mrs. Mihm crossed the border."

●

And so, as the seventies began, it was an unequivocal fact that Canada provided a safe refuge for U.S. Armed Forces deserters. Whether or not the border would remain open for them under a new government or in light of the serious unemployment besetting the country was not entirely clear, but it was certain that a man would never be refused permanent admission to Canada on grounds that he was a military deserter. A tighter border would mean only that Canada was accepting immigrants with exceptionally high qualifications. Deserters could still come as visitors and discover, with the help of the aid groups, what their chances were of becoming landed immigrants. As visitors (the Kreeger "three" were not landed immigrants at the time of their kidnapping) they would not be bothered as long as they didn't work. In the end, it was the vagaries of capitalism, not bureaucratic prejudice, that would decide how many and which deserters could stay legally in Canada. As the economy took a serious turn downward in Canada in 1970, the deserters would be the first to suffer. (In a later chapter, the attempt to remedy this unfortunate situation is examined.) Meanwhile, in Montreal the ADC was organizing the first Pan-Canada Conference of American Exiles. In the U.S. the GI movement was suffering severe repression (despite the navy's relatively mild sentencing of underground journalist Roger Priest) and movement activists like Fred Gardner were discussing desertion and referring to Canada as a "potential Yenan." And everyone agreed—basing logical extrapolations on the fantastic numbers of ex-servicemen whom the thirty-two exile aid groups across Canada had processed in the past two years—that there were no less than six thousand, if not ten thousand, American military deserters in Canada.

On January 2, 1970, the *Washington Post* carried a UPI article by correspondent Darrell Garwood in which the Pentagon said 576 American deserters had gone to Canada and only 107 of them had left as a protest against the Vietnam War. The manner of irrefutable certainty in which the Pentagon released these figures caused some exiles to think again about the official number of American casualties and battle deaths in Vietnam. The *official* figures were 45,000 killed in action, 300,000 wounded, and 9,000 deaths attributable to accidents and sickness . . .

FOUR

Poetic Justice

Canada has gained from the Vietnam War. Canada has gained thousands of artists, writers, musicians, photographers, poets, and craftsmen. A great many exiles, perhaps a quarter of them, can fit into one of these categories. To name a few: Tom Hathaway, draft resister, heir to the Hathaway shirt fortune, musician, former student at Toronto's Royal Conservatory of Music; Ross Hazel, deserter, photographer *par excellence*; John Sandman, draft resister, novelist—his novel *Eating Out* was published by House of Anansi; Peter Anson, draft resister whose anthology of poetry was published by Anansi; Doug Featherling, draft resister, his book of poems published by Anansi; Erik Moore, deserter, publisher of Winnipeg's underground paper, *Omphalos*; Jack Todd, deserter, writer with the *Vancouver Sun*; Greg Schiffren, draft resister, announcer for CKGM, Montreal's "free form" FM radio station; John Phillips, draft resister, photographer, owner of Baldwin Street Gallery, a successful Toronto photo gallery attracting wide attention; Tom Needham, draft resister, writer for Toronto's alternative-politics newspaper, *Guerilla*; Jesse Winchester, draft resister, song writer and singer, who recorded an album for Ampex. There are many others. In Montreal most of the leather workers in the small craft shops are exiles. The original staff of Montreal's underground paper, *Logos*, was entirely American save one. (It is now run by Canadians.) A deserter does sports cartoons and illustrations for the *Montreal Gazette*, the morning English daily. In Toronto several war resisters work for radio stations as announcers and reporters; there are exiles with the Canadian Broadcasting Company (CBC). In Vancouver one of the city's major art galleries is owned by an American exile. The Canadian Council for the Arts has given work grants to a number of war resisters: writers, poets, artists. Also among the war émigrés is an ice skating champion who will be skating for Canada in the next Olympics and a twenty-six-year-old American bull fighter from California known as the "draft-dodging matador." He has killed two hundred bulls in the bullrings of Spain and Mexico, but he refused to kill human beings in Vietnam.

Peter Milord is a poet. He is also a deserter and an English teacher in Eastport, Newfoundland. He is married to a stunningly beautiful French Canadian whom he met in a park in Montreal and who now teaches French in a school in Eastport. Before leaving for the provinces and the clean ocean air, Peter spent a year working at Sir George Williams University where, following a brief stint as a book sorter, he was put in charge of compiling the papers of Irving Layton, Canada's poet laureate. Peter is twenty-four, from Stamford, Connecticut, and a graduate of the University of Connecticut. He majored in English. He is tall, with blond-to-brown hair worn long and parted in the middle, and has serious, deep-set eyes and a handsome countenance. He has a superb wit and a quick, wide smile. He left the army after six months—after receiving orders for Vietnam. He says he is glad he is in Canada and that now his roots are here. He says he would only make use of an amnesty to *visit* the country which forced him out.

I was a personable, nice kid with a good sense of humor who liked to play sports and was good at it. I was a big fish in a small pond, however. I wasn't that fantastic. Yeah, sure, OK, I was captain of my football team in my senior year, co-captain of the baseball team, one of the better hockey players—I just did the whole thing. I mean like my whole story is like typical American kid growing up. My roots were middle class, but by the time I was in my teens my father was making a lot of money in New York. I grew up in Stamford, Connecticut. I'm oldest, one brother, three sisters.

My father was in New Guinea as an infantryman. He was a hero in Korea, silver star, bronze star, purple heart. He's a self-made man worth about eighty thousand a year.

In college I did a fraternity bit. It was a Jewish fraternity. I was a goyim among the chosen. It was a whole new thing for me. I got to know what Jewish kids were aspiring towards and what their worries were as opposed to what I was worrying about. I enjoyed studies, but I hated math, the sciences. I enjoyed something you could get into, have sensitive arguments over; I enjoyed poetry. Overall in college I did fairly well—my grades were poorest when I worried about them. When I said, fuck it, they were all A's.

I started wearing my hair long in 1964—that was kind of funny 'cause I'm not an innovator. But I got turned on to these things early. I got turned on to pot; I got turned on to a whole new aspect of life. I started hanging around more with the art students and the English department than with the fraternity kids. I threw the fraternity away and went out and did a Walden Pond thing with a couple of guys for my senior year and that set the stage.

I remember when Johnson started escalating the war in the summer of 1965. I think the thing that really turned my head was that the draft calls got bigger and I talked about this with my friends. Realizing that this would affect us, we decided to investigate. I did some research on the Geneva Accords of 1954 because I'd heard that that was one of the things the antiwar people were using to point out the illegality of the whole thing. So I read all this, see, and I said, damn it, I'm not going to swallow this whole thing hook, line, and sinker. Yeah, you know, it *is* kinda questionable . . . and then, it's not only questionable, it's wrong. And then the movement swelled, and on my own campus I joined it—we sat in once in the administration building, but it wasn't much of anything. I used to go to teach-ins. I got more into my literature, and I got to reading poetry and a lot of things that said that, you know, that there are other aspects of life besides this side of the coin—there's another side, and not only is there another side, but there are edges that go around, and not only that, but there is something inside the coin—great! The whole thing when you study literature, when you study a novel, is that you extrapolate and tear the things apart and learn the motives of the characters. And so perhaps I applied this new outlook to the Vietnam war—I moved from almost nothing to liberal and then from liberal to quasi-radical.

OK, we all know about the war, the draft, the inevitable duty of every man to go in and defend his country without uttering any thoughts of his own but just taking on the general premise that it's all right to do it, that that's what you're supposed to do. So, it came at a time in my life, after having gone through four years of college and being immune from the draft: *conscription!* The war was raging in the back of my schoolbook somewhere, but it wasn't very real. Of course it never is. We don't believe the television set. It's a fantasy. Cronkite was fantasy; so were David and Chet. So I was just sitting around during those old college days not doing anything but getting fat and happy.

And then time came when you get word from the draft, and they say come down for a physical. Now I had thought because of an early heart condition that I had as a kid—which was fairly severe—that perhaps I would be deferred so I wasn't too worried about it. But I went down, and, as it turned out, the final results were that I was acceptable for the army. So boom, boom, boom—things start ticking in your head. I hadn't received the final notice of approval from the medical board and the draft board so I said, well, I'm going to start out to wandering awhile to see what I can do about thinking things over. So, my friends and I, soon after college—all of us were faced with the same situation—went off to Nassau, down to Florida, bumming around, spending a few days here and there trying to get over the fact that *it's all over* and that now it's really going to be hot on our backs like hounds, the draft and everything. We do that for awhile; come back; can't stay at home, it's a drag; can't look anybody in the eye because I know I want to bolt and they know I wanna too; and it's all very tense. So I take off to Europe with another friend and stay over there for about a month. Came back, picked up odd jobs around Connecticut for awhile. Got itchy again. I heard in July that I was acceptable for military service, that I was 1-A and that I could be drafted anytime given twenty days' notice. So I said, look, I'm not going to hang around home. My old man was getting a little more tense as things were getting closer to conscription time—it was the election of '68 and he was ranting and raving against Humphrey—of all people to rant and rave against—and he was just being ornery. I was just fed up with that situation, and so I bugged out again and went out to Colorado. I had a sister going to school in Boulder so I drove out there, stopped off on the way and saw a few friends in Kentucky and places like that. Got out to Colorado and for about a month and a half just buried my head into the mountains, trying to figure out just what was going to happen. But I really wasn't very cognizant of the actuality—well, it's not really going to happen. I rushed off an application to Vista and thought, well, it's the easy liberal way out so why not do it?

And while I was out in Colorado doing various things—enjoying it tremendously of course, really forgetting about the whole situation—I received a telephone call from my father. He said I received a notice in the mail and he took the liberty of opening it and you are to report for induction December 10. So I said, No, I'm not coming back to Connecticut to report; I'm going to Canada. He was quite upset, he was babbling on the phone, very teary-eyed, very emotionally overwrought with the whole thing. "You can't go to Canada, I'll kill myself, I'll blow my brains out, what'll it mean, da da da da. Do you know what you're doing? *You're going to be here!*" I'm *not* going to be there, I said, because it's wrong. I've known it's wrong ever since I started reading about it in the papers; I've known it for a long time; it's not right. I'm not going to do it.

Well, this was me speaking after having the freedom of roaming about the hills of Colorado, roaming about the various countries of Europe, being footloose and fancy free. In fact, I knew nothing of Canada, I didn't know who to see, who to go to. I'd never been really close to the political movement so I didn't know any draft resistance people or places, and I had no literature, no information about Canada. A friend of mine in Colorado whom I'd met, a rather scatterbrained wildman, on the spur of the moment when I told him I was going to be drafted said, "I'll go to Canada with you. We'll hop in my Scout and take off." I probably should have done it then. But I didn't because—not that it wasn't right—but it just wasn't right for me at the time. I couldn't face doing it. My father, through all his senseless haranguing about blowing his brains out, made me still feel that perhaps I should go back to Connecticut and try to talk it out.

So I abandoned the idea of going to Canada upon getting my draft notice. I got into my old beat-up car, and I made it back to Connecticut in a couple of days. The drive back was a long one; I was all alone for 2500 miles; I didn't pick up any hitchhikers. It was quite a reflective time. There were a lot of things pulling and working, a lot of fears that I thought I had overcome in my supposed maturity, that I hadn't overcome. One was the fear of not reporting and having my parents suffer the consequences, directly or indirectly, from the government. I wasn't sure I could make it in Canada 'cause I didn't know anybody. I was afraid to go up there blind. It was a situation that lots of people find themselves in one time or another in their lives, not only with the draft—a time of great decision. I was having difficulty. So I figured that since I could adjust to almost anything if I had to, I would go in the army, reluctantly, against my will . . . My father said give it a chance, but I didn't believe any of the stuff he was saying because I knew he was just talking through his hat. He didn't know what else to say; he had lost all touch with me long ago. My mother was a bit saddened by the whole thing. She was against it then, more now. But she was afraid of my father 'cause he's a very strong figure—his personality, his will, his weight carries a lot.

So, I went in. Took the train to New Haven, reported—on time—and shaved off my moustache the night before because I didn't want the army barbers after it, but I still had my long hair. Kind of reminiscent of the wild, free days. So here it was, boom, the Vietnam War, something that had come right directly to my attention, let's say in 1964-1965, when it started to get in the newspapers. So you become aware of it. In my sophomoric reveries I knew nothing of the causes, the justices or injustices. It meant nothing, it was a far-off war, another thing we were getting involved in—I kept thinking of Lebanon. I had known about that in '57; I knew something was going on over there, though it wasn't like Vietnam. Now here it is; it hits you, you're there; the whole thing that in your mind, through abstraction, you've been denying, putting back, the demon you keep driving into the cave, not with any real tools, but with just your thoughts, your mind—and now it comes out, and it bites your ass. So, it bit my ass.

Like in my last couple of years of college, the States got rolling, things were happening. Sixty-seven was a hell of a year; a lot of things were coming to the surface. Sixty-eight, the convention, for example—Chicago, there were so many things pointing to the many errors that were being made in America and outside of America by Americans, not by the people, but by the government. The policy makers, the guiders, the people who guide us in and out of wars every twenty years, the economy makers, the whole thing—the whole thing that is not the people, that is not the body politic, the *con-trollers*. It was all going a bit sour. We'd seen it on the horizon, now it was . . . now it was right on top of me. With a kind of Jack Kerouac abandon I said to myself, well, here goes another experience . . .

The supreme rationalization. I had lost the battle with my wits and my mind—I wasn't able to say no, I'm not going to go; I'm going to Canada. Not at this juncture was I able to say it. So I gave in to it and almost with a maniacal twist of wit, I just said, aw fuck it, I'll go in and . . . ah . . . just enjoy it, you know; I'll play the game and see what they're doing; I'll see what the army's like. Then I had these flashbacks of when I was eleven, twelve, thirteen years old, and I used to be the commando, you know, my friends and I would run around playing jungle fighter and stuff like that. This was the mythology, the thing that's built into you by the mass media, built into you by the popular literature, everyone aspires to be a Sergeant Barry Sadler; you gotta do it. I figured well, here I am now, I've committed myself, unwillingly, to the situation. I have to go in. I wasn't about to hop off the train in North Carolina somewhere. I had it in the back of my mind that because of this heart thing I might get out in a while because they'd discover it, and I'd do anything in my power to feign sickness, fall down in the field, white and everything. I should have known better of course, but I didn't. I thought I could talk my way out of the army once I was in it, you know, just go up to a doctor and say, look . . . But this isn't the case—you're in, you're *in*, that's all they care about.

There were about a hundred of us from Connecticut, and we all went down by train, down to South Carolina. Wooo! I'd never been in South Carolina before except *through* it on my way to Florida once—I'd never stayed there—*South Carolina!* Boy! Fort Jackson is the base, and the town of Columbia is built around the base, not vice versa; I'm sure of it. It's a basic training-type fort. They train you; they do all kinds of weird things there. So I get down there . . . Like I said, since I was sucked into it now, as is my tendency most often when I get into situations that are beyond my control, I started acting out a part or adapting a certain way so that it would be most comfortable for me. I couldn't go in with a total bummer attitude—but, I mean, I was still very depressed. It was very bad; this thing had won over me. After all the lip service I had paid to dodging the draft—to this, that, and the other thing—now I thought I had been quite hypocritical, but the truth was that hypocrisy is based on fear, and now I was scared, man, and I couldn't get out of it . . . So you get down there and you don't know what the hell is going on, but you have strength because you're with a bunch of other guys who don't know what the hell is going on either. You put your heads together, and everybody's your friend, and you're everybody's friend because you're in this whole thing together, you know. You're hogs before the butcher; you know what each other looks like but you don't know what the butcher looks like yet. So, you get in there and you get your head shaved—I had long locks and a sergeant said, "Hey you, you, where you from?" and I said Connecticut. He said, "You know you look like a girl?" I said thank you sergeant.

You go through an orientation period. They assign you to a basic training unit, and then the fun begins. Then you learn the various things that you have to learn in basic training. You get closer to the people that you have to be sectioned off with. You look into their heads. You see how the military is run from the lower echelons and you see the kinds of things that come down from the upper echelons. Because I had a certain amount of intelligence, I guess—I saw a lot of my fellow soldiers who didn't, guys who were brought out of the New York ghettoes, guys that were from the coal-mining towns of Pennsylvania that didn't have the benefit of an education that I had, weren't able to receive the information that was put out, digest it, and make their own judgments on it—I knew everything was bullshit to begin with. I knew it all had to be taken with tons and tons of salt—not with a grain, my boy. It was easy for me to decipher between what was right and wrong, and I knew that most of what I was doing in the army was wrong. In the army you meet people; you become friendly with people, and I became friendly with people who, of course, were "of my kind," people who had been to college, let's say, although I made friends with countless other guys that were from totally different backgrounds. I enjoyed talking to them so much just to see how they felt about this thing because I knew how *I* felt about it. I knew I hated it. I was against being here although frankly I didn't have the courage to say no, but I wondered what made them resign just as I had resigned, in fact, to going in.

Everybody had a different opinion of why they were there—from "I didn't know what was going on," to "This was a natural thing to do," to "Hell, man, there's a war on and we got to stop communism." It was incredible, the mélange, the mixture of people thrown together under these circumstances. It was a great experience, it was, really. I was able to intellectualize it well enough to know exactly where *it* was and where *I* was. But I wasn't ready to get out. In basic training I was thinking that perhaps after basic I'd be shipped to something in the States; I'm the world's greatest procrastinator. The life wasn't hard: many of the things I saw were very stupid and senseless, they made me sick; other things I saw were very good, the most basic aspects of human relations were just exposed rawly in the army, the cruel part and the comfortable. There was a guy in the army from Baltimore, I remember; he was overweight, and not just for dietary reasons, but morphologically he was just built in such a way that he was a bulk with very spindly legs and arms—he spoke with a lisp which immediately everybody took up as faggot, which he wasn't. He was very sensitive. He was a social worker from Baltimore and he couldn't understand why they took him 'cause physically he just wasn't in shape. And we talked about it, and he said, "Well, perhaps they had to fill their quota and that's why I'm here." That boy all through basic training was harassed and harangued beyond what is necessary. He was browbeat; he was called names, insulted all the time. It's not enough just to be insulted by the cadre, the sergeants, this is expected, but when the cadre take you and put you in front of your own men and *they* begin to talk then you know that it is a very, very sad situation, a very hopeless and cruel situation—man *at his worst*, torturing his fellow man, not with knives, not with sticks, but with verbal venom. Yccch! It's so bad because it's such a subtle killing. This kid kept his head. The whole time he stayed so cool. He asked the sergeants to please stop doing this to him. Finally, he got sent away to the Special Processing Detachment (SPD), a special camp. I've never been in the stockade, but they say SPD is the next worse thing. So they sent him there. The guy who bunked under me in basic training was from Pennsylvania. He was eighteen years old. He could hardly speak the language because he stuttered, and he was slow in his head. He didn't know how to make a bed. He could not make a bed. He was the guy who was always lagging behind. Because I was his bunk mate, I took it on myself to, like, try to get him straight. I'd talk to the guy and ask him what the problem was and I could see it was just in his head, like he wasn't an idiot—he was just *not quick*. His fate was that he got sent to SPD too. I never saw him again.

You get time off in the army, and they warn you not to go into town and go into this place called the UFO, the famous GI coffeehouse in Columbia. Our captain would stand up there, and he'd say, "Now you boys, I'm gonna give you your first pass; now when you go into town I want you to act like soldiers and gentlemen. Make sure you fellows have a good time; get it all out of your system. And by the way, I don't want to see any of you people going down to this place called the UFO. Got a bunch of weirdos, hippies, a lot maragewhanna down there and stuff . . ." The thing I liked most about the army was picking up on these people and imitating them. And many of the people I'd imitate, I'd do it right in front of them and they wouldn't catch it. And my friends who would pick up the subtleties would laugh. We used to goof a lot. This is the only way to stay sane; the only way to stay above water was to create some great Candide out of the whole thing; make it into a travelogue of idiocy . . . So we weren't supposed to go to the UFO. Needless to say, everyone went to the UFO. I met some of the people there that I needed to make my later escape into Canada, my exit.

Basic training was like a book in itself; you can't describe it, so many weird things went on. Got stoned a lot in basic, everybody got stoned. Everybody was getting wrecked in one way or another. Either they were juicers—or they were shooting horse—or they were smoking Js—or they were just going into town, to the whore house, the Hotel DeSoto—and every weekend one of the guys would go in and get rolled for his whole paycheck and not even get laid. I went through the whole thing. Kill! Kill! Kill! "To kill without mercy is the spirit of the bayonet!" Learn how to shoot an M-16. Learn how to reload an M-16. Learn how to clean an M-16 in five seconds, put it all back together and scream "Uncle Sam is the Best." They taught you how to do everything, and not only did they teach you once, but they repeated it nine times. Not because it was that important, but because they had to get the people who weren't quick, which was a lot of people. I mean they were just taking everybody in—two years ago I wouldn't have been drafted because of the heart trouble—they were taking people whom they wouldn't have taken two years earlier because they needed the manpower. So you go through the whole thing; you learn how to dig a foxhole, the whole thing. I was goofing all the way through it.

I know that what I see I really don't like; it's very incorrect, to say the least—quite wrong, quite audacious of my government to do these kinds of things, so stupid; they have no brains it seems. I was goofing the whole time through it, and because I dig certain aspects of physical competition between men, I was doing pretty well despite my outlook on everything. In my mind I was being a cynical, satirical wit, you know; I was always being called a wise ass for making comments to the sergeants they couldn't understand. The biggest joke of the whole thing was that my platoon sergeant said, "Well, Milord, you're a pretty smart boy aren't you?" and I said, well, I don't know, and he said "Come on now—you're going to be the platoon leader." I goofed on that too. I didn't care. It was obvious, and the sergeant said, "What the hell's the matter with you talking like that, Milord?" I said, I don't care one way or the other, and he said, "Well, you're gonna be caring where you're going, *boy*, and you know where that is, *Nam!*" I was quite used to that kind of threat 'cause it was always hanging over our heads. We used to do marching, and we'd march in cadence and the overweight E-6 drill sergeant who had never been west of the Mississippi River would say things like, "On our way to Vietnam, gonna kill the Vietcong, that's the Fort Jackson boogie. What a craaazy song."

"If you're a bad boy you're gonna go to Nam." This thing is always held over your head. You hear stories by some of the cadre who've been to Nam. Our sergeant, our assistant platoon sergeant, was an E-5 draftee; he was drafted two years ago, sent over to Nam for a year, and he was so fucked up in his head over there that he used to pick brains to make empty souvenir skulls. He was a brain picker and an ear collector and he used to talk about it and would show us pictures. He was just a savage. But he had something about him; you could talk with him and make sense. He'd say, "I don't know what the hell is going on; I don't like being here anymore than you guys, but we gotta do it." Well look, sarge, you don't *have* to, I said. *I'm* not planning on doing it if they give me orders for that. "Well, damn you, boy, you better, you don't want 'em on your ass." He actually believed that, you know, if they said jump, you had to jump.

Wow, so basic training ends. You're out of it and you get orders. Where do I get orders for? I get orders for infantry. Advanced Infantry Training. All college boys go straight to infantry. I was really pissed, and I called my parents up and I said Hi, how are you. I'm not getting any leave time between basic and AIT. I'm going straight to infantry. And my father says, "Ah, yes, I was in infantry," and I said, I know, I know, I know. And my mother said, "Well," she said, "damn it, why didn't they put you in clerks' school?" I was quite disappointed. Not only was it infantry, but I wasn't even gonna get to travel around the country. They were sticking me right across the fort. By this time, things were progressing fairly rapidly. I was able to laugh and stone my way through basic, staying above it, getting used to it; I was on top of it at all times. It never got to me. I maintained a certain level of comedy that can almost always win out over most tragic situations. But then I knew, well, the game's up. Talking to myself as I used to do a lot, I'd say, well, now they're sending me to AIT, and you know that Fort Jackson is a training fort for Vietnam. You know you're going to end up eventually in Vietnam so what are you going to do? So I thought about it awhile and I said, well . . .

I hadn't learned yet about the Canada thing, and I hadn't had any real experience with the UFO yet. I'd heard about the UFO in basic, I'd visited it once, but I felt badly 'cause I was a bald-headed GI and this was supposed to be, like, a coffeehouse atmosphere—I didn't know at the time that it had been set up expressly for GIs. I didn't know anything yet, so I said, shit, I'm still stateside; I'm still going through training; so I'll go into AIT. But I said, I'm going to start using my head a little bit more to try to get out of this thing. Because up until then I thought something would work out. Like my old man at one point had interjected half way through my basic training, he said he knew somebody in the Pentagon who was a lieutenant with him in Korea, and he had saved his life, and that he was sure—this guy was now a colonel and a head of some very important thing having to do with troop placement—that he could get me a nice desk job somewhere. I said, shit, I didn't want it. Crap, man, my friends have to go through this; I will too. Like, if the army says, without any outside pressure, this is where you go, well, that's where you go. I don't want that shit with your friend in the Pentagon. I want it to be my own stand, I told him.

So I go to AIT. This is it. This is where you begin to learn a little bit about what it's going to be all about. It was tough; the people were meaner, the psychosis, the neurosis, the schizophrenia was more ingrained in the soldiers; everybody was uptight, paranoid, big brother, 1984, all crashing in on us, and it was a drag. It was a supreme drag. It was so frightening. Like here we'd had these old 1935 barracks with the coal stove, you know, at least I could sit there in my fantasizing head and say, ah, the romantic army period. But in AIT it was brand new sterile barracks with the white light up in the ceiling, eight men to a room, your own little cubby hole where you had to put all your stuff in order. Because they were new barracks they would keep saying, "Well, boys, 'cause these barracks are *sooo* new, you're gonna have to keep them *sooo* clean." It was a constant harassment. It's very stark; it's very naked. It's very hard on the nerves. There isn't the freedom that there was in basic. You get into AIT and it's a whole different bag. You get a certain gang of people who think more or less the same way you do and all hang together because everybody else is out of their skull. Our captain was a madman; Christ, he was a madman. He went out one day with an M-16 and blew the head off a bird that was flying overhead just to show how well the weapon fired under semi-automatic. He was crazy. He was nuts. And guys were freaking out; our company was going AWOL all the time. I never did 'cause I didn't want to hassle with it; I didn't want to be thrown in the stockade; I figured if I got thrown in the stockade then any chances of getting out are gone. It's not too easy to escape, and I'm not that great on just raw nerve courage, bolting my way through the gate and spitting at the master sergeant at the same time.

OK, so it was AIT and it was miserable. In AIT they give you very specialized training. You learned how to set up a Claymore mine, and the best way to set it up to make the most destructive impact. You learned how to use a rocket, antitank weapons, how to throw a handgrenade. In the last week you simulated an ambush. You went out in a mechanized unit; you jumped out of the truck and swept across a field as if it were an LZ [Landing Zone]. You waited on the other side, cleared the perimeter; a helicopter came down and picked you up and took you to another LZ; then you started your patrols; you dug in for the night, started shooting your enemy—you get the whole realistic thing. A lot of guys were really digging it—they'd signed up for AIT in hopes of getting to Nam. I was about as happy as a pig on the way to the sausage factory.

Here's where I learned that there's help for those who want to say no. I went down to the UFO—I got over the shyness about being a green, raw, bald-headed GI. The bald head strips you completely of your personality—you're a complete robot. I didn't become a robot, but you can get so close to being one it's frightening. You go downtown and you don't want to look at people. Especially people who were like you before, the hips that run around down there and freak with the coffeehouse. You were like them before; now you're not. You had let yourself get changed; I was very down on myself for letting it all happen. So I go to the UFO and I get to know the guys. I got to know a lot of the guys on the fort. There was a lot of resistance going on down there at Fort Jackson. There was the Fort Jackson Eight. A group of guys in another company were causing quite a stir—GIs United, they were called. This was where the army was having its problems, 'cause these bright inductees were the boys in the political scene that were organizing, participating in the organizing, and getting those people into it who hadn't been exposed to it before. They were good with their mouths. Up until this time I never got involved with anything of an organized political nature—I investigated the UFO, however, and I found out things could be done. Two of my friends and I had said, look, we've got to get out of this; this is complete insanity. I was going a little nutsy. The fun was over. This was very serious. I was feeling very bad about the whole thing, and I hated it. So while I'm at AIT I'm getting involved with the UFO coffeehouse, learning about RITA, Resistance Inside The Army, the general tone of the movement. To get the necessary information depended very much on these people at the UFO.

So my friends were freaking out, I was freaking out, so we said, look, we know we were against this thing from the start, but for one reason or another we got into it, and that's it. There's no use pouring over the past, why we didn't do this, or didn't do that. If the bullfrog had wings, his ass wouldn't be sore—if, if, if. We said, look, there is a thing called conscientious objector, and you can apply for it in the army—wow!—let's find out about it. Sure it's possible, not only is it possible, but there are people in Columbia who've got lawyers, the whole thing, they'll help you fill out an application. We went to see this one guy; there were three of us and we said we wanted to file for CO. He gave us the name of a priest to see in Columbia. Now the priest—Christ almighty!—he wanted to know the reasons why we were conscientious objectors. It wasn't enough for him to know that we were against the war, that maybe at any given time we'd be against any war, that we were against the whole thing—he just wanted to know if in your hearts it was a *Christian* motive. Ha ha. It's a human motive! Don't give me that brand-X label. But he was trying; he was very concerned. He was all right. I'm finding out the statistics. Something like two percent of all COs who apply within the army for CO get it. How long does it take? A very long time. Very itchy feet—gotta get out of here, gotta move out. I can't wait around for a CO. And then I got to thinking, you know, the priest's questions got to me. I said, look, I'm a CO, but in this war or all wars?—you know—I was getting all hassled with the definition of CO. You've got to have a showable ideology. You can have an ideology in your head, but if you can't verbalize it or write it down, you've had it. Anyway, I said, well, this isn't going to work . . .

So we found out about Canada. We found out Canada was good; we found out that you could go up there, that there was an organization there called the American Deserters' Committee, and the UFO had literature about it; and I met a kid who was back in the army who had been up in Montreal for three weeks and then came back and got caught. He was telling me about it. So I said, damn it! I had Canada on my mind before I got drafted—and I said, shit, it's gonna work out. It's gonna be able to happen! Damn it, I said, this time I'm gonna make it happen. Come hell or high water. So I wrote to the ADC in Montreal, and they sent me brochures and I read them and passed them around to my friends. I went and I got very enthused about the whole GI movement thing and I went to the coffeehouse—used to be there all the time—I would run CO papers back into the fort. I got caught for going AWOL one night. I hadn't wanted to go to this thing they had called Escape and Evasion, E&E, where you run around all night and these people try to catch you and torture you—it's supposed to be a Vietnam-training-type thing. So I said, I don't want to go to that; that's weird; let's go to the UFO. And we got caught. They called in CID, Criminal Investigation Detachment. What had got them most uptight was not the AWOL but the CO applications. This CO thing was really getting to them 'cause the movement was getting very big. Our battalion hadn't had too much trouble with this, and, all of a sudden, here were two of us. Something's starting here so we better nip it in the bud. So the captain interrogated us. But we only got an Article 15—you can't go anywhere—restriction. During our last two weeks of training the CID men were coming around, military intelligence and military police were coming around asking a lot of questions about the people we knew, but we told them we didn't know anyone. They left us alone after awhile. We finished AIT and I collected my travel pay to Fort Lewis, Washington. I got my two malaria pills. The orders came down. Practically the whole company was given orders for Vietnam. I think out of two hundred people, five were given Korea, two were stateside, sixteen were chosen for NCO school, and the rest to Nam.

So, that did it, of course. I corralled about eight of my buddies and told them I was going to contact them during leave and that we were going to do a Canada thing together; like, seven of us were going to go up. I was able, during basic and AIT, to sock away a little money and send it home and my mother put it in the bank and I had accrued about 150 bucks in my savings. Plus they'd given me 170 dollars in travel pay, plus special pay of 60 dollars so, all told, I had something like 350 dollars saved. So this was enough. I told my mother that I was splitting; she was a lot easier to talk to than my old man. And my brother and sisters all knew. I had twenty-eight days. I went home. I'm feeling badly about it because I knew what it was doing to my father. It was shooting him right downhill quickly. Because he in no way could understand, let alone accept, what I was doing. He was a veteran of two wars. Now for myself it was a test of my own—how can I put it?—*rights of passage*. I had to do this thing, not only because I didn't want to go to the Vietnam war and because I opposed the Vietnam war and opposed everything the military did, but because I had to assert my will. I had a fear of him because he was a very strong figure; he had a well-defined character, and when he said go, you did it. It gave me a little bit of anguish to confront him and sit down in the living room with him . . . He'd say, "You're deserting," and I'd say yes, and we'd go through it, and we'd try to talk it out, but it would only end up in a very emotional outburst. It was a big jump. There was certainly nothing I could have done by going to Vietnam. There was certainly nothing I could have done by going to a military stockade. And there was nothing to be done by hanging around in the States waiting to get clamped on by the military police or the FBI. So off to Canada.

I had to leave surreptitiously since my father threatened to have me stopped at the border. It's not so much that parents want their kids to go to war, but that they want to keep them from doing the *wrong thing* as defined by the whole national mania. And also his own world was a world that had worked out quite well even with *two* wars in it. So he couldn't see why I couldn't conquer that. And also he saw it as a proving ground for a man. So, on the twenty-fourth day of my leave, with four days to go, after having my suitcase packed in my car for four days while I was tossing and turning, I got in my car and just started driving. I left New Haven at midnight and wound my way north through New England which I knew so well. I was getting a bit saddened; but I was also getting very elated over the fact that I was free. The minute I got into that car and started driving north, the minute I made the decision to *do it*, I felt good. It may or may not be easy, I said to myself, but only time will tell. But I gotta do it, and right now I feel damn good about it. I crossed somewhere in Vermont and a guy with a French accent came out and said, "Hello," and I said hello. "Where you going?" Montreal. "Where you from?" I said, Connecticut. "Where were you born?" I said, Connecticut. He said, "Could you open up your trunk, please?" I opened my trunk. He said, "Well, have a nice time."

I really felt free! Wow! I wasn't going to be caught. I had picked up a hitchhiker in Connecticut and I'd told him I was taking off from the army and he said good. He was a German hitchhiking around the world. He knew somebody in Montreal, and he gave me a telephone number. So I said, well, I've got a phone number; I've got the telephone number of the ADC; I've got 325 dollars in my pocket; I've got my old car. I'm not too bad off I don't think. Before I knew it, on May 18, 1969, I was right downtown at Dorchester and University, and I got out of my car and called this telephone number and told the guy I just got into town from the U.S., I left the army; and the guy came down and picked me up. He let me stay at his place for three weeks until I found a room of my own. I got in touch with the organization, and they helped me get landed. After all the UFO people had done for me at Fort Jackson, I felt I had to get involved with this—I've got to do something for the guys back in the army; I've been through the army; I know what it's about exactly; I know what it can do to you. So I said I've got to help try and get out as many people as I can. So blindly idealistic, enthusiastic as hell, I went into the ADC office when they were down on Wolfe Street and I wanted to know how you do this, and how you do that, and who should I meet to do this, and deedly-deedly-doo. My enthusiasm for them betrayed me as an agent in their minds. I came just after the Canadians had reversed their policy toward deserters, and the committee was expecting an influx of agents to come up and see what was going on, now that deserters were allowed in. I tried to pick up as much knowledge in the shortest amount of time so I could be the most effective the quickest. Apparently it seemed that I had come on too heavy for these people who were running the organization at the time, and it was being passed around that I was an agent. People who trusted me in the beginning were telling me that I was being taken for an agent—I would talk with Jerry Boornstein and just to be a human being with him, I would ask him what he was doing besides this work. Little did I know that he was a so-called professional revolutionary, as he called himself, and he would snap back at me, "It's none of your damn business."

So, here I am in Montreal, and I'm meeting these guys who are deserters from everywhere. The place is fantastic. The weather is getting warm. It's May. I'm free. God, did I feel good!—'cause I knew I made the right decision and I knew I carried it through. Like I should have done back in Colorado. The army was behind me. It was an experience, its training; it was insight into a world that I might have never been in before had I refused to go, and I knew it. So I felt that I had certain insights. I met a couple of guys, and we decided to get a pad together up on Saint Urbain, and we lived up there for awhile—and I just let my head unravel for a long time, mainly with drugs—lot o' grass, lot o' hash, some acid, stuff like that. I just let it roll. I just let it all come out, and it was good. It was like a purging of the inner demon that was tormenting you while you're going through all these changes down in the States. From here on out it was a new life, and I was glad.

I went down to the immigration office; I had all my stuff together. The fact that I had a degree from a university helped. The guy who interviewed me was in sympathy with deserters, draft dodgers, everybody. He said,

"Welcome to Canada," and passed me. I did a little stint at McGill working in the English department for the summer to get a little bread—I assisted in a couple of courses. A good friend from college sent me up two hundred dollars for "one of the best damn causes in the world," he said. An old college professor of mine sent me up thirty dollars and said "Spend it on wine, women and dope." I said, yes sir! The reaction was good—my father was going out of his skull—but my mother was in sympathy, and now that I had made the move she was getting really activated on my behalf. My brother and sisters were clapping; my cousins were clapping; everybody was glad I did it except my father and the older people of our family who didn't quite understand yet. My mother understood because she's very good in the head—very hip. My mother said when I left, "A mother does not raise a son to go to war. The whole premise of raising a child is for exactly the opposite reason. To make him cope with life in a more human context than slaughtering each other."

Canada, yeah! . . . Montreal, the French, St. Jean Baptiste Day back on June 24, 1969. I became aware of a whole different world. The French, they were in trouble up here; there was a book by Vallière called *Le Nègre Blanche de l'Amérique du Nord*, about the French—I began to realize that things were happening here too, just like they were all over the world. The year before that it was Paris in May 1968. So I was getting into a political thing, the ADC, and the French thing, which wasn't a comfortable thing for me because I just don't work that way, I was always a loner of sorts, at least intellectually. I held no allegiance to any cause or movement because I had felt that once allegiance is sworn to one thing, you were kept from trying another. Allegiance means total involvement. My reasons were just to help everybody else get off the ground when they got up here, to help guys coming to Canada. I wasn't in it so much to do the whole radical political thing; I was into doing a more humanitarian thing. This is what eventually made me quit the ADC after working as the office manager for the summer.
working as the office manager for the summer.

In the ADC I was mostly the corresponder. We'd get forty or fifty letters a week. I was very embroiled in the organization, doing my main thing which was answering letters and telling guys it's cool, come on up. Like, "Dear ADC, I am nineteen years old. I've been AWOL from the army for two months. I have to move around a lot. Is Canada safe? I've heard it is; the army told me it wasn't. What do I do?" I'd write back and say bring this, this, this, this, and this and come on up; and don't be afraid 'cause the border's open. People in Montreal were calling up and offering help. By this time my head was getting into writing a bit. I wanted to get things together, you know, start looking around a bit, get myself straightened out. By the end of the summer things were going fairly well for the ADC, so I didn't feel badly getting into my own thing. I began falling away from the ADC a bit because I'd done what I thought I could, and should, and I wanted to get into finding out where my strengths were. Also, the ADC started getting factioned. There was this radical political versus the humanitarian aspect, and, like I had never had a head for politics. I feel I can do just as much as an individual human being *being*; I'm not going to bring the political revolution any quicker by that kind of attitude, but I certainly will help a lot of people understand what my age bracket is about and what *I'm* about and what a deserter's about—like, I did some interviews, talked at high schools, a junior college.

In the meantime, I was blazing through this fantastically beautiful summer, completely free. I had met this girl. Ah hah! A French girl who was like the sun, the moon, and the stars. She was really fine, and we decided to live together as we're still doing. Now it was time to look for work. It had always taken very little to make me satisfied. So I was living with Ghislaine, and she wanted to go back to school and I said, yeah, I'll get some work and you can go to school. I said that I'd just work enough to pay the rent and eat—I wasn't even going to buy clothes. So I did, I got this job at Sir George Williams Library working in the stacks at thirty-five bucks a week, part-time. I still wanted to have time to write 'cause I had all this poetry I brought up with me and all this stuff I'd written during the summer and I wanted to get it together. I was reading a lot, reading like crazy, smoking a lot of hash, and getting into the great black artists, Baudelaire, Poe—it was my melancholy period.

As far as the States goes, I sense something very foreboding. I don't know what it is. If repression comes, it's going to be horrible. And if the revolution comes it's going to be equally as horrible—that no matter who comes out on top, people are going to be shot in the streets, thrown in jail, put up against the wall. I fear people of the left who say without reservation that if you're a pig, you'll have to die. I fear people of the right who say if you're a hippie, you'll have to die. In the U.S. it's the government which is fucking up the people. Headlong speed is going to kill America; pollution is going to kill America; bad government is going to kill America. The thing that's going to save America is going to be its people, if they ever get their heads together. The direction of things can be changed, I feel. For me, the revolution goes on, in a life-style manner. For others, it goes on in the way they want it, if they want to organize themselves into units, viable movable units, *do it!*—if they feel that's right—but don't insist that someone else do it who feels it isn't right in his conscience. Don't berate the people who are not willing to join in a collective effort, in a collective revolutionary effort. I'm willing to join in a collective *humanitarian* effort.

I have a concept of history that makes me not want to join the violent revolution. Everything to me in history—as Yeats pointed out in his poetry—is cyclical, that is: man is always possessing the good and bad that he's going to have, and these things are always flipping over and turning in and out of each other and winding and unwinding and revolutions come and revolutions go and people change and people don't change, and it's all part of the continuing story of the species of man, and I, I want to find something a bit different. You can't deny that you're part of the whole thing, that you're part of the human race, but what you can deny are the follies of the human race, if you want to. I think the real revolution when it comes about is going to change the make-up of the face of the earth; it's going to change the way people think, it's going to change the political structures, it's going to change priorities . . . *if* the revolution is successful.

My time on earth is going to be spent sorting out my life and relating to other people. I get into a very basic Christian ethic, I guess, you know: do to others what you would have them do unto you. I get into a lot of trouble over that. People say it's naive . . . If that's naive, it's also very human too. And it's also being just as human to go to Vietnam and shoot people. Yccch.

Jesse Winchester is a song writer, a guitarist, and a singer. He is twenty-six years old and he left his home town of Memphis, Tennessee, three days after receiving his induction notice. He has lived in Montreal since then where, unfettered by the demands of war and the constrictive pressure of the American "super-hype," he was able to develop his talent as a folk-rock musician. He is from a large, close family with a brother and a sister and lots of cousins. After attending a Catholic high school where he was a "crackerjack," he received a music scholarship to Williams and graduated in 1967 with a degree in German. He is a walking encyclopedia of rock-and-roll music and his style embodies the best of nearly two decades of rock-and-roll but draws primarily on a unique genius and a restless soul. His music is like no other, and in Canada it was quickly recognized as something beautiful and different. In 1969 he appeared with The Band in Montreal's cultural center, *Place des Arts*, in a performance which the press called a "night of really superb music. The Winchester-Band concert was one to remember." The audience responded as enthusiastically, both nights, to Winchester as it did to The Band, an eminently successful and well-known Canadian group (which records in the U.S. but lives in Toronto). During the winter he cut a record which did, and is doing, very well, especially in the United States. *Variety* called it the best first record of 1970. The following spring Jesse appeared with Jethro Tull and The Jefferson Airplane at a rock concert in Montreal's Autostade. His lean frame, gently undulating, was barely visible to all the thirty thousand rock fans, but his melifluous voice lost none of its rich feeling in the big stadium as he sang his simple and beautiful songs: "Yankee Lady," "Rosy Shy," "The Brand New Tennessee Waltz." Jesse Winchester's soft brown eyes, slightly worried, stare out at you from the four sides of the folded cover of his album and tell you of an intense inner sensitivity and a warm and gentle goodness. He is every bit what the photographs say.

The Winchesters are an old Family. James Winchester was one of the three founders of Memphis. By most people's standards we were wealthy, but we weren't really. The thing that we had was more of a pride in the traditions and that kind of shit, much more than we had money. We certainly didn't have a whole lot of money; we were upper middle-class I guess. My father was very together; my parents are very together people. My mother certainly is a good Christian, she does the things that Catholics do, but she does 'em with devotion. My father, also, was a true Christian if there ever was one. My father fought in the Second World War. He was a navigator and bomber in the Pacific, and he came back just tremendously fucked up, a shell-shock type of thing. He eventually came out of it, but my mother told us about it all the time. My father had done an idealistic farming trip when he was younger; he wanted to get back to the land. So after the war he got a farm and left the city. Later, he had a heart attack and died when I was nineteen.

I thought I'd probably go into the army. The army was a different thing when I was in high school; it was kind of, you know, gettin' drunk and goin' into town, that kind of shit. At Williams I really hadn't confronted the idea of the draft in my mind. I went to Germany for my junior year—the University of Munich—and that's when I think I started to look at a lot of things, like the draft, you know . . . I got a kind of new perspective on the States—football, hamburgers, jeezuz! what have I been doin'! I was always very conservative, I still am a very conservative person, I never did anything political. I've almost made a career of being different, just to be different somehow. Sometimes that means I don't want to be part of the radical crowd and I don't want to be part of the reactionary crowd. I had more friends among the left—that's for sure—'cause they were talking more my language, but some of the things they were concerned with were crazy and childish. If I could have voted, I probably would have voted for Johnson—if I would have voted. I really didn't care much about politics, not until I got to Canada anyway. Now I do. Now I find myself liking politicians for the first time in my life—I'll be happy when I can vote here finally.

After graduation I just waited in limbo for the draft. When it finally hit me I just packed my bags and left—impulsive is the right word. Something told me that Canada was the place to go. I knew that I didn't want to play like Conscientious Objector 'cause I knew that I wasn't a pacifist. I figured Canada was a groovy place, and I was right. Canada was on my mind, but I didn't really know anything about Canada. What really made up my mind was a combination of being sick of the States, you know, the whole thing turned me off, and it was the letter, the whole army trip, going down and seeing the sergeant and things and taking the physical. Canada was something new, some kind of a change, I guess. Memphis was driving me crazy. I'd already been to Europe and I knew I could get along fine in foreign cultures. And I could already speak French. It wasn't a reasonable or logical thing though—I just packed up and came up.

I couldn't have gone to Vietnam. You *feel* it and you know when a fight is your fight, you *know*. Otherwise you're gonna get your ass shot off if you don't have the proper morale to go into battle with—it has to be right. I mean, I just wasn't involved in that fight at all; it just wasn't my fight. It touched me in no way. If it touched me in any way, I felt a kinda sympathy for the poor guys going around barefooted in black pajamas. I felt sorry for them more than the guys who had all the bigger guns and shit, the Americans. Ho Chi Minh seemed like a friendly sort. Friendlier than the one we had. Anyway, I'm not the fightin' type; if I have to fight—I realize that sometimes you have to fight—I hope I have the courage to recognize that time and do it. But basically I just hate it completely. My folks saw the Vietnam War as a case where it was a man's duty to fight, and I didn't. It wasn't really a question of conflicting morals for them, you know: there's a time when a man has to go off to war—it's as basic as anything—if your liberty or your family is being threatened, it's the only thing you can do. So, it wasn't really a conflict of morals in my family's view. If Lyndon Johnson told my grandfather that they were there to fight communists then that was good enough for my grandfather, but it's not good enough for me. As far as their own standing in the community goes—if it's done anything, I'm sure it hasn't helped. I had a cousin who was killed, an air force pilot shot down in Vietnam, so maybe that balances it out for the family.

While I waited for the draft, I just quietly made plans for gettin' tickets to Montreal, gettin' my passport and things ready. I knew nothin' about The Resistance or that I could have hid out easily in the States, at least for a while. I knew when I was coming through Kennedy Airport and I had a two-hour wait, that every cop I saw . . . wow! I went up to the ticket counter at Air Canada and said, I want a ticket to Montreal please; and I whispered, I didn't want anyone to hear me getting this ticket. I was scared. The ten days you've got to report for induction weren't even up yet, but I thought they were going to bring the iron curtain down, you know. All I knew about Canada was what I had read in an article in the *Memphis Commercial Appeal* about a month before I came up, and it was about how these two draft dodgers were gettin' along in Canada and it said there was a group that was helping guys but it didn't give a name or address or anything. So I figured what I would do was to go to McGill University when I got up here and find a guy with a long, long beard and long, long hair and ask him if he knew these people. It turns out that I got in touch with the Montreal Council and they were a big help. They really were a big help, they got me right through. I got landed almost immediately.

Before I left I made the stupid mistake of telling this guy I worked with in this office where I had a two-month job, filing or something, what I was gonna do. He used to go out drinking with us—I didn't tell anyone except my mother, and this doctor friend to get his reaction—but I did tell this guy and so, by the time I got to Canada, everybody knew where I was, and there was a big noise . . . wow! And I've got a religious family, like I said . . . oh wow! One guy in the family is an Anglican bishop, and he came up to plead with me to come home and not be a "traitor." My grandfather was the worst hurt; it just broke his heart. He was a patriarch type and it really hurt him. It hurt me, 'cause I really love my family, and I really love my grandfather, and I didn't want to hurt them; I didn't want my grandfather to think I was a coward. But there wasn't much I could do—I've got to lead my own life. I wrote a lot of pious letters and tried to talk in their terms—tell 'em what I did and tell 'em in their language—but I don't think I got through. But they still love me, everybody writes to me, they all write to me. It's usually the women in the family who understand something like this. My mother's been up and my grandmother and sister. My brother, who's twenty-two, came up and is staying with me. I don't think my family feels he's being subverted by being with me.

It was a little lonely at first. There weren't too many of us up here then. I met a few guys but not too many. You'd meet a draft dodger every month or so; now you meet 'em every day. It took me a while to get adjusted. It took me a long while because, well, the first summer I got up here, it was in '67 when everybody was doing acid and growing his hair, including me, just freaking out—that's what was happening. Not only was my life completely shaken up by the draft, but also with that LSD business and all; it really took me a long time to kinda get my feet on the ground, and now maybe that I've got 'em on the ground, maybe somebody's gonna pull the rug out from under again. I took maybe ten acid trips over a period of two years. You know, it was that time—kind of an experience a lot of us went through then, the whole freak-out thing. The last trip I took, I got bored; I wanted to go sleep and not be high anymore. So I figured, well, that's that, so much for acid. Acid just shakes you up completely from top to bottom, and it's up to you to put the pieces back together. I was smoking before I came up here—but I got into acid here.

During the drug thing I was playing with a rhythm and blues band and playing lead guitar with a Jimi Hendrix imitation group; we were really freaked out, that's what was happening during the drug thing musically; it happened to a lot of people. For money I got a job with a French rock 'n' roll band and we played in Trois Rivières and Chicoutimi and all over the place—just started working as a musician. This was the first time I made a living just doing music, but I'd played in a lot of bands in high school before. The name of the band was *Les Astronauts!* . . .

I had no idea I'd be doing what I'm doing now. Which is writing songs and making records and gettin' my name in *Rolling Stone* magazine. I thought I'd make a living more as a professional musician than as a celebrity, a star or something. Canada had a lot to do with it, but just how much, I don't know. My guitar technique and my singin' technique got to the point where I could carry the ball in a small club. I started out on my own simply because I could get a job in the New Penelope if I played alone. Then there was the Yellow Door and the Back Door and I got a lot of jobs playing for high schools. There were still some very insolvent periods—I used to live right down there on Mount Royal Street in absolutely the dingiest, dirtiest, cock-roachiest piece of shit you've ever seen. You know—"paying your dues." Capital P, capital D.

My music is rock 'n' roll—what I'm playing is best called rock 'n' roll. It's rock 'n' roll and it's twenty-six years old. The new album is basically rock 'n' roll, but there's some extraneous stuff in there. It really expresses myself. The music is everything, all kinds, pop music mostly. Like I've always liked Elvis Presley and Jerry Lee Lewis—they're both from Memphis—people like that, you know; they influenced me, and the station disc jockeys and listening to the hits at the A&W, you know. There've been pressures from people to go back so I could do my music trip in the States—a doctor wanted me to go back and have myself declared insane, but I told him I didn't want to do that. I want to remain true to my convictions about the draft. Americans can't believe that everybody up here doesn't want to go back to the States. It was just assumed right away that I was desperate to get back. It wasn't pressure so much; they were just trying to be helpful. But I told 'em, no, I don't want to go back. First of all, it's written into my contract with Ampex that they can't make me go back to the States. If a company ever started getting heavy like that, then that's the same trip the draft board was into. If they don't want to make my records, I'll find somebody else who will. I just realized that having my record produced in the U.S. was a decision without that much integrity involved. It would be nice if it were a Canadian company. But at least Ampex has got another Canadian act, Ian and Sylvia, so, if the finger of blame is going to be pointed, point it at Ian and Sylvia too. Maybe if I'd put this out on a Canadian label and Ian and Sylvia put a record out on a Canadian label, maybe we could build a good Canadian record company. Same story with The Band. I had a chance to do it too. There's a deserter up here named Chuck Grey—he owns Studio 6 down on St. Antoine Street. At one point Chuck and I were going to make an album on his four-track recorder, but then along came this big producer with The Band and I saw "fame and fortune" staring me in the eyes.

I got another album in the making. It's coming along pretty nice. I've also written a couple of songs in French. One of 'em's pretty good if I do say so myself. Maybe I'll try and record it on a single. The problem with all this is that sometimes when you get into one of these trips—being "Jesse Winchester"—it's hard to break away and go back and back-up somebody else, get my guitar back where it was. I just want to do some simple things, but sometimes being an entertainer kinda works a thing on your head, you just get so self-centered and eccentric. I've got a lot of plans. One good thing that came out of this Jesse Winchester thing is that I'm gettin' a little money to play around with, and I think I'll take some of that money and start a nice little club in Montreal, have a good little dance band, just a good place to have fun. It'll be a very traditional club in the sense that there have been a million clubs like it before and there always will be. You know, a little hole in the wall with wine and good funky dance music. Not too much beer—all those bottles are a hassle. Wine mostly, buy it by the gallon and dish it out.

I didn't know what I was doing and I still don't know what I'm doing, but it sure worked out nicely. I can say that for it. Because it was a decision that came from something really real . . . fear! Whenever I read statements about us, by people who don't like us, again I feel afraid; you know, you read a letter to the editor that says, "get those pinko queer commies out of here," something like that. I don't hate the guy, but it kinda upsets my stomach to read it. I'm still sort of uneasy about being a draft dodger and I think Quebec is the best place to be.

And then some of the things goin' on in the States get me upset. Like when Spiro Agnew starts talkin'. I try and take it off my mind as soon as it gets on. But I'm not really angry at the U.S. I just stand back in awe, you know . . . wow! . . .

There are things wrong with America, of course, but I still really love America. It's impossible to stop. But America as bully, that part of America I was certainly sick of—takin' everybody's natural resources, bleeding all these little countries and shit like that, imperialism et cetera, building cars so they'll fall apart, the whole waste-greed trip, you know, was a drag. And that part I was definitely sick of, but you can't say that's America. I hope not anyway.

I don't miss being in the States, *not at all*. There are a couple of people and a couple of places I'd like to see again, but I just put them out of my mind. I'm really starting to identify with this place, not just musically, but in every way—music is just a part of my life—in every way I really like it. I plan to stay as long as they let me. I certainly prefer Montreal to Toronto. And that's putting it kindly, man. Montreal has a lot of life in it; it's a very vital scene. It's an extremely beautiful city to look at. Every street is beautiful. It just really makes it for me. Whereas in Toronto, there aren't any restaurants that serve you anything but fucking junk. Toronto's a very American city, you know; people are expressionless. Toronto's a very, like, "make it" type place. All musicians want to "make it." In Montreal you never hear the term "make it." What's there to make? There's some nice people in Toronto, though; that's for sure. Everybody seems to like Montreal. Everyone I talk to. You have to kinda like the quiet pace—I love it. Montreal is such a good city.

During the acid thing I really reacted against the city, but now I'm beginning to enjoy it again. I'd still like to get a place in the country, but that's money.

The main thing is that I really dig it here. We tend to take Canada for granted 'cause there's not so much happening—I mean on a certain level. But wow! It's a good place. And for me now, because I chose Canada, because I made it my own out of a conscious act of my will, I feel that I have more of a stake in it. I feel like I want to be a good citizen, I have a reason to be a good citizen 'cause this is my new country. And I'm sure Canada will survive no matter what happens in the States. I mean, wow!, Trudeau is such an incredible diplomat. He rolls with the punches. Couldn't have a better guy . . . I think he's really good. Canadians don't know what they've got. Canadians really don't have a clue about how good they've got it. I'll take citizenship out as soon as I can—two more years. If I go back it will be as a Canadian.

Right now, I want to find a wife and have a couple o' babies. That's about my number one plan on my mind right now. That, and to continue to give as much as I receive.

F I V E

The Antiwarriors

Richard Perrin joined the army when he was eighteen, a logical choice for a young man who had no thoughts of college. The army was his college, however, and he quickly learned things about his country that many Americans still refuse to believe. "Before I enlisted in the army," he said at a press conference that received nationwide publicity, "I had been to only one antiwar meeting, and I'd seen the film *The Time of the Locust* and had heard the tape of Bertrand Russell's *Appeal to the American Conscience*. I couldn't believe the atrocities I had seen and heard and pushed them into the back of my mind. However, at Fort Leonard Wood, I overheard two sergeants joking about Vietnam and the barbarities one of them committed there. He told of torturing a prisoner in order to extract information. Later I heard other accounts of equally inhuman actions." After explaining to the press how he came to be associated with Andy Stapp's nascent GI organizing efforts at Fort Sill, he closed by saying, "I hope the people of the United States will wake up to the fact that they are being led through a period that will one day be called the darkest in our history. The world's people will condemn the United States, just as they condemn Hitler. I hope we antiwar GIs can count on support in our efforts."

Perrin found support, but not from the brass. For a trivial pass violation inadvertently discovered three days after his press conference, an offense that never brings more than verbal reproof, he was sentenced to thirty days in the stockade. After that experience, coupled with what he—and the nation—continued to learn about Vietnam, he knew he could not serve three more years in the United States Army.

The extraordinarily good-looking Perrin, tall, dark, with short black hair, spent his first year and a half in Canada operating two hostels and a counseling service for the Union of American Deserters in Regina, Saskatchewan. Presently, he and his Canadian wife are working at a center for retarded children in Moose Jaw, Saskatchewan. "I was getting tired of deserters," he said. Now twenty-two, Perrin is still a radical, though his anger against the U.S. has cooled somewhat. He feels he can be of no use in the United States but that there still remains the hope of building a revolutionary consciousness in Canada. Unlike many former movement GIs now in Canada who are planning to return "by any means necessary," he is not.

I was born in Massachusetts. We lived there until I was five years old, then we moved to Vermont, and I lived in Springfield until I graduated from high school. My mother is a registered nurse, and she works for a veterans' hospital. My father is a barber and has his own business and he's in the American Legion. He's a disabled veteran. My mother is in the DAR. Outwardly conservative people but their thinking didn't suit their image. They were more liberal than their friends. They had a hard time with my brother and his civil rights activities, but they tolerated it. Like they were a little bit uptight about me taking part in civil rights demonstrations at fifteen but they let me. If I wanted to do it, then it was my decision. With my folks there is sort of a basic humanism which sort of stuck in my head. They wouldn't tolerate me saying nigger, polack, anything like that—pretty liberal people generally. I was always truthful with them, like, anything I did, I would always go home and tell them about it. When I was fifteen I went to Chicago to visit my brother who was a student at Northwestern University and he was involved in some civil rights work, North Shore housing project, stuff like that. I started doing a little bit of work with these civil rights people. I went to a demonstration where Dick Gregory and Martin Luther King and a bunch of other people were speaking. It really meant a lot to me, the togetherness of the people and all. Marching down through the center of Chicago, it really felt good. I learned a lot about the ghettoes. Like I'd never seen a ghetto before in my life; in fact, I'd probably only seen three or four black people before. I discovered what living in the ghetto was all about. That left quite an impression on my thinking. I did this for two summers, the civil rights thing.

I went to California right after I graduated to live with my brother who was then in San Diego. Worked in a filling station—turned eighteen while I was there—registered for the draft in San Diego. I decided I'd better figure out what to do. I drove back to Vermont to see my folks and decided there that I ought to go in the army, enlist in the army, take a trade so I wouldn't have to be in the infantry, right? I went into the army in January 1967—went through the in-processing at Fort Jackson, South Carolina and took basic at Fort Gordon, Georgia. After basic I went to my first AIT at Fort Leonard Wood, Missouri and learned wheeled-vehicle mechanics, truck mechanics. That's where I started getting interested in the war, as I started getting closer to where I was going to be stationed—which was going to be Vietnam I thought. I talked a lot with guys who'd been in Vietnam and heard some pretty gruesome horror stories which really shocked me. I'd heard a few things before from my older brother, but I didn't really listen. He was a professor at the University of California and was involved in the antiwar movement. I started reading stuff in *Playboy* magazine about the war, liberal stuff against the war, and decided I was pretty upset about going to Vietnam.

After I got out of that training period I was given a month's leave, and I went home to Vermont, and I went to California for a couple of weeks and talked to my brother about what the hell I was going to do. I talked about deserting. He said, no, I shouldn't desert, but that whatever I decided to do he'd help me with it. Then I went to Fort Sill, Oklahoma, at the end of June 1967. I was there about two days and my brother phoned me and said he'd heard about Private Andy Stapp and the work he was doing there—he'd recently been court-martialed for having some leftist literature in his locker.

So I went out and looked for him that night and found him and Paul Gaedtke and Dick Wheaton, a couple of guys who were working with Andy. We spent the whole evening talking, and Andy gave me a big armful of literature, and I went back to the barracks and read every night. I'd sit on the toilet reading all night. Then I decided I'd go and see a chaplain and see if I could get CO status. I went to see a chaplain and he told me to forget it; CO status hadn't been granted at Fort Sill in something like five years. He told me I didn't know enough about the war in Vietnam to have an opinion. He also told me that things crossed his desk every day that he disagreed with but he went along with it anyway. I didn't even try to apply for CO after that.

I went back to see Andy and he gave me more literature and more books. I went down to the book stores and the base libraries, went everywhere, getting books about Vietnam. I read *Street Without Joy*, Felix Greene's *Vietnam, Vietnam*, all sorts of pamphlets. One that stands out in my mind particularly was written by Carl Oglesby, a speech of his in Washington, D.C. I told Carl about it when we were in Montreal for the conference [Pan-Canada Conference of Deserters and Resisters] —told him it meant a lot to the direction of my life. I read *Behind the Lines* by [Harrison] Salisbury. A book by Stokely Carmichael. Then I started getting into some really heavy organizing on the base there with Andy and the other guys. One night we went to the University of Oklahoma and talked to some students there. The first time we made it, we got there OK, talked to the students, professors, anyone who'd listen to us. It was an antiwar seminar. We didn't talk about organizing in the army, just our view of the war as GIs. Another time we were prevented from going.

I was going off-base every night, going to the Holiday Inn in Lawton every night, to see Maryann Weiseman and Key Martin from New York, people who were there sort of helping us from outside the base. They were from Youth Against War and Fascism in New York and they were helping us organize; they were the only group who would do it. The thing was that Andy had been affiliated with the Progressive Labor Party and they didn't want anything to do with him now that he was in the army. So he left them and asked all sorts of people to help, base people for the outside, resource people, and nobody was interested. SDS wasn't interested, the Trots weren't interested because he wasn't a Trot. Finally Andy found YAWF and they were right on top, they really wanted to help. They printed all sorts of literature about the struggle at Fort Sill. They were a great help. So they came out to Lawton while I was there, and we went out and talked with them every night, had our supper there, rapped, rapped, rapped . . . and read. Sort of had our own little struggle sessions.*

With Andy, at Fort Sill, we'd turn out leaflets, go around and hand them out. They'd turn up everywhere, under pillows, in dayroom book racks, in the library, in the cafeterias—antiwar leaflets. Andy was a little more militant than I was, more than the other guys. He was anticapitalist, antiimperialist; I was antiwar. But we worked together really well. Andy is one of the people who's been very influential in my development—my thought development. We reached a lot of guys—there are 40,000 GIs at Fort Sill, and we reached a lot of them. Most of our leaflets were printed in New York, but we printed some on the base. We were distributing *The Bond,* which was then a West Coast thing published in Berkeley. Andy Stapp later took it over.

One night I didn't sign out on the pass register. I had a pass, could have left, it was legal for me to leave the fort after duty hours. But I neglected to sign out on the pass register. Three of us were picked up by detectives, Dick Wheaton, and this other fellow whose name I can't remember. We were put in handcuffs, handcuffed behind our back, and thrown into the back seat of the police cruiser and taken down to the city jail. They charged me with being AWOL since I didn't have my leave paper. Dick Wheaton had his and they let him go. We were turned over to the fort authorities and then turned over to our company commanders, and then we were put on restriction. We had to stay inside the barracks and couldn't go more than fifty feet around them. This went on for two days, and finally I went into the commander's office and said, look, you going to charge us or what? He said he'd let us know the next day. The following day he informed us we would get an article 15, nonjudicial punishment, more than you usually get for a pass violation. I refused to sign it and demanded a court-martial. Sort of blew his mind.

I got my court-martial. The witnesses all perjured themselves; some of them couldn't even identify me. I was found guilty. Usually that type of thing is a slap on the wrist. The thing we wanted to point out was that guys for the most part don't sign out on the pass register—they just leave after 5

*Stapp's full story is told in *Up Against The Brass*, Simon and Schuster, 1970.

o'clock. It's an open fort; there are no gates. You just drive through. We weren't picked up for not having passes. *We were picked up for our antiwar activities*, and, as a result, it was discovered that we didn't have our passes. They were following us around. We wanted the court-martial so we could get this thing out in the open and could bring out a lot of stuff. It was really good because the fort authorities were really uptight about us. People were driving in from all over the country. Students from Madison, students from California and New York coming down in cars, from Oklahoma, from Texas, all converging on Fort Sill on July 31, 1967. Andy and I were being tried the same day. He was being charged with breaking restriction also. He had been put on restriction for no reason by his CO [Commanding Officer] —he always made sure he had his pass. He got off 'cause his restriction order had conflicted with another order he'd been given from a higher officer. We wanted to do this court-martial thing 'cause we wanted to publicize our activities, to let people know that we were organizing against the war and that we were being harassed for that. And the thing is that the command of the post did all our advertising for us; they called every GI on that base into formation that morning—each commanding officer—and told them what was going on and told them not to go near the place where our court-martial was. Some of the guys didn't know about it before this. It was really good advertising. Anyway, I was found guilty of the charges and got thirty days' hard labor.

The people who were coming to see us were followed by helicopters from Oklahoma City and the state police and FBI cars. Most of them didn't get there. They were stopped on the Interstate ramp by the military police and state police. Maryann Weiseman and Key Martin had been ordered by the commanding officer not to come on the base and when they tried to get on for the court-martial, they were arrested for trespassing and put in the city jail. Their trial came up after I left the States. They got six months each in federal prisons for trespassing. They served it, six months, each of them. The judge at the trial told them that they were being put in jail not necessarily for trespassing but for causing dissension within the armed forces.

I was taken to the stockade and put in a little cage in the middle of the stockade grounds and all the prisoners had the daily newspapers and my picture was on the front page saying I was a commie. They were beating on this cage and shouting at me. Then some guards came to get me and took me into the stockade commander's office, and he told me they were going to send me to a security cell area to protect me from the other prisoners. I told him I didn't need protection from the other prisoners—that even if I got beat up a little, I could still deal with it. He gave me all sorts of shit, tried to get me to hit him so he could get me for assaulting an officer. So I went down to the security cells. Same deal there. All the prisoners were waiting for me; they had the newspaper with my picture on it, beating on the cell doors trying to get at me, "There he is, the commie, let's get him." In the security cells I got to know the guys, got to like the guys, built some pretty good relationships down there. But some of the guys I was afraid of—pretty mean. The second lieutenant would come around in the daytime and beat up the prisoners, the guys he didn't like, beat the shit out of them. Like the lieutenant brought in a letter from home and showed it to me one day, holding it ten feet away. Then he put it back into the envelope and took it with him. The latrine had crap on the floor, the toilets were overflowing, you had to call a turnkey when you wanted to use the toilet facilities. You had to take showers in shit. It was a messy scene. It left a deep impression—I kept thinking about what I'd read and heard back home in high school about prisons in Russia, and North Korea, and in China, you know, and the type of thing that was going on in the stockade was the same type of thing that was supposed to be going on in these communist places, right? It sort of blew my mind. I thought the stockade would be a sort of liberal place where you could read books, watch TV—the idea I had of an American prison.

So anyway, after I was in there for awhile, I had a lot of visitors, chaplains, officers, Vietnam veterans, guys who were trying to talk me into seeing that the war was a good, groovy thing. Telling me all about their missions in Vietnam. They kept sending all these people into the stockade to talk with me because they thought I was still young and still a salvageable case; they said I'd been brainwashed by the commies. They even flew my parents in from Vermont. They tried to save me! The chaplain would come in for several hours at a time, and I'd sit and bullshit with him. Some things I compromised on, some things I didn't. I wasn't really radical then, anyhow; I was pretty liberal. When my parents came in they got a tour of the fort from the commanding officer—they tried everything trying to get me back on an even keel. They would use me as an example, maybe, once I repented. They could have had me going around speaking to soldiers about the communist menace that I was almost a part of. When they thought that I'd repented, they made a deal with me. If I stopped working with Andy Stapp, if I had no more contacts with commies, if I didn't talk to GIs about the war, then they'd guarantee to send me to Germany instead of Vietnam. Also, they'd release me early. So I said, OK, and they released me after fifteen days. On that day an officer admitted to me that it was a stiff sentence and the reason I was in there wasn't for breaking restrictions or pass violations but for my political activities. As if I didn't know it.

I saw Andy the first day I was out. Then I flew to New York and saw some of the people there and then went to Fort Dix. All my friends came down from New York to see me before I left for Germany. In Germany the first thing I was aware of was the racism there on the bases—much more acute than in the army in the States. The first thing I was told when I got off the plane in Frankfurt was, "better forget the German girls because black guys get the German girls." It seemed like it was true—blond girls and black GIs everywhere. The first Saturday night I was there a black guy walked into the EM [Enlisted Men's] club with a German girl and a fight started. There were more white guys than black guys so this other guy and I were fighting with the blacks against the whites. That night, my friend, who lived in a predominately white barracks, got the shit beat out of him. I lived in a barracks with mostly blacks, only five or six white guys. Nobody touched me. All this time I was getting really turned off. I was hearing stories about guys running their tanks through German farmers' fields, that sort of thing. I started getting really ashamed to wear the uniform, and that's really the basis on which I deserted. I would walk around in a German city and just be completely ashamed to be in the army anymore. It was no longer just the Vietnam War, it was the whole fucking army, the racism, the memory of the stockade, the whole thing. I was disgusted, totally disgusted, ashamed.

When I got to Germany I was all alone. I wouldn't have deserted if I had been with someone strong enough, like Andy. I wasn't that much of an organizer and didn't really think I could do anything in the army—I wasn't that committed. I didn't really become radical until I'd been in Paris a few months, and then things started moving fast. I was sort of hanging on to the old American myths for as long as I could until the contradictions became so great that I couldn't hang on to them any longer. I was sort of hanging on to the old liberal myth: There's-nothing-wrong-with-the-U.S. . . . This-war-is-just-a-mistake . . . We-can-stop-this-and-elect-a-new-administration.

So I finally deserted. I went to the train station and split for Heidelberg. I got a ride from Heidelberg to Paris. I couldn't find anybody in Paris. I went everywhere, I went to the Communist Party and they just kicked me out— they wouldn't help me at all. This was in the fall of 1967, even before the four went to Sweden from the *Intrepid*. I finally got in contact with a guy named Max Cook, a draft dodger from the Korean War, and June, an expatriate, fairly rich—a left-liberal woman who since that time has become quite radical, giving away a lot of her money and so on. These were part of a radical-left group of Americans in Paris. I was the third deserter they had helped. In December Stokely Carmichael showed up. He was arrested by the French police at the airport and held for a few hours. I phoned Max and said I'd do an interview with Carmichael on TV—I think it would be worth it. Before, I had refused TV and films and interviews because I had signed an agreement with the French Government not to engage in any political activities. This was after the four guys from the *Intrepid* deserted to Sweden. We wanted to keep desertion in the headlines, and we figured this was a way to do it. Stokely said fine, he'd like to do it. We did an interview with CBS and the *New York Times* and *Newsweek* and Swedish TV—nothing in France. Before, we had done several interviews behind screens with Terry Klug, myself, and two other deserters. [These appeared in *Newsweek* in February 1968.]

So we did the thing with Stokely. That was when I started getting turned on to radical politics; I spent three days with Stokely rapping with him. After that, I read *Revolution in the Revolution* by Regis Debray. Started reading about the Cuban Revolution. Anyway, right after the meeting with Stokely we formed RITA, Resistance Inside The Army. We were always trying to avoid working politically in France because of the agreement that we had already signed. So we called ourselves Resisters Inside The Army and decided our main focus wasn't going to be to get guys to desert but to encourage resistance from inside the army. We could get away with encouraging this because we were not in the army. Then another group sprang up in France, very opposed to our group, called the American Deserters' Committee. Their stand was uncompromising revolution, and they turned off so many deserters who ended up going back to Germany. Besides that, during the May revolt they were sending out press releases condemning DeGaulle's government—we wondered, my God, are you crazy? We were out fighting on the barricades sure enough, but we weren't publicizing it.

Most of what we did in Paris was to publish *ACT*, the first GI underground paper, and we'd send them all over the world. Terry and I and Phil Wagner started *ACT*. We weren't that deeply involved with deserters—we'd help guys out—but our main interest was talking to guys still in the army. It wasn't a very good newspaper, but it served its purpose. It turned on a lot of guys and opened up a lot of avenues. Like, Terry and I were writing letters to the *Stars and Stripes*, having arguments with the editors and so on, really carrying on a good forum, and all the GIs were reading this. We were pushing all the time—three or four hours' sleep a night. We were trying at the same time to set up an American Serviceman's Union in Germany like Andy Stapp was organizing in the States. I'd get on the train and go to Strassbourg and talk to GIs there, at the German border. Always doing interviews, German radio, and so on. But mainly, we were getting out *ACT*. It was really successful. We distributed *ACT* by mail—we had an incredible mailing list of about ten thousand. The press run was ten thousand.

That went on until January 1969, when I flew to Canada. I decided to leave because after the May revolt I didn't trust the French government at all. I sort of expected at any time they'd be turning us over. In fact, Max got arrested shortly after I left.* And we couldn't count on expatriate Americans

*From the *Paris Herald-Tribune*: "Mr. [Max] Cook's arrest has caused consternation among the approximately 200 American deserters living in France who believe that the policy of allowing them to remain might change with the departure of General DeGaulle . . . Mr. Cook supervised the underground railroad that brings deserters from American units in Germany and helps them set up life in France, finding them homes and often providing money. The French position, a reflection of the government's position against the Vietnam war, has been to tolerate the deserters so long as they do not become active in French politics. They had been free, however, to express their views on the war and to encourage desertion. The underground railroad is still in operation. Mr. Cook, who is employed as a research scientist, was arrested Thursday on the Boulevard St. Germain . . . Mr. Cook was forced to return to Austria where he holds citizenship."

for support. The Paris American Committee to Stop the War in Vietnam wouldn't help us, they were very uptight about deserters. In fact, we were sort of the niggers of the American community in Paris. I was glad to leave finally. Terry Klug left Paris the day after I did and returned to the States. He was going to turn himself in to organize inside. He was getting very frustrated in Paris. He wanted to work with Americans and he was separated from them. So he decided to turn himself in so he could talk with Americans. He did, and he was involved in that riot at the Fort Dix stockade. I was afraid that in going to prison something like the riot would turn up and they'd get him in there for another twenty or thirty years. Which is what could have happened. It didn't happen to him because of all the publicity he got. Klug was acquitted of charges stemming from the riot, but many of the Fort Dix 38 were given long sentences. After that he decided to cool it and get out of the stockade. They didn't break him; he's still really strong. He's at Fort Leavenworth, Kansas now. He got three years for deserting. He'll be out in another year or so and then he'll be free to travel around the States . . . and of course I can't. I don't know how he'll come out of it. I'm sure it changed him just like coming to Canada changed me, only differently. I can tell you right now that I'm not as militant now as during the first few months I was here; I still do political work but just mild stuff. I'm sure that when he gets out I'm going to be in the position of trying to slow him down. He's going to be really bitter. We're really good friends—I consider Terry to be my best friend—and we respect our different choices. He says the first thing he's going to do is come up and see me as soon as he gets out.

I didn't know if Canada was safe for deserters or not—I came to Canada before the law had changed here—but I was still committed to doing some political work so I was willing to live underground. My brother had some friends in Regina so I came here. I discovered that there were a couple of professors helping guys out as they came through. I went through the immigration thing—it took me a long time to get landed. When the RCMP came around to see me they had about a six-page letter from the Department of the Army, the U.S. Army, and all sorts of reasons why they shouldn't allow me to stay here. I finally got landed, anyhow. I originally had a job at the university teaching a seminar on the U.S. Army; now I'm paid fifty dollars a week by the Canadian Council of Churches to do counseling for the committee. We started the committee, or the Union of American Deserters, in June 1969 and got a farm out in the country and we had guys staying there who were passing through. By the end of August '69, we got going full steam. I've counseled about ninety guys who have all been landed in the area since. We get a few new guys, but mostly referrals from the Vancouver committee.

I like Saskatchewan because it's a secure place to live. Because of the socialist reforms that took place during the past twenty years. Things are much more right-wing now, but as inflation and unemployment get out of hand, people are turning back to the social democrats again. My father-in-law, a carpenter, says that if the NDP [social democrats] isn't reelected, he's going to leave the province. Regina can be kind of interesting. It's not as dead as you'd think. We've had quite a few antiwar demonstrations in Regina. Also, pro-Panther demonstrations. We marched through town in a Panther demonstration when Fred Hampton was shot; we even got a police permit for the demonstration. Fred was here about two weeks before he was killed, touring Western Canada, speaking.

For the most part I still want to see a socialist revolution, but I can't see a socialist revolution without people making the socialist revolution, and too many times people in North America who call themselves revolutionaries can't even talk with people. If they're completely isolated from people, how the fuck are they going to make a people's revolution? What I want to do is start a very small commune with one or two other couples, integrate into a small community, and just get to know people. I don't feel like getting into this sort of "do your own thing" trip, the hippie commune thing; I don't dig that at all. In fact, I don't even like long hair 'cause I'm a greaser and when I'm working on cars the hair gets in my eyes and I can't stand it. Long hair is only practical for people who don't do any work, I mean manual work. I'm sort of in the middle between the cultural revolutionaries and the political revolutionaries. I think they both have a lot to say. I don't see why there has to be such a split in the U.S. between them. As for the Weathermen, I think they are totally suicidal.

Revolutionaries in the U.S. cannot talk to people; they just cannot talk to people; they can only talk to each other. That's the bag I was into for a couple of years. I couldn't talk with anybody. I'd meet a guy my age, and, soon as he said something reactionary, I'd jump down his back so fucking hard that he'd never come near me again. That's incorrect 'cause these people are the people we're going to try and make a revolution for—we can't keep turning them off. But the radicals say, well, it's going to be a revolution of young people anyway. But I'm trying to point out that the majority of the young people are still with the establishment; they would still stand up and fight for it. They're doing it in Vietnam right now. Then I hear people like Tom Hayden at the Montreal Conference say we need a revolution in the next three years. Horseshit! You try to make a revolution in three years and you're going to find yourself dead. You can't make a revolution until you have a fairly good number of people fighting with you. Everybody is trying to do revolutionary work but they're not doing any ground work for revolution. You've got to do a lot of preparatory work first. They're talking to themselves or disagreeing with one another in the States. I mean things like that with the "liberated *Guardian*" are suicidal. If the *Guardian* had been forced to close up because of that shit that went on there, it would have set the movement back a lot because of everything that is in the *Guardian*—like Wilfrid Burchette for example. The *Guardian* provides the only real truth that Americans can get about the war—and these fools came close to cutting it off. [In Canada, Wilfrid Burchette is carried from time to time by the large English dailies.] I think if those people didn't dig the way the *Guardian* runs, then they should have started their own newspaper, for Christ's sake. It was counter-revolutionary to nearly close it down like that. These people running around trying to make a revolution within three years are going to cause a premature repression. The government is going to react. The government *will* kill them off.

In Canada, I see a national liberation struggle as important. There is a nationalism growing here. Just talking to people in the streets, Canadians are beginning to turn against Americans like the rest of the people in the world. Many people on the Left here won't recognize this nationalism because they see it as not progressive, not internationalist, but my point is that if the Left doesn't grab a hold of it, then the Right will. I think that the Canadian and American revolutions are going to have to be separate. There are different traditions. Another mistake Americans make here is to isolate themselves from Canadians. I'm married to a Canadian; I live with Canadians; I intend to become a citizen of Canada. Canadians are now talking about leftist cultural imperialism. Before I joined with Canadians I was always being attacked about that—"This is our movement and we're going to run it the way we want to run it, not the way you run it in the States." You know. Also, I don't understand American radicals saying that political work in Canada isn't important because Canadian people are just as important as American people. Like in the U.S., too many organizers head for the cities, and nobody goes out in the country and works with the people. I'm disgusted by that. Here we are out in the hinterland of North America, but there are people here.

My parents were up here a couple of weeks ago. They support my desertion, and they sort of support the idea of revolution. The type of revolution that I've been talking to them about is the kind of revolution that I believe in, that is, sort of going back to the principles of the Declaration of Independence and the Constitution with a few amendments here and there—though I think it is basically a good document. I think that's pointed out by the fact that the North Vietnamese use almost the same document—copied much of it word for word. I think just to return to the principles of Thomas Paine is really revolutionary. I think we never *reached* the level of Thomas Paine and I think it's about time we did . . . So my folks are really good, saying the future of the world is in the hands of the young people. We were sort of comparing the type of struggle that we have now as young people and the type of struggle they had when they were young. My father was young in the twenties and thirties, when it was a struggle just to get a meal. And when your main struggle was to eat, you really didn't think a hell of a lot about political stuff, or the world's problems. We've grown up in an affluent society, and, using the basic principles of socialism, the situation allows for people to think in socialist directions . . . I can remember when I came home from the army one time telling my dad that he wasn't free to say what he wanted to say. I kept saying the Constitution says that in this country we can say and write what we want, we can go to the church that we want, we can do anything, but you *can't*. He would say, oh yes, I can, I can, I can, and we'd argue and argue. When he came up here two weeks ago he said, I can't! 'Cause as a barber, talking about me, his son, a deserter, he'd lose all his customers. That's what I was trying to point out to him before.

After the months in Europe, and now, I consider myself to be more a foreigner than American—like I talk about *those* Americans—so I wouldn't have come back to the U.S. from Europe even if I'd been guaranteed no more than two years in prison. It wouldn't have been worth it. Exile is by choice, really, though of course I'd like the right to go back and visit. In relationship to the length of my life, it has been a long time since I've been in the States. Things have changed a lot since I've been there. Like when I was in California you could drive down the street without being hassled; you could have long hair and you wouldn't get hassled. But now they stop you with drawn revolvers. It's no longer my country.

Laurence Svirchev is twenty-three years old and aging rapidly. The burden of revolution weighs heavily on him for that is what he is committed to. It is not a passing thing. He will remain a revolutionary until America changes or he dies. Whichever happens first. He is relatively new to the movement, but he learns quickly. Like thousands of his contemporaries, he is a bomb child, raised in the warfare state and formed in the crucible of the Vietnam years. Had he not been forced into exile—it was that or five years in prison—he might not have become what he is. He might still be working for the Chemical Bank in New York. Although it can be debated whether being forced into exile is reason enough for one to become a revolutionary, there is no question that being a revolutionary is a far more suitable occupation for a political refugee than working for a bank in exile—if one must make such a choice: between banking and revolution.

There are elements in Svirchev's past which would indicate why he became a revolutionary to the professional people who reduce young people to specimens useful only for their "professional" conjecture. There is a strong father figure—his father is a Marine Corps colonel and former commanding officer at Fort Schuyler in New York—and there is a strong Catholic upbringing including several Jesuit Schools, Brooklyn Prep, Holy Cross College, which, it is said, either turn out saints or Martin Luthers. One could say that his "revolution phase" is nothing more than rebellion against this authoritarian upbringing, but that does not help us to understand Laurence Svirchev any more than dismissing President Nixon as an egomaniac helps us to comprehend that man. The point is that America had better worry about what men like this, at opposite ends of the political spectrum, are saying and not who they are. For what both are saying, and doing, will determine what happens to America in the seventies.

Svirchev arrived in Montreal in the late fall of 1969 and following the usual period of readjustment took over the job of office manager for the American Deserters' Committee. He stayed with the job and the committee paid him a salary of thirty-five dollars a week. His girlfriend, Stephanie Durant, an art graduate of the University of South Carolina and a former staff member of the UFO coffeehouse near Fort Jackson, joined him from the U.S. She left shortly before the UFO was closed by court order and the remaining staff arrested and sentenced to up to six years apiece—for "creating a public nuisance." Svirchev and Durant shared the same revolutionary fervor and worked hard for the ADC during a difficult and extremely cold winter. While other ADC members dealt with deserters' problems like immigration, housing, counseling, and jobs, they became more and more involved with the political end of the committee's operation which meant forming an exile voice which would begin to have an affect south of the border. Svirchev proposed a national exile conference for May of 1970 and with money from a U.S. peace group traveled across Canada to secure support of the other exile groups. He successfully managed to convince over fifty deserter-resister counselors and exile leaders from all over Canada to convene in Montreal, along with approximately fifty U.S. draft counselors, GI organizers, peace movement leaders, and radicals who came from as far as Berkeley, San Antonio, and Nashville. The conference turned out to be the most important event in the political life of the exile movement in five years.

At this writing Svirchev was arranging for an "exile contingent" to be part of the next *Venceramos* Brigade to Cuba.

Larry and Stephanie will continue to raise their political consciousness and that of deserters in Montreal and in Canada as well, and then, no doubt, they will return from exile and join the underground in the U.S.—when they feel it is time.

At first I supported the war because my father always used to say, "If we don't defeat them in South Asia, pretty soon they'll be fighting in San Francisco, at the Golden Gate Bridge." I was always curious about Vietnam. For instance in my freshman year we had a woman who had come back from the North [Vietnam] —and she came to the college and was talking about the fragmentation bombs that just rip the shit out of people. And there must have been about a hundred people there, and nobody believed it. Nobody believed her. They'd say, "No, we wouldn't do that, and besides, they're communists." You know. And nobody was able to accept just plain people being ripped apart by American bombs.

A couple of weeks later about four people got together and they called for a meeting. This was in the fall of 1965. They called a meeting of all the people at the college who were against the Vietnam War. I went with the attitude of, maybe these guys have something to say and I might as well listen to it—very wishy-washy position 'cause I didn't know anything about it. And that was my first experience with any kind of movement activity. I was just up in the room listening to what these dudes were saying. That was my first and last contact with the movement until I went into the army. I didn't know much about the war—I didn't read the papers.

Then I left school and went to work for a year and worked for the corporate trust division of the Chemical Bank of New York Trust Company at Broadway and Eighth Street, right on the crossroads between the East and West Village. I didn't know anything about capitalism or socialism; I just did a good job. I really found out a lot about the way capitalism works. Like, I wanted to work for the bank, you see; I wasn't working for me—I didn't need a fantastic salary; I was working for the bank and I wanted to make my bank a good bank. It was really naive, and later I found out why. Because everyone in that fucking bank was out for themselves, and they were all juggling for position and more money at the expense of each other.

I wasn't aware of any of the anti-Vietnam demonstrations during that year in New York. I was a hip capitalist who really dug rock and roll, a weekend hippie. I could come out of that bank at night and go over to the East Village and go to the Fillmore or go over to the square and listen to the bongo players or the freaks playing their guitars.

My job was external coordination. What I would do was, say Sperry-Rand needed a job done, well, I'd have to contact a representative of the firm who was usually a president or vice president or one of the elected managers so I was dealing with very heavy people in the capitalist structure, and I started reading annual reports, and then when I got into the army I looked back and I said, holy shit!—something just clicked—I got myself drafted because of that fucking system, and every one of those corporations that I helped out in my own little way—mine was more direct than other people—every one of those fucking corporations had a stake in keeping the war going. Every corporation had war research grants, whether it was research and development or actual production. Weyerhaeuser Corporation, for example . . . the amount of lumber they ship to Vietnam!—boatload after boatload.

I was conscripted. I was reclassified 1-A three months after I dropped out of college. I was attending Fordham night school, but I didn't take enough credits to keep my 2-S. I delayed the army for about a year. I had made up my own mind not to go, but I felt I had a responsibility to inform my parents, so about a month before I was to go in I told my father I was an athiest and I also told him I wasn't going into the army. Basically, I didn't want to go in because of a simple gut reaction, you know, why should I give my life to a country that was not going to win a war. I couldn't weigh the values of the Vietnamese struggle versus American capitalism; all I knew was that the U.S. was never gonna win that war. I can't analyze the process whereby I arrived at that conclusion except that, well, Westmoreland kept using the phrase, "the light at the end of the tunnel," and he said that about four different times and I said, wow! jack, don't you understand that unless you go in there with nuclear force or unless you make a total commitment and wipe out North Vietnam there's no light at the end of that tunnel? It was obvious; I had read Mao's tactics in high school, the three point program, and I knew what the NLF was doing. It was obvious that America was not going to win.

It didn't make sense that America was drafting me for this. It was a very selfish thing. At the time I wasn't a pacifist. Which I'm not now—I went through that stage to rationalize why I was against the war, and also it was really my only option and still stay within the system which I wanted to do then. At the time I wasn't really against armies, or even the army experience, but I couldn't see the army in the context of Vietnam. Why should I give my life for this? But I decided I'd go in anyway since I had little contact with the movement and I thought my only options were to go to jail and lose my job or go into the army.

I was drafted February 7, 1969. The day before I left the bank, the people I worked with gave me a going away present of some grass. It was the first time I'd ever had enough grass—I'd only smoked a few joints before. So I went out to visit some friends, and we smoked and stayed up late, and I missed the midnight bus back to New York where I was supposed to be inducted at six A.M. I didn't feel like taking a three A.M. bus back just to be at the draft board at six A.M., so I said fuck it and took a morning bus back and got there too late to be inducted. Which was just as well 'cause all the guys inducted that day had been taken into the Marine Corps. This was lucky for me 'cause I would have refused induction into the marines. I'd thought about it for a month before and knew I couldn't take the marines, but because of the social pressures that my parents were putting on me and the shame that they'd feel, I said, OK, I'll go into the army . . . You know, there are a lot of things to do in the army. In the marines they tell you what to do and that's Vietnam, I knew that. But in the army you can go to Germany or Greenland or somewhere and stay out of Vietnam if you're smart . . . So I said I'd go into the army. Well, that night, since I was late for induction, they sent me down to Fort Hamilton by myself and told me I had to stay there. I was smart enough to know that I wasn't in the army yet, so I took the grass that they'd given me at the bank and I went over the fence to a very hip place in New York where Johnny Winter was playing. It was the most fantastic music night I've ever had because I was stoned out of my head for the first time and Johnny Winter's playing and, out of nowhere, Jimi Hendrix walks in and jams on bass and Buddy Miles picks up on drums and some freak plugs in his violin and Country Joe McDonald walked in and played piano. At four o'clock in the morning I went back to Fort Hamilton, climbed the fence, and went back to the barracks.

Then we got shipped down to Fort Jackson. Basic training was a physical adventure. All this time I wasn't faced with a real decision, I mean, I knew everything was wrong and I was starting to fit the pieces together on how come I was drafted, why the United States was in Vietnam, the whole capitalist structure of making money. All these things are in your head, yet what are you going to do about it? The opportunity for making a decision of yes or no or drawing the line someplace hadn't come. So, when the army posted our orders on the bulletin board and I saw mine were for Advanced Infantry Training, the whole fucking world caved in.

I made a phone call to a friend, a law student, and he told me of a lawyer who had won some CO cases for guys at Jackson. So I talked to some people at the Columbia draft information center, and they gave me a whole bunch of pamphlets to read and I found out that you could get a discharge, theoretically, and the grounds for the discharge were to be against all wars. I knew the Vietnam War was wrong, and so I decided all wars must be wrong which, I guess, is the ultimate thing anyway, and that became my principle. I went back to the base and read the stuff over. Then I got my orders; I graduated, and General Hollingsworth made up my mind for me. I was almost eighty percent sure that I'd become a CO, but when I heard Hollingsworth give his graduation speech—what fine young men we have been trained to be! how we were the future of America! and that there was just a minority, a very few people, who were trying to fuck it up for everybody else! At that point, that fucking General decided for me. Just listening to his rap I decided that if *he* is representative of the U.S. Army and the U.S. system, then I was now committed against that.

So the next morning, shaking like a leaf—I could barely talk I was so afraid—I went in to see the first sergeant and told him I was a conscientious objector and wanted a discharge. The sergeant said I'd have to apply at the next base. He said they were all rushed and too busy to do anything. He really screwed me up, so I called the lawyer in town whose number the people there had given me, and he said there was one thing I could do and that was to copy down the regulation over the phone and then just read the regulation to the officers and say I'm not going anywhere until my application has been accepted.

I got to see the commanding officer, and told him I was a CO and he blew up and told me I had to go to the next base. I told him his information was incorrect and then I read the regulation: Furthermore, "An individual desiring to apply for con . . ." and his mouth just dropped. And he said, "Lieutenant Schmidt, get me the regulation book . . . Well, Svirchev, according to this regulation, you're *right*. Would you like to see a chaplain?" I said, yes, I'd like to see a Jewish chaplain. And he said, "But you're not Jewish," and I said yessir, but Jews are against the war; they're really against the war, and my father's a Catholic and he's a colonel in the Marine Corps, and ninety percent of the officers in his command are Catholic, and I've known plenty of chaplains and all Catholics are *for the war*. He said I should see the Catholic chaplain anyway, and so I did. I heard the captain in the next room say that this chaplain really hated COs. So I went down to see him, and he said, "Well, Svirchev, I understand that you think you're a CO. Want to tell me a little bit about it?" He pulled out a little pad and said, "You know, I always like to take notes on these occasions." I said, "Well, sir, I feel that most Catholic chaplains are for the war and I really don't want to talk to you if you're gonna take notes." He said, "Well, if you don't want to talk to me you don't have to," and he picked up the phone and said, "Captain Vabriskie, Svirchev doesn't want to talk to me 'cause I'm a Catholic." All this time I had a guard with me and so they finally took me down to the Jewish chaplain, and I talked to the Jewish chaplain for two minutes, and the Jewish chaplain said, "Yeah, I guess you're sincere, I'll write out a recommendation for discharge."

And so the whole time I was under guard. They made me move all my belongings into the orderly room, and I had to stay there, and I was under twenty-four-hour guard for four days. My friends brought out some subversive Quaker literature to the base and then some people from the UFO came out and said, "Look, don't worry about it; you've got a lot of people behind you." That's when I met Stephanie. She popped out of the car with her hippie bag and long hair and short skirt and looked like something out of Greenwich Village—something I'd never seen in South Carolina . . . The people at UFO were the first people I could trust. That was my introduction to what they now call an alternate life style . . . I could do whatever I wanted within the confines of this room, and I had the Quaker literature and it said in words what I had been thinking. It was beautiful. That's when I wrote out my application. I wrote—I'm really proud of this—what the lawyers said was a legally perfect application. Peter Weiss [of the Law Center for Constitutional Rights] said I should have been discharged on the basis of that application.

I complained to the judge advocate's office about the guard, and they finally took it off and put me into a headquarter's detachment where I wouldn't have any effect on anyone. Most of the guys were just back from Vietnam and were short-timers. I spent the summer while the application was being processed driving a truck and talking with any recruits I would meet. I had been under orders to Fort Lewis, Washington, but when you put in a CO application you're taken off orders. I started going down to the UFO and talking to people. Then I realized, hey, something else is happening. Over a period of time I underwent a complete transformation from doing this individual act to realizing that my individual act meant nothing in the context of the war. It didn't matter if the army discharged me or not 'cause I'd just go back into the capitalist system and they'd get some other sucker who was probably not a middle-class kid like me, but some poor white or poor black who never had the opportunity to observe what I had observed and who would just take it totally as a matter of course. I sat down with the other GI organizers and we tried to figure out what we could do. Finally we figured, if I had gotten stabilized (not transferred to infantry training) why couldn't a thousand guys do the same? And so the idea was born for the Fort Jackson Committee of Conscientious Objectors. We knew that if twenty-five people put in an application it would help to screw the army up. It was a tactical step.

Before we were through we had fifty members. I saw the files, finally, before I left, and there were over five hundred applications for CO. Yet, when I originally filed, the army said I was the first one in the history of Fort Jackson to apply for CO which was a lie 'cause there were lots of guys doing it at the same time. When we realized that, it was beautiful. All these people were doing it individually. Over this period of time I started going AWOL every night and staying out until three or four in the morning. I went to the UFO or one of the houses and worked for the committee. I got caught on one of my AWOLs and got a thirty-day restriction. Those thirty days, not going off base, are what made me political. It was a final chance to think about all that had been going through my head. It was at that point I decided that I had to become committed to radical politics or I wasn't fulfilling my duty towards myself or my compatriots. I wrote up this handsheet entitled "The Revolutionary Tactic of Conscientious Objection," and it told you the ins and outs of being a CO, whether in fact you were or not. And that was distributed at the UFO to everyone who came in.

The CO provision was made for, like, a dude who would marry a Jehovah's Witness, or a Seventh Day Adventist and so on. These guys would get discharged. When Vietnam came along and Vietnam became a problem to the army, they had to submerge this provision. Less than one percent of the guys who apply for CO discharges actually get out. Lots of movement people and even movement GIs were down on me for organizing COs—they saw it as an end rather than a means, that we were just trying to get out, just like the early bourgeois draft resistance. Just to filter guys out of the army *is* very bourgeois, because just getting guys out of the army—well, they're just going to take another *poor* kid and another sucker and get him in your place. So you're caught with relative values—what's good for the individual and what's good for the movement. I tend to think what is good for the movement should be good for the individual. But I felt that organizing COs who would make work for the army by applying for discharges and forming a back-up group of support that would permit these guys, including myself, to take each case to the highest court—this would be a threat to the way the army operates. We all became a threat. The end, of course, if any of us *were* successful—very few are, never usually—was to get out. This was not the end, however, for which we were organizing. None of us really thought we'd actually get out. As I said, it was a tactic in the fight against the army and the war.

On the Labor Day weekend of 1969 I was informed that my second application had been turned down and I was put on orders for Advanced Infantry Training at Fort Lewis, Washington. Then I put in my third application, which is perfectly legal. I called my lawyer to see if he could get a restraining order. Meanwhile I was shanghaied, put in handcuffs, thrown into a car after going limp, and driven by a circuitous route out to the airport where a Delta Airlines jet was waiting parked behind some construction. There were three seats left—nicely reserved by Delta officials for my two guards and me. I was flown to Fort Lewis. To preserve the integrity of my latest CO application for discharge, I couldn't train at Fort Lewis. So I refused to train and that's when I was put up on a court-martial charge. The court-martial would have been bad since the hierarchy already knew about me—the commanding general had been expecting me. That weekend I went down to the Shelter Half coffeehouse, and I spoke, and I began organizing the Committee of Fort Lewis Conscientious Objectors.

At this point I felt I could be most effective *in* the army and not by getting out. I wanted to stay around and fight this thing all the way through the courts and harass them by my own actions at the same time. So I'd be harassing them on three levels: publicly, the courts, and whatever infighting I did on the base. Well, the army effectively shut that off by shanghaiing me, putting me up for a court-martial—refusing to train can bring up to eight years in prison—and, well, I said, fuck it, I'm not going to go to jail.

The decision to desert came after I read Jessica Mitford's book, *The Trial of Doctor Spock*, and what that trial said to me was that Spock got out on a technicality—so I go to jail and finally get out, and out of the army, based on a technicality, well, what have I done, 'cause it wouldn't help anybody except me. If I had won my case, it would have been won on a technicality—that the army fucked up by shanghaiing me. One more thing. I started thinking about Howard Levy who had just gotten out of prison. It seemed that he had been a sort of martyr to the movement—a necessary thing at the time—and that his kind of testimony to his beliefs was only good during a certain period and by 1969 we were past that point. Anyhow, what would America be like in three years when I got out? Or would I ever get out? Wouldn't political prisoners, GI dissidents, be the first to go, especially if they were already locked up, following a right wing coup or simply an all-out law-and-order government? Finally, a sweet little old lady who processed court-martial COs showed me a list of people who had gone to prison. The cats who were politically active went to prison for four and five years, while the rest of this list of thirteen people got one and a half to two years.

So I left, and flew to New York and looked up some movement friends who got me enough money to get to Canada. It was complete serendipity that brought me to Montreal—the bus was cheaper to Montreal than to Toronto. Before I left I called Stephanie at the UFO—Stephanie and I were comrades at the UFO more than anything else, then we fell in love—I called Fort Jackson, and I said, hi Stephanie, listen, I'm going to Canada, wanna come? And she said sure. She came up two weeks later. I looked up the ADC when I got here—I had a three-piece suit and twenty-five dollars. That first month was pretty hard—we got awfully hungry. We lived on a diet of bread, cheese, honey, and water.

There is going to be a revolutionary movement forming up here, getting ready to go back to the U.S. It seems to me, at this point, that the most logical course is for revolutionaries to grab the American power structure wherever it is most vulnerable and then literally destroy it by whatever means necessary. Militant exiles are going to have to come to grips with this and realize that OK, this is a sanctuary; Canada is a sanctuary, but sanctuaries are always looked on as a *temporary place*. Deserters, to be truly anything more than liberals in exile, can only go back to the United States.

I figure it's either a live or die situation in this world. Che says in revolution one wins or dies. Perhaps that's applicable to the whole world right now, because if we don't have a revolution, we're going to die anyway. And if the rationale for a revolution is *just* that, it's a good rationale. Because if we don't crush American capitalism and institute a socialist system, the world is going to be destroyed and everyone's going to die.

Since I've been up here, my father won't talk to me. Only my mother writes. My sisters are against the war. My youngest sister wrote and told me—she's ten—that she wanted the war to hurry up and be over so that maybe I could go home and we could go sleigh riding together.

Buffy Parry is a unique person, unique because he senses being unique, a sense which many people have lost in the modern collectivization of life. He is the antithesis of what Jerzy Kosinski calls "denial of the self." He wears short hair, conservative clothes, and balks at using the vogue words and phrases. He is on a very nonbohemian search for self-realization and personal identity; the search itself is a life-style, and it must refuse the widely conformist life-style of the counter-culture. His even, thoughtful manner is supplemented by an open smile, a radiant warmth, an apparent contentment, all of which are often lacking in the vacant or cynical faces of America's demoralized young.

While he was in—exiting, rather—the U.S. Air Force he organized the most famous of all the war protest church sanctuaries in a Honolulu church where he was joined by thirty-three other servicemen from all branches of the armed forces in Hawaii. The sanctuary lasted six weeks, was widely covered by both the underground and the straight press, and, when it was broken up by military police who smashed their way into the church doing extensive damage to people and property, only six men were there, the rest having been smuggled out of the islands a few days earlier by antiwar groups. The sanctuary grew larger than anyone had anticipated meaning that the military would have handed down stiffer sentences to participants than if it had only been AWOLs doing a week-long protest. For this reason, nearly everyone chose to desert rather than become forgotten martyrs.

Buffy Parry ended up in Canada along with another deserter, Lou Jones, with the help of Clergy and Laymen Concerned About Vietnam. In Ottawa he quickly found work in a government agency called CUSO (Canadian University Service Overseas)—Canada's Peace Corps—and settled comfortably into the quiet life of the Canadian capital. He lived in a small cabin with a friend about ten miles out of the city. Following a year of work, he enrolled in Ottawa's Carlton University to study genetics, and he plans to complete his studies at the University of Toronto. He has been offered several positions with international development agencies in Africa, but he neglected to apply for a U.S. passport before deserting and so he is unable to travel. Canada, as has been said earlier, insists on treating the American exiles as normal immigrants and will not recognize that they are therefore denied international travel documents. Concessions are made to East European refugees who are normally given special travel papers if they do not have valid passports. Many American exiles do have passports, but those who do not must remain in Canada for five years, until they can become citizens. In any case, Parry is not bitter about this; he hopes the Canadian government will recognize this problem and do something about it. Meanwhile, he enjoys Canada. He even likes the winter.

I was born in San Mateo, California and grew up in San Jose. My father was a sort of ombudsman for the Electrolux Corporation. My mother is Catholic—a staunch, staunch Catholic. I went to church every Sunday and to Catechism. I have three older sisters—married. My father was a Eugene Debs socialist in his prime. My father was a very enlightened man, self-educated. He refused to acknowledge the educational system as a real means of becoming educated or of searching out the major questions of the day. He always traveled in, sort of, very erudite circles. He once wrote a few articles for the *Saturday Evening Post*. I think I had a very stimulating environment. He died of a heart attack. He always said the family should have some sort of a dance ceremony over his grave after he was dead. He resigned himself to the concept of death and thought it was very amusing what this culture did with death. He was opposed to it. That's why he asked that everyone dance on his grave.

In high school I was very erratic. I would go from A's in subjects I was interested in to D's in those I didn't care about. I went to a very unique high school. It took in almost every cultural force in California. San Jose High. There were a lot of rebels there. Many of my friends, in fact, turned out to be student leaders at Berkeley and universities like that.

During high school I wavered between Right and Left. I was a rebel, mainly, in that I couldn't see the administration being nearly as powerful as it was, and shams like student government in high school I found hard to stomach. I didn't like, for example, the administration controlling student funds. I thought students should be in full control of that. I thought the students should be in full control of any kind of political decisions that were to be made, with the advice of faculty and administration but not this ruling parental authority that they symbolized at the time. In 1964 I was a Goldwater fan. I was so idealistic. I worked for Goldwater, helping to organize youth groups for Goldwater. I was even in Young Americans for Freedom at the time. Goldwater's statements were either so hard to believe that I didn't pay attention to them, or I was so carried away with my idealism that I never listened to them, statements like making Vietnam a large parking lot, paving it over after defoliating all of the jungles.

Politics, that is left politics, first came home to me when I participated in a civil rights march in the center of San Jose while I was in high school. I had a very close friend when I was a junior, and she was negro, and we used to go out a lot, have dinner together and so on, and I never thought that the blacks had it as bad as I was reading about until I started eating out with her and dating her. It gave me a whole new perspective. I decided to investigate this, and I found, yeah, Fillmore district in San Francisco really exists, and it's not just a thing to ignore, and that East San Jose really exists—that's the biggest ghetto for Mexican-Americans. So I participated in the civil rights march and that really politicized me.

At the time I was really ambivalent—I still am in some ways—I couldn't see the difference between marching for civil rights and working for Barry Goldwater. I couldn't see a clear demarcation line at all. He represented the real ideals that I believed in, as a symbol that is, and so did the civil rights march. Now I can see the difference. Ha! Goldwater believed too strongly that he was right—in his heart he knew he was right—and he's the kind of person who doesn't leave enough marginality to see where he might be wrong. That's why I have some grave misgivings about the New Left today, they don't leave themselves enough marginality to sort of explore their commitments—not everyone, but many of the people I've met don't give themselves enough room to become introspective and to really, you know, measure their own values.

Then I went to San Jose City College. I supported myself for one semester with all kinds of jobs, working in bookstores, theaters, nightclubs, MacDonald's restaurants. My family didn't have a great deal of money at this time, and I had to pay my own way, working full time, and I tried to go to school full time. It was quite impossible. Finally, I took off five months and lived on the San Jose State campus and audited classes, a lot of sociology classes and so on.

During college I went to Stop-the-Draft-Week in Oakland in 1967, and I was there for a full week. It didn't, in the vernacular, "radicalize me" as it supposedly radicalized so many people. I was clubbed and I was maced, and at one point, being very chauvinist and full of male chivalry I threw myself over this chick and said, "You ain't gonna club her," and they clubbed her anyway after they beat the hell out of me. And so it was quite an experience, and I could see and sympathize with a lot of the objections that some of the organizers and demonstrators had against the police, but I still suspect that their tactics were all wrong. All wrong. You know, what's Mao's statement, "All power comes out of the barrel of a gun." I don't really believe that, at least not in the U.S. If there was a large, large proletariat, a huge sector of the population that was poverty stricken then maybe, but there isn't. The police forces are too well armed, too well organized, they're far too committed for one to oppose them on their level of power. I think another level would have been massive civil disobedience, which is what Stop-the-Draft Week was supposed to be, but it rapidly became violent. It's hard to tell who provokes the first violent act, but there are people on both sides who use violence in these situations as a tactic. Violence became the tactic of that demonstration.

The demonstration didn't radicalize me because I know that the police don't wear clubs and handcuffs and tear gas and mace with the intent not to use them, and I fully expected that possibility before I even went. The fact that they did use them as much as they did was a bit of a surprise. It was the more naive people who were radicalized.

I would say that I wasn't an activist. But I respect my individuality enough in the society to stand up for something I think is wrong. And if you have to go out in the streets and demonstrate or whatever, then that's the only way to do it, if it is the only way.

You can't get away from demonstrations in college, if for no other reason than they're so interesting. Most of the time the ideal that people are rallying around is *worth* rallying around. One being, like getting Dow Chemical Company off campus. I was in full support of that, just as I'm in full support of seeing it burned to the ground. I think that's the most despicable corporation that there is in the world, one of them anyway. Napalm, defoliants and so on—a corporation dedicated to destruction, de-foliating another people's whole country. Really, what kind of a mind is that? I protested against Dow. I didn't throw stones or anything. At the same time, I thought, well, they do have a right to recruit as would a university department or government agency have a right to recruit, but not on campus.

I don't like to think of a college as an employment agency for the society. That to me is not the value of education.

While I was auditing courses, I was of course open to the draft. I didn't want to be bugged by the draft so I enlisted in the air force, took some tests on which I scored quite highly, and they put me into administration.

Before I went into the air force, I was politically cognizant, but I wasn't politically active. I had investigated SDS and found it wasn't exactly to my liking, *in toto*; of course there's good and bad in everything. I could see the value of SDS, but it was so poorly administered, with everyone on ego trips, you know, with everybody wanting to be a great heroic leader and get their heads busted by the cops, you know, purposely going out to get their heads beaten. It was the most foolish thing I'd ever seen. I didn't really find a group that I could align myself with. I went into the air force, despite these previous beliefs, this early awareness, because, well, I thought I'd been given a lot of crap, that a lot of things I'd read about the war and the military were just not true. I couldn't think of military people as evil men, as devils, I couldn't conceive of that. I couldn't conceive of a lot of things. I couldn't conceive of the VC being all good and Americans all bad. The only way I could find out would be working in the system that was supposed to be perpetuating these horrible evils. So I enlisted.

I considered the army, and I'd considered jail and Canada. I thought very seriously about the latter two possibilities, jail and Canada, and decided neither of those was really worth the knowledge that I would be denying myself by not going in. The air force is easier than any other branch of the military, and it does provide better educational opportunities. I resigned myself to eventually going back to college as a registered student and using that system for what it's worth. But at that point I said, why should I shackle myself, I wasn't ready for that. Also, I was out of money and couldn't afford any more college. I wasn't ready for college, not after working for so many years and going to school for so many years. I saw the air force as a break from all that.

I enlisted in May of '68. Basic training was at Amarillo. I was grossly insulted by the dehumanizing process there; I had never conceived that it would be quite as severe as it was—in the air force yet! The subtleties! If you've read Kazantzakis you remember his trouble coming to grips with man's evolution from animals; in a sense, I had the same trouble coming to grips with our collective animal nature, as manifested in basic training—and that after all, maybe it's not quite so collective. Anyway, I was insulted at becoming a number, at having my head shaved every other day. I guess in every empire, every military has to have this kind of system or the empire is not going to survive. I had a lot of questions as to whether the empire should survive or not, for one thing, and I respected myself too much to be reduced to that denominator. I was shocked by the treatment.

After basic came Biloxi, Mississippi. That was by far the strangest experience I've ever had. Living in a truly closed society. A really inner-directed, endogamous sort of society. And the sort of fiery patriotism they had didn't correlate at all to the treatment of military people down there. It was sort of a funny contradiction—the young men in Biloxi would constantly travel in large gangs and beat up servicemen or run on base and stab a serviceman. Yet there would be big red, white, and blue signs in the banks and stores that said, "Support our Servicemen." I don't like to put south-erners in a bag, however, and I found a lot of really great people down there in the bayou country, really earthy kind of people, poor people, peasants, really very poor people, but cultured in a sense. They seemed to reject the redneck's ideals. They chose to live on the bayous, away from all that.

Again my ideals came into conflict with what I saw. I had thought that civil rights acts were really being implemented, at least on a very legal basis. I never dreamed that in 1968 I would see drinking fountains still for whites and for blacks, or signs on restaurants that said for whites only. These things were constantly coming into conflict with my ideals. My roommate was from New Orleans, he was half negro and half white, and this was an advantage. He showed me a lot of the countryside, a lot of the gutty things about Louisiana and Mississippi which most servicemen get few chances to see, or wouldn't want to see. So that was an advantage, seeing the south from his point of view.

Then I went to Hawaii. At that point I decided that it was going to be hard for me to hack this thing. I had doubts from the beginning, but I thought I would be able to stand it. Not until I'd been in awhile did it begin to occur to me that I couldn't take it. In Mississippi I went to this coffee-house that a few like-minded servicemen would go to. It was an opportunity to leave one womb and go into another, so to speak, the other womb being a "groovy," political leftist atmosphere which I believe is also a womb. But too, it gave me a chance to study in a freer environment than that which was given to me in the military—I could read what books I wanted to read without someone coming into my room and saying, you're a dirty communist or why are you reading this kind of trash. This was the first time I was confronted with the idea of taking some kind of political action within the military. I was politically active in terms of vocalizing my beliefs from the very beginning. I went through questioning sessions in basic training about whether I was a communist or not. One of the group leaders called me into his office and said, "You're the kind of guy that would allow the communists to come onto our shores and rape our mothers and sisters." I said, oh yeah, now that tells me a lot about the Vietnam War. I burst out laughing when he said that. I was just uncontrollable, 'cause I had to stand there at attention while he sat there with this vicious madness in his eyes, his face turning red and purple, and I'm laughing under my breath. He hated that. So I suppose I was identified as a troublemaker from the beginning. This one fellow used to study sociology, and he'd stand in front of our group, and he'd hold up his sociology book and say, "Now I know—now I know which one of you is gonna cause trouble." He was really mad. Sociology had sort of become his bible, a real religion to him. As if you have to read a sociology book to find out which is an individual in a group, who is more outspoken in a group than other people. I have some real questions about the behavioral sciences and their misuse.

In Hawaii I was doing administrative work. I think they had a hunch of my political leanings. I had taken a test which qualified me for deciphering codes, and so they wanted me to go and work in Southeast Asia, and I refused. I will not do that, I said, and they knew at that point that I would refuse duty in Southeast Asia.

When I first arrived in Hawaii I was positioned in a room next to a fellow who used to be in OSI, Office of Special Investigation, and he asked me to come over to his room, and so I came over and he poured me a scotch and asked if I'd like to see his scrap book. He had been a photographer in Vietnam for OSI. He brings two of his scrap books out and they're all pictures of mutilated, napalmed people, so I'm drinking my scotch, gulping it down while I'm turning the pages. I said, "Gee, this is quite interesting, a very strange collection—this hobby of yours leaves a lot to be desired." He walked back to my room with me and he started looking at my books, and I had an issue of the Young Socialist magazine, and he shouted, "Where did you get this trash?" and I said, I'm subscribing to it. I brought out a Black Panther newspaper and said I'm also subscribing to this. I suspect that he dropped a few lines to my commander saying he had a weirdo in the ranks now. The Office of Special Investigation searched through my room after it was learned that I had this literature. They didn't suspect me of being any kind of powerful subversive force, but they thought I had potential in this area. For this they put me to working everyday with the garbage collection, and I got to meet some really good people collecting garbage, except for going to the officers' houses and having the officers' wives call the Hawaiian and Samoan garbage collectors boys. The major reason I was given garbage duty was because I hadn't showed up at the firing range, and they thought it was for political reasons. I wasn't going to go to Vietnam anyway, so why go and learn how to fire a rifle? It was senseless. Later when my father died, the air force investigated to find out if it was true. They wouldn't believe me that I needed a leave to go to the funeral.

Hawaii was a very profound experience for me in all ways, more so philosophically. Just the ocean and the weather, the immersion into nature. I had a Hawaiian girlfriend, and she introduced me to a different perspective. She being Hawaiian and showing me what the onward march, the manifest destiny of America had done to the Hawaiian culture—it's amazing, really amazing. I had an extremely easy job, worked six to eight hours a day, had weekends off, so I moved off base, to the other side of the island, as far from the base as possible. I knew at this point that eventually I would make some kind of a stand, try to exit gracefully as a CO, or do a sanctuary. I sort of set these limits. I felt there was no sense in exploring the military life-style any longer when I could live Hawaiian, life in Hawaii for a while. With the people. So I moved out to a section of Hawaii that was slowly turning into a hippie community; North Shore, Halveeva, Kenoui Drive. That again was a new and profound experience for me, living with very, very middle-class kids who weren't emotionally screwed up but had very real objections to the systems they were brought up in. The difference is, of course, that they could afford to move away and live in such an environment. The contradiction between individuality and collectivity was gnawing at me, really gnawing at me, and living out there sort of reinforced an existential philosophy I was developing. And that's why I think I eventually chose a sanctuary over anything else.

Prison was within the scheme of options that I had constructed in my mind before I even went into the air force. But the time finally came to leave the air force and that took precedence over jail. I chose the sanctuary thinking, of course, that I wouldn't go to prison—for a great length of time at least—for many reasons, one of them being that I would have stirred enough support and attention so that they wouldn't give me a very severe court-martial should I decide to stay out the sanctuary, to continue on until I was arrested. I didn't think I'd get a severe court-martial on the grounds of my stand—not doing anything that I considered extremely chaotic, just being myself and stating my position. Just before that, I tried for a CO discharge, and in the red tape, it was never allowed me. The chaplain had said, "Well, you're the kind of guy that can realign himself with the military and sort of hack it out 'till it's over." The CO option was denied me. It is one that I would have done, not on a Christian basis but on a conscience basis, an existential kind of basis—that I could no longer live a lie, participating in this machine which perpetrated the war and also suppressed individuality.

My association with the peace movement had no effect, to the disbelief of the military. The military thought I was a pawn in the peace movement's games, but, I wasn't. I had come to my decision on my own. The sanctuary was my idea, for example; I proposed it to the peace groups. I used to go to Resistance meetings, and I really didn't participate much. I just listened more or less. While I was in the air force I took some classes at the university and that's where I heard about the Hawaiian Resistance group at the Church of the Crossroads. Also, we used to go out to a professor's house every Sunday afternoon where he hosted encounter sessions.

I was in Hawaii for fifteen months and for the last three months I thought very seriously about how I was going to channel my exit. At this point in history I didn't consider military service in the United States to be an honor. The sanctuary started out by my inquiry into the activities at the Church of the Crossroads. I had also heard about the Kanehoe marines who had done a sanctuary and what a catastrophe that was. I thought, well, if I'm going to do this, I should plan it out a bit more, and I should be the planner instead of being the person who is allowing himself to be manipulated. The Kanehoe sanctuary had been a bit too controlled by people outside. The two marines turned themselves in eventually and got two years in a mainland prison. I studied the concept of sanctuary and looked into the history of sanctuaries in Italy and Greece and the rest of Europe. The concept, in the Christian tradition, of a sanctuary is exactly what the word implies—a place where a person is immune from any kind of punishment. The churches were known to put people up for the necessary period of time so the person could avoid persecution. After sanctuaries were no longer recognized legally in the west, they became symbolic only. In essence, this sanctuary became a symbolic sanctuary. All it really was, was a means to address the public; it was not a sanctuary in the true sense of the word. You're not immune from legal incrimination. I knew that.

So I inquired and I found out that if I truly believed what I was saying, that I could go ahead and do it. I could use their church as a sort of platform. I did that on a Wednesday in August of 1969 and the following Sunday we marched from the Church of the Crossroads to a park in Honolulu, and I marched with the rest of the group, and it was all very dramatic. I was surrounded by a bunch of people—I didn't wear my uniform, of course, that was asking too much. I gave a speech at the rally at the park, and at that point a serviceman joined me and he said he could no longer tolerate the military. The sanctuary had already been made public, and there had been a lot of discussion and the military had read statements. So at the rally five servicemen joined me on the spot. It was impressive, these sort of very emotional fiery speeches coming out of these guys. We were surrounded by agents and MPs and police. There were about one thousand marchers which is a lot for Hawaii. After the rally we fled back to the church; we six servicemen poured into a car which marchers surrounded and we were then driven back. The city police were extremely cooperative. The city police of Hawaii have a lot to teach the police on the mainland.

Just before I went to the church I was AWOL for about a week, and I went to live in a rain forest and brought a few books with me and really sort of did some soul searching. I was thinking about the different possibilities and what would be the best thing to do, and what would be the result and would

I be willing to go to prison. I came to the conclusion that yes, I would be willing to go to prison, but I didn't think I would be arrested, and escape was in the realm of possibility—although I said and thought differently during the sanctuary and in some of the speeches I made. I did give it a lot of forethought. It wasn't something I jumped into.

I knew that in other sanctuaries the people weren't arrested for at least two weeks, and I knew that, if I had to, I could split. I had the finances to do it; the arrangements were made. If I had been arrested earlier, I would only have gone up on an AWOL rap, though I could have been charged with some of my statements about noncooperation in the military. I wasn't at ease with myself about going to prison; I wasn't at peace with the fact that I might go to prison, but it was within the realm of possibility. I thought I could stomach prison for a year if I had to. But as the sanctuary progressed, it was clear that the whole thing had become much bigger than I had thought, hundreds of people sleeping in the church, more sleeping on the grass.

The thirty-three guys in the sanctuary ranged through every life-style possible. It was unbelievable, the cross section of American society that was represented in that small group of servicemen. A lot of the guys were dopers, of course, kids of the counter-culture. There was a myriad of emotions and commitments. Some guys were there just because they liked the girls and the food and the rock bands. At this point I stopped feeling responsible for drawing men here. Many had come out of personal commitments against the military and the war while others had come for other personal reasons. There were many different avenues of enticement going on at this point—most of them without my knowledge, and as a result I was not directly responsible for most of the guys who were there. The only responsibility I felt was that of a leader, the one who made most of the press releases, participated in most of the interviews, the person that was on Huntley-Brinkley and Walter Cronkite— in this sense I felt responsible, as spokesman. We always told the press that we were planning on staying there indefinitely. The Hawaiian papers gave it good coverage and were especially outraged when the church was finally busted by MPs. A lot of editorials were written about the military control over the island, that the military felt they had the right to do whatever they pleased. When the sanctuary was busted there were only about eight guys left.

Some of the guys were smuggled underground; some chose to come to Canada; some paid their way to Canada; some managed to find enough sources of money to pay their way. Six guys chose to go to jail.

Since it had become a major event in the antiwar movement, I was offered an option by Clergy and Laymen Concerned About Vietnam to go to South Bend, Indiana, to present my position to the assembly of the National Episcopal Convention at Notre Dame University. They were discussing what kind of social issues to get involved in and Clergy and Laymen thought it would be good to have me surface at South Bend and talk about conscience and the military. At this point I sort of did become a pawn, but I knew I was very close to Canada. The sanctuary got big enough to where I was very excited about its potential, although, as chaotic as it was and as totally disorganized as it was, it still had a lot of potential. I became committed to it and felt very responsible. The sanctuary lasted over six weeks. I left a little before it was over, before the bust. The result of the sanctuary was that it set up a strong branch of the American Serviceman's Union and attracted a lot of guys who wouldn't make this kind of commitment but who would join the ASU, so all the organizers rushed out to organize new kinds of on-base activities.

When I left the sanctuary I hid in a car and was driven out of the church to the airport and took a flight to Los Angeles and then to Chicago and South Bend. The sanctuary had gotten to be existentially anarchic, too anarchic for any kind of cohesive continuation that could have had prolonged effects. I still attached a lot of hope to what we had done and what the result was, but for myself, the state of sanctuaries—there were several others by then besides at the Church of the Crossroads—was such that I didn't feel at ease in the evolution that it, they, had taken. I was not happy with the sanctuary as it had evolved just before I left. Looking at it in a collective way it was an effective exercise, but for my own personal input I figured that that input had been exhausted at the point that I left. There would have been no point in going to prison; it would have been anticlimatic. The protest was the sanctuary itself, and nothing was to be derived from whatever punishment came from it. Had the sanctuary not expanded as much as it had, I might have gone through the court-martial phase and even gone into prison. But after the sanctuary had gotten to where it had, and had even exhausted itself, a court-martial seemed a bit futile. I had expended myself in terms of the movement. Any further actions, at least in Hawaii, would not have been effective. To publicize his act, that of refusing to train Green Berets, Howard Levy had to have a court-martial. I had already publicized, more than I'd hoped, what I was trying to say about the military and the war.

There were long sessions on what should be done after I arrived at South Bend. At one of the general sessions we marched into the main arena with huge banners—sort of like the Christian crusaders! I was introduced and I spoke to the bishops; Lou Jones spoke also. The body of bishops was asked to stand if they supported me and over fifty percent stood up. I don't suspect it was for political reasons that they stood, but more for humanitarian reasons. Then it was over. We moved to one section of the arena and sat there for about three days, completely surrounded by clergymen. I wasn't sure at this time what the outcome of this sanctuary would be, and so I stayed, thinking perhaps that maybe through radiations out through the media it would reach a lot of people. I thought we may be in the verge of a very large kind of civil disobedience in the military; I'd heard that there were quite a few other GIs about to do the same thing. We discussed doing other sanctuaries in other cities, moving east and popping up in a number of churches, continuing to defy the authorities. At the same time I felt that the history of martyrdom is not that earth-shattering as it effects social change, so what good would I be if ultimately I had gotten arrested at another sanctuary. This really wasn't much of a fear in Hawaii, but it was now at South Bend. In Hawaii I wasn't really worried. There is something very strange about islands in general. Just studying the culture of island peoples gives insights into the consciousness that is evoked by an island setting. You have more individuality and more confidence in self-actions. Oftentimes I acted spontaneously in Hawaii, feeling secure in a sort of bond between the island and myself. If I'd have been court-martialed there, for example, I don't think I would have had much to fear. Back on the mainland it was different. The day after we left South Bend, thirty FBI agents descended on the convention.

Canada has been one illumination after another. Coming across the border was quite a feeling, knowing that there was no way I could be caught.

It was a psychic relaxation. The groups in Toronto asked me to come to Ottawa to get landed—they seemed to be worried about me—so I came to Ottawa and got landed through AID.

I was offered a job as assistant to the medical director for CUSO. I had the opportunity to learn something as well about the Peace Corps since CUSO did parallel work in many countries, and from this I could see CUSO seemed to have a deeper understanding of culture in a nonmanipulative sense. I think I might learn much more by living in Canada than I would have in the United States. For one thing, the universities I've seen here are not as wombish as those in the United States. There's a cultural sophistication about the youth in Canada that I think surpasses the youth in the U.S. Politically, Canada has the New Democratic Party, socialist, which is many steps ahead of anything that exists in the United States. I would support a socialist party in the U.S. but there isn't any. I think the NDP has a lot of potential here. At least there *is* an officially recognized left party.

The only kind of political statement—or *state*—that I could carry on now that I've come to Canada is conscience and consciousness and what that means in this day and age in a given society. That is to say, that a society should be structured so that each individual in a society can have a full grasp of what conscience and consciousness means. If that doesn't happen, then any kind of progress mankind could make just won't come about—if people can't be reflective and introspective and really question their existence constantly throughout life. And I suspect that a society that allows for that will be ultimately successful. The United States allows for this to a degree, more than many countries, which is to say that the U.S. has a lot of positive aspects.

I do feel bad that I cannot be in the States assisting change, not affecting a revolution, but assisting effective kinds of change, which I think can still be done through institutions. It is unfortunate that the U.S. is on the verge of taking a downward plunge in terms of personal freedoms and, you know, the creative base from which people can explore their own existence. It could go either way right now. That's why I regret what Agnew is doing with his polarization techniques. It could bring on a totalitarianism, either right or left, depending on who wins out. But I'm not saying this is what is in the future. Basically I'm optimistic about the United States. I see a liberalization coming on in certain government circles, in government welfare circles, even in the military, making the nature of institutions much more flexible for the changes that have to come about. There is this dimension of individuals and institutions changing—becoming open—and I think there is a whole segment of the so-called silent majority who will be a force for change. My family is in that group.

My family isn't radical, which is not to say that they won't be if things don't change soon in the United States. They support me; they've been up to visit, and they defend what I've done. They've had to question their own position in American society. It's easy to pass off demonstrations, it's easy to pass off people's stands of conscience until it comes within the limits of your family. I think that they really searched themselves out. They've come to what I think are surprising conclusions about the United States' intervention in Asia, the whole policy, the foreign policy of the United States. My mother had an amazing transformation politically in the last two years. She's gone from a very conservative, right-wing position—she voted for Goldwater—to a liberal sort of leftist position. She's getting angrier and angrier at the continuation of the war, at the government's refusal to acknowledge the demands of certain sectors of the society, the blacks, the Mexican-Americans. My mother didn't vote in the last presidential election. She didn't vote for either Nixon or Humphrey.

Ideally what I'd like to see is an amnesty. I feel we all deserve an amnesty. That wouldn't mean that I'd go back to the United States right away. I'd just like to have the right to travel across the border. I think many people in the U.S. who might mobilize behind support of amnesty feel now is just not the time to do it. Right now, up here, I don't think there is any sense in making a furor over amnesty. It's just not time. As long as we exist I don't think the liberals in the U.S. will forget us—in fact, I'm sure they won't.

SIX

Liberated Prisoners

Dave Weise, after a long and tortuous odyssey, has retired with his girlfriend to the remote corner of a forested island in British Columbia's Straights of Georgia. Weise doesn't want to see the so-called civilized world for a while but would rather hunt and fish and plant some vegetables and chop firewood and read some books. He has fixed up an old cabin where he lives with Susan Casper, a New York schoolteacher and Brooklyn College graduate whom he met traveling in California. Along with a dozen friends, mostly draft dodgers and deserters and girlfriends, they form a little community of youthful settlers who ask for nothing more in this life than to be left alone to be themselves. They pay little rent, and food is cheap, so money is not a problem. Weise was living under a false name in New York after managing a daring escape from the prisoners' special processing center at Fort Ord, California. He had been picked up for being AWOL after he refused to board the plane for Vietnam. After the strains of being a fugitive became more than he or Susan could bear, they moved to Montreal where Weise spent the winter generally relaxing and working for the American Deserters' Committee, overseeing the production of a film and managing several fund-raising benefits. In the spring he rebuilt a Volkswagen camper and along with another American couple in a VW camper, set out for the Pacific Northwest and the gulf islands. David and Susan hope to be able to buy some land cooperatively with several other American exiles, and they talk of perhaps one day starting a progressive school in the mountains. For the present, they merely wish to live, something which common sense tells them most people in the great metropolitan centers are no longer doing.

I was raised in western Oregon in a small community. My background is mostly lower-middle-class, even poor you might say; my stepfather, for as long as I lived at home, which was until I was twelve, was a laborer. My parents split up when I was twelve, and neither of them stayed around for long, and, from the time I was twelve until I was eighteen, I lived with seventeen different families, foster homes. I'd live with each family on the average of three months. For a while I tried to adjust every time I moved to somebody else's house, and I tried to live according to their values, but after a while it was completely impossible for me to play musical heads; I couldn't keep up with it all. It sort of forced me, I think, to start thinking for myself a little bit younger than a lot of people have to. For that, I think I'm very fortunate because, looking around at my nice Jewish friends from New York City who come from very strong family backgrounds, a lot of the hangups—not that I don't have hangups too—are too deep seated for them to overcome. I didn't have to contend with that since I was forced not to listen to all this bullshit that kids have to listen to from their parents. It was difficult, at times, when I was living with these people. I was naturally considered a rebel, a black sheep, whatever. But nevertheless, I had to—in order to make it—I had to think for myself.

Upon graduating from high school I received a scholarship in wrestling from the University of Oregon. I had been a state wrestling champion. During the summer of '65, following high school, I packed my belongings in a laundry bag and hitchhiked to San Francisco and went to work on construction and spent the summer there. Before going to work, I went to the Sierras for the first time. Every summer since then, including the time I was AWOL, I always spent a lot of time in the High Sierras, as much time as possible.

I was going to the University of Oregon in 1965 and there was no protest then. I remember in 1965, I wasn't where I'm at today; I was eighteen years old and at that point Vietnam, the military, and everything else was not my concern. I was interested in what I've always been interested in, which is basically enjoying the environment around me, and living in a way that is not harmful to other people—I dig life, I dig living, I was not concerned with the antiwar movement. First of all, I was as straight as anybody was or could be. I had just come out of a really right-wing environment—Yamhill County, Oregon, where people talk about those dirty niggers and communist bums. This environment still had a strong effect on the way I would look at things. When I looked at somebody with long hair, I didn't hate them, but I didn't understand what was going on with them. I was a thinking person then, but I was thinking about entirely different things.

While I was going to school I broke my leg skiing and lost my wrestling scholarship. I didn't have any money to continue so I had to drop out. Anyway, I felt there were more important things to do right then besides go to college—basically, travel, and to learn from people, and so I set out doing that. I ski-bummed for four months in central Oregon, and hitchhiked all over western United States—all the time realizing that since I had temporarily dropped out of school after the first year, that eventually I was going to be drafted. I'd been reclassified 1-A after the first three months that I was out of school, so after that it was a nervous period of time, though I wasn't really worried about it because I still didn't really understand the concept that I was going to be inducted into the service. It was still pretty remote and I didn't worry about it. However, as things progressed it got closer and closer—I knew the draft notice was coming. I was working up in Yosemite—this was in September—and I decided to go down to Berkeley and enroll in a college again—Merrit Junior College in Oakland. I went there and it turned out that I had three weeks to go before I finished the semester when my draft notice finally caught up with me. I had notified the draft board that I was back in school and told them to send my 2-S. But they denied me a 2-S since I hadn't stayed in school. I then asked for a 1-S so I could finish the semester—and they refused to even let me finish the semester, so I lost all the credits at Merrit. I got drafted.

I objected to the army on the level that it went against my understanding of life, and what I think it is all about, and the way I think people should be able to live. I don't understand, nor can I accept, the idea that exists in the U.S., that is, that when you're eighteen years old you are conscripted into the army, and there is a very good possibility that you'll have to go to Southeast Asia or Korea or whatever the case may be at the time and die for something that you have no conception of, die for a lie, die for something that is totally absurd. My objection to that is that I have to be able to be free to determine my own destiny, to determine exactly how I am going to live, what I'm going to do with my life, and it doesn't involve going into the military for two years—if I live two years—and putting my head through the torture that these young kids who go to Vietnam have to come home with.

I had received my notice. First of all, I transferred my induction and it gave me about a month and a half and all through this period and for four months preceding this I had been to various counseling groups, the Central Committee for Conscientious Objectors and other Bay Area draft-counseling groups, and I had strongly considered making a CO claim. Finally, I did make a CO application but, as I had already received my draft notice, it was too late. Since I couldn't get the CO status, I really strongly considered refusing induction. But again, the way my head was structured at the time, this was in 1967—in the Bay Area guys were getting three years for refusing induction—I just couldn't justify losing three years of my life in a prison. I assumed that since things gradually worked out for me I would go in the army and I would avoid going to Vietnam. I had sort of predetermined that if I went into the military and I got orders to go to Vietnam, I would definitely refuse but up until that point I wasn't willing to go to jail. So I went into the army.

I went into the military with the idea that it would be a total waste of two years of my life. I couldn't see how I could benefit by spending two years in the army, nor how I could benefit mankind in general by spending two years of my life in the army, if I lived that long. And I couldn't really justify my pointing a gun at someone; there was no such thing as the reality of me understanding what it would be like to point a gun at people and kill them. Now I was raised in a rural community and I've had guns all my life. I've hunted deer and I've hunted birds and I've learned to, you know, subsist through nature. I know a lot of pacifists are on this trip of how it's evil to kill animals. But I've been in the situation where if I didn't shoot deer I would starve so I shot the deer and I ate it and I enjoyed it. But killing a man just doesn't appeal to me. I realized that not going to Vietnam might make my life difficult, but not going to Vietnam, regardless of what happened thereafter, well, I would be able to live with myself. If I went into the army but got out of going to Vietnam then I wouldn't have to kill. It would be a very hypocritical thing, I realized, but the thing that was going on in my head at the time was that I thought, I sincerely thought, that America was a beautiful place to be and a beautiful place to live, and I didn't want to leave. So I went into the army.

My first reaction to the army was—I laughed. I thought it was pretty funny. When I first got to Fort Lewis I had this hairlipped drill sergeant and he got out there with the same speech problem that these people have and said, "Ghhhad dgghammit, shtand at attentshhhin," so I laughed, not because he had a hairlip but because I apparently wasn't standing at attention right, and he kept shouting at me in this manner and I laughed—that's a problem I had all throughout my entire seventeen weeks in the army. I couldn't really accept the idea that these guys were serious, that they were going to bust your ass and knock the shit out of you and kick your fucking teeth in, this whole business didn't make sense to me. Well, I could understand the ego problems that these 5'2" drill sergeants had. Really, though, I could stand at attention and have sergeants all the way up to lieutenant colonels yelling at me and I would have to laugh. I really had a hard time keeping a fucking grin off my face. It was that absurd. Like I said, though, I found out it really wasn't a good idea to laugh. It really wasn't. I don't think anyone ever has or ever will accurately and sufficiently describe what going through basic training and infantry training in the army or the marines is like. I think it is an experience that has to be experienced to be understood. You know the saying—the whole patriotic trip—that going into the army will either make a man out of you or destroy you. Well, if that's what being a man is all about, I decided pretty shortly that I never wanted to be a man.

As far as the training itself is concerned, I'm not a masochist and I didn't enjoy having them hassle me after they're on your back for sixteen or eighteen hours a day so the less that you hassle them, the less they hassle you. So I was a model soldier; I won three trophies when I was in the army. I was real good with an M-60 machine gun, physical training, and G3 proficiency—I did this because I thought it would be the easiest way.

The service isn't Gomer Pyle, U.S. Marine Corps—it's a pile all right, piles and piles of bullshit. And it's awesome. How can you expose what the army really is when, whether it's on TV, radio or in the newspapers, people won't believe it? What can you tell them about the military—how can you tell them the truth when they refuse to believe it? How can you tell them that kids are driven to suicide. How can you tell them that you have to march around sixteen hours a day screaming at the top of your lungs, "I want to go to Vietnam, I want to kill the Vietcong." Or at Fort Polk, the huge billboards showing a GI sticking his bayonet into a Vietnamese with blood running down and at the bottom a sign saying, "Kill The Cong"—how can you tell people that. They won't believe it. I don't think that a military structure such as the United States has been paralleled except perhaps by Hitler Germany. And it's becoming more dehumanizing every day.

I remember in basic training and Advanced Infantry Training there were three people with whom I was very closely associated in my own company who shot their heads off, like committed suicide, because they didn't know what else to do. They knew too when they went in the army that something was wrong, but they didn't want to go against it; they didn't want to go to jail either. One of the people in my company who shot himself—he slept in the bunk next to mine—was so messed up that he couldn't take an M-14 apart which has nine parts and put it back together, after eight weeks of training! This guy just didn't have it; he couldn't do it, but he wasn't processed out, he wasn't anything—like, the sergeants cheated on his proficiency tests, on the range they all marked down the minimal score and shoved him right on through. While the gun was still on the rack, the guy put a shell in it and shot himself and for two weeks the guy didn't die; and constantly, as a daily reminder, the drill sergeants were standing around warning us that this guy had better die because if he doesn't he's going to get court-martialed for destroying government property.

In AIT I was in a company of virtually all draftees. There weren't any regular army guys in my platoon 'cause we were the next group of cannon fodder for Vietnam, and it's obvious that guys who join the military generally don't go to Vietnam unless they want to get another stripe; in other words: they get the training they want; they get the station they want; they don't have to go unless they want to; and when they do go, there is a good likelihood none of them will ever see combat because they're career material and the army doesn't want to waste all this money on training them and then have them shot up in Vietnam. So they take these eighteen-year-old kids over there who don't know a fucking thing. And they don't want college graduates if they can help it—although they're getting plenty of them in combat areas since they're not career material—they think too much, they're too much trouble. They want young guys.

At Fort Lewis, Washington, there are eight inches of snow on the ground and we're going around with a whole pack full of cold weather gear which we don't wear 'cause the army says it's not cold out. So, after the second week, a third of the guys are in the hospital with pneumonia—the army gets to you in a very real way. First of all they can't get to your head until they get to your body so they wear you down sufficiently to the point that when they throw a bone you're going to jump for it. And when you're tired—and you are tired—your body gets to the point where your mind doesn't function; it just reacts to whatever they throw out. It's obvious that this kind of military is necessary to perpetuate the kind of things that are happening and that the awareness level today, even in the military, is to the point where people know they're getting snowed, they know they're getting fucked over, yet once you're in you can be controlled. It's like conditioning a rat or a pigeon. Something that had a very strong effect on me while I was at Fort Polk: I had toothaches so bad I couldn't stand it and I asked them to fix my teeth. They gave me some pain pills and then in a few days the pain came back. I asked them again and the reply was, from a first sergeant, "If you get back from Vietnam, we'll fix your teeth."

I think organizing in the military is a very vital part of the whole struggle 'cause if the time comes when the kids in the army are going to have to shoot their brothers in the streets—I don't think all of them are going to do that. But organizing within the military takes strength, strength parallel to the strength that Mao had or Ho Chi Minh had. First of all, when you commit yourself to organizing within the military there is a good chance you might die at it. Of course, as soon as you become effective, you're transferred, busted, and I can't see it as being the answer unless one is really strong.

I was in the army seventeen weeks, eight weeks of basic and nine weeks of AIT. Right after that I received orders to go to Vietnam, 11 Bravo (light weapons infantryman). And it was very . . . you know . . . that was it! I had a twenty-day leave before going and so I went up into the Sierras with my Kelty pack and camping gear so I could get my head together. I had orders in my pocket to go to Vietnam and kill people—unbelievable! I realized I couldn't do it. I was due to leave on May 22, 1968, and I still had a little time so I went to my brother's high school graduation. I went to see my brother and my family and to tell them that I couldn't go to Vietnam. Now this was sort of a whole family gathering—I don't have parents, but all my aunts and uncles and grandparents and brothers and sisters were at my brother's high school graduation. There was sort of an interesting reaction. I told them all that I wasn't going. At this point I was seriously considering—since at that time Canada wasn't open to deserters—I had tried to realistically consider the idea of going to jail, facing court-martial and going to jail and refusing to go to Vietnam, which would have got me at least three years in Leavenworth. So when I was at the graduation I explained to them all, and they got quite emotional and gave me the communist traitor bullshit and broke out crying and said they didn't want to see me anymore. These were the people I had lived with for my last two years of high school. The reaction from most of my family, as it is a conservative family, was that from that point my aunts completely disowned me. Some tried to understand and said, "Well, you're crazy but if that's what you have to do, you have to do it." But most of them weren't really very understanding. Therefore, as far as family relations go, I've only got my brothers and sisters. My brother got out of the military in sort of a half-assed manner in that he did manage to avoid Vietnam by joining the National Guard, but that's cool 'cause I would not like to see my brother killed in Vietnam. He'll be twenty in July.

I've met many kids who were beautiful people before they left, but because they couldn't tolerate the pressure upon them to go into the military—like I said, I avoided these pressures because I didn't have the parent thing pushing me into it—I mean, they went and they came back screwed up in their heads for the rest of their lives. As far as my objections to the military go, this gets right back to it; I had a pretty good idea, however abstract it was, that I didn't want to go over there; I had pretty good imagination of what it was like. And I had two cousins who had been there previous to me. My cousin who joined the army went over for a year, and he came back pretty screwed up—he was shot over there. I was pretty close to him when I was young—we were really close as a matter of fact. We lived in the same town, and we lived together in the country. When I came back up to Oregon on leave, I told him that I wasn't going to go to Vietnam. I said I didn't know what I *was* going to do, I was scared shitless, I was really frightened, but I wasn't going to go. I had just told him that, and his reaction was really moving. When I asked him what he thought, he just kind of hung his head between his legs and started bawling and said just don't go over there, whatever you do, just don't go over there. It brought me down, it really brought me down.

After my brother's graduation for which I was AWOL by this time—May 22 had passed—I was driving down the coast back to the base and I was hit head-on by another car and went through the windshield. The police took me into town and threw me into jail without any medical attention since they discovered I was AWOL. I still have this scar on my nose. The MPs came and picked me up four days later—still covered with blood and bruised ribs—and shackled my legs and handcuffed me and threw me into the back of this van and took me to Fort Lewis where I finally got my nose stitched up. I talked my way out of this summary court-martial for being AWOL by telling them that I was still going to go to Vietnam but that I wasn't going to go until I saw my family and my brother's graduation. This guy thought I was a real patriotic guy. They gave me a ticket to Oakland Army Terminal to report for transfer to Vietnam. I thought I could perhaps delay it again since I wasn't healed up from the car accident, but the Red Cross wouldn't OK it so I got my ass off that base as soon as possible since I would have had to get on the plane to Vietnam. At the Oakland Terminal I saw all these kids running around in circles getting ready to get on the plane. I had to make a decision right there—I knew I wasn't going to Vietnam, but I wasn't ready to turn myself in and go to jail. So I split.

I stayed in Berkeley with friends and met Susan—I wasn't exactly conscious of the fact that I was a deserter, I was only conscious of the fact that I wasn't going to Vietnam—it's called survival. For a while it was hard to understand that I was now a criminal and if the cops pick me up they're going to throw me in jail for five years. I didn't really clearly understand that I was a fugitive—it didn't seem real, it didn't make sense—but I understood when the cop started shooting at me. Susan and I had hitchhiked down the Monterey coast and crashed at a motel with some people we'd met. It was noisy and the manager called the cops, and, since we were near Fort Ord, the cop suspected I was a deserter and decided to check my ID. I told this cop that if I went back they would put me in jail since I wouldn't go to Vietnam. I made this whole emotional scene about refusing to kill and refusing to go to jail. I told Susan—the cop walked back to the car to radio in—to tell the cop that she had met me hitchhiking. At that point I slipped my knapsack off my shoulders and started running. The cop immediately fired three shots over my head and I really thought this was it. I ran down the beach and kept running for a couple of miles until I came to a rock formation that blocked my path and there were these guys camping there. They looked OK so I ran over and told them what was happening and asked for help. They put me in the back of their camper and covered me with a mattress. Then the cop car pulled in and the cop asked them if they'd seen me and they finally gave in and said yes. The next thing I knew, there was a gun in my face and I was under arrest.

The MPs picked me up from the San Luis Obispo county jail and leg-shackled me and handcuffed my hands behind my back and took me to this Special Processing Detachment at Fort Ord. They said, "Go ahead and run, motherfucker, this time we won't shoot over your head." The SPD is like a big warehouse with cyclone fence wire over all the windows. They put me there at eight o'clock in the morning, and a day of that was enough to convince me that the main stockade was no place to be. They said they were going to transfer me to the stockade the next day. But this place was bad enough! There were six guards and about thirty men, most of them seventeen or eighteen years old, who'd gone AWOL to see their parents or girlfriends. It was an absolutely vicious scene. There were these small boxes on the floor, and the guards made you sit in them, and if your legs went outside they'd come by and hit them. There was a tiny cage in the middle of the compound, bolted to the floor, about three feet by three feet by five feet, and they had a guy in there they didn't like, all curled up. They wouldn't let him out to go to the bathroom. They made the rest of us stand at attention against the wall, holding a piece of paper on it with our noses, and we got beaten if the paper slipped. One guy they taunted 'cause he stuttered, and the more they teased him the more he stuttered until one of the guards said something like, "You're pretty mad aren't you? Come on, why don't you do something about it. Just you and me." The kid swung at the guard, and then all the other guards jumped on him and beat him to hamburger with their clubs. It was terrible. When the guards changed in the afternoon, most of the kids just sank to the floor and broke down crying.

The amazing thing about all this was that it took place in full view of a bunch of civil service girls typing in the next room who could hear the screams and see the beatings and just kept right on typing. I figured if this can go on here, what must it be like in the stockade? I decided I had to get out. The only part of the compound that didn't have cyclone wire around it and over the windows was a small window in the front door, only a couple of feet square. I planned to go through the window somehow. I talked about this with another guy that evening and he wanted to go too. We planned to throw the fire extinguisher which was next to our bunks through the glass and jump out after it. I sat there all night and watched that window knowing that I had to do it—if I didn't do it there would never be another chance. I could see that this other guy wanted out just as badly, but he hesitated too long when I said, OK, here goes, follow me. There were three guards in the room so I had to move quickly or they'd shoot. I grabbed the fire extinguisher off the wall and went running toward the entrance and literally dove right through the glass with fire extinguisher and rolled down the cement stairs on the other side. With the adrenalin flowing like that, I wasn't hurt at all except that I cut the hell out of my legs flying through the window. I only had on the bathing suit I'd been wearing on the beach when they picked me up and a field jacket and some thongs. Fort Ord is right on the water, and after running up and down rows of barracks with the guards after me, I ran toward the beach and crossed Highway 1 and ran along the edge of the water for about six miles so I wouldn't leave footprints. It was foggy, and that saved me 'cause a helicopter came over shining its light and I heard it above me. I crouched down in the water which didn't feel so nice on my gashed legs. After dawn, I covered my bleeding legs with my field jacket and went out on the highway to hitch. I got a ride miraculously enough with a vegetable grocer who told me to get in the back. He didn't have to see my legs. He took me as far as Santa Cruz, and I went to the bus station and asked this hip-looking girl to buy me a ticket to

Oakland, and she did. I called Susan, and she sent this guy to pick me up. We hid out in the Bay Area with friends while my legs healed and then we went to Susan's home in New York.

In New York I got a job as a bookkeeper. I'd like to say a little bit about this job. It was capitalism at the very ugliest, the very ugliest level. I was working for a temporary employment agency as a payroll clerk for immigrants, drunks, Puerto Ricans doing work by the day for which they get the minimum $1.40 an hour. When they got work, even for one day, they had to sign a contract saying that the employer wouldn't hire them as regular employees even if their work was satisfactory and the employer needed permanent help. In order to work full time, they would have to quit for three months. There were a lot of Puerto Rican immigrants who didn't speak English who had been working for six days a week—I filled out their income tax things so I know—for two years! . . . six kids, and yet they couldn't go to work directly for the people who were hiring them. They had to come down in the office every day and get a little sheet of paper, a dispatch sheet, at six o'clock in the morning and then report back to the office at the end of the day and turn it in and get paid. They were being sold for three dollars a day by this agency for two years! Slaves! I tell you there is nothing sicker. These people were beautiful people. I tried to treat these people like people, make sure they got the right amount of pay on time. I'd go downtown after work to take deposits to the bank, and I'd see these guys and they'd insist that I go with them and have a beer even though they were only making $1.40 an hour. It would break my fucking heart because these were such beautiful people. It was criminal—I was glad to get out of being a part of that place. At least while I was there they could maintain some kind of dignity. The agency treated them just like the military treats the Vietnamese.

Then I worked for a gypsy cab service driving cars in Brooklyn Heights. It was run by the mafia and was a real example of exploitation. The car service exists—it's actually illegal—because crime exists. It's exploiting people's misery. People, like nurses, maids, waitresses who couldn't afford it, would take the car service because they were afraid to take the subway, or if they took it, were afraid to walk to it. They would be afraid to wait for a taxi in the morning. It cost plenty.

One time I picked up these two dudes who got into the car with three pounds of heroin under their arms all wrapped up. The cops were staking their place out and so we were soon stopped. They took me down to the station, but I was able to convince them that I had no part in it and that I worked for a gypsy car service. Fortunately they didn't fingerprint me.

Another time in New York I had all my money taken by two kids at Washington Square. They pulled a knife. I talked them into leaving me my false identification however. I told 'em I needed it 'cause I was a fugitive too. The whole year and a half down there was probably the most detrimental thing that ever happened to my mental state. I withdrew. I'm shy for one thing, but I wasn't only shy, I was frightened of everyone, I couldn't even relate to people—I couldn't talk normally, I had to repress everything.

I went out to Squaw Valley and skied for two months and then went back to Berkeley to see some friends. My friend's mother called the cops when she heard I was a deserter—my friend thought he could trust his mother—and one day in Berkeley two cops and two MPs came to the door while I was shaving. My friend opened the door and I saw them through the mirror. I had to crawl through the house on my hands and knees—there were cops outside too—and then I ran out the back door, across fences and backyards, and finally got a plane back to New York.

It was getting to be too much, hiding out like this. The whole tension was mounting. I was trying to build a life with Susan, but it really wasn't building a life, it was living in a nightmare. She couldn't continue to live under the idea that the doorbell rings one day and I'm taken away—and I couldn't live that way either. I would jump at everything, the phone, the doorbell—it was a degenerating process, and I knew much more of it would fuck me up. So finally in November I realized I had to do something. Then I was reluctant to leave the States so I was preparing to turn myself in and go to jail. What I was going to do in hopes of staying in the country and minimizing the jail sentence was to do a sanctuary thing. I got in touch with the GI movement in New York, and they found lawyers to defend me and got all ready for it. They really wanted me to do it too. I was seriously thinking about jail—I was trying to be optimistic; I was kidding myself so I could do it. I couldn't take much more of running or New York for that matter. Spiritually I was dying and I couldn't take it. So after nineteen months, that was it.

Before the sanctuary was supposed to take place, I went down to Washington D.C. to take part in the November Moratorium. In Washington I worked for the New Mobe for a few days, and I met this attorney whose office overlooks the steps of the White House and this writer for the *Washington Post*, two beautiful people, and we spent the whole day talking about this sanctuary. The lawyer said, "I'll defend you, but you're crazy." He really wised me up. He said I'd get at least eight years having been a deserter for almost two years and doing a political thing. Previously, Susan had already made plans to quit teaching and get a job teaching in Kansas so she could be near Leavenworth and come and visit on Sundays. We had really planned to do this. But the lawyer talked me out of it. So some people at the New Mobe helped me get enough money together to get to Canada.

That weekend I was really awestruck at being there with 400,000 people—I remember going down Pennsylvania Avenue and all the streets with marines lined up on top of the buildings, soldiers on top of the Treasury Building, and the Commerce Department, and the trucks full of soldiers, and the White House barricaded. This whole thing was so powerful to me, but it was such a down, 'cause the next day Nixon was saying business as usual as if nothing had happened. He had watched a football game on television. It was all so futile. This is what I saw of America the week before I left. I mean, I saw hundreds of thousands of people saying stop this insanity and the leaders of the country saying "what insanity? . . ." and I left. That's the last thing I saw of the United States. I drove to Canada on Thanksgiving Day, and I had a lot to be thankful for.

I went through and I'm still going through a very difficult time because I first chose to do what I've chosen to do as a human being—that's refuse to kill people. I've chosen not to participate in this mass murder, and therefore now have no home, have no country; it puts me in a situation, since my awareness has increased, of making me very angry. And it made me very angry for a long time. I've finally lost a lot of the anger, but I still feel a responsibility to the United States and a responsibility to myself even though I've been thrown out of my home to try to help save my home before it destroys itself and destroys the rest of the world. And I think any intelligent person realizes that this is what is happening, and, unless more people take this responsibility seriously, destruction is precisely what is going to happen. It's difficult to justify. Now when I went into the military I mentioned that I couldn't accept the idea of killing, intellectually I couldn't accept the idea of killing, which I still can't, yet throughout history there have been wars and people have died, and now, in my mind, I can understand what it means to really die for my country. And not in a fanatic unrealistic way. It's just that I really realize that it's not going to be able to sustain itself; it's not going to be able to exist much longer without destroying everything including the earth that we walk on—it's not even going to be inhabitable very shortly, so I can really see what is necessary, and what is becoming more and more necessary, and what is going to have to happen in the States . . . and I do feel that I will be going back when the time is right.

When the liberal intellectuals who now think everything is groovy in the States find out that everything isn't groovy, then it is time for me to go back to the States. Because when these middle-class liberal intellectuals find out a little bit more—and they're finding out too—then there's really going to be a problem 'cause they'll have to take the front off this whole thing and show people where it's at—that this is Hitler Germany nineteen-seventy whatever. When this point comes, with the great liberal tradition that the United States has had, then maybe the people will have enough guts to do something. But right now we can only pretend that this is a great free society when the cops can come into your house without warrants, open your mail, tap your phones, and take you to jail, and arrest you for no fucking reason whatsoever just because they don't like your looks—the liberals don't understand this because the cops aren't doing it to them. But when they start, when cops move a little closer to these people, when these people too become oppressed, then wow! Like, I wasn't oppressed until I was nineteen, but now I'm really oppressed; I've become really victimized by a completely unjust system—and when more people become oppressed in the United States—and they're going to—then they'll commit themselves to changing this thing. I hope. Right now it doesn't look so good, however.

I realize that I'm not an intellectual and I don't have a great analysis for this thing, but, in very simple terms, I left the United States because I had to leave the U.S. or go to jail for five or eight years. But I have friends who got honorably discharged out of the military and were free, but *they're* coming to Canada or going to Europe to live because they really understand and they really see what is happening, and, since they're not revolutionary people, they're doing the only alternative thing possible for them; they're leaving. They know where it's headed, they know Reagan isn't joking when he's talking about putting these people in jail, and he's not talking about putting a few people in jail, he's talking about trying to isolate the whole "cancer"—to quarantine it. I know people who are coming to Canada not to flee the military machine but to flee the fascist state that is developing in the U.S.

The great American brainwash worked perfectly on me for nineteen years. It's beautiful that I could finally realize this and that I could finally accept the idea of what the United States is and what it really stands for and what it is actually doing to perpetuate the society that exists down there. It's incredible. I've spent hours and hours and hours just freaking out, thinking about it. How can I better describe it? It's really a brainwash; it really blows my mind. It blew my mind to realize that America was not what I thought it was, what it always had been.

I once was able to enjoy very much what I was doing and not even realize that what I had materially was being paid for in people's blood, a lot of different people's blood. At the same time I had a sportscar and a motorcycle and a whole closet full of nice new clothes and lots of things, and I really thought that was great. I was living the good life, or I thought I was living the good life, but, upon realizing what was really going on, I could no longer live like that. What later happened was that, from rural Oregon to Berkeley and the subculture that I really related to, I moved to New York, and this made me further reject this way of life and completely destroyed any possibility of me being able to overlook the knowledge that I gained about this system. The reason America is what it is, is because of the standard of living—most of the people are *too* well off and they don't want to hear the truth. They don't want to upset the apple cart. I was the same—is what I'm trying to say—my whole reason for going to college was to get a good job and make a lot of bread. It's unlikely now that I'll get a degree. I don't need it.

This whole new idea of low-energy living—I guess you'd call it—when people are really getting back, coming down to earth, not spending half their salary on horseshit they don't need, replacing these plastic values with things that are vital to everyday life, this is what the revolution is about. The revolution is happening; it's happening in people's heads. The next generation is going to be a serious threat to the power structure that exists today—not by the threat of destroying it but just by the fact that people aren't interested in living like that—and a growing number of people aren't going to live as this society says. It's going to do strange things to the economy at any rate. It looks at this point as if the United States is willing to write off a whole generation—and not a generation of idiots, they're losing the intellectuals, the whole group of thinking people. These people are going in another direction, a new direction that appeals to them *because it is real*. They're getting their heads together. It's taken me nineteen years and a lot of people I know the same amount of time to really understand how much of a victim of this whole pile of shit they've become.

Just to give an example of the hypocrisy of the whole Anglo-Christian ideal: I went to a Methodist church while I was growing up. The minister of that church was my bus driver in high school, plus I saw him three times a week at church. I was very intimately acquainted with him; he was a very close friend. When I came to Canada I wrote him asking for a letter of recommendation concerning my character—would I make a good Canadian citizen. He didn't have the fortitude to return the letter because he was also on the draft board in Yamhill County when the board completely overlooked my application for a 2-S deferment, even a 1-S so I could finish school, and drafted me into the army. And he had been standing there in front of me for two years preaching, "Thou shalt not kill," and "Love thy neighbor."

I had much less of any sort of home than most people, therefore I think my need for grasping something to call home was much stronger than most people's. That's why I think it was harder for me to leave the United States. Because I had so little of what home really represents that what little I did have, New York and Susan, meant so much that I didn't want to leave it. But it wasn't really a home since I couldn't even write my brothers and sisters. I wrote my sister once, and she turned me into the FBI, although she later apologized and now understands what I've done.

Most of these guys I've met up here have really inspired me—they have understanding—you know, they're just really down-to-earth beautiful people who say, "I was getting fucked over, man, and I had to leave." It's really pathetic what a lot of them are having to go through. I was more fortunate; it was easier for me. Things always work out for me, somehow.

Linden Blake made a dramatic escape from the prison ward of the Presidio army hospital in San Francisco. Earlier, he had been placed in the Presidio's infamous stockade on September 9, 1968 for refusing to board a plane for Vietnam. On October 11, while on a work detail, he saw his fellow prisoner, seventeen-year-old Richard Bunch, shot to death by the guards for walking away from the group. To protest the killing of Bunch, twenty-seven prisoners, including Blake, sat down in a circle outside the stockade and sang songs. This became the well-publicized Presidio Mutiny.* The Presidio is not the army's worst stockade, nor was the mutiny the first open rebellion against prison conditions, nor Bunch's death the first killing of a prisoner. In 1966 a Private Might was shot dead attempting to escape while en route to the Fort Jackson stockade; in 1967 there had been a serious riot in the Fort Dix stockade, the scene of many later revolts; in early 1968 there was the riot in Long Binh Jail in which several men died; in 1969 Sandy Hodge, a marine deserter now living in Canada, took his story of atrocities in the Camp Pendleton brig to *Life* magazine which published an exposé on October 10. By early 1970 a Congressional committee was investigating the military's prison system. However nothing was changed by all the publicity and the remarks of senators and representatives. All one needed to do was talk to fresh escapees from army stockades and marine brigs who were showing up in Montreal, Toronto, and Vancouver by the dozens—nothing had changed. They told of prisoners' fingers being systematically broken by guards, of relentless beatings, of guards witnessing suicide "gestures" and not stopping them, of sending men near death to solitary confinement instead of to the hospital. One deserter testified to having seen a man in the Fort Polk stockade who couldn't stand it anymore simply walk over to the

*For a complete account of the Presidio Mutiny Case see Fred Gardner's *The Unlawful Concert*, Viking, 1970.

fence and try to climb out. A guard, without giving an order, calmly walked over and blew the top of his head off with a .45. The *New York Times* never learns of these incidents. They are easy to cover up; like My Lai.

It is not as new a problem as people may think. In 1961 Julian Beck of New York's Living Theater indicted the military penal system in a play called *The Brig* which played widely in the U.S. and Europe. But this only served to enlighten a very few people to the sordid realities of military discipline. By 1970, however, largely because of the trials of the Presidio 27, the conditions of military prisons were brought to light in a barrage of articles appearing in many newspapers and magazines: *Time, Life, Newsweek*, the *New York Times*, *Playboy*, not to mention wide publicity in the underground press. The TV networks, too, provided thorough coverage in commentary and interviews. No one could help but be informed about what America's military was doing to tens of thousands of innocent young people whose only crime was a brief AWOL or refusing to kill in Vietnam. It was no secret; yet nothing changed. By late 1970, Seymour Hersh, who had uncovered the My Lai massacre, was writing syndicated reports of what he called a "concentration camp" in the 197th Infantry Brigade at Fort Benning, Georgia, where Vietnam veterans were confined to "correctional custody" and forced to suffer beatings and eighteen-hour days of hard labor for nothing more than missing a bed-check which normally brings punishment little worse than pass restriction. While *Newsweek* was devoting an August 1970 cover article to military justice and the need to reform it, the army was cynically instituting even greater repression of human rights by establishing prison camps for nonjudicial offenses to which men were sent without so much as a court-martial. Much was said and much was written, but nothing was done. The men who run America ignored the situation; the men who are in a position to press for change did not act. "Yet I asked no further questions," Albert Speer has written, discussing the time when a colleague intimated that he had seen something terrible at

Auschwitz.* Unlike the German people who didn't know what was going on in the prisons, both civilian and military, and unlike Speer who didn't care to find out (but whose position demanded that he did), the American people *knew*, they could have known, they did not have to ask, the information was there, yet they failed to act.

Linden Blake acted; he could not tolerate these conditions any longer and so he left. He is one of the lucky ones. He now lives on a commune called Sundance in central British Columbia. His straight, shoulder-length hair has been bleached bright gold by the sun and his long, lean back is bronzed from working the vegetable plots. He has become a vegetarian out of necessity and says he has never felt better in his life. There are four couples and two single men at Sundance including five Americans: two girls, one honorably discharged serviceman, one draft dodger, and one deserter. At a commune where the "family" lived before locating Sundance, Lindy Blake met his wife, and shortly after moving to the new farm, she gave birth—without a doctor—to a baby whom they named Jules, after the old Indian who had given them the land.

I'm from Los Angeles. I was born in the downtown part and when I was six we moved to the suburbs—that trip. My people were sort of middle-class. Everyone says that. My father worked at a defense plant, North American. Spends all day building missiles, you know; doesn't know why. Doesn't know what he's doing. Graduated from high school in 1966. After that I started to travel, I started traveling around. I worked now and then. I got stoned a lot. I worked in Arizona for a contractor for a while. I did some nice things. A lot of the time I was really confused. Like kids are, I guess. I went to college for a while; I was going to do a full-course trip. I only went for a couple of weeks then left. I kept two night classes, psychology and philosophy, which I finished. College can't teach you the right things; only you can. The right things are learning about people, not learning about things.

I was dropping acid, things like that. I was doing acid in high school and

*Albert Speer, *Inside The Third Reich*, Macmillan, 1970.

after. I was busted four times for possession of drugs both in high school and after, but it never stuck. It never got past arraignment, until the last time . . . I was walking out of a friend's apartment, out to my car with a lid sticking in my belt. I closed the door and turned around, and there were these two cops standing there. One of them had busted me before, but couldn't make it stick. They were very happy to arrest me.

It was in my mind to refuse induction, but I didn't know what I was doing. I didn't have any preparation. I didn't know what would happen or what my alternatives were. I knew you could refuse, but I didn't because my trial for possession came up the day before I was supposed to be drafted. It was just circumstance that both things hit me at the same time. The judge said, "Well, the army will be enough punishment for you," and everybody in the courtroom started laughing. And I started laughing . . . oh well.

When I got in the army I knew . . . like they were sick, man, really sick people there. And they were making me really sick, even if it was just in my reaction to them. Really weird way of living. I took basic training pretty much as a big joke because there were other heads there, and we just laughed—you know: KILL, KILL, KILL, ha ha ha. We just went crazy. But we had a talk one night, me and this other guy, and we both decided we'd have to draw the line someplace, and we both decided it would be when we went to Vietnam. We'd be able to draw the line then; it would be really easy. We'd both not go to Vietnam. I don't know whatever happened to him. The last I heard he was going to Vietnam. I went to breadbakers school after that, by some lucky accident . . . I just saw it on the list and said, wow! that's what I want to do, I don't want to go into infantry. And that's what I got. I must have set up some strange vibrations. I went to Virginia to go to breadbakers school. It was really depressing, they can really confuse you until you think you don't know anything. Then you're just open for their propaganda, their brainwashing. I guess it's the same way they accuse the Chinese of doing. Anyways, I went to Virginia, and that's where I got orders to go to Vietnam. And that's when I decided that I wouldn't go. It was kind of a relief because I knew then, that at that point, I could draw the line; I could say no.

In Virginia, after I got the orders, I went to Virginia Beach which was near Fort Lee where I was stationed, and I met this chick who was from Canada, and she wanted me to go to Canada with her. Oh fuck, and I didn't! I said no, you know, there are things I have to do here. I have to do this really hairy thing—I told her I had to refuse. I think it was because they burned me out of so much time, so much of myself, that I had to burn them out of something to make myself feel balanced. If I just ran away, I would have left unbalanced. So I had to do something back to them, and refusing was really a good thing because, like, when I did it, I did it all completely in my own head. I talked to some people from the ACLU and some other lawyers 'cause I wanted to see some of the legal trips that were going down. But I didn't try to publicize myself; it was all for my own satisfaction.

The peace movement originally wouldn't give me much help. The lawyers I'd called never came through, wouldn't even write back. They didn't have any advice. I don't know—peace people always really disenchanted me, the nonviolent type, peace-protest-marcher-demonstrator-let's-get-out-of-Vietnam trip, you know. They reminded me of a bunch of pussies. If they really believed in what they were saying or if they really had the guts to stand behind what they were saying—all you have to do is say, fuck it, and just walk away, and don't pay any attention to it, and don't contribute to it in any way, but you don't have to scream about it 'cause that just makes people mad; it doesn't accomplish anything. There are lots of little things you can do, you know; you can fuck with the establishment's heads just by being your own self and not by being your anti-self. I talked to some other peace groups, Women for Peace, Grandmothers for Peace, or something like that. They weren't helpful at all, in fact they were downright rude—I talked to some other people who'd say, well . . . ah . . .

Like when I was escaping from jail—it was really a tense time—I had dreams, really far-out dreams. I had one dream where I just discovered there was a door in the wall. Wow! Look! I can just walk out the door! So I walked through the door into the next room, and I found a bunch of chicks lying in bed and it was a co-educational jail, how nice! That was really great, and what's this? Another door! And I walked out the other door, and—Look! it just led right out to the outside. I thought, wow! I was standing there on the outside in this alley, and here comes this giant peace demonstration, these people with big placards and everything. They're walking down the street—you know—stomp, stomp, stomp, and I'm standing there, and, uh oh! I'm trying to escape from jail, and here comes this peace demonstration—and they trampled me. Yeah, they trampled me. I'm lying there all fucked up, and these guys come from the jail and take me back inside. I was right back where I started from.

I'll explain another dream I had. When I first came to the jail I kept having this recurring dream that I was walking down a dirt road; it was nice and green—birds singing—free—and it was early spring. I kept having the feeling that it was springtime, and when I woke up I had a profound feeling that I was going to be out of jail by spring. I didn't know how, but I'm going to be out of jail by spring.

When I went home on leave, before I was supposed to report to Oakland to go to Vietnam, I told everyone that I was going to refuse just to see what the reactions would be. And every single person said, "Oh no, don't do that; you'll go to jail. *Do what they say. Just go along with them you only have a couple of years and then it'll be over*." Only one person said it was a good thing to do, that it's your life, do what you feel you have to. That was my mom. She was really good to me; she was really a head. My mother said, "Well, you gotta do what you gotta do, and I'll just help you as much as I can."

Anyway, I finally reported to Oakland. My head was really fucked up. I was all ready to refuse, but every army person tried their hardest to talk me out of it. It's really difficult to refuse; you have to go through a bigger procedure to refuse than if you just go. They made it really difficult—they wouldn't give me a CO application—they lost all my things. I wanted to go along with them right up to the last and then refuse to get on the bus to the airport, but they were making it difficult so they could charge me with more things than just refusing to go to Vietnam. The suspense was really terrible. Finally, I just decided, look, I've thought this through logically before, but I can't think logically right now 'cause I'm too emotional, so I just did it. It was so satisfying! It was so great!

First, they called my name, and I went up to the CO's office and said, look, I'm going to refuse, I'm not going to Vietnam. He gave me a direct order and I refused. He told me to wait in this room, and I waited there for six hours, and when he called me back he had a written order ready and he wanted me to refuse the written order. He had a bunch of witnesses, a colonel, a major, a couple of captains—I won't forget it. He read me the order and I said, well . . . and just as I was going to speak one of the officers started giving me his rap of, "You know, you're going to get five years in jail," and "You don't really want to wreck your life, just go along with us." They'd been feeding me this rap for a long time and that's what had been confusing my head and finally I just said, Fuck You, Fuck You—I started ranting and raving, "*You can get fucked, man. You can all go and get fucked.*" Anyway, they called in a couple of sergeants who took me over to the Presidio and the stockade. They wouldn't let me call a lawyer. When they took me to the Presidio I knew that I had done the right thing; this was the right road. From then on I was always sure.

The first night I was in the jail, there was a riot, and it was fun; it was a fun riot, not a hatred trip, prisoners just getting off. We were just having a party—*they*, I mean—it was my first night and I was just sitting there watching it all. "This happens every night you say?" Finally the MPs came charging in and lined everyone up against their bunks with their bayonets and all. Actually it was a pretty big joke; we were just having fun.

When I was in jail I received a letter from my father saying just horrible things like, "Your kind belongs there." You know, it really made me sick to my stomach; I couldn't take it. So I wrote him back a hate letter, and he wrote me back a hate letter. Finally one of us cooled it.

The Presidio stockade is the Black Hole of San Francisco. When I first went there and there was the riot, I thought, gee, what a neat place. The subtle psychological things they do to degrade you, it takes a few days to realize that they're doing it to you. But it's terrible, man, like just little, itty bitty things, like if your cigarette pack—they gave us cigarettes in those days—has cellophane they would take it away from you and say you can't have cellophane on your cigarette pack. Unconscious psychological treatment is really bad, sickening. Like I witnessed a bunch of suicide attempts—what the army calls suicide "gestures." They both happen: real suicide attempts where a guy really tries to kill himself and times when a guy just wants attention or wants to get out. But to the army they're all suicide gestures. I witnessed quite a few people, five or six, suicide attempts, people who really wanted to do it. Like one time when I was in the box—a segregation cell where they put you when you're a bad boy, when you don't stand at attention properly or call the guards sir—when I was in the box the first time, the guy in the next box, his name was Lee, he had a stock of razors and kept slitting his wrists, and they kept taking him back to the hospital and bandaging him back up, and he'd do his wrists under again. Then they took him to the hospital and stitched him back up and this time put him in a straight jacket and brought him back to the box. One time I undid the straight jacket for him—you could reach around between the boxes though you couldn't see through—and he did his wrists again. Then there was a guy named Donald Heaston in one of the boxes who slit his throat. Heaston was really a beautiful person, and he—he wanted to die. He'd had it. He was about four feet tall and six feet wide, really muscular. He was really a gas. He'd torment the guards, but he'd never hit one 'cause he was afraid he'd kill 'em. He dropped a whole bottle of morphine tablets one night and slit his throat. He slit his throat three times in all; one time he got his jugular vein but they got to him in time and sewed him up and brought him back. He was so innocent. This other guy, Reidel, tried to hang himself, and one time he almost succeeded. They took him down—he'd hung himself with his sheets— and took him to the hospital and pronounced him DOA but later found he wasn't dead so they brought him back to the stockade.

I was just reading in a book the other day something about a concentration camp in Germany, and it reminded me a lot of the Presidio—just the general feeling, the feeling of the writer, and even some of the atrocities, they're just the same. Like when a guard shoots a prisoner he gets a promotion and he gets to choose whatever base he wants to go to and gets a thirty day leave. Things like that are pretty much the same. The feeling is pretty much the same. The only difference is in degree.

I think the reason so many people in the Presidio tried to commit suicide was because of the type of people they are: I mean, the army was the last chance to make it in a lot of ways, to make it in society; and they'd be trying, you know; they'd been really trying. And mostly they couldn't handle the army; it was too much; it blew their minds completely. Army people were really into hating, and they just couldn't do that and so they ran away and went AWOL. Or maybe they just couldn't stand it and they ran away to see their wife or something, and then they'd be put in jail. All their lives their fantasy life trip just kept getting taken away from them; they really wanted to make it, but they couldn't, and they ended up in the army, and then they ended up in the Presidio stockade. There are no discharges; no one ever gets discharged. And these people are just going to keep going AWOL and getting put back in jail. They finally give up and say, "What the fuck," I guess.

One day the inspector general came through for a tour, this was right after the mutiny, and he shouted through the bars, "I don't suppose you guys have any grievances," and walked away, and we began to shout and holler because we had a booklet of grievances about half an inch thick, mostly individual cases of this or that happening, and so he came into our cell block and asked us what our grievances were, and so we told him, and he said, "Well, look, what I want is someone to lay charges on. Now who's been hassling you guys, and I'll lay charges on him like that." So I went up and explained to him, lookit mister, we don't want to lay charges on anybody. If we lay charges on someone then they'll end up in the same place we're at, and we don't want to put anybody through this shit man, 'cause this is really bad. What we want to do is just make things more liveable 'cause it's intolerable to live in this place; you can't exist in here. You can't exist; you can't stay alive; you have to die; part of your soul has to die to exist in here. So he got down on me really bad. Later I filed a complaint form in which I complained about the inspector general's attitude toward us prisoners, and he called me into his office and ripped up the complaint form in front of my face, so me and him had a screaming battle . . . Yeah, it was a fun one, he'd slam on the desk and I'd slam on the desk. I told him things like he was a *bad man*; like I was really unsubtle—You're evil, man; you're no good; you're what your mother warned you against, you're anti-human being—So I went into the box for that, too. For two weeks.

Two of the boxes were black boxes and had absolutely nothing in them, no light; they were black. You had to sleep on the floor, no mattresses. There were also white boxes if you weren't quite so bad or if the black boxes were full. In the box they gave you what they called rabbit chow which consisted of bread and water and mashed potatoes. They'd give you an orange once a week. Like, when you're in the box, there's nothing more they can do to you so it's really the freest place—until they started taking prisoners off to Treasure Island, which was a marine brig, a local marine brig, and they started taking people there and beat the fuck out of them for three weeks.

We had a lot of dope in jail. Most of the time you could get anything you wanted. We were getting in acid, grass. People were getting in smack; there were junkies in there who kept their habit. Every Sunday there would be shipments of speed. Sunday night we'd be screaming and rapping and carrying on the whole night. At the same time it was completely intolerable. It's a hard situation to explain. I had a realization right after Bunch was killed that, fuck man! we're all going to die; there's no use in hating them; you're not going to awaken them. I got to the point where I could fast for a week at a time, and I'd chant at the wall for a whole week. For the first couple of days in the box I'd shit and they'd drag me out to the latrine, but after that I wouldn't have to go anymore, and I'd just piss on the floor outside the bars 'cause you could yell, guard, guard, all day and they wouldn't come. I could exist just within my own self, and they could take everything else away from me. Not only that but they could hate me, but I was in a space where I could still be happy and exist—I mean, be really happy and love. And this could really get to them. I could lay something on them, if only my innocence. If they asked me to do something, I'd say why—I never got hostile to them; I'd just ask them to explain. What they couldn't stand most of all was somebody rationally opposing them like that. Like some people would say, no, I refuse to do this, I'm for peace, man, and that's the kind of thing they could write off as a type, "These peace freaks." I just opposed them rationally for as long as I could, but I couldn't keep my head in that kind of a space for too long; I finally broke too. I managed this for a couple of months anyways—until I got hepatitis and I was really down and they thought, ah ha! now Blake's down and we can really get him. Like I wouldn't get out of bed in the morning, because I couldn't get out of bed. When I'd stand up, I'd just fall down, so they kicked me, you know, put me against the wall, trips like that. At that point I sort of lost something that I had, but it was also at that point that I got to go to the hospital.

I never knew Bunch at all until the day he was murdered. He was sleeping in a different cell block. Usually, when there was somebody who was really crazy like him, everybody knew about it, and it was just sort of a basic understanding, you know, that everybody tried to help this guy get along because there was pretty much of a togetherness feeling, among the heads anyway. So the day we went out on work detail—like there were four prisoners and a guard with a shotgun, and the guard with the gun wasn't letting any prisoner get more than fifteen feet away from him or closer than five feet. So he marches everybody around in a little group. We were marching down to go to work to put wall lockers together for somebody or other, and all the way down Bunch was watching these MPs driving around in their cars and he goes, "Fuck you," to the MPs—first he'd given the peace sign. That was really freaky. They looked at him really stern, and then he'd say "Fuck you," and so they drove over and said, "Hey kid, don't give us any trouble," and they were bitching at Bunch so I played the mediator and said, look . . . um . . . this guy's about sixteen years old or at least he looks it—he was seventeen—and . . . ah . . . he's just a little kid, just a little kid, let him go, huh? Most of that day I was trying to play mediator between him and everybody else. Like, when we were putting the lockers together, we went into the next building to have a drink of water, and the guy with the shotgun was following along behind us, and Bunch was saying things to the guard like, "If I run would you shoot me?" and that was a pretty common thing to say to the guards because everybody always says that to find out if some guards would shoot—and some guards actually wouldn't and you could tell. This guard, I could tell, was really weird, and I could tell that Bunch could tell it too. Like the guard was just back from Vietnam, and he was really shaky. And Bunch kept hassling him and kept asking him, and I didn't know what Bunch's motives were, or where his mind was. You shouldn't hassle that guard, I told him. So I took him off and, while everybody else was drinking water, I just said, look kid, that guy's got a gun. Don't fuck with his mind 'cause his mind's really messed up already. I guess I knew something was going to happen. So we walked back across the street, and I was standing on the sidewalk and I started tearing open these cases of wall lockers and I just heard, "Aim for my head, be sure to hit me in the head," and then, just as I turned around, the guard was aiming, and he fired. I can still see it. Like flash, Bunch is hanging there in mid-air with a perfect Christ pose and this big blood hole in his back, blood gushing out. As soon as he hit the ground he was dead—pow, you could just feel it, his spirit took off. Like, he was ready to go, I guess, because he was committing suicide I'm sure. His insides were just ready to split his body; he was just all prepared to do it. As soon as the guard shot Bunch he turned the gun and pointed it at me and said, "Hit the ground or you'll be next." So me, I just stand there completely frozen. Then I dove behind a truck. I didn't know till later, but the guard's gun had actually jammed with the second round in the chamber. So I was the next one—I haven't told anybody about that before. Afterwards we're all standing there, and the guard was shaking and saying, "I—I—I didn't mean to do that,"—and he was trying to unjam his gun. "I didn't mean to kill him." Things like that. It didn't dawn on me until later when one of the other guys said, "Yeah, and the guy's gun was jammed with the second round in the chamber."

They took us to an office building after that and they left us unguarded 'cause we were in a complete state of shock. We were in one of the buildings connected with the jail, and all these people were sitting there and typing out shit, you know, as though nothing had happened. They don't even give a fuck that someone was murdered ten minutes ago I was thinking. Murdered, man! So I ran over to this guy's desk and pushed all the papers off and ran around the office kicking over wastebaskets and pushing typewriters off desks and things.

When we finally got back to the jail with the prisoners the whole place was in a state of mental shock. So we talked. "What the fuck are we going to do?" And I knew personally that I had to do something. I wasn't too interested in organizing anything; if anyone else wanted to do something, that was fine, at first. And then we sat down and talked—just completely about Bunch's death and nothing else. We sat down that night and said we'd fucking well better talk about this because there are people already starting to crack, do weird things, like they're going to start really blowing it, a really violent riot, not just a happy riot—I mean, a kill riot; and nobody wanted that to happen, you know, we all knew that's not going to do anything. So we sat down and rationally decided that we'd better have a discussion, and so we did. We had a big, giant discussion and decided that what we would do was all sit in one of the cell blocks and take off our clothes and sit there—that was Walter Pawlowski's idea. The other idea was to go and sit on the lawn 'cause that way we could have people take pictures of us, and that was really important. We wanted to get the thing publicized. I started thinking about other things that were happening in the jail, our list of grievances. Mostly, there were insane guards, guards who were off their rockers. We wanted our say in who guarded us—that's kind of ridiculous come to think about it! Actually, it was an out-and-out mutiny—ha ha. Nobody instigated the protest.

Some people said Pawlowski did, but that's bullshit. We were just all sitting there, and we all knew we wanted to do something. It was an entirely spontaneous thing.

. . . Like I was so fucking naive about politics when I went in there. Then I started finding out some things—like, oh man! they'll do anything, they're murderers, the government is evil. Except for a few good intentions, there is nothing good about the United States Government—the whole thing is set up to promote separatism between human beings, and that's evil. Maybe *bad* is a better word.

Anyways, we made up a list of grievances and decided that when they read off the first name on the roll call we'd all yell out "Here" together and go out and sit on the lawn. We really didn't know what we were going to do after that. But it worked. While we were planning it we felt that it should include the whole jail, not just twenty or thirty of us who were stalwart, who were really going to do it. So we went around and talked to everybody, about 130 people altogether. Just about everyone I talked to agreed, but then they chickened out at the last minute.

So we did it. When we sat down I started chanting 'cause we had to do something. I was chanting Om and Rick Dodd was chanting Om 'cause we just wanted to get ourselves elevated because it was such an elevating situation. Then someone started chanting, freedom, freedom. We were making a lot of noise. We had it figured out before that we were going to make enough noise that, one way or another, if they read us a direct order we couldn't hear the direct order. When they were reading the mutiny charge we thought they were giving an order to go back inside. We never heard the order to go back inside. Some of the guards standing on the other side of the captain from us, about twenty feet away—they couldn't hear it. They testified to that at the pretrial hearings, but the army struck it from the record later.

Wow! We were really amazed when we learned that they read a mutiny charge. We didn't know until a few days after. They had read it through a bullhorn, but we were all singing so loud that we hadn't heard it. When they read it in the jail later they said it was punishable by hanging or whatever punishment the court chooses to give. We couldn't believe they were serious. But not only did they read it seriously, but they threatened us with hanging for a long time after that, and not only the guards but top ranking officers and lawyers who would come by and who would say, "You can be hung, and you probably will be because that's the military way. Because we can't have this insurrection in the ranks. We just can't have this happening."

After they read us the mutiny charges and said it was punishable by death the main sergeant of the jail, Sergeant Woodring, came up and said he had inside information and he hoped that we would get the maximum sentence. Which was hanging. Woodring was a former L.A. County sheriff's deputy. That describes him. Just a big pig like they had at the L.A. County jail. He'd do some weird trips, man. One morning he pulled me out of bed, and he and two guards carried me downstairs, me and two other guys, and started threatening us with the box—we'd all been in the box before—and, like it wasn't the box, it was him, man, the hatred, like I've never before or since sensed or felt anything that bad. It was worse than somebody in a fight who's trying to kill you. I don't know why, but it was more lethal. Worse. It was terrible, man. He's really a hairy person.

They separated us after the mutiny, and they put us in a big cell together. This was supposed to keep us away from all the other prisoners since we were contaminated people. Keep the innocent people away from insane people like us. That really made us so together, 'cause after we'd done the mutiny we were in a state of elation, twenty-seven people in complete elation. "We've done a fabulous thing," though we didn't know exactly what it was we'd done. We were so together—like I've lived in communes a lot, and I've never seen people so together as we were then. We ran the jail, and we did what we wanted to do, and then they started separating us and putting prisoners in different cells, and, when they got the prisoners in different cells, they'd do different trips to them. After the mutiny we never fell out for formation 'cause they were afraid we'd do another mutiny; they were afraid of us, so we'd stay in bed until breakfast was ready. They didn't know what to do with us. We'd have some KP who'd come up and say, "Breakfast is served." And we'd all get out. We took over the place.

Terry Hallinan came and saw us that Sunday morning, before the Monday of the sit-down. He came because of his client, Randy Roland, who'd just been put in jail for appearing in uniform at the GIs for Peace march in San Francisco that weekend. When he came, Randy told him what had happened and that we were going to do something, but he didn't tell him what we were planning. And so I went down and told him all about Bunch, and he wrote it all down and said he was going to read it on TV Monday night, which he did. That started the publicity rolling. What he read was my affidavit, or what he calls an affidavit—law is really weird. We told Hallinan to have the press there Monday morning. But they didn't come because the army knew something was going to happen, and they closed the base. The pictures got out 'cause an army photographer sold them later to the press. After I saw Hallinan, someone brought him down Bunch's notebook. That was the most pathetic thing. That's when I found out that Bunch was committing suicide in fact. It didn't alter anything that he wanted to commit suicide. In fact it makes it worse—that he had to use that method and it worked . . . so easily.

There were about five or six other guys there who had refused orders to Vietnam, but a lot of others got out and went to SPD for doing the same thing I did. I don't know why they went to SPD and I didn't. I finally got a court-martial, right after the mutiny—not the mutiny trial. I was court-martialed for refusing a direct order—to board the plane for Vietnam—disrespect to an officer and missing shipment which were three charges. I got two years for that. By this time we all knew we had been charged with mutiny and that those trials would be coming up so I couldn't be moved to Leavenworth until after that.

At the pretrial for the mutiny charges—the army's equivalent of arraignment—there were blackboards on the walls and I wrote, "Circus of Lies," on the board. One of us sat near the board, and every time the army lied we'd chalk it up so the press could see. We didn't count any of the minor little petty lies, but by the end of the day we'd chalked up 113. There were all these congressmen there too, and the guards couldn't very well walk up and wipe this off the board when it was our way of communicating with the congressmen and the press. We had got two lids of grass on that morning, and we got really ripped before we went to trial. There were fifteen of us at the pretrial. When we got in the courtroom everyone was so solemn, the solemn judge, the solemn people, and we started laughing and laughing and laughing. It was beautiful.

On Christmas Eve, eight people slit their wrists and elbows and they also had a wham-bang riot and burned all the bunks and mattresses. The riot started because all these people were supposed to be getting out for Christmas, and none of them did. The officers had promised certain guys that they'd be out by Christmas, and then they didn't let them out. It set off a lot of things.

Right after Christmas this guy had hepatitis. When that happened everybody would take the guy's blood 'cause it's better to be in the hospital than in the jail—anybody knows that. If things weren't too bad nobody would do it, but if they were bad everyone would, and things were getting pretty bad in those days. So I took his blood, and I got hepatitis—we did it with a straight pin. It was good I got it 'cause by this time—early January—I was getting in a bad way, my third escape attempt had just failed. One time we had a hole dug under one of the buildings, and they discovered it. We had a wall knocked out into the boiler room another time. Then we knocked out a wall underneath a staircase. Walter and Keith [Pawlowski and Mather] escaped Christmas Eve. I knew they were going to escape, and when they left on their way to their carpentry job which they master-minded to get them out of the stockade periodically, they waved to me, and I said see you in Canada. And they said, "See you in Canada." I went into the hospital after I'd reached almost the climax, the point where I could die. I was all yellow, but they kept me two weeks before they put me in the hospital. I was really weak physically and mentally.

At first I didn't know what was going to happen. Would I spend the rest of my life in an army jail? I didn't know what my future would be. I didn't know what was happening so I wasn't really frightened. Hallinan seemed to think that we'd either be acquitted or hustled out of the army with a dishonorable discharge since we'd caused such a stink. None of us knew what their intentions really were. But then, when I got in the hospital, we had a newspaper brought to us by one of the good guards, and there was a big write-up about Nesrey Dean Sood who had just been to trial, the first one, and he'd got sixteen years.* And Sood was considered by most of the jail people not

*It was this unconscionable sentence which Dean Sood received that outraged liberals and radicals alike and prompted a nation-wide campaign on behalf of the Presidio 27. Pressure on the army forced them to reduce the long sentences to five, six, and seven years apiece; further pressure got the army to grant a commandant's parole by early 1970 and most of the men were freed.

to be a leader. But me and Rick Dodd and Larry Zaino and Randy Roland and Walter Pawlowski were considered to be leaders of the mutiny. We thought if Sood was getting sixteen years we're going to get thirty. And that's the rest of our lives. That was the boot that kicked me out. Then Osczepinski and Reidel got tried and they got fifteen years each.

It was a hard decision for me to escape. Partially I wanted to stay there and see the thing through, you know, 'cause I'd done so much I wanted to see the rest. And I didn't want to leave my friends 'cause we were really good friends now and we really wanted to stay together. But I knew that I was going to die if I stayed in there. One way or another it was going to end up killing me. Maybe only to a degree, but still killing me. I was really confused because Terry Hallinan had come in and tried to talk us out of escaping, and he talked Randy out of it. I don't know how Terry knew, but he did. I wanted to help him too 'cause he was really in a bad way—he was one of us too. I didn't want to let him down 'cause I was his star witness as far as Bunch's death went. And I also knew the name of the guard who shot Bunch, but I never told anyone—I could have said that in court. I didn't want to let him down. I had special information on suicides I could give and so on. In the end they didn't accept any testimony about suicides anyway. Finally, it just came to me: here die; there live. If I escape, I can go to Canada and I can be alive; I can live.

The escape started in the hospital with this guy who was in the cell before us and who had got a butter knife in and had tried to work the bars with that. All he did was scratch the paint, but it gave us the idea. I don't think I would have even thought of it. When I first came to the hospital, Richard Gentile was still there and he said, "I'm going to escape. I'm going to escape"—he had hepatitis too. The ward was really weird; it was like a dungeon, you know, in the basement of a hospital. I think it was for shell-shock people in World War I who went nuts; they had things to chain people up on the wall. Not only that, they had incoherent scribbling all over the walls like "A second chance, a second chance, to lie is that we have more than one . . ." Wow! that's really true. It was really a weird place. Like, doctors and nurses were really afraid. They didn't know us; they didn't know what we were. The doctors had to put on the whole authoritarian trip, but underneath they were really afraid to come in there. We tried to be friendly with them, but it didn't help. So, after we had the idea to escape, I got a blade in, a hacksaw blade, through the window. There was a guard that walked around the hospital every fifteen minutes so that left time for someone to get a blade in. We could communicate with visitors on Sunday.

After about a week and a half of sawing away, we got a real hacksaw in, like a real hacksaw. By that time I'd gone through about three hacksaw blades. Made 'em too dull to even scratch your fingernails. It was spring steel in the bars, and it's really hard to saw through. I don't know exactly how it works, but it expands when it gets hot and seizes the blade. We ran the showers all the time to cover up the noise—I mean, hacksawing makes a lot of racket. The guard must have thought we were nuts 'cause we were always running the showers and singing. One time a guard walked in and walked right up to the window and looked at it and walked out and over to his guard phone and called up and said, "I want to report a window knocked out—one of the window panes." I heard him repeat that it would be fixed by the end of the week. So we had to hide the hacksaw in the laundry room. Two or three days after that, when nobody showed up, we went back and got the hacksaw. Meanwhile we had somebody waiting all this time outside every night for us. We thought it would be easier, but it took two weeks of sawing. We used paint chippings and soap to fill the saw cuts. After the guard looked at it we had to fill the cracks really well. The last day—I'd finished the night before—I had to wait for this chick to come; she came and said through the window, "Do you think it will be tonight?" She was getting really depressed 'cause she'd been coming for fourteen nights. I took the bars and bent them back and said, da daa, da daa—how's this?

By this time Gentile had been taken back to the stockade so he couldn't go, and Randy couldn't make up his mind. Right at the last minute, like, I went out first and said you better come, man; I just wanted him to get out of there. I got stuck going out; my hips stuck, and I had to scrape skin and blood off to get through. I thought oh no, I'm going to get stuck in this window!—and this chick's pulling, and I'm squirming, and finally I popped right on through. Randy was supposed to hand me out the bar—we had that planned 'cause I was going to keep the bar as a souvenir. It weighed about fifty pounds. But he didn't hand me out the bar, and he wouldn't come to the window anymore. All of a sudden he just disappeared. And these guys across the hall; they'd been sawing too, and we were supposed to escape together. They'd been ready five days before us but were waiting so we could all do it together, but then, just at the last minute, the window wouldn't come loose. So they didn't get to go.

I'd met this chick at the pretrial one day and arranged for her to meet me. We went into Haight-Ashbury, and I danced in the streets I was so happy. We spent four nights in San Francisco with these people. It was really weird being able to take a bath, being able to drink hot chocolate, being able to look at a tile floor, being able to talk to somebody. Really weird. Really neat too. Then they took me to this guy's house in Berkeley 'cause it was really hot in San Francisco—the people were too well known. From this guy's apartment in Berkeley I could look out on the Sather Gate, and it was during the big strike and the first day they ever used pepper gas. And I was sitting there watching out of the window 'cause I couldn't go outside all day and I had a first-class seat right there to watch the war. Then I went to Palo Alto for a few days and came back and stayed with these Buddhists. I was really weak. I wasn't over the hepatitis yet, and I was really weak from escaping. There was nothing left in me, but these Buddhists fed me macrobiotic food, and, like, in four days I was all better, really good. They were really fine people.

Then the girl who'd waited for me at the jail and her sister drove me up to Vancouver. I thought that when I got to Vancouver there would be happy people there, that it would be a completely different trip . . . and it isn't. It's really just the same thing. Only politically it's just slightly different, a little bit—it was really down. Like Keith and Walter were already in bad spaces. The people I was staying with were such super political activists—just looking for things to cause trouble about, and they'd sit around and discuss Marxist philosophy . . . oh man! So sick. I told 'em that a few times, but they didn't dig it. All of the people from the Presidio stockade got a house together—there were some other people from the Presidio who hadn't actually escaped but who deserted when they got let out of jail. There were eight of us from the Presidio, including Keith and Walter from the 27. One day me and this other guy got fed up with the city and decided we'd go to the country. So we're sitting there with these other Canadians who'd once had a farm in the country and who were trying to find another one. Then one of the guys walked in with this paper and an ad that said, "Farm for rent in Central B.C., $110 a month. 185 acres." The next day two guys went up and rented it. That was May 1969. I went up a few weeks later. It's really a fantastic place. When I got there it was like going home. I was walking up the road, and that's when I saw that it was the same road I'd seen in my dream, with the same mountain. And it was spring.

When I got to the OD Ranch there were about six people there, and eventually all those people left except Gordy, the Canadian who'd signed the lease, and me. We stayed on. New people came, and by winter over two hundred people had come there and lived there awhile before moving on. I mostly ran the garden last summer, but it was pretty disorganized with so many people coming through. This summer they're getting about thirty-five to forty-five people a night up there for dinner. So last winter a bunch of us decided, look, we gotta stay in the country; we gotta do it, but the OD Ranch isn't the place. We got to find a place of our own. We need a place that's quieter. Our family at the OD was getting too big, and we needed to be separate—have two places instead of one. So now we have the OD and Sundance too. Gordy decided to stay at the OD and keep it for travelers, hitchhikers, you know, to show people how to live in the country. A place where people can get together.

Last winter was cold. It was the first time I'd seen snow, being from L.A. I was always frozen. But we rented a chain saw before the snow came and cut down a bunch of trees. We kept pretty warm in the main house. You burn a surprising amount of wood when it's really cold. It shouldn't get as cold here at Sundance; we're a lot lower here. It's only 600 feet, yet that mountain right there is 9,500 feet. Beautiful!

When we came down here looking for land we were staying there, across the Fraser, and our tent was parked right on the edge of the cliff, and me and Charlie and Leona were looking down over the cliff one day and wondering what in the world we were gonna do—like, every day we'd been looking for farms to lease. So we looked down here and saw this place and it looked really good. So we came over and talked with the owner, this old Indian, Jules, and we told him we wanted to rent it from him. He wouldn't hear of it. So we went back and thought about it and then decided, wow! we'll have a get-acquainted party with Jules. He'll rent it to us if he knows us. So we went back to see him and brought him some fruit and had a party with Jules and told him we really needed a place to live. Finally, he said, "Well, go put your tent down there." Then he came back the next day and said, "It's yours." He said we could work it for a year for nothing. "And if you don't eat all the fruit off the trees, you're fired."

The way I look at things, there are too many people in the cities, and the people who I see in the cities are starving to death; culturally, spiritually, they're starving. Like, people have got to get back to the country because they really can't exist like that. They have to get in touch with the ground, the basic survival trip. The human race has got to get back to learning about the land and how to exist on it. They've got to learn where the earth is really at; people walk around like they own the earth, but we're just members of it. I feel like we're sort of an advance group. Like, there are going to be a lot of people moving out of the cities. Something's gonna happen to the cities, and people will have to get out. Everybody knows something is gonna happen soon; everyone's got that feeling. And when they come out here to the country, I want to be in a position to know enough myself so I can help people and teach people. Also, I'm interested in my own survival.

We live. We fight forest fires. Last fall we picked apples for the Chinaman down in town. We picked apricots today—off the reservation. We make out. If you want to make it, you can. But I can see that we've got a lot to learn, a lot of conscientious work to do learning about the earth again. We've all been fucking the earth, all of us. We're going to have to get back to the earth. There's no where else to go. We're not that together right now; we're not doing that much for the land right now, but when the tragedy comes or the catastrophe or whatever happens, then if we're together physically, we'll get more together and be able to do what we have to do. We've got a headstart.

SEVEN

A Revolution of Consciousness

A relentless consciousness drives many of the American war resisters in Canada into social service and youth organizations. Exiles
are scattered through such organizations as the Company of
Young Canadians (akin to America's VISTA), Brown Camps for
retarded children, urban children's aid societies, the YMCA (the
North American movement was founded in Montreal by Sir
George Williams), a number of summer camps and dozens of social
welfare agencies. Draft dodgers work as probation officers in
several cities; a deserter and his wife operate a house for delinquent children in Vancouver; a political exile (wanted by the FBI
for "subversive" labor organizing) is employed by the YMCA in
Toronto as a social worker in the Italian ghetto; a draft dodger is
the recreation coordinator for the Toronto borough of York; a
draft resister in Montreal works as a community organizer for the
Rotary-endowed University Settlement. Most of the drop-in and
drug-aid centers, community switchboards, and youth clinics in
Canada are partially staffed by American exiles—the government-
subsidized Toronto Free Youth Clinic was organized and is managed by a U.S. Army deserter and former medic. A number of
army medics work as hospital orderlies. Several thousand war
resisters and their wives are teachers, many of them working in

small towns in the north. And of course there are the exile aid groups and the social service people they employ, such as Sylvia Tucker, a counselor for the Toronto Anti-Draft Programme, and Larry Martin, housing coordinator and hostel manager for the Vancouver Committee to Aid War Objectors, whose stories appear below. One person who understands youth problems, the counter-culture and the new renaissance is draft resister Peter Turner, president of the Elected Council of Rochdale College.

Peter Turner left the United States rather than become involved with violence which is what he thought would happen if he remained. He received his draft notice on the same day that he received a subpoena to appear before the House Un-American Activities Committee which was investigating people who had participated in radical factions of the McCarthy campaign. Turner had worked for McCarthy right through the convention and later worked with the Coalition for a Democratic Alternative which attempted to elect independent candidates following the splitting of the party at Chicago. Pessimistic about the direction of things in the U.S. at the time, essentially the growing repression of youth, Turner chose Canada rather than the underground. In Canada he quickly saw that the government, in contrast to the United States, displayed an extraordinarily receptive attitude toward its youth. He became involved with Toronto's experimental Rochdale College, which is run entirely by the people who live in the college, and he was elected president of the council and chairman of the board of directors.

American war resisters have played a significant role in Rochdale's development since it was founded early in 1968—or Rochdale, rather, has played a significant role in the lives of many war resisters. The college has an important place in the affairs of Canada's youth; it qualifies for Tom Hayden's definition of a "liberated zone." Rochdale is a long, zig-zagged, eighteen-story structure which dominates Bloor Street in downtown Toronto. It houses approximately 850 students. Its first floor contains a cooperative bookstore, a co-op record store, a co-op cafeteria, the "People's Gallery" for contemporary art, and a cynically placed branch of the Canadian Imperial Bank of Commerce. The halls and elevators are a graffiti museum, a fierce assault of revolutionary slogans and gentle poetry. Within the building are a printing shop which turns out a weekly paper, a bookbindery, a bakery, and myriad craft shops. Innumerable projects in the arts are underway throughout the college. On weekends in the summer the outdoor second-floor terrace is the scene of free concerts by the Revolutionary People's Concert Band. The roof-top sundeck is reserved for nude sunbathing by day and by nightfall becomes a campground for transient youth, including many Americans.

Peter Turner's job is that of politician and liaison officer between this controversial institution and provincial and federal authorities, some of whom would like to close it down. After much bad press which concentrated on drugs, and failed to explain the "Rochdale experience," a federal grand jury was appointed to investigate the college and make a report to the federal government. The jury concluded, "It is the opinion of this grand jury that the community life of Rochdale exemplifies the problems and desires of a large segment of today's youth. At the heart of the problem are the lack of effective communication and understanding between our young population and the rest of society. The existence of Rochdale therefore provides an ideal opportunity for the rest of society to investigate these problems and begin to develop effective and workable solutions for them. For these reasons we feel that a real effort should be made to determine the feasibility of supporting Rochdale's continuation as a social experiment." In the council's report to the federal government requesting a grant to help pay off the mortgage, a section described the need of a subsidy for two floors to be allotted to American war resisters and exile aid groups to enable Rochdale to provide short-term, inexpensive accommodation for American refugees. The report reads:

One problem we face and are dealing with is the increasing number of immigrants from the U.S. This year we can expect three times as many immigrants from the U.S. as last year. We had many pass through here. They have many problems in common. a) They face a new environment. b) They must make new friends. c) They must find housing, employment, and provide for themselves. They have lost one country but have found another. When they first arrive, many suffer from paranoia, feel strange and tend to keep to their own rooms in town. When finally they socialize, they go to the easiest group—the transient population. Once this occurs, they generally become useless to themselves and useless to Canada. There is a great deal of concern over what becomes of these people and we feel we can provide intermediary solutions.

Turner, twenty-five, is of medium height, small-boned and has a great shock of red hair. He is intent, but quietly so, as he manages the most unique project of the alternate culture in North America. He is not a hippie, or a freak, or whatever, but more of an independent intellectual; his bookshelves are lined with the classics, ancient history, not much Marx or Lenin, lots of early philosophers and contemporary psychologists. He shares his apartment with Bill King, a draft resister from St. Cloud, Minnesota, who is treasurer of Rochdale. Together, they patiently deal with the difficult internal problems of the college and the very real threat of Rochdale folding. Rochdale was originally set up by some young developers as a profit-making cooperative housing project. As Turner explains, "The way they had set up the rent structure, the project was bound to collapse. The Rochdale Council was originally just a figurehead organization. It was supposed to manage the project, but didn't. Finally, however, the council took control—we kicked out the developers, took over the mortgage, and now the Council runs the college." As this is written, certain people in the city of Toronto are pressuring the federal government to foreclose the mortgage and close Rochdale. As these times prove to be more of a transitory Renaissance than a new beginning, there is a good chance that Rochdale will no longer exist by the time this reaches the reader. So it goes.

We lived on 9th Street in New York most of my life, from the time it was a Ukrainian ghetto. I watched the neighborhood change. I was sent to boarding school since I spent too much time on the street. After boarding school I went back for a year at the public school—I found I didn't have to work. I just knew everything. I went to Downtown Community. We had a fascinating music teacher, Pete Seeger. I went into Brooklyn College and majored in chemistry and I was really interested in the sciences. Eventually, I came to the conclusion that man was merely nothing more than a pure piece of carbon and water. That freaked me out. I was also doing a day job in an attorney's office, very large. I became the managing attorney which is just docketing and arguing motions, as opposed to cases, and keeping files up to date and keeping lawyers informed. I learned a lot about the federal system. I dropped out of school after two years, dropped the firm, and spent six months doing absolutely nothing but reading. I went to Berkeley after the six months of reading. I was there from about the middle to the end of the Free Speech Movement. I got all involved in the FSM. I was doing a nonstudent thing at the time, taking courses and so on, without credit. In Berkeley I picked up Kierkegaard. His leap of faith, et cetera, is interesting, not religiously, but just in terms of one's own ability to continue to live. For awhile, spending that six months when I was reading, completely absent from anything, it sort of gave me that "dangling man" perspective—I sort of felt vaguely that I was insane. I went from Kierkegaard to Camus, Camus to Satre to Ortega y Gasset, Dostoyevsky, Kazantzakis, Gide, and various other people. I always come back to Camus. I went back to New York and enrolled in Brooklyn College again and decided to major in philosophy.

While I was thinking about all of that, philosophy et cetera, McCarthy came along. At the same time I was very, very interested in the political thing. I picked up on McCarthy and went to work for him. The main reason I picked up on McCarthy was that that's all the chance there was to make something of the war issue. Rather than letting a small group of people get crushed to death—radicals—polarizing a nation, McCarthy had something to say to the country; "Give the people the facts, they'll give you an answer; give them the correct facts, and they'll give you the correct answer," he would say.

I wasn't surprised at what happened in Chicago. I *was* very angry. I was in the Hilton at the time the police burst into the McCarthy staff floor—the police came flying in, grabbed all sorts of people and threw them up against the walls. Then Curt Gans came stomping out, yelling at the top of his lungs to the police and telling them to get out. He shouted at us to come with him and three of us piled into the elevator while the police were still at a slight loss, and we went up to McCarthy's floor. Just as we got in the elevator we heard a lot of screams and by the time we got back down and McCarthy got down from his floor, there were a lot of kids very badly injured. They were dragged out and beaten all the way down the elevators. It didn't influence me so much as it did, perhaps, McCarthy. He came in and started putting his hands on various people's shoulders, grasped them tightly. Mumbled something about, "Can I do this to them," sort of taking the blame. Chicago was the first time that I saw police really take on a political role, to take on vested interests. It was the first time the police ever attacked middle-class kids and the political situation from here on was going to become quite intolerable.

A lot of kids I knew working in the McCarthy campaign were SDS members. The higher up in the McCarthy campaign you got—until you got right to the McCarthy level—the more radical the people were, which is interesting. And we saw that whole structure as being potentially a movement structure, something that was national already, something that could be converted to a more radical politics. This, if it had lasted, could have had a very profound impact. But most of us who were near that level, and who had been very active at the convention, got really hassled, very heavily, by the FBI, police, and so on.

I worked in CDA—Coalition for a Democratic Alternative—and for a very short period of time CDA controlled the Democratic Party in New York. We were so bloody subversive, having taken over a whole State Democratic Party that has forty-three electoral votes. Perhaps we were *dangerous*. I held a number of jobs. I helped coordinate activities in the 28th Congressional District. Just after the election there was a sudden move of the government coming down heavy on the more active, heavy radicals of the McCarthy campaign—a lot of those kids had ended up in CDA where they worked for independent candidates. It was just complete persecution, as such. There were two Con-Ed trucks parked in front of my door at all times. With these funny men who earn a lot of money per hour just sitting reading newspapers. Just after the convention there were a lot of Con-Ed trucks sitting on Eighth Street, which is the center in New York.

It was just a few weeks after the convention that a lot of things broke out at my place—I got the draft notice and a subpoena to appear before the House Un-American Activities Committee. And, like, the police were going through my apartment while I was gone. They even planted grass which I found. At that point I decided I didn't have the energy to continue, I didn't have the energy to fight all of this. I felt it had gone beyond where I could do any good. I got the feeling that the situation was becoming intolerable—I was no longer useful to it. It required commitment in areas that I really wasn't willing to commit myself to. And Chicago really determined it for me—I could no longer condemn any reciprocal violence on the part of the kids in any way.

I applied for a CO about a year before the McCarthy thing. It was rejected but then I appealed—meanwhile I worked for McCarthy. When the appeal came up, I convinced the appeals board officer—the interviewer—that I was a legitimate CO; I mean he was on my side. The Justice Department's view that I was a subversive prevailed with the group, and I lost the appeal. I was drafted. I was going to do alternate service—I didn't see anything wrong with that—if I got my CO. There were several camps I had worked at for retarded children, and I knew that would have passed as alternative service.

Canada was the only alternate thing. It was still close enough to modern issues for me to get involved. So here I am. Now, I'm interested in Canada. I see it as a potentially flexible nation. You talk about bi-culturalism, bi-lingualism here; I can see multi-culturism, multi-lingualism. In terms of Canada's government versus the kids, I see a very wide-open area. I really don't know how much influence it will have on the States, but I can see the influence up here as creating a very good basis for interaction, interrelation, intercommunication between factions—and Canada's still a young nation. What I'm hoping is that Canada goes the exact opposite direction that the United States is going. I feel very strongly that it will. I'm optimistic about it. At this moment it seems that way. I've had talks with members of the federal government and they're very astute men. I've also heard provincial men speak, and they're some of the most ignorant people. But I'm wondering what makes the federal government so astute. For the next five years, anyway, it's my feeling that youth groups and other people will have a free reign.

Trudeau himself is merely a reformist. It's useless. He doesn't compare with Eugene McCarthy. I was pretty close to that situation, and there were a number of cases in which McCarthy could have compromised and didn't. Trudeau very much compromises. Trudeau is probably flexible and young-thinking and all of that because he's astute to a certain extent. One thing that worries him right now is the U.S., very much. Much of his commitment to youth is because, probably, youth is simply the most nationalistic group right now in Canada. Canada is still young enough so that you don't have as many major concerns running it as you do in the U.S. If people like McNamara and the others—several hundred people—didn't actually run the U.S., you'd have a much more flexible situation there too. I give Trudeau a certain amount of credit but not that much credit. As for who's available in politics to run a country right now, he's the best. But it's that old thing of who do you vote for, Humphrey or Nixon. I voted for Dick Gregory. I would vote for Trudeau, however, but what I'm saying is that I never had that tremendous a romanticized vision of Trudeau. I always felt he was merely another reformist. What I see is that they're astute enough to be able to use the youth, the feeling that youth has, and a number of the open issues, the issue of the U.S., in order to gain a certain amount of national character. I think the move to make the voting age lower [eighteen in Canada] is to give the constituency that any man would have in office a more nationalistic character. And to preserve Canada. To stop it from being the fifty-first State.

Yet I don't hold the same pessimism about Canada that many Canadian radicals do. I've dealt with youth here, Canadian youth and also American youth. And when an American youth says there's an inability to communicate with one's government, I believe it. I *know* it. But when a Canadian youth says that—it's couched in the same words—and you get down and argue with him about it, you begin to realize that he never tried. And that most of this is osmosis, pure osmosis, absorbed from reading about the U.S. I don't really believe what the Canadian New Left is saying most of the time.

When I came up here, I went to Rochdale. I was offered a scholarship by one of the radical groups in the U.S. to go back into the university of my choice but they wouldn't accept Rochdale. I was eligible because any person who had stopped going to school in order to engage in political activity could have this scholarship to go back in school—re-engage himself in school. They didn't give scholarships to Rochdale because it wasn't accredited. I came here anyway. At first, Rochdale was a very negative trip. I was profoundly disillusioned with the college. I walked in, caught the vibrations, and hid in my room. I got my mind together. A year later Rochdale began to have some positive attributes about it. Got interested. Bill King convinced me I should run for Council. I did. Got elected.

The building itself has forced the people into something good. The building was probably the most destructive thing to the initial concept of Rochdale. The building was originally designed as a residence, completely. There wasn't enough room for the original concept to be realized, for seminar rooms and so on. The building on the other hand is very *con*structive to community in a high-rise situation. The doors in the halls here are rarely closed. The experiment turned out as an experiment by accident, was recognized as such after the fact. It's built for 850 people. There are several commune floors, several collectives et cetera. Over half the students are University of Toronto students, part- or full-time. In 1969 we had over four thousand people living here in the period of three months. We've had from 50 to 100 thousand people visiting. We have a fair percentage of people who don't pay rent and who eventually get thrown out of the building. University of Toronto dormitories have one hundred percent rent payers because they withhold grades. We can't do that. You have to get into the alternate economy to figure where a lot of the rent comes from. Of course there are professors who teach and doctors and lawyers. One of the janitors has a Ph.D. in English. Makes eighty a week. We have a tremendous cross section of people, a great variety of skills. All the people, from the Ph.D.'s right down to the high school dropouts, basically share some of the same values. When you get a professor from the U. of T. sharing the same values as a kid, it sort of adds to an interesting relationship, an interesting building.

There were originally resource people here, instead of professors. People would teach on a voluntary basis. Seminars. A lot of kids came to the building very, very appallingly damaged. They were damaged by the urban community. Suddenly, all of this free university concept was wrong—let's teach Elizabethan poetry "on our own." Education is supposed to be relevant to the majority of people. Then you get into that whole rich education, the sciences et cetera. But there are two very strong areas of education. One of them is that education has to be relevant to survival. Beyond that education is supposed to provide the abstracts for engaging in new discoveries, progress, all that shit. But if you don't provide the initial basis for education, providing the secondary basis is absolutely useless. What's the use of worshipping progress when there's human misery? So Rochdale sort of developed a new form of education. A free university wasn't enough. We were learning that same shit, only in a different way. It wasn't relevant. For a long time, for example, we used to engage in seminars and we discovered that seminars weren't relevant to this situation. I'd had a lot of relevant seminars at college, but I never found seminars in here to be relevant.

In the meantime you had a tremendous need. First of all you had a community here that was being damaged by speed freaks. What brought them here was the press's immediate reaction to the college when it opened—"Let's look for drugs in Rochdale." So they advertised it—so they attracted kids who were interested in drugs. The first thing the community realized was that they couldn't handle the speed freaks. So finally they rejected them. The freaks got thrown out of the building. The community at this time was still fairly negative . . . we are against the establishment, period. What *are* you?— we're not this, we're not that. When at the beginning they say you're a free university, a progressive university, and they outline exactly how you'll function, you're *not* a free university. You're not a progressive university. You have no ability to discover anything. Later a community developed here that functioned with very little program and many people in Rochdale and a lot of people who hadn't come in yet claimed that nothing comes out of Rochdale and that Rochdale has no direction, no goals. Isn't making any contributions to anything. But an interesting thing is that because we were goalless, directionless, getting hassled, a community developed here, solidarity. People didn't recognize it, some still don't. Rochdale has community because it's not conscious. A consciously developed community is one where everyone is sitting there trying to be part of it and never really being part of it. Education is suddenly realizing you've learned something, you've experienced something.

The initial concept of what education is has dissipated, but the idea of us being a college as such hasn't. I mean we engage in far more original projects, community projects, and research without really realizing it. People learn by doing. We're using society, the whole building, as a learning program. The first thing that people realize when they get in here is that this is an urban situation. They begin to rid themselves of that alienation that an urban situation normally produces. They communicate. In their communicating, they learn the problems of an urban situation. Problems of the regular urban situation, problems of the alternate urban situation. When the nature of a problem is realized, it isn't so difficult to find some way to solve it. And this is where our projects develop. Throwing off urban alienation is a big part of the experiment—learning how to cope with the city, how to live in the city, developing alternate things to hospitals, to police, and so on. Rochdale would be like a research department in a university. But it's less expensive than a research department in a university.

There's a certain amount of real freedom here now. Freedom works two ways. If someone comes up and really disturbs and pushes in the community, the community pushes back. If someone comes up and demands that he will act in one certain way and still demands that everyone play with him, they won't. They simply won't; they have the freedom not to. Some pretty obnoxious people have gained a great deal of humility passing through here. The May 4th Movement [an extreme-left Canadian group] which operates around here—isn't based here—has been tempered by the experience. On the outside the establishment is against them so they get angrier and angrier, losing all perspective. In here, when their own peer groups say, "What the fuck are you doing?" they listen. They gain a much more objective view.

Like when cops come in here. There will immediately be shouts of pig, pig. But then there will be ten or twelve people standing around lecturing and saying what are you calling them pigs for, you're making them into niggers, cop as nigger. Do you like that? And the kids go, huh, huh? That wouldn't have happened on the outside. I think kids are better off here than in the streets. Moreover, I think people are better off here than in the University of Toronto. Originally, the community was not very together, and it was very easy for police to come through here. Right now, we have an agreement that if the police come in they have to pick up the security guards. It keeps the police from getting killed. And it limits the type of people who get busted. Usually they come in for hard drugs. Dealers who get caught aren't at all cool about it. The life expectancy of a dealer is usually about two months, then they get caught. We've never had a heroin case. We evict speed cases. We had a suicide here. She managed to commit suicide. But she'd tried it seven times before and locked herself away, not telling anyone. But she was caught seven times. In any other building she would have succeeded at the first try.

Rochdale couldn't exist in the United States. I hope it continues to exist in Canada. The Province would create a polarized situation in this city if they objected too strongly to Rochdale or tried to close it down. I think the federal government feels you can have Rochdale or you can have chaos and violence. In terms of Rochdale College and the federal government, unless we can get federal aid, we might have to close it down within a year. With federal aid I think we'd be open another five years before any power is exerted against us. People like Pierre Berton, Alan King, Ivan Illich have been through offering encouragement. I think we've gone beyond Marshall McCluhan. He got heckled when he came here. The kids didn't want to hear a speech; they wanted him to either walk around and talk with them or else shut up.

Before John Munro [Minister of Health] talked about community clinics, there was one in here, and it had been operating effectively for over a year. It arose because the community itself had a need. It later became the Toronto Free Youth Clinic, and now it is almost exactly what's been described as necessary by people who've studied it. If you look at all the organizations in Canada dealing with youth that are even halfway effective in dealing with youth, you'll discover they're either wholly or partially staffed by Rochdale people: the Youth Clinic; Trailer [a drug-aid center] ; the Crisis Intervention Center; Project '70; Red White & Black. Theater groups have developed out of Rochdale. There are six farms up north where the people are engaged in the whole concept of going back to the land—they're actually supporting themselves. Kids from that are now engaged in putting together Canada's *Whole Earth Catalogue* here in the building. We have a dome city out in the Vancouver hills that came from Rochdale. The pollution groups in Vancouver are headed by Rochdale people. There are dozens and dozens of groups all across Canada that are staffed by Rochdale people. People here came in, didn't know anything, said, wow! groovy, a free university, but in here things became important. A number of these people are Americans—perhaps sixty percent—who've gone through Rochdale and out into Canada to do what they saw needed doing. They see themselves as Canadians.

Canada is getting excellent people here from the U.S. They're getting very moral people—people here to help with the environment, not people who come up here and work for an American company and help ruin the environment. A great many Americans—deserters and resisters—came up with that paranoia that so many Americans suffer when they first get here, and they locked themselves up in their little rooms around town and were afraid. Rochdale opened them up to Canada, turned them on to Canada. Rochdale has saved a lot of them from falling in with the least critical group, the transients, the underground where they are lost to Canada, wasted as such. Passing through Rochdale has such an immediate impact. A situation that would develop for someone in the course of four years "out there" develops in the course of six months in here. Things develop so rapidly here that they're very obvious. It's the same thing as being able to read a book in half an hour instead of over a period of two weeks—you understand it, you've got the beginning and the end right there. So Rochdale gives you that sort of understanding, that perspective, you begin to understand some of the social problems here. And you go out and carry this knowledge with you. One of the things about it is that people who've developed this type of education here don't realize it, they see all these problems and then they try to solve these problems or relate these problems to "out there." And they don't realize that that is an education.

We've discussed with the federal government the possibility of having two complete floors subsidized. A lot of dodgers get rooms by passing a value judgment; we'll say to them if they can't afford a place that they can stay a month and then make up the rent when they get landed and work—there's a certain amount of leniency but we really do want people who are able to pay so we can pay off the mortgage. I would say we've had at least five hundred draft dodgers and deserters living here altogether. A lot more visited, and we referred them to other places—every day they come in and ask around, and we refer them to the various organizations. We put them up for a night or two.

My own politics? At this point, between the two groups, the political revolutionaries and the cultural revolutionaries, I'm supporting the cultural because I do not see a tremendous distinction between repression from the right and repression from the left. Camus—a person whom I very much greatly admire—it was often said of him that he was neither the right wing nor the left wing but was the whole bird. To most of my friends, interestingly enough, I don't sound very radical. But I am a radical. I'll call myself a revolutionary when the revolution comes. There's an antipathy between me and Progressive Labor and the Maoists. I take issues separately, examine them one at a time. I don't like dogma. For example, I was for Israel. So were a lot of other radicals I know, *until* the party line came down. They changed. The New Left line is that the Israelis are the aggressors. Yet, even by the Soviet Union's own definition of aggression written several years ago—that it is a primary act of aggression to close off a waterway to another country—the Arabs are the aggressors. According to dogma, the Israelis are the aggressors. I am very much for Abba Eban who is a very articulate man. A very sane man. And I'm not Jewish.

I return now and then to the U.S. The border up to now has been no problem in going back and forth to see what-the-situation-is-down-there. People talk about repression. There is. I can see it. People are dying. There is repression, yet I don't believe it. Lindsay won in New York for example. People are crossing over. New coalitions are being formed. People are being aroused from their apathy. What I'm saying is that I think if Lindsay picked it up in '72, I think there would be a great movement to back him. That one office, the presidency, can influence the mood of the nation. I think that if Lindsay were there, the mood of the nation would be reversed. I would work for Lindsay if I were there, if I could go back. I'm not so pessimistic. But you can still get killed down there.

Larry Martin, twenty-five, runs the best hostel in Canada for American war resisters. It is on a tacky street in Vancouver's Kitsilano district. The hostel is self-supporting, and Martin draws a weekly salary from the Vancouver Committee to Aid American War Objectors. Martin is an upper-class draft resister from San

Diego who gave up being a professional musician, gave up teaching music, and gave up management of a Vancouver audio shop in order to open a hostel in early 1969. He ran it on his own before being hired by the committee. At the committee's office he also handles the housing of newly arrived émigrés with Vancouver families. He must separate the exiles with severe emotional problems and adjustment problems—those whom he assesses as being a liability to the Canadian families on the housing list—from the relatively stable, well-educated middle-class resister. Therefore, along with many well-adjusted war resisters who prefer the freedom and community of the hostel, Martin's house takes in all the "problem cases" as such. Martin's real interest lies in social work— his college major was the behavioral sciences—and he is expressly interested in the process of liberation among the lower classes, the wasted, the oppressed. He feels that the young men who end up at his hostel have in every case—as in his own—taken a psychologically liberating first step in their decision to leave the army or refuse induction. The personal liberation of this group of disadvantaged people is especially visible, especially beautiful, and more significant perhaps than the liberation experienced by any other group of young Americans except the blacks. As Angela Davis has said, "The path of liberation is marked by resistance, mental resistance, physical resistance, resistance directed to the concerted attempt to obstruct the path." The hostel has a special value in Vancouver, Canada's most polarized city, where young people experience alienation almost as great as that in California. Despite the liberating force inherent in the act of coming to Canada, for the poor, the uneducated, it can be blunted, destroyed even, when the young exile cannot find work and feels oppressed here as well, in a strange land. At this point many young Americans who end up in British Columbia decide to return to the United States. Larry Martin's "main thing" is to convince them that they must not return. That what they will face as a fugitive in the States will be far worse than the mild if unpleasant intolerance of Vancouver.

My father's deceased, died when I was eight. My mother's been a vegetarian since she was eighteen; like, she's that much against killing. I wasn't allowed to have any toy guns or war comics. And she voted for Nixon. There's a super conflict there. She wanted me to go to jail; she thought that was cool. I did something I believed in, and now I had to pay for it. She was against me going to Canada. After refusing induction and a year of waiting around after refusing induction, I was finally contacted by the FBI. During the four-year period I was trying to get out of the draft, I was preparing myself for jail all that time. Then the FBI came around on a Friday, and Monday I left for Canada and came to Vancouver. It was a gut reaction.

Since I had about four or five years of working experience, it took a very short time to get landed, about four weeks. During that period of time I lived in Mark Satin's hostel—Satin finally got fed up with running a hostel. We moved to another one, but it got busted—it was in too wealthy a neighborhood, and it got busted for not having enough bathrooms. So far no one's been able to run a hostel for more than six months because of the emotional pressure. I really respect Mark; he helped people out quite a bit. I had a straight job running an audio-stereo shop here in Vancouver, managing a branch store for a larger company. Eventually I decided to drop out and rented a house myself which I turned into a hostel. When I walked into Mark Satin's hostel everyone thought I was a narc 'cause I had my 180-dollar business suit on, and my 50-dollar shoes. Mark was extremely surprised that I stuck around as long as I did. He was even more surprised when I opened a hostel of my own. Since I've gotten to Canada, my life has begun to straighten out so I wanted to help some other people do the same thing. It's been going well ever since coming up to Canada. Feeling freer and more relaxed. Compared to Southern California, I find life a lot calmer.

My real interest is people. I prefer to work with people. Like, in music you get close to people, and I worked as a radio announcer, and I worked very closely with the people at *Psychology Today*. At the same time I was sort of a successful businessman—I ran a hi-fi store in California. I was on the edge looking both ways. I really wasn't a typical businessman in the States, I was borderline, and then coming up to Canada, I got to where I didn't want to be in it anymore. So I got out. I come from a very professional family, three generations of insurance brokers. Fairly well off. Mercedes Benz when I was sixteen. I didn't think I could go that way. So I got into music. Music is good expression; it's a good outlet, but I'd really rather have the kind of direct contact with people I have running the hostel and working for the committee, doing the housing, counseling.

The reasons I do it are basically to keep people out of the war machine and I like to see people get into the Canadian scene, that is, becoming Canadian because I think it's helped me out quite a bit. And I also like to see people get involved, to remember what's happening down there, to try and see that it doesn't happen up here. Also, they need a place to go. I'm not concerned with the guy with the degree who went into the army right after college and then deserted and then gets put in a private home here, stays with the family—he's always had a mother—the army, college—and now he's got another family and gets a job and becomes a Canadian citizen. Like we can't help those people—the majority—they can help themselves. I get the guys with the tenth-grade education. Like one guy got put in the army by the orphanage where he grew up. Now I'm not talking about the whole hostel, only a small group who we always see, the fuck-ups. And I get the lower-middle-class, middle-class guy of average intelligence—maybe he would have been a factory worker ten years ago, but now he's becoming aware through the drug scene and the revolutionary scene and the left political scene. There are more and more people becoming aware of what's happening to society, to western civilization, especially to the United States.

All the fairly straight people I house in private homes. So all the absolute fuck-ups end up at the hostel, *and they're some of the nicest people I've ever met*. All the training, the reading in the science of psychology and sociology hasn't changed too much my love for these people who are really open with you and who are on their first step toward being a freer individual—like we're talking about that lower- and lower-middle-class type people who really look to your warmth and my warmth toward them, the close feeling. I'm really involved with them; like, they're trying something; they've taken their first step. Refusing induction to me was my first heavy decision, and like, coming up here was the second; like, doing something against God and country and your mother. Coming to Canada for a lot of people is the first thing they've done in their whole life that really means something. Besides the humanitarian thing of helping guys to get their heads together, I think the hostel helps make guys a little more politically aware. While the hostel isn't "political," there's enough of it going around so that people are becoming a little more aware. Like in the hostel I've seen dozens of guys go through their first acid trips. One guy came up, and he was an "Ayn Rander," and then he did his acid trip and got into Zen, and, a few months later, he was a freak. There's another "Ayn Rander" in the house right now. In six months he won't be an "Ayn Rander." I found an Ayn Rand book in my house, and I played Fahrenheit 451 on it and tore it up. You have to be involved totally for this type of work, but you also, for your sanity, have to be uninvolved. But I do get emotionally involved. I like to see guys go through these changes. I'm encouraged by what I see at the house. I've seen a lot of people get their heads turned around.

Like we have meetings every once in a while at the hostel. We had a dope problem—and like, the situation is that you can't operate the house with dope in it and jeopardize everyone. So that really hurts when someone doesn't respect themselves enough—they can't feel enough for someone else's situation. I always bring up at the meetings that twenty-five deserters equals 125 years in prison for one joint of marijuana.* There were twenty-two people at the meeting. Four people had dropped mescaline in the house the week before—like, dope's my biggest hassle; I really sweat it—some Chinese guy brought in seven tabs of acid, and then seven guys dropped acid. At that meeting I was really pissed off; my voice was really shaky. Like how can you do that to yourselves, to me, to us. Like, the neighborhood is really hot, the Haight-Ashbury of Vancouver, and like, as soon as that happened I asked this person if he'd dropped mescaline—I knew who had dropped acid—and his voice completely cracked, and he started crying; he was that emotionally upset and sorry for doing it in the house (they know I don't mind dope, just do it outside). So that's just part of the involvement between me and thirty-five other people twenty-four hours a day.

*Canada rarely imposes sentences for possession of marijuana, only moderate fines. But possession is grounds for deportation, and a landed immigrant is subject to deportation until he becomes a citizen. Therefore, the "125 years" refers to the five years that each deserter would face upon being returned to the U.S. by Canadian authorities. So far there has been no reported case of that occurring.

The hostel is self-supporting. Like, if I collected all the rent at a dollar a day, I'd make six hundred a month and the rent is only 150. But I don't collect all the rent. Some guys don't have it. Right now the city is giving free feed-ins so the guys walk down there, but before that we cooked communally. The food bill was running 350 dollars a month, but now the economic situation is such that guys can't get casual day jobs as easy as before and can't afford to contribute toward food. So the city feeds them.

I guess about 600 people have gone through the hostel. Plus there's another 200 whom I've housed in private homes. Every type of personality you can think of has been through here. One guy was around for about two weeks, and he sniffed glue until it affected his mind quite a bit. Then there's the normal guy from Southern California—white, Anglo-Saxon—who's father might be a butcher and his mother a nurse. And there will always be the two or three strange people who offset the whole scene. Like, I don't know if you met the guy with the light beard, blond, but, like, he isn't too bright. Everyone enjoys having him around, but a lot of people are just making fun of him. Another guy, five years a junkie, came up here, and he's been off for three months now, very heavy into tranquilizers—like, he's trying to get his head straightened out, and he's doing a really good job of it. Another guy, John Doe, he was in court at fourteen years old, burglary or something, and they sentenced him to nine years in reform school, and he got out when he was twenty-one, stole a car, got busted on a dope charge, and blah blah blah, and ended up here. We got a lot of Americans who simply screw up down there. It's a lot easier to screw up in the States than in Canada.

One guy, seven years Vietnam, marines, his nickname around the hostel was "killer," and—like, I had to wake him up once to move him to another room 'cause a couple was moving in—and he assumed the karate stance immediately, and I thought I was gone. It was really scary. This marine corps type—like, he was still really militaristic—threw somebody off a bed once; and I walked up to him—and I'm not an authoritarian at all—I walked up to him the day after he threw this guy off the bed, and I said to him in my manner, "Well, I've sort of been thinking of kicking you out, like please, I'm gonna have to ask you to leave." He left in three minutes. Said goodbye. I've never had a physical contact with anybody.

Another guy was CIA in Vietnam—we checked his story out; there's a guy who deserted from army intelligence who works for the committee who checked his story, so we believe his story. His mother's the president of the DAR in Louisiana; his father is general somebody or other, and like he's afraid of being kidnapped. He's really paranoid toward everyone. There's another guy, seven years air force, reenlisted three times, thirty years old; he just split, and now he's in Toronto doing social work. His case was a slow realization of conscience; it was a moral action when he deserted. He came to the door, and he had a suit on and had a 160-dollar AM-FM radio-cassette tape recorder in one hand and a bottle of Jim Beam in the other so everybody thought he was a narc. Which is ridiculous. They don't send narcs like that. But guys were seriously thinking he was a narc. There was this whole aura of paranoia in the house, and then one of the guys downstairs ripped the guy off for his tape recorder 'cause he thought he was a narc and it's cool to rip things off people who are narcs. But it turned out later that he was really a nice guy; about a month later he sort of calmed down and got off the air force thing. He was a little older, mature, and he seemed to get out of the military bag in a hurry. He showed the rest of the house what assholes some of them were. Like if they're going to send a narc, it's going to be somebody like me or you.

Then there's my token black; graduate of Chicago conservatory of music, guest soloist once with the Chicago Symphony, bachelor's degree, fantastic classical musician, now plays electric violin, practices all day. He's a deserter.

I'd say the majority of the people who come up here melt into the walls. Even the majority of the guys in the hostel get jobs. Still, I don't know very many people who would stay if an amnesty were granted. I think a lot of people would go back. Like, they're not Canadians. I hate to see the straights who come up and just fall into suburbia. Sometimes a deserter will get fed up and want to go back. I try to talk to him and talk him out of it for his own sake and because that keeps one more person out of the war machine. Like, I'm really fed up with America. I wouldn't go back. I really try to stop people from going back before they do.

Future? Is the war over? Perhaps I'll run a group-home for Children's Aid, a home for delinquents. A good friend of mine, a deserter, started the present house for Children's Aid with his wife. Like I said at this big meeting recently between Bill Spira and the five Unitarian ministers and the whole committee—what I'm going to do when I get older: I'm going to run a house for retired draft dodgers.

Sylvia Tucker is one of an estimated ten to fifteen thousand American women who have left the United States with their exiled husbands, becoming exiles themselves. Miss Tucker's husband chose Canada over the draft in 1961, three years before the Vietnam war. After their separation she chose to remain in Canada: "If you don't like a place when you live in it, you move on. If you like it you stay. I stayed." Following several years of being housewife and mother in a Toronto suburb, she joined the theater and ended up with the lead in a number of plays: *The Travelers*, *Two for the Seesaw*, *Faces*, eventually starring in Toronto's first production of *Futz*, an experience which put her on the road to political action. The new American exiles first came to her attention when the director of *Faces* invited fifty draft dodgers to his home for a backyard cookout. Ultimately, she was drawn to radical politics and was invited to work for the Toronto Anti-Draft Programme where she has been working as a counselor since January 1969.

Miss Tucker presently lives on the spacious, middle floor in one of Toronto's immense old residences that fill up street after tree-lined street near the city's center. The decor is unpretentiously hip; there are lots of original paintings on the walls. There is a huge poster-advertisement of her appearing in *Two for the Seesaw* in 1966. She looks slightly younger now than she does in the picture—one guesses about twenty-three; she is thirty. Her unaffected and cheerful face and huge, disarmingly bright eyes that demand honesty from anyone who looks into them express not so much a woman's liberation as a very real *human* liberation, a liberation which few men achieve even though for them the struggle is easier.

Below, Sylvia Tucker explains how she came to view life as a "political act" and whence she derives the intense commitment necessary to exist for a year at the Toronto Anti-Draft Programme where the four counselors see a total of twenty new men a day. It is a rewarding yet emotionally draining job, a far more demanding business than the draft or military counseling done in the United States. Miss Tucker and her colleagues carry on the work begun four years ago by Mark Satin at the Student Union for Peace Action.

You start out in New York City with a middle-class Jewish background, a typical, very straight middle-class Jewish girl. When I decided to go to college I chose Antioch which was a very pretty far-out place. I feel like I was reborn then in a very real way. I was not a political person at all at Antioch. I was one of your arty types. I ran around spouting all kinds of philosophy and I was in the theater there—I was a theater major, did lots of plays. Graduated in 1961 after doing Antioch's five-year co-op thing during which I worked at the United Nations and at the *Cleveland Press* as a copy girl. I taught. I went to Europe on a writing project which I got credit for. I knew I was a kind of versatile person, but I had no area that was really stronger than anything else—I was just searching and jumping around which was great. And then when it came time to graduate I realized something very weird, that all of a sudden my life was over. It was really true. And I cried my eyes out 'cause I had no idea what I was going to do out there.

I got married, moved to Toronto, became a teacher, and lived in the suburbs and it was really weird. I didn't understand what was happening. Had a baby, so that kept me at home for a couple of years, and I was freaking out; I knew that I wasn't in any way the person that I wanted to be. I was dying. Here I was twenty-two years old, and I was doing the same things that a woman of fifty was doing with her day.

Suddenly I kind of broke loose, and I started to get involved in almost anything 'cause I was searching so desperately. Because my training had been theater—I realized that what I was going to do was get directly into straight theater, which I did, and I immediately started acting and worked for a season with Toronto Workshop Productions which was a good company. And then I left that and started to act around and still had no direction and no sense of what I was doing or why. Then, when I went with Toronto Workshop to Brandeis for an international theater festival, I met the people from Café La MaMa [experimental theater club in New York] that were into a new kind of theater that had to do with communication and physical contact and freeing, and you as a human being could not participate in that theater unless you as a human being began to grow. The original director of *Hair* was there, and he participated in workshops. So a year later I was wandering around Rochdale looking for something that was going to wake me up, that was going to excite me, and I met a friend I'd met at Brandeis, and we started talking about theater in Toronto, and we started talking about La MaMa and the plays that they were doing and why Toronto was somehow not doing these things, and we realized that one of the reasons was that everybody assumed that we weren't going to be allowed to do these things in Toronto, *Toronto the Good.* And we decided that that was an assumption that was kind of ridiculous. He had just started working with a group of kids in Rochdale, and he asked me to come and help him and kind of teach and get the thing together. And we were just going to do it for fun, for our own benefit. And so we got these kids and we were all working together and really having fun and we created a production of *Futz* because we both just dug the script and thought it was fun. And the powers that be heard about it, and these producers decided we should take it to the Central Library Theater. Here were people who had never acted, who knew nothing about the theater, and who were into searching and freeing themselves, and we did it together, and the result was really nice. I don't think at any time we stood up and said, we-are-going-to-do-this-immoral-play to bug the authorities. The play just emerged. We kind of decided lackadaisically that we'd do it. And so we did it. And the next thing we knew, all of us were smeared across the front pages of the Toronto papers. "Obscenity Comes To Toronto!" People were very upset, very polarized, and everyone was discussing *Futz*. The morality squad was in there every night, and every night they served us a summons; each of us got a summons every single night. And we got a little stubborn about it, and we kept running it. We thought they were going to close us down. It was a very strange experience to see my face on the front page of all these newspapers—I was like *the* obscene woman in Toronto. I had never considered myself to be anything but a middle-class girl and suddenly to be, like, notorious! It was so incredible; it was a mind-blowing experience. And all these like really hip people would wave at me on the street; suddenly I was like—a *cause*. Not only me but the other kids in the troupe found the same thing. Suddenly we realized that people were really upset and that they could really hurt us for this, and I was shocked. I think that was the first time I became angry. Because I had honestly, simply been doing something that I thought was worth doing, and there were a lot of people telling me that I wasn't allowed to do it, that I *couldn't* do it. And a lot of people telling a lot of other people that they were not going to be allowed to come and see this show even if they wanted to. That was the first time I became aware of the fact that we weren't free at all.*

I became polarized with a certain group of people who were very antiestablishment. And so that was when I began to become involved with what I supposed could be described as groups who were in one way or another politically oriented. I guess I'm someone who's kind of slow to get angry, but that was definitely when it started. Then I decided to do shows and work with groups who were trying actually to do the kind of theater that we felt should be done, and it had to be free theater. So you automatically become involved with writers and people who think a certain way. The group that I was with formed a theater group called *Théatre Passe Muraille*. The whole thing was to break through walls, to say hello, to look people in the eye, and this was part of this whole living theater thing that we were doing. After *Futz* I went to work for a new group called the Global Village. What they were doing was a whole concept, a way of life, not just plays, not just theater, but everything happening everywhere. It was completely open and it amazed me how people, when given no direction, could operate so beautifully together—that's when I think I started to realize that anarchy was really so beautiful. You didn't have to have a head, an organizer, but if you trusted people they almost always returned your trust with creative activity. And I also, in the meantime, had gotten to know people in the other areas of the movement, that is, people not involved in theater but who were saying the same thing. It didn't matter whether you were in theater or whether you were in the Toronto Anti-Draft Programme or whether you were painting; we had something in common, we were all working toward the same thing. And one

*Charges against the cast and producers were eventually dropped. Toronto today is a very different city from what it was four years ago.

day I was rapping with Naomi Wall and she said she needed another employment counselor to help at TADP, and so then I started working at TADP.

I came into TADP 'cause I believed in what they were doing, and it was a worthwhile way to spend my day. I got there and, as a result of being in that spot, started to talk to people, meet people, and a whole new series of ideas which I'd never touched before rushed into my brain. You cannot work there without becoming very involved with the basic questions of American identity. I hadn't thought about being an American very much; I think about it all the time now; I try to understand why I never changed my citizenship. I could have changed it anytime, I've been here for nine years. Why don't I change it now? There's something in me; I can't do it. So when you're working in that office—anyone who's interested in America or American affairs somehow comes through that office—you start talking and there's a constant interchange. For example, a deserter who's been in Vietnam and he has seen things there will come in and tell you something about what he's seen which will shock and dismay you. And then, a very political person, revolutionary, will come into the office with some incredible fantastic story which five months ago I would have laughed at but, because I just finished talking to a deserter who is *not* political and who backed him up in terms of his facts completely, I start to put the two stories together. The next thing you know, you're thinking about it all the time; you're becoming more political every day, more frightened every day. Suddenly the work has become very immediate.

Working at a place like the TADP, even though to a great extent you're doing social work, you're helping people who must have your help; they have nowhere else to turn. You meet so much courage in that office; you meet so much confusion—a good half of the kids you meet cannot ask their parents to mail their birth certificates because their parents have cut them off—you come to such basic questions about parent-child relationships, integrity, decisions. The people are constantly making decisions of conscience about their lives, and they're asking you to help them. You have to make some very honest decisions about your own life. It forces that on you. So, working there forced me to become a very honest person, and, once you do that, I think you become more political. You can't sit on the fence because you start to see things and you have to act on them if you're going to have any integrity.

You have no choice. You can either get out and stop doing that kind of work, therefore stop being faced with those questions every day; or, you're going to stay in it and you're going to find yourself getting angrier and angrier and more and more determined to get at the core of the problem.

This is always the hassle. Because I went to college and went through the whole intellectualizing process I find myself constantly wondering whether the truth that I'm seeing is the whole truth, always wondering about the other side. I used to be so much like that I could not *act*. You get to the point where you think you just have to sort of plunge in and say maybe I'm wrong but I cannot sit on the fence forever so I'm going to act on what seems rightest to me at this point in time. If it turns out that I'm wrong, OK, I was wrong; big deal, I'll change my course of action. But I'm not going to sit on the fence and not act because of a small possibility that I may be making the wrong decision. That's your intellectual trip, and it's no longer my trip. *Today, the way you live your life is a political act.*

I probably counsel twenty people a week, and my main concern when I'm counseling is to make sure that the guy that's up here is aware of what kind of decision he's making, to make sure that he's ready to make it, that he knows what he's talking about, that he knows all the alternatives, other alternatives, that he's ready to make the leap he thinks he's ready to make. Now a good part of the time, that involves saying, look, you've got many alternatives, you've not been inducted yet, why don't you go home, there are a number of appeals you can make. Are you aware of what it's like to try and make it on your own here? Canada is not the only alternative, and, as a matter of fact, it should be the last one because it's a fairly final decision.

Also, I can point out the culture shock. People don't think there is one, but there is; there's a difference. And then of course establishing the kind of rapport which will make it possible for the guy to be honest enough and then if he has any real problems they will come out. Once it seems apparent that he is going to stay, then comes the practical thing, how to go about it, and my speciality at the office is helping him find a job. He then goes to someone else for border counseling. Once he's been landed, in essence, we kick him out of the nest which makes a lot of people say that TADP is cold. But at that point he has as much chance to survive as anyone else in Canada. And that's really all the counseling involves, but you realize nobody is routine. It's a constant job. Each person presents a different problem. Sometimes they've been busted in the States which means they can't become landed—even for a possession charge. The saddest situation is when you're talking to someone whom you realize can't get landed. He doesn't know it yet, and he comes up and says, oh, by the way, I've got a record for such and such; and you know that's gonna keep him out of Canada. One gets the idea that they're going to stay anyway. They're not going to go back to the U.S. and jail.

We're getting more deserters now and they're a very different kind of people. The only problem this is causing is with Canadian public opinion—Canadians were very happy to get the American brain-drain, going the other way for a change, having all these nice bright college-educated Americans coming to Canada. But all of a sudden they're realizing that a lot of those Americans who are coming now have a grade-ten education and no skills and are taking jobs away from blue-collar Canadians. It's harder to get jobs for these guys. They're really refugees. Some of them aren't even old enough to get landed—they're under eighteen.

The beauty of the dodgers and deserters, even the totally apolitical, is that at some point it occurred to them that they didn't have to do what they were told, and that's a beginning. The deserters particularly are terrified, really paranoid; they're really afraid, and they can't believe that they're not going to be chased by the police for the rest of their lives. At least twice a day there'll be someone in my office and he will say—he's afraid to say it because he feels almost silly and yet he's got to say it—"Which name should I use?" and I'll say, well, what's your name? And he'll say, "Well, you see, I've got two sets of identification." and I'll say, what's your name? OK, that's who you are, right? "Yeah, I know, but isn't anyone going to? . . ." And I'll say, no, you haven't broken any laws here, no one is going to hassle you. You are a legal person. And it's so beautiful—that's the best part of my job—to see the look on that guy's face, there's just this incredible disbelief and relief, and he says, "No shit! You mean I could, like, get a social security number? And I can do anything I want?" And I say sure, and it's just beautiful. Those are the nicest moments, and it happens at least twice a day, usually more than that, when you talk to a guy who honestly can't believe that he is free.

If you present this idea of going back to the dodgers, if you say, "Don't you want to help screw up the draft system so that other people won't have to go?'' it goes like water off a duck's back in most cases.* I always present it, but I had a real struggle between being political and being honest. I wanted very often to say, oh, by the way, if you go and do this, or if anyone did this there wouldn't be a draft, and you wouldn't have to be coming up here in the first place—that would be in the back of my mind. And sometimes I felt that I should say it. But I *always* say, when the time comes and you no longer have any alternatives, come up. I *never* say, why don't you go home and be a revolutionary. How *can* I say that? I'm an American living in Canada. Why don't *I* go back? Why doesn't anybody? We're individuals.

Counseling itself is no longer satisfying my need to do something political, and that's the problem with everyone at TADP, particularly since the Montreal Conference. We'd been asking the question for some time before the conference—are we or are we not political? are we related to America and Americans and the movement or just to whatever poor unfortunates the world may hand us? what is this all about? Most of the people have felt very strongly that they weren't doing anything political by counseling *en masse* and felt a very strong need to do something that was more positive toward the situation *down there* because we were becoming more aware of the fact that the situation there was worse than people thought three years ago. But then, can one do anything within the confines of the TADP which was set up as an aid organization and which, for example, is getting money from the churches? How do you do that? The solution for most people was to quit when they got to that point and get into something they thought was more political, more active. However, at the Montreal Conference we were reminded very strongly that we, in our own way, as an organization could do a great deal to help. We were feeling very guilty, as a matter of fact, about the

*Because of the large number of American war resisters residing in Canada and the serious unemployment problem besetting the country, most exile aid groups were encouraging draft resisters by 1970 to return to the U.S. if possible, explaining to them that deserters now have first priority. A deserter is automatically a fugitive, while draft resisters only receive that status following indictment, and indictments for draft evasion in the U.S. were in some areas running two and three years behind induction refusal. This policy of dissuading draft resisters from choosing Canada also fulfilled a secondary political thrust which was to encourage young men to fight their induction in court, thereby increasing the backlog of draft cases to an even greater degree. Ultimately the system would become inoperable.

fact that we weren't doing more, but the Americans who came up to the conference like Oglesby and Hayden made us feel less guilty by pointing out in what way we could help. They pointed out that we can help by just making guys aware that they are not doing anything political by simply coming up here. You see a lot of people up here, and they think they're just incredible, they think, "Oh boy, I've done this incredible political act. Here I am." And they expect the red carpet to be rolled out. In fact, all they're doing is leaving the U.S. and making it easier for the establishment to function with less opposition. If the opposition all leaves the country, then you don't have any opposition. What Nixon really wants is for you to get out of the country so he doesn't have to bother with you. Now when you present that to people, it really surprises them to a great extent, when they see it; but then only those that are politically minded, who have a *political* conscience, have second thoughts about coming here. But I don't think that everyone is geared to be a political human being. I'm just talking about those people who *are* geared that way who didn't realize that they were doing the administration a favor. But who wants to change people who don't think that way? People are individuals.

After all this is said, in the case of the deserter it doesn't make any difference what his motivations are. He has no other alternatives. He's doing his job by deserting. *That* is a political act. Now in the case of the dodger— when I get some guy up here who's got ten thousand dollars, a B.A.—it really becomes frustrating. We're working our guts out for fifty dollars a week, and then we get some person like this who loves to *act* political and talk about how terrible things are in the U.S., and you know they really don't give a damn. But you have to realize that we're in it up to our necks. Our perspective is altered. I try very hard not to let this frustration out on the guy, but I can't deny the feeling of just meeting so many intelligent young minds who not only don't know what's happening in the U.S. but who really don't care. I refuse to play god so I talk to them. Changing people is a pretty heavy job, and I don't really think I'm capable of it.

People in Canada who object to our constant talk of revolution are thinking still of a different kind of revolution than the way I think of it. I'm thinking of a mind revolution that will probably happen almost at the same time in all the western countries—there's a certain type of mind that is becoming obsolete, and that type of mind had better realize that it is being threatened now. My concept of the revolution is that, simply, a human being has got to free himself from the kinds of fears, hangups, and binds that make it impossible for him to make his own decisions. And once you've freed yourself, you're a revolutionary, and everyone you run into is influenced—I believe freedom is quite contagious. The antidraft movement has been a contagious kind of thing, thousands of guys deciding to free themselves; like the deserters now coming to Canada, they are making a revolution in their own minds because they have freed themselves from bondage. But I also believe that real freedom is the most difficult thing to achieve. I think that the kind of peace and happiness that comes from working through the processes of freeing yourself is somehow apparent in the human beings that you talk to, and that's what makes it contagious. You want to know what makes this person so able to look you in the eye; what makes his voice tone so calm. Healthy vibrations. I know that is the kind of thing that drew me in, somehow sensing that whatever it was that was coming at me from the people who were radicals or whatever was somehow honest and calm and sure. There's such a certainty. People don't need to get into ideological arguments —there's such a peace. I don't think the radicals *hate* anyone who is in the establishment; I think it's a matter of honestly not being able to believe that these people can still be where they are mentally. I think there's a tremendous feeling of pity, a tremendous desire to bring them across the line. And the difference it seems to me between the new type of revolution and the new type of revolutionaries and the other type of living is a lack of fear. It is to be unafraid that is to be alive.

I've been back to the U.S. three times. I was raised in New York City, and I thought of myself as a New Yorker for so long that it is hard to come back to that city and see the changes that have occurred since I left. Is it New York which has changed, or is it me? Something has happened. I can't believe that human beings will stand for what New Yorkers stand for and not shout. How they have been pacified is completely beyond. It's as if everyone in New York has become numb. I really believe the city is grinding to a halt. After being away and coming back you can see the breakdown of the whole system, that nothing's working. And nobody's screaming. They've lived this for so long that they believe that this is the reality, that this is the way life has to be, that they can't rise above it. I get deeply depressed. I saw so few bright faces. The only happy, good faces I saw were the Black Panthers who were selling their paper and buttons on the street corner—they were realizing that there was another way. One of the things that impressed me about New York, however, was that people were talking to each other on the streets. I didn't find it so cold as it once was. Everyone wants to talk to you, to each other, but I think it's a little like a concentration camp where people huddle together.

It was strange 'cause I was also frightened there which I'm not in Toronto. I was afraid to walk down a dark street. I was afraid of the hostilities. Also, I feel comfortable wearing absolutely anything here in Toronto. I can walk down the street in a dress that is absolutely see-through, and nobody will turn around. 'Cause I feel like dressing that way and that's cool with them. You can't do that in New York. It's like waving a red flag in front of a bull. If you wear a see-through blouse in New York and you walk down the street, what you'll invite is rape. And you'd be a fool to do it. You are *not* free in New York to wear what you want. Women dress very conservatively there; they're very uptight. I couldn't wear half the clothes I brought down with me, and none of them were very "shocking." I'd put a skirt on, and suddenly it would seem so short, whereas it didn't seem short in Toronto at all. It really surprised me. I mean I'm really free in Toronto.

There's a hopelessness in New York. We saw old men falling off park benches like in Allen Ginsberg's poem about old men dying in the parks. Well, it's true. Watching men literally falling off benches with cuts all over their faces—we saw that! And no one seems to care, or maybe they care but there is nothing they can do—it's a sense of hopelessness. It's that incredible feeling that fate is larger than man. And then on the same streets are people in these fashionable restaurants spending hundreds of dollars a night—they don't want to look. We walked into one restaurant and had to walk right out again; it was so disgustingly vulgar. Lavish food, people dressed in the latest chic fashions, very expensive, and then just down the street are these bums, sores all over their bodies, lost, sick.

Right now I'm really becoming more and more convinced that the situation in the U.S. is incredibly frightening. Because I came from an immigrant family that was grateful to be in the U.S., because I was the first

American born in the U.S. in my family, and because I grew up being told what a privilege it was to be an American, when *I* said, I pledge allegiance, my heart would palpitate; I was really into it. I could never see that flag waving without feeling some very strong emotions. And now, you know, I go to New York, and I see the flag pasted on the helmet of a construction worker who I'm terrified of because I'm walking down the street with a guy who has long hair and I get the feeling that if we turned the corner he could get beaten up—suddenly the American flag has become a symbol of everything that I despise.

My father is a Russian Jew; my mother came from the free city of Danzig. They left through Germany in 1939—my mother had been in a concentration camp. My mother would always say to me—but she said it for the wrong reasons, so I would stay among Jewish people—she would say, "When I was a teenager in Germany I felt every bit as secure as you feel now. My friends were not Jewish; I believed that the government was democratic; I believed that I was a free human being. If anyone had told me that things were going to happen as they happened, I would have left." Actually, what she was telling me was: you never know; you can really feel that you're in a democratic situation, but you never really know when one way or another your circumstances may change completely. So I never felt as secure as a lot of people did 'cause I had always had this feeling that even in America it *could* happen.

EIGHT

Vietnam Veterans

The words of an average Vietnam veteran as he denounces the war and American militarism weigh much heavier as an indictment of the U.S. than all the great tomes by Noam Chomsky or Bernard Fall or David Halberstam. After a few months of combat he has usually arrived at the same conclusions about the nature of American imperialism as those reached by the outspoken journalists and angered academicians after years of study. He has done it without listening to Radio Hanoi, without reading Marx or Ho Chi Minh, without hearing the impassioned speeches of movement leaders, but by simply observing the armed forces of the United States in action in Southeast Asia. He watches the air strikes, hears the B-52s, sees the results of the round-the-clock artillery fire, feels the agony of the villagers, flinches at the torture of a boyish NVA (North Vietnamese Army) prisoner by an American captain, smells the smoke from a freshly burnt village and talks with any English-speaking Vietnamese he can find. As one deserter in Canada put it:

> I started sneaking off-limits and going into the villages at night and talking to the Vietnamese people to find out what was going on. They always greeted us with open arms 'cause we never took weapons out there. They were beautiful people. I was introduced to VC and they were beautiful people too. And we'd sit and talk for hours and they explained how they thought about the war and I started to realize I felt like a British soldier and these were the liberty boys of 1776.

When a GI in Vietnam begins to analyze the war in the same terms as the antiwar professors and journalists (who do not have to fight it), he is ultimately faced with the predicament of what to do—he is on the front lines of a war he knows is wrong. He is killing for no purpose and he chances to die for no purpose. Caught in that position, no man has a greater reason to refuse to fight; the draft dodger's opposition pales by comparison. If this war has produced any heroes at all—if the antiwar forces have produced any heroes—they are the combat infantrymen, both enlisted men and draftees, who have left the war at the front lines, refusing to participate any more in the killing of Vietnamese people. It is not stretching a moral point nor indulging in impossible analogies to compare them to German soldiers who might have left the Waffen SS after Lidice, or who might have deserted their units during the blitz of the Warsaw ghetto.

How many men have done this? Judging from the number of men in Canada who deserted from the front, there are many (not counting other Vietnam veterans of which there may be three to four thousand in Canada). One can meet them every day in the large Canadian cities. There must be many more that one never meets. There must be a great many more who have chosen to remain underground in the United States. The Japanese Beheiren has hundreds of combat veterans living with Japanese families, waiting for some means by which they can make their way to Canada or Sweden. There are over two thousand deserters living underground in Saigon, mostly infantrymen.* And there is the occasional GI who chooses to fight with the other side.

Thanks to the army's own policies, it has been fairly easy to desert from the front lines in Vietnam. All one had to do was reenlist and one was automatically pulled out of combat and given a thirty-day leave and a bonus in pay. After exceptionally heavy engagements, the recruiting officers would be the first people to

---

*Author's note: I gathered these approximate figures of the number of deserters in Saigon from military police. I also witnessed a number of infantrymen, most of them black, being escorted to the Long Binh stockade for refusing to return to combat.

greet the returning unit, often flying out to the firebase to see how many men now felt that four more years in the army would be better than another week of combat. It is hard to believe that any army could use such cynical recruitment tactics. At any rate, for many GIs this was too tempting to resist (the army ended this practice in the spring of 1970 but replaced it with something better; providing two-week "holidays" in the U.S. to Vietnam GIs). The other method was to wait for Rest and Recuperation, sign up for Hawaii, buy a ticket to the mainland, then scrounge some money and hitch to Canada. And, of course, thousands of deserters made their decision to desert while in combat but waited for their rotation back to the States before leaving.

Oddly enough, in almost every case of front-line desertion that one encounters, it was not a question of the individual fearing for his own life that prompted it, but a concern over what he was doing and what he had seen. Deserters have run for their skins in every war when faced with odds in favor of being killed, but this has not been the case in Vietnam because the odds of being killed spread over a year of "humping" in the field are not very great in comparison to the big battles in other wars. Helicopter pilots have a greater attrition rate than infantrymen. Also, despite terrible morale and a serious discipline problem among front-line GIs, within the infantry companies in Vietnam there has existed a powerful camaraderie instilled by the unique fraternity of a combat assignment. Men who hated the war yet had experienced combat felt closest to men who wore the Combat Infantryman's badge; it distinguished them from those for whom duty in Vietnam meant typing in an air-conditioned bunker; one had at least seen something of life. And of death. So for an individual to fear only for his own life was to break with that comradeship. Moreover, when the entire unit hated the war, hated combat, and tried as a unit to avoid contact and firefights, trying to save one's own skin would be tinged with plain cowardice. But a moral consideration set one apart. It was true that not every GI objected to the barbarous crimes he was forced to perpetrate. But some did. Some would not go along. And thus it was usually GIs who had witnessed a particular atrocity who later decided they could no longer serve; knowing the war was wrong but serving anyway was not enough—not when one finally learned just how wrong it was. There are atrocities in all wars but the tolerance level for them in this war was not high enough for people who had seen them to accept them.

With the revelation of My Lai 4, many Vietnam veterans in both the U.S. and Canada decided it would, at last, be of some use to bear witness to their experiences in Vietnam and many came forward to do that. GIs all over the States held press conferences to help prove that the perpetration of war crimes in Vietnam was Standard Operating Procedure for many units, even whole divisions. A GI war crimes committee was started at Fort Benning, Georgia but was quickly suppressed. Many other GIs and ex-GIs were intimidated from saying anything by fear of prosecution. Among the Vietnam veterans in Canada, however, there was no such fear, and a number of press conferences were held in Montreal and Toronto where it was clearly stated that prisoner torture, throwing prisoners from helicopters, shooting prisoners, and shooting civilians including women, children, and old men was consistent, de facto policy among the front-line units in Vietnam.

In Montreal, former 1st Infantry Division medic, Jim Weeks, who helped Private Bruce Peterson put out the *Fatigue Press* at Fort Hood following a year's combat experience and who deserted after being ordered back to Vietnam for engaging in antiwar activities, told of his company tripping a Claymore mine on fourteen school children who walked by their outpost one morning. All were killed and Weeks had to load their shattered bodies on the helicopters—he never forgot it. No one was ever held accountable. Weeks reported, "We used to go into Vietnamese villages and disobey direct orders not to help these Vietnamese villagers—we were supposed to work only on our unit. Officers told us explicitly, You're not to treat gooks . . . This gook business inflames the black GIs. They can see very easily what is happening to their people in the States and what is happening to the Vietnamese."

Weeks, one of the original founders of the Montreal ADC, read American news reports of a particular operation and then read reports of the same operation by Australian journalist, Wilfrid Burchette, sent to him from a friend in the U.S., "Burchette was traveling with the VC, and he, not our reporters, was telling the truth. I was in those operations, and I know what happened, and only Burchette reported it." Weeks had an opportunity to meet Burchette in Paris in December 1969, when he represented the American Deserters' Committee at one of Sartre's war crime hearings.

Another deserter, John McCullough, described army interrogation procedures:

> First, prisoners are interrogated by GIs. The guys try to talk to them normally, tell them not to be afraid, they're not going to get hurt. Then the officers say, "Why are you treating them this way. Get out of here. You're not doing any good." If they don't talk after the officers have worked on them, the captain will tell you to shoot them.

Twenty-one-year-old William Whitmeyer, a good-looking Californian who had served with the 172nd Armored Regiment—"which isn't exactly known for its humanitarian activities"—was outraged by the "standard procedure of killing Vietnamese civilians" and he deserted immediately after returning to stateside duty and promptly joined the Young Socialist Alliance, later emigrating to Canada with his young wife. His tank crew had participated in mowing down twelve Vietnamese villagers, all over sixty, including several women: "No one had to answer for it. I never heard any more about it, except in the *Stars and Stripes* I read that the 69th Armored near Bong Son had killed twelve VC. The officers thought it had been a good way to release tension and get some kills. They were always pushing our unit for kills, more kills." A marine deserter talked about watching U.S. jets put napalm on a village across the road from his platoon's outpost.

I don't know why they did it. We'd been working in that village doing pacification work. I was part of a medical team and we'd been helping people in that village. After the strike we went into the village with two trucks and found about seventy or eighty badly-wounded Vietnamese and about fifteen people dead. We loaded 'em onto our trucks and drove them down to Dong Ha and the medical officers wouldn't treat them. *They wouldn't treat Vietnamese people.* They said they needed the facilities for American boys yet there weren't any American wounded coming in. So we had to drive them all the way down to Da Nang, about a hundred miles. About ten people died on the way. This is against humanity, this insanity, it's all against the natural flow of energy. I decided I didn't want to have anything more to do with it and that I could serve mankind in a better way.

Jerry Samuels (a pseudonym) organized the Toronto press conferences. His personal participation in atrocities in Vietnam caused him to change his mind about the war. He felt he was going insane thinking about what he had done, and tried to get out of combat but was repeatedly sent back to the front lines. He finally reenlisted and took his thirty-day leave—thirty days plus a lifetime in Canada. He feels a private guilt for his actions in Vietnam, but does not entirely accept the blame. In his words:

It's almost the picture of some guy walking up to some innocent kid and manipulating his patriotism, whatever feelings he has, manipulating them, twisting them, making him commit a crime, somehow enticing him, fooling him, fooling him into thinking that if he commits a certain crime or if he does this certain thing that is a crime but we won't call it a crime that he'll be rewarded and people will be proud of him for it. So the kid commits the crime, but the guy who's twisted him is really the one to blame.

After arriving in Canada, Samuels joined the staff of the newly-formed Toronto American Deserters' Committee and also began collecting documentation of atrocities from other Vietnam veterans for the Citizens' Commission of Inquiry into War Crimes in Vietnam headquartered in Boston. He believes, perhaps naively, that it will do some good to help make the American people aware of what has really been happening in Vietnam these past six years. Samuels quit high school after the tenth grade but he is better educated than a lot of people about the American reality. He has a machinist's license, and there is work when he needs it, but he spends most of his time reading philosophy, political works, Marx and Lenin. He lives with a Canadian girl, a dental assistant, and shares a large apartment with a draft resister and his girl, a Canadian who teaches retarded children. He plans to continue collecting all the testimony he can about war crimes for the Citizens' Commission. Like many of the exiles, his original activist zeal may wane, but the revolutionary spirit within him never will. Jerry Samuels is a changed man.

I was born twenty-four years ago in Los Angeles. My folks split up when I was four or five and from the time I was four until the time I was seventeen I was in foster homes. I was kind of rowdy when I was a kid, kind of incorrigible. At sixteen I got an apartment with a friend and worked at a car wash. I dropped out of high school after the tenth grade. When I was seventeen I enlisted in the Marine Corps just out of desperation. I lasted seven months and then got a medical discharge because of a heart problem I had and pains in the chest. I was still seventeen. That kind of broke me up a bit. I felt like a real failure. I went back to work and became a machinist and got pretty good at it and was making pretty good money. I got a class B machinist's license which is worth three-fifty—four dollars an hour. I got married when I was nineteen to a chick who had just come to California from Detroit. Then marital difficulties ensued, and we decided that maybe we should be separated a while. I decided to join the army. It took me about two months to appeal my draft status which was 1-Y after having been discharged from the marines as medically unfit. I appealed to get into the army. I was red, white, and blue all the way. It really made me mad to see these war statistics—two, three hundred guys getting killed every week and people protesting this war. Of course I was anticommunist. It was a really patriotic thing coupled with the marital difficulties that I was trying to run away from. So I finally got into the army. I was twenty-two. After the basic training and radio teletype school I got orders for Vietnam. I really wanted to go to Vietnam.

When I was growing up, my father was a bad guy as far as all my foster parents were concerned. Social workers had the same attitude. My father was so hung up on my mother that ever since their divorce, for twenty years now, he's been living in the same little room in Los Angeles and driving a taxi cab and taking home his sixty or seventy bucks a week—doesn't have anything. He just isolated himself like that over grief over losing his wife, my mother. I hadn't seen him for three years. Finally, I went to him for help. I was going to get thrown in jail for a traffic citation which I wouldn't pay. He told me to pay it, in fact he helped me pay it. So, he sensed a kind of father-son thing that could possibly happen. We assumed that he and I could have a relationship, and he didn't want to lose me. He didn't want me to go into the army and when I did and got orders for Vietnam he wanted me to desert. He begged me not to go. I thought he was crazy, man. I practically spit in his face for telling me to desert. I said what are you, some kind of a commie bastard, really. He's just against war, he's a real pacifist type.

When I came back from Vietnam and I told him what happened there and I started crying; then his tears started and we cried on each other's shoulders—for the first time we were close. He didn't want to lose me, but now I was a deserter and had to come to Canada. I told him to come to Canada with me, to move up here. But he chose not to come 'cause he didn't want to interfere with my life or be an authority over me in any way. He wanted so bad to have someone to live with, to be with, yet he gave that up so that I could be a total one-hundred-percent free person. I begged with him, pleaded with him, to at least come up here for a visit. But he doesn't want to interfere with my life.

On my twenty-third birthday I set foot in Vietnam. I was assigned to the 65th Engineers Battalion whose base camp is at Cu Chi, the 25th Division. I carried a radio for the company. I was assigned to the communications bunker—we had the network control station. I was a radio teletype operator; I did a lot of cryptographic work, a lot of code. I was in the bunker for the first three months except for a couple of body count sweeps around the camp perimeter. Later, I went out a lot with all kinds of patrols, company, platoon, squad-sized patrols. Part of our battalion was at Cu Chi—my company, headquarters company—and part of it was in Tay Ninh so I went back and forth a lot. I legged it a lot like a regular infantryman—the 65th Engineers is nothing but a glorified infantry battalion.* I pulled a lot of bunker guard. I had a secret security clearance so I had a little priority and didn't have to pull any dirty jobs. The first five months I was there it went pretty well. Things got kind of different in my head the first time I saw napalm. I didn't see it being used, we just had to do the body count afterward. This was at the base of Nui Ba Dinh, the big mountain in Tay Ninh province. It looked pretty bad, you know, there were a lot of little kids burned and pretty well messed up. I don't know; I didn't consciously think anything, like wow, Uncle Sam is a sonofabitch, or anything like that. But I think it was a subconscious or unconscious type of thing that said Uncle Sam isn't supposed to burn babies or, golly, this is what it looked like in the old films of the Nazi thing. I didn't really scratch my head and say, I want out of this, but it was a kind of doubt that set in.

Up on Nui Ba Dinh I finally got hit in the head with a little bit of shrapnel. We got a ground attack there through the fog in the middle of the night. I got hit and I got sent to Cam Ranh Bay hospital. I was there for almost two weeks. There, I got a letter from my wife, the first letter I'd gotten in Vietnam. She had got a letter from the Department of the Army saying I'd been wounded, she was listed as next of kin. Believe it or not, her letter was only concerned with one thing and that was the benefits of the insurance policy in the event of my death or disablement. I knew I had to give up on her now 'cause she didn't think anything about me. Let me tell you, that really broke me up bad. I got a really gung ho feeling after that. I wanted to go out and really do my thing—this was a conscious thing. I decided, fuck the world! army all the way!

I finally got back to my unit and we went out on what was supposed to be a seventy-two-hour patrol and we ended up being out thirty-one days. Thirty-one days in the field, skirting Nui Ba Dinh, into Cambodia a couple of

---

*Author's note: In Vietnam I witnessed the total destruction of a village of five thousand persons by the 65th Engineers which blasted and bulldozed it into extinction. No camp was set up for the refugees; no reparations were made. It was done to provide an alternate convoy route between Cu Chi and Trang Bang village which lies on the main highway to Tay Ninh. See "The Destruction of An Thinh" by Roger Williams, *Ramparts*, May 1969.

times, made contact a lot, saw a lot of guys get messed up, killed. One time we went into this village that was south of Tay Ninh, not far from the Cambodian border, in the parrot's beak. There was a second louie there and he had this thing about treating everyone as if they were VC. It was a free-fire zone and the way we were pushing and slapping people around . . . I was doing it too . . . every once in a while a burst would go off and a Vietnamese would go down, and the way that was going on, it really started the wheels turning. I started thinking. Again, this thing about the Nazis came back. I felt like a real Nazi. I felt like a criminal, consciously.

A guy feels guilty when he watches anyone being slapped around by somebody bigger, you feel guilty until you're doing it yourself and then you get involved with it. Sometimes you get outraged and you start kicking and slapping and punching at this little guy. But when you turn a burst on this guy, when you spray him a couple of times and you see him drop dead, there's an instantaneous feeling of satisfaction, then there's a feeling of doubt about yourself. And in order to justify what you've done you've got to do it again. You've got to keep doing it. This is how I felt, looking back at it.

So we went into this village, and we were herding these people into one corner of the village. It was obviously a friendly village 'cause it had wire set up around it, American-made razor wire on the perimeter. Man, we went into that village and we were dragging the people kicking and screaming into this one corner of the village [for interrogation]. All of a sudden it was mayhem; there was no order at all; it was just a sudden thing of, wow! man, these people are resisting. Bursts went off; people hit the ground; GIs were firing into the crowd of people now and then, and there was yelling and screaming and biting and kicking. Yes, there were pregnant women, kids. I was having trouble with these two boys about fourteen or fifteen, trying to get them into the crowd, and finally I shouldered them into the crowd and kind of lost sight of them. I was so pissed off at them as they'd been kicking me in the stomach and biting me that I unslung my weapon and fired a burst into the crowd. About four people dropped. I let off about eight rounds, a two- or three-second burst. Instantly, I felt shitty. But I was still pissed off at these people, they were almost fighting us and I heard the sergeants yelling, "Vietcong bastards! You little motherfucking commie gooks!"—I pictured them as the enemy. Finally, things started calming down after about two hours of this bullshit, laying people on the ground, standing on their backs, slapping them around. Things calmed down, and me and one of the buck sergeants and two other guys took these four chicks in the elephant grass outside the perimeter, and we were all fooling around. We balled these chicks. They were forcibly willing—they'd rather do that than get shot. Then one of the girls yelled some derogatory thing at the guy who'd balled her, in Vietnamese, but he knew what it meant. He just reached down for his weapon and blew her away. Well, right away, the other three guys who were there, including myself, picked up our weapons and blew away the other three chicks. Just like that. It was just a spontaneous, instantaneous type thing. The first word that entered my mind was murder. I thought I was going to get in trouble for it, but I didn't. You know something? I was disappointed, man, I wanted some kind of bolt of lightning to come out of the sky with Uncle Sam stamped on it and strike me down. But there was no punishment; there were no second thoughts about it except that me and this other guy—one of the other three guys—we got high together in the bunker a lot, and we talked about it a lot and why we did it. The thing we couldn't understand was that when this other guy shot the first chick, we just picked up our weapons without giving it a second thought and fired up the rest. This all came at the time when I was into being a foot soldier, a leg, really gung ho.

As for why this Nazi thing occurs, shooting down unarmed civilians, torturing prisoners, and so on, I've tried to figure it out psychologically, socially, spiritually, the whole bit, but all I can come up with is that there is a thing about a man holding a weapon over somebody smaller, taking another person's life in his own hands. Whether it's a basic human trait, I don't know. Whether it's the result of a violent society, I don't know; all I can tell you is how I felt. There is a certain amount of satisfaction in killing somebody— everybody knows that. This little gook is out there shooting at you, he's the enemy, OK? Now, in Vietnam you identify every gook with the enemy, unless it's some broad you're laying in Vung Tau or Saigon. You feel it's their fault we're there. If it weren't for the Vietnamese, we wouldn't be there. It's hard to explain, but all I can remember is the temporary satisfaction of defeating something, of making a conquest type thing. It's not an enormous, fantastic, majestic thing at all; it's just a way of life that allows you to have the satisfaction of holding the power of life and death over somebody for the year that you're there. Why do people join the police force? Why are there lifers in the army? Why do people extend their tour of duty in Vietnam?

As for the tremendous pressures a guy's under being the reason that GIs do these things—well, it's true, but it's more of an excuse; it's the thing that allows it to happen. You can assume, especially in a free-fire zone, that you can fire on anything that moves. Now there are some officers that will say, naughty, naughty, you will get an Article 15 for that, or you will be court-martialed for that, but it never happens. When it does happen, it really makes the news and makes it big, so it looks like an isolated incident and that the person responsible is being punished accordingly. Believe it or not, there're a lot of young officers, especially a lot out of ROTC, who really preach against the genocidal thing. The old World War II veteran, NCOs, first sergeants, or the old-timer major himself is the guy who will say, "I want kills. I want them gooks to be wiped out. I want to see you guys come back with kills." You know, this type of thing when they're prepping you for a patrol. It's the patriotism, the World War II type of patriotism that is no longer valid in Vietnam—it's not even valid in the States anymore. They still feel this red, white, and blue patriot sort of thing, and they say, "They're commie bastards, so let's wipe them out so San Francisco won't be overrun."

They don't differentiate between VC or civilians. When those body counts come in—like I say, I was a radio operator and I had to call in body counts—those body counts come in and everybody who was killed in a village, civilian, or otherwise, is VC body count. Men, women, and children, the whole bit. If there's an airstrike on a village and it's wiped out, if three hundred people lived in the village, it's VC body count. If there's, say, a U.S. patrol out, a company patrol, and they make contact with two snipers and they end up blowing away the whole village, it's written up in the *Stars and Stripes* as an engagement between a three hundred-man VC outfit and an American company with maybe one U.S. wounded and three hundred "enemy" dead.

Killing gooks is a way to release a lot of pent-up feelings. Psychologists might tell you every time you kill a gook you're killing authority or something like this. I don't know; those gooks didn't look very authoritarian to me. But I felt the animalism come out in me nevertheless. It just comes out when you're in the field. I've always been self-conscious, simply because of my background, shifting from one place to another, wondering why I wasn't stable, you know. So in Vietnam I was always trying to figure out why I was doing what I was doing. It was so easy to use the excuse of being an American and having the right to do it—it's so easy to do that. When you're walking through that stinking, hot jungle with this M-16, all this power all over your body, all this ammo and stuff, it's almost a god-like thing. Sure you get scared, that little gook is out to get you; he wants to mess you up, and this justifies it even more—he's a dirty commie bastard. This feeling of justification carries over to all gooks, I mean Vietnamese, when you're going through a village and pushing people around during the prisoner interrogation thing. It carries over. But scales were tilted when you see babies, young children blown to pieces, or burned by American napalm.

We used to do a lot of Personnel Damage Assessment [PDA]. You go to the area where the napalm struck and you do the body count—of course you're always on the lookout for any kind of contact. Anyway, we went into this village and I was assigned the detail to get a couple of Vietnamese together and bury the bodies. There were all kinds of burned bodies, of all sizes and sexes. Burying the little children and all got to me, I got pretty emotional about it. There were only a few hootches that were untouched; I guess there had been a total of fifteen or twenty hootches in the whole village—about a total of two hundred people lived there. The body count was 88 VC. Even in the *Stars and Stripes* they had the audacity to print the same body count, "88 VC." You read it; you halfway believe it—you spend more time staring at the pin-up they have on the back page instead of reading the article.

In another village, in Cambodia, near the Vietnamese border, we were taken in by big Chinooks for PDA. There was an elementary type school there that had been hit by napalm and was partially burned. It was a strike on an elementary school and the outskirts of the village. In the school a fire had swept through it and the children or what was left of them were still sitting at their desks, burned, like the kids had just died in their place, they were just sitting there dead. There were a lot of adults in the village too, civilians, all dead. What got the wheels turning upstairs was that the 5th Mobile Strike Force, Special Forces, was just entering this area as we were completing our body count. They were there with press people, Americans, and the Special

Forces were proceeding to rebuild things and do a lot of nice, wonderful things while the press was there. We weren't allowed to talk to the press or the Special Forces people, that was out of bounds. Now this came out in the *Stars and Stripes*—I don't know why so late but almost a month after—but it said that the NVA had completely massacred a village which was "common procedure for the NVA," naturally, and Special Forces had moved in to help out and rebuild the village and they were trying to find this NVA outfit that had done this. It was clearly, when we went there two days before the Special Forces, a napalm strike. I never heard of the NVA or VC having napalm. *It was a napalm strike by U.S. jets, man.* It's the simplest thing in the world to tell the difference between flame throwers, which the paper said the NVA had used on the village, and napalm. Because when napalm is through burning it is still hanging around; it looks like snot hanging from the trees. We had to clean up the napalm that was left and clean up the bodies and then, as we were burying some of the bodies the second day, the press was brought in to take pictures. If any of the GIs were seen going near one of the reporters, he was shouted at by one of the sergeants. All the while the Green Berets showed the press people the school building and the destruction. The whole thing really touched me; it really got to me. This was a Nazi thing as far as I was concerned.

The GI in the field, the average soldier in Nam, is there as an American. He's not there as Joe Blow from St. Louis. He's there as an American, wearing an American uniform, and he's got the right to kill gooks 'cause he's an American. We've got the right to have bases in Germany, in Korea, in Japan, and everywhere else because we're Americans, man, and we're protecting the world. But that individual son of a gun if he's got any kind of conscious, humane feelings at all—and usually it's a black guy—he is gonna really say, fuck it, it's a racist thing; it's genocide. Something I noticed . . . the vast majority of GIs over there when they're going through a friendly village they get a kick out of throwing a can of C-rations or candy or something into a crowd of little kids and watch them scramble for it. You know who won't do that? The black guys won't do that. The Puerto Ricans won't do it. Any of these guys who've been oppressed at home won't do it; they can feel kind of unconsciously the way these kids feel, and they won't do it. And they'll cuss out whitey for doing it. On another operation, I think it was in Cambodia, we saw this little girl who had somehow lost all her fingers and they were bandaged up with blood coming through the bandages. She was standing there trying to hold her damn rice bowl. I really got emotional about it; me and this other guy, this buck sergeant, a black guy about six foot five, real big guy, got to crying about it. He started crying and that started me off. I had headaches for a long time after that just thinking about it.

I don't know . . . if a soldier can possibly make the connection that I made, seeing a buddy get shot up, the feeling for him, and then shooting up a Vietnamese unnecessarily, an unarmed civilian or something, and then thinking, wow! the grief I felt for my buddy and I was only his friend, and this Vietnamese man, this guy's got a family; he looks different, he's a little guy, he lives in a little village out in the sticks, but still man, he's a human being; then possibly, you get the feeling they have when they lose one of their relatives, or get the feeling of what it's like to be a prisoner and be interrogated by U.S. troops. I made the connection, and this thing really got me to thinking. The feelings I had snowballed so that I couldn't wait to get out of this shit, to turn my back on it, spit on it, and say the hell with it.

The thing of kicking around civilians a lot, of firing up civilians, really got to me. I went to mental hygiene at Cu Chi about six months after I got there and told them my head was getting pretty messed up. I was scared I was going to go completely insane, out of my mind. I was shook up, man. I went to mental hygiene feeling like a kid who's just done a very bad thing and I wanted them to either justify it or take me under their wing and tell me, yes, you are messed up and we'll see to it that it doesn't happen again. I wanted either this or I wanted them to justify it and show me it was the right thing to do. I was going batty. I was fantasizing the wrong things, having weird dreams, identifying with the wrong things. I tried mental hygiene 'cause I've never been a religious person. That failed, and I really felt alone, isolated, so I went to the chaplain—well, maybe God can help. That's just a big joke. So then I was just left with only one thing, myself, man, figuring it out, asking myself: am I going to identify with this killing? am I going to stay in it? am I going to keep it up? is this me? is this how I'm going to be? shall I be a part of this? I decided I wouldn't have worn a Nazi swastika, so what am I doing wearing the American eagle? It's doing the same thing—that thing really hit me hard. I had to make my choice, make my decision and carry it out and do it. It was an inability to relate to things going on around me—I wasn't rational anymore; I even stopped eating. I was fucked up.

I was changing, I could tell by looking at incidents that occurred even when I was at base camp. I had a different attitude toward the mamasans and papasans around the mess hall and around the shit bins—I looked at them like the enemy. I lost friends. I started smoking more grass—I wanted to get stoned and feeling good 'cause when I smoke pot I get on a laughing trip and that was a real escape, man. Then I made the big mistake of doing some speed. I got on this horrible trip of everyone in the world being against me—I was having fucking nightmares that I was being dismembered. It was guilt, I guess, more than anything else. I just wanted out of that; I didn't want to go crazy. I was already unstable because of the shifting around in my childhood and I'd found the army to cling to; I'd found a really groovy thing and that was great, man, the nation type crap. Now, all of a sudden, it was down; it was a lie; I couldn't even hang on to that anymore. I would rather—it really sounds trite—but I would rather, sincerely, have had both legs blown off than have had my head messed up as bad as it was. I feel sorry for every guy that had his head fucked up even one tenth as bad as mine. For every guy in the hospital crippled physically, there're two running around that'll never be the same again in the head, crippled mentally. And for every two of them, there're at least five hundred Indochinese people who are really in grief over severely wounded or dead relatives or friends.

At mental hygiene I dared not tell them how I felt about the war in general. I was talking to a major who was some sort of psychiatrist. He just gave me some pills to take to relax me and slapped me on the back and said not to worry about it, "son." So I went to the chaplain, a Presbyterian, and he just grinned. The whole time I was talking to him, tears streaming down my face, he just had this grin on his face and reassured me that I was doing what was right for my country. So finally, I opened up on him and told him I hated war, I hated him, I hated officers, I hated the whole bit. He said, "Relax, why don't you sit in the chapel awhile and figure yourself out"—let Jesus take care of it. So anyway, I went to my communications chief, a second lieutenant who was two years younger than me. I said, *Sir,* and I opened up on him. I told him everything. He was in ROTC, had been to college. He was generally a pretty cool guy. He knew a lot of the guys smoked pot, for example, but he didn't care; he didn't smoke it himself. He'd come in the communications bunker—we had incense burning in there a lot, we smoked a lot of grass in there—and he'd say, "Is there any writing on that cigarette paper? What brands are those?" He was just a college kid who was now in the army; he showed me a picture of his wife, and she looked like a hippie to me . . . I had been to see him before and he'd said I should play up the head wound, faint a lot. I said, I can't do that. He told me to go to mental hygiene some more. So after that didn't work I went to see him this time, and he said, "Well, have you thought about reenlisting?" I said, wow! Are you crazy, man? I called him man instead of sir. He says, "No, if you re-up you get a thirty-day leave and you can go to Sweden or maybe Canada." I took him up on it. I reenlisted the day after.

I didn't tell anyone about my plans. Except I did tell one guy whom I thought I could trust. But he told the section chief, a sergeant who was a speed freak by the way. All I could do was threaten him and I said, look man, don't go rapping to anyone about this; you do and I'm gonna tell 'em about all your speed. There was two months between the time I reenlisted and the time I got my leave, and I had to go out in the field a couple more times. It got to the point where out in the field I felt guilty about just being there. I felt guilty toward my buddies since while I was doing my job I wasn't sincere about it any more. I felt guilty because I still had to kill the enemy; I still had to protect myself; it was still combat. It was really an enormous relief to get on that plane and leave Vietnam; it really felt good. I went home, all the way home. I was thinking of just one thing, Sweden. My father was overjoyed. Then I went to the Los Angeles Resistance which I heard about through the *L.A. Free Press*, and they told me about Canada so here I am.

Something allowed this to happen, something is to blame. It's not the weapon, it's the ones who pull the trigger. And I believe that the army in Vietnam is the weapon, and the guys who are pulling the trigger are in Washington, the policy makers. The soldier is the weapon. I don't know if it's a cop-out or a justification thing, but I believe, or I try to believe, that the policy makers are to blame for allowing this to happen, or that there should be another Nuremberg for majors and above . . . But I don't know; I saw a lot of animalism in the field that was unfounded, a lot of "legs" who'd been out there for a long time sort of forgot about the world. All they think about is

Nam and their way of life there. And firing on a gook, man, is like firing on a dog or a pigeon. It's not murdering a person, that thought doesn't enter your head.

I guess it's only the higher officers and the generals and policy makers back in the States who are aware that this is a guerrilla war and that the only way you can win a guerrilla war is to kill everybody. So they have to try and do that legally. So they establish free-fire zones, they use napalm, they use antipersonnel devices that are so *illegal* it's pitiful, outlawed by the Geneva Conventions. They have some of the most incredible weapons you can imagine, and they use them all over Vietnam every day. It's a war against a people instead of against an enemy. It's professed to be against an enemy called communism, but it's gotta be against a people. You've gotta wipe out the people. You've gotta kill *all* the guerrillas.

I think the blame goes all the way up to the fact that this patriotism thing that is taught to the people in the States is taught to the people for a reason. Now this is going to sound like a really rash, radical, communist statement, but I really believe that the Americans in the Pentagon and the government are scared to death that they're going to lose their power, their prestige, and they've got to have these big imperialist feet stomping around on little people all over the world to retain this power. The trouble is, they're using Americans to do this, young Americans, kids. The policy makers in Washington and Saigon and MACV [Military Assistance Command Vietnam] are saying hooray for the red, white, and blue! fuck communism! we're gonna wipe them off the face of the earth. They're undermining democracy is what they say, but actually they know they're undermining capitalism. The communists are saying, you cannot be rich and manipulate people anymore— we're going to stop that; we're going to level off wages, we're going to level off resources; things like this, and this totally undermines capitalism and men like Rockefeller are shaking in their boots—good grief, stamp it out they say. So we're taught this in the schools.

If you've ever seen an American convoy rumbling along some road and looking at all that steel, man, all that power, all that fire, all that gunpowder, all those rockets and things and then realizing what that power is being used against . . . and looking at an airstrip at Bien Hoa, or Cu Chi, all the money, the jets, watching U-2s taking off from Bien Hoa airbase, the millions of dollars that plane is worth, the millions of dollars being spent. Somebody's profiting from it, somebody's making money—and for what purpose. Why!

From the first day an American sets foot in school he is the victim of this American propaganda thing, man. If you have to live outside the U.S., you're poor, you're bad, you're sick. If there is any enemy of the United States, he's undermining everything that's good in the world, see, and it's got to be a communist plot, anything that's un-American or nonwhite—it's got to be bad and dirty and filthy. So, you go to Vietnam and you have the opportunity to see what's happening in Vietnam, that what the Americans are doing in Vietnam is the very thing, *the very thing*, you were taught was wrong in school. If you can somehow relate what's happening in Vietnam to the documentaries on the Nazi thing, the prisoner thing, the genocide they engaged in, then you're going to become aware. Of course a lot of the guys in the field over there just kind of put it all under the rug. They get under the wing of this bald eagle, and they want to stay there because it's nice and clean and safe and white and groovy.

Here's an analogy. Supposing a person's parents tell him how horrible it is to start smoking yet they're always puffing away on a cigarette, lighting up, and telling him the evils of it. The kid will sense a lie which will result in disrespect which can only bring on dissent later on, which is almost a type of hatred. Now this is happening on a mass scale in the United States, not just against parents, but against parent government. This parent is telling people how horrible it is to commit genocide, to burn people, how rotten it was the Nazis did it, and then they're asking this poor guy to go over five thousand miles away and do that very thing, man! Most of the guys put it under the rug 'cause they want to still believe in their parent, their government, or else they have nothing, they don't have anything to cling to. If they never had anything to cling to to begin with, a guy kicked around in foster homes like me, or some black guy who's never believed in the big white father image anyway, he's gonna dissent, he's gonna be against this thing, he's gonna speak out.

The guys who question it consciously are the ones who've unconsciously dissented from the time they were in school; they couldn't grasp this red, white, and blue thing; it never made total sense to them. Now on the outside they might appear to be a very patriotic individual, but on the inside—this applies to a lot of guys—they just aren't going for it. I mean, they see Mickey Rooney singing the Star Spangled Banner in some old 1945 movie—they can't identify with that. They can't identify with apple pie and white picket fences anymore. Then they go to Vietnam and they really get it thrown in their face, what a lie it was.

I look back on my schooling and how real education is being suppressed. I look back on my education, my *lack* of education, even the black history of the U.S. It's really a laugh man; it's a pity. I wouldn't have learned these things in a million years if I hadn't gone to Vietnam or if I had never gone outside my base camp in Vietnam. I would have gone on reading the *Stars and Stripes* and being overjoyed at the glorious victories, you know.

If America was so wonderful and if the American dream was so fantastic, don't you think the people of North Vietnam and South Vietnam and all over the world would cling to it? Don't you think they would swarm to it, man? No, they're fighting it tooth and nail in their homes and their own land. They're saying, fuck you, we like it the way it is. But it's only the manipulation of the masses by a choice few that keeps this system going. No one else wants it. Do you know I talked with literally dozens of Vietnamese—I'd talk with people that could speak English—who were saving their money *to go north*. They hated the Saigon government, let alone the Americans, and they only wanted to go north. For Christ's sake!

So anyway, I came to Canada, took the train to Chicago and Detroit and crossed over at Windsor in November '69. In Toronto it was snowing, the first time I saw snow, and it was like being on another planet. I thought I was the only American in Canada, let alone the only deserter. One day I was walking down Yonge Street, taking a walk in the snow, and I walked into this book store and there were a lot of longhairs in there. Finally, I just sort of broke down, and I asked one of the guys, "You're going to think this is silly, but I just deserted the U.S. Army," and before I could even finish the sentence, he says, "Oh yeah? I'm a deserter too." Wow! Then he gave me the address of the Union of American Exiles over on St. George Street and he says go over there and they'll clue me in. I went there and they talked to me and then sent me to the Toronto Anti-Draft Programme and they gave me immigration counseling. I met the people at the UAE who were putting together the American Deserters' Committee, and I began working with Harvey Maurer. I later moved into the house that the ADC had rented. Helped paint and clean the rooms.

While living at the ADC house, I'd make an attempt to get away from it all once a week and go up to Rochdale and make a point to get stoned. I ran into this chick there who was pretty conservative, really, from a small town in Ontario. She was nice and eventually she moved in with me at the ADC. I became one of the staff at ADC and worked mainly on the war crimes thing. Did some counseling. At the time we were in the process of getting all the professional help we could for the ADC and we got a hold of this girl, Judy, who had a bachelor's in theology and a master's degree in psychology, and we decided that she would be pretty good for helping guys to get their heads together. So she came to the ADC house and lived with her husband, who happened to be a draft dodger. She helped me get my head straight—I was one of her first patients so to speak. She's been giving me every kind of psychological test; the only thing they point to is guilt, guilt, guilt. She says, and I believe, that everything that I do from this day on is going to be as a result of this guilt. The guilt is the foundation now.

Number thirty-seven is my guilt number, as a lot of GIs call it. It's the number of Vietnamese that one's certain to have killed, civilian and military. Guys keep a record of all the gooks they killed in combat. I only kept track of the innocent people I killed, the civilians, prisoners, a lot of NVA and VC who we'd captured and who I'd been told to "take care of." It came to thirty-seven.

If I was there now of course I would not pick up a weapon. I'd refuse. But it took me a while to get to that point. It was not a decision made overnight, or even in Vietnam for that matter. I had to be away from it for a long time before I could really see *how* wrong everything was, *how* wrong I was. I knew I was wrong when I was there, but now I *really* know. I've been in Canada seven months and only about two months ago I got out of the army, I stopped being a soldier. It was only a few months ago that I could spit on the street or put my hands in my pocket in front of a cop. I used to stand at parade rest while waiting to cross the street at a light. I was a good soldier, originally, "outstanding" as they say in the army.

It doesn't erase what I did, to work against it. But it's a reason to live. Sure, I've thought about suicide; I don't have any reason to live. I've already killed all these innocent people, and there's nothing I can do about it. But I think that I have the duty, what's the other corny word, *obligation*, to try and do as much as one guy can do to stop that war. It's a crime against humanity. The only way I can see stopping it is revolution, man, in the States. The people making profits off it aren't going to change their minds.

I want to help bring out a public awareness, to tell that immoveable Rock-of-Gibraltar, apple-pie-eating, red, white, and blue bald eagle sitting on his couch with his feet up on his naugahyde footstool watching the war on his color TV that what he is watching on TV is a very sugar-coated genocide. It's an advertisement for the bald eagle to see GIs trudging through the jungles of Nam all sweaty and filthy, you know, fighting communists. But if these TV cameras could pan the whole area and see what's really happening, these hard-hats marching through the streets of New York with the American flag tattooed on their chests—if they could be in Vietnam instead of France or Germany or Korea or wherever they were, if they could be in Nam and see the prisoner interrogation, the napalm, the effects of napalm on children—I'm afraid they wouldn't give Nixon any kind of trophy.

Believe it or not, after all I've said here, I still get angry when I hear about somebody burning an American flag because it's still something that I respect. I'm an American and I won't ever renounce my citizenship. But I don't want to see this old World War II patriotism come back. What I do want to see is this bullying around the world, this genocide, the killing, the cultural rape of an Oriental country like Vietnam—I want to see this stopped. I'm going to help and see that it stops. But it's going to be difficult. For the very reason that Americans have already committed the ultimate atrocity, which is Hiroshima and Nagasaki, it's going to be even harder for them to grasp what's really happening in Vietnam. Okay, they can know the facts about My Lai, but they're still not going to be able to realize it's a crime. It's going to be harder for them than it would be for another nation perhaps. Unless there's another Nuremberg of some kind.

Jim Riehle was reeducated in Vietnam. Following graduation from the University of Dayton where he received a degree in business management, he was drafted and reluctantly went. He was an unlikely candidate for desertion, but then serving as an infantryman in Vietnam might make a deserter of the president.

Riehle found himself in Vietnam just as he was beginning to formulate his opinion, fraught with doubt, about the war—and the army's action and his own sensitivity helped speed up the process. One day he resigned and refused to fight anymore. He wrote to his wife that he would probably end up in Leavenworth, that she would have to prepare herself for that. Instead, he ended up in Toronto, with his wife. They lived for a while in one of the American Deserters' Committee cooperatives before finding an apartment. They both found jobs. She is a teller in a bank, and he was hired as a management trainee by a large, Canadian-owned financial institution which took him on even when he mentioned he was a deserter. "I want to work to change society from the inside. I think I can do that even in finance. I wouldn't be against a socialist system, but you've still got to have banks. I don't need a lot of money—I don't need clothes for example. I'm happy with what I've got on, cut-off jeans and a T-shirt. Too bad I can't go to work like this." Radical exiles would be critical of his choice of employment. However, he is not to be compared to them, but rather to the thousands of young veterans who have chosen to remain silent despite their opposition to the war they fought in. Riehle chose not to remain silent and made his protest, an enduring one, which more than likely will last a lifetime. One more exile to make Americans question their militarist system.

Riehle's background is that of the thought-stifling, small-minded, puritanically self-righteous, white upper-middle-class. It is the oppression of homes where *Life* magazine is considered radical journalism because it criticizes the government from time to time. It is a class of small factory owners, bank managers, insurance brokers, and highly-paid engineers, and they live in the suburbs and in small towns in gracious frame or stone houses with an acre or two of lawn. They are Respectable People, and they go to church, and they voted for Goldwater and for Nixon. They have supported the Vietnam War from the beginning since their sons didn't have to fight it. And so it was with Riehle's family, even when the draft did take their son.

Jim Riehle is twenty-three, son of a president of a middle-sized Cincinnati engineering firm. He is one of three brothers, one older and one younger. His open, semiserious, college-sophomore visage has been in no way hardened by a year of Vietnam combat. He was destined to carry on his father's image, to work his way up in finance in Cincinnati, buy a big white house, and become a paragon of the community. But the Vietnam War changed all that.

I was born in Cincinnati, raised in Cincinnati, went to Catholic schools, lived in the suburbs. I went to a Catholic university, liberal-Catholic university. Very conservative politics. I worked for Goldwater in 1964 and I was a member of the Young Republicans in my freshman year in college. I was really caught up with the Goldwater dream, you know, the thing with America, this courageous western attitude. And I was really fed up with Johnson. I thought Johnson was a crook. I mellowed through '65, '66, and '67, though I was still for the war. When Johnson made his big buildup in 1965 I was in favor of it. I really believed that the South Vietnamese people were down on the North. And I was for Nixon in '68. People in the Republican Party, I think, knew Nixon was the one, all the people I knew did anyway. We knew Goldwater was dead. And nothing is worse to a Goldwater Republican than a moderate like say Rockefeller or Romney, so we considered Nixon to be the one that we'd back. I considered McCarthy not really down to earth. I considered him to be too idealistic, too concerned with philosophy, the old philosopher-king problem. I thought he couldn't deal effectively with the problem. And I thought Bobby Kennedy was more concerned with Bobby Kennedy. However, now I think he would have been the best choice. You've got to remember, I was molded in right wing thought; I wasn't really open; I wasn't informed either; like, I considered military people to be the heroes of our society. I mean, I knew the army was a lot of shit from what my brother had said, but I still considered generals and colonels to be great men, the whole West Point thing. I always considered myself a Republican, and when the boys would get together to shoot the shit, I'd always have all these facts, these names of congressmen and senators and what they were doing, and I could win any argument; these guys weren't informed on the political issues. But it's a common tool, I guess, that people use when they're debating, to throw out all this high sounding information like you really know what the hell you're talking about. Like Bill Buckley. Later I got into Camus and Teilhard de Chardin and learned to forget facts and let the overall thing go into my Zen mind so to speak.

I wasn't, like, actively Republican; I was sort of like into the Jaycee thing more than anything. Like when Nixon went out to St. Louis the other day and all these Jaycees met him at the airport, I just thought that's where I would have been, that could have happened to me if I hadn't been through the army. I could just see it. I was all ready to go into the air force as an officer, but a month before I was to go I got drafted, and it really pissed me off 'cause I had voted for Nixon in November 'cause he said he was going to end the draft and the war and everything, and, like, I wasn't any longer the Goldwater Republican. I was the liberal Republican. But deep down, I still had these strong ties to the Jaycee thing—Stand up for America.

But then I was drafted, like wow! I couldn't believe it. Like all my life I'd been yea America! you know, go to the football games and sing the Star Spangled Banner. I remember I was really shocked when one day in basic training I was running for some senseless reason and, while I was running, I noticed an American flag and I felt contempt for it, and it really shocked me, you know, because this is my country, this is my flag—I'd always been extremely patriotic; I'd read every issue of *Reader's Digest*. So it shocked me, this brutalizing, inhuman—stupid—military training, and it was hard to admit that it was America that was doing this to me, that this is the sum total of our society right here. I couldn't believe it, that I would feel contempt. I came home on leave and I told my wife to check on getting a passport to Sweden. I said, I can't live with this, this is insane, how can people live like this. How, in 1968, with all the thinking that is going on in the U.S., can the army do this to people, and how can officers, people who are educated, do it, live like this. But during this leave I calmed down and said, well, it isn't really so bad—I can take it. And like it was fascinating in terms of education; like I've never been oppressed, and all through history people have been oppressed, so let's see what it's really like. I felt like this is one way I could get the feeling of what was really going on in the world. And also, my whole generation was going through the army, and, like, even in two weeks in the army I could see that I'd probably end up as an infantryman and probably go to Vietnam, but I wanted to see this, share this with my whole generation; like, I would really know what it was all about.

I didn't really think the army was wrong, just the methods. But as I went through basic and went through AIT I started to feel more and more contempt for the army, more and more contempt for the establishment that was paying for this army, allowing it to continue. And I think I was really starting to build a lot of contempt for myself 'cause I didn't really have the courage to, like . . . desert. But I remember in AIT every time I'd think about deserting, I didn't know where to go. I didn't think you could come to Canada. I mean I didn't want to go to Sweden 'cause I'd heard guys were coming back from Sweden.

I was reading things that showed me that Vietnam wasn't all the army said it was. And like my views on Vietnam changed drastically just before I got drafted because, well—the elections in Vietnam—I'd finally read some stuff about the elections in Vietnam which sounded pretty accurate. I began to believe the elections were maybe a fraud, and I decided on that basis alone that I had to find out more before I could go and shoot people in Vietnam. Even though I was a Republican and even though I was anti-Ho Chi Minh, anticommunist, I still thought, well, maybe these people who are always writing about Vietnam and what a corrupt place it is are right. And then they showed us a film on Vietnam—why we were there—and it shows all these people running around and voting for Diem back in like '56, and I said, well, I know *that* is a complete lie and so I thought, hmmm, what's the army doing? That's what really convinced me, their film with all the lies in it, that we shouldn't really be in Vietnam. I realized there was another side and the army was trying to cover it up. I realized I had to be more informed. I was really embarrassed watching this film; I mean, my whole basic training company was really intelligent, mostly college-educated people—fifty percent of us had degrees. We had one lawyer who refused a commission 'cause he said his practice couldn't wait four years. Anyway, what eventually occurred to me was that it was not that you have to be convinced that a war is immoral before you *refuse* to fight it. What *should be*—is that you should be convinced that a war is moral *before* you fight it.

AIT was as bad as basic, and it gradually worked on me that I was going to go to Vietnam, and at times I would think of refusing and saying, no, I'm not going to go, but then it would trip in my mind that if I do that, I'm gonna go to jail, that means I'm a criminal and, like, my ties to the Jaycees were too strong to accept the fact that I'm a criminal. So what I did was pull rationalization number thirty-five out of the air and repressed the idea that the Vietnam War is immoral. I knew I had doubts about the war, and by the time I had graduated from AIT I hated the army—I was completely disgusted with the army—but I felt that Vietnam was something I had to do. My subconscious was telling me at the time, all right, you can refuse to go to Vietnam and cut your ties with the Jaycees . . . but I couldn't let go of the Jaycees, it was an ego-support thing; like I'm better than the working class, I'm in the Jaycees, *I have my degree in business*. So I couldn't go to jail. So I knew I was going to go to Vietnam, but I didn't want to go.

I was really paranoid. I didn't want to die. I was really scared to death, and to get over this fear I had to make up this thing, like, *this is something I have to do*. A Holy War. I had to forget my doubts about the war. I still hated the army and thought by this time that the draft was wrong. No man should have the right to hold another man's life in his hands. But I had to suppress my fear so I forgot all about this stuff. In fact, I knew guys in Vietnam who were so afraid of dying and who worried so much about it every day that the only way they could get over it was to become very concerned about killing communists.

Vietnam. When I first got over there, I was really afraid. And yet there was a certain fascination there; like, I was back with Caesar on the day he overcame the Nervii, that's what I felt—all through history men have been marching to war, all through history men have died on battlefields, and now I'm one of those guys. This is *the* most basic human thing. When you first get there they send you through the whole Long Binh deal, and then they sent me to the 1st Infantry Division at Di An, and they put you through a week of training, typical army training, except that it's good in the sense it gets you ready. Like, people could go to Vietnam with a month's training and that would be plenty, but they give you that whole six months' training deal, I think, just to get you ready psychologically to go into battle. Like it really makes you *army*. So I was soon out in the field, fighting the goddam war but vehemently antiarmy . . . like, I considered it immoral to be an officer. The whole while the real thing with me was the draft, like it's slavery, it's wrong, and officers support the draft, in fact they wouldn't be officers in many cases without it. It is involuntary servitude, and it's prohibited by the Thirteenth Amendment—if the Thirteenth Amendment is real. If there weren't a draft, there wouldn't be a war. Our whole infantry company was made up of draftees. There were no regular army men.

Like these guys in Vietnam would tell you that you're going out there to die for *freedom*, and nothing seemed more ridiculous to me than someone enslaving me for freedom! I used to get enraged. Talking about feeling oppressed, I mean, like, when I was in Vietnam and after Vietnam, I could feel down deep inside of me the rage, and I could remember reading stuff in the black movement by Eldridge Cleaver and Stokely Carmichael and I could remember them writing about the rage they feel. And I always thought these people were crazy; like wow! it can't be that bad, but that was just a lack of education on my part. And now I saw how the black man was oppressed, whereas, when I was in the Jaycee thing, it had always remained hidden.

I would try and get to my officers and say things like the army is slavery and my lieutenant would say, well, it's only slavery if you want it to be. I would radicalize my battalion, my group, by talking about aristocracy and that in the U.S. you can't even have a title, and then I would relate that to the army where the officer corps is really an aristocracy. To the infantryman the war isn't necessarily as important as what he's lost—his freedom and the fact that he's treated like a piece of shit by this elite class of stupid men who love to fight but never go into battle themselves. The war isn't worth all this sacrifice, like World War II was to GIs then. Back in 1965 when I'd argue with people over the war, I'd say look, they're fighting it with volunteers; the marines are volunteers, Special Forces are volunteers. Everyone over there then was a volunteer and that was a main point in my argument.

I was brought up learning that communism is wrong, communism is a totalitarian system. That was my rationalization when I first got over there— well, maybe it's a fascist state in the South now, but maybe ten years from now these people will be better off under Thieu and Ky than they would have been under communism. But fighting communism was, like, way off in the distance. Like in firefights I wouldn't really fight. I'd always turn around and look to the rear while most guys were blasting away up ahead. Like my buddy and I would shoot at the big red ants on bushes instead of at the enemy; I mean, we really weren't warriors. Like I couldn't see shooting these people unless they came running at me. We weren't really there in self-defense, killing communists in self-defense, because it was *their country*. I just used the idea that I was there to stop communism as a rationalization for being there—that's why the U.S. was there—and *I* was against communism ...*but in the field we weren't really stopping communism*. We were just killing people. It was their country. I couldn't shoot at them.

I ran into very few people when I was in Vietnam who really thought that we should be there, who really thought that we were accomplishing something. And even those people wouldn't admit it right off, only when you got them into a defensive conversation where they finally had to say what they believed, and then I'd shoot 'em down with arguments like: if there had been free elections everyone would have voted for Ho Chi Minh, and why the hell do you think we can't win this war with all of our troops and fire superiority if people didn't support the VC; look at the political repression in Saigon—that dude who talked to his brother who was a communist and who got thrown in jail simply for that. And there was Dzu who had been sent to jail, one of the candidates against Thieu.

I had been in the field for about five months and had seen a lot of combat. One time five guys and I were pinned between a group of VC and a bunch of Americans, the 11th Armored Cavalry Regiment, the old Patton people, all maniacs—anytime they hear anything they usually shoot for about two hours and just destroy everything. Anyway, we had walked out in front of them and they didn't know it, and we ran into some VC. They got our squad leader in the back and shot the radio operator. I was really lucky. I dove down behind a tree and said, well, this is great, I'm alive and now the Cav's going to come out 'cause they were about seventy-five yards behind us—I figured they'd come out and save us. But when they heard the AKs [AK-47—automatic rifle of either Russian or Chinese manufacture] open up, they started firing at us too. I laid there with these dudes opening up with fifty calibre, fifties going all around us, and I really started to go insane but then I just faced it, I'm going to die, *this is it,* tough shit. It was good because after that whenever we got in bad stuff I could maintain my self-control because I had faced it and said, if it happens it happens, there's nothing I could do about it. It was important in giving me more composure. I was no longer afraid. This was one of the reasons I was later able to refuse to fight. Like I said, most guys are so afraid when they get over there that they realize the army is their only salvation; I mean, the army's all they got. By now I was beginning to get away from that.

I came in from the field one day and was reading *Newsweek* and read where Nixon had said, "The American people should match the spirit of the men in Vietnam." This just did it with me, man, I just went freaky! So I sat down and wrote this letter which was printed in the Asian edition of *Newsweek* and I said: "I'm writing concerning Nixon's statement about the spirit of the men in Vietnam. I'm a combat infantryman; I see men die, I sleep in the rain, I eat food that isn't fit for pigs. For what? Mr. Nixon should know the answer to this and he should know that the only time there is morale in Vietnam is when a unit finds out it is going home." I had to go back and change all the pronouns because five other guys signed it. I went on R&R and then returned to Di An on my way back to Dau Tieng. At Di An I picked up a *Newsweek* and, holy shit! it was in there!

I came back from R&R to my new job at the PIO [Public Information Office] in Dau Tieng. I had my own little office, turned out this garbage copy for the division newspaper and magazines, shit like "GIs take orphans to Saigon Zoo." I would finish pieces with stuff like, "as the sun set in the East the Chinook went off into the sunset with a load of kids all smiles"—my CO ate it up. But I didn't have the job very long.

At Dau Tieng, it took my CO fifteen days before he saw a copy of *Newsweek*. Finally, one day he called me in and said, "Sit down. What do you have to say about this letter." And I said, well, it's just an honest expression of how I feel. He asked me what I would have done in World War II and said that in World War II they had it a lot worse than this, a lot more people were dying. And I said but in World War II you could concern yourself with the fact that you were fighting for a real cause, fighting for *something*. And that's what it kept getting down to in Vietnam. It kept getting down to the fact that we're *not* here for a cause, we were here for, as far as I was concerned, no reason; we were here because Nixon doesn't want to be the first president to lose a war. That's the way I saw it. And like we were killing people right and left for nothing, and American guys were dying right and left for no reason. He said, "Well, what about your position here in the PIO?" I said, well, that's got nothing to do with my position here because I'm just reporting news here, my own personal feelings don't enter into it. He said, "You're fired. Go back to Alpha Company." So I sat down and wrote another letter to *Newsweek* and said, guess what happened, that letter I wrote got me sent back to the field. My CO said it's not because I wrote the letter, it's because he says it shows I have an antimilitary antiarmy attitude. So that was printed in *Newsweek* too, Asian edition, about three weeks after, under a headline, "Writing and Rights." I mentioned the battalion executive officer, Major Kelly, and everyone knew who I meant, including him, so he was really down on me. I gave a shit 'cause I was back in the field. What else could he do to me?

So I was out with the infantry again. One day we were walking along through rubber in the Michelin rubber plantation, and we came into cut rubber which was still running down the trees, and I said to our platoon leader, there're rubber workers ahead. It wasn't just a few trees, like the VC might cut as a ruse, it was miles of cut rubber, and we were heading toward where the Michelin employees were working. So we hear some noises up ahead and the CO calls battalion and asks if there are any friendlies in the area and battalion said no 'cause they had called Michelin to get their people out of there. Well that happens all the time, and Michelin usually forgets to tell their employees not to go to work. So the CO calls the M-60 machine guns up on the line and we open up. We killed a little girl and an old man. When we got up ahead and found them it made me sick. I shouted at the CO, You *knew* they were rubber workers, you dumb son-of-a-bitch. Couldn't you see all this cut rubber we were going through?—typical West Point mutton-head robot out there for body counts and rank. All the Vietnamese families and workers were shouting and screaming and crying. How would you like to be out with your family working and six M-60 machine guns open up on you, kill two, and wound thirty? I could see that these people were really angry. They really hated us.

One of the things that really tripped me over so I said, yes, the U.S. should get out tomorrow, was just looking at the face of the farmers. Or looking at the face of a woman at the fish market as she looked at you in your American truck as you barrel through their village at fifty miles an hour and everyone helter-skelters and the truck driver is sitting there with his can of beer thinking this is really cool, making those little slanty-eyed bastards jump. I would see this and I would look at the people. I would see this farmer plowing his field and he would look up for one instant and then look back down, and in that one look his face touched me so far deep down that it was much more powerful than all the intellectual reasoning I could go through to state my position on the war. I mean, that said it all. It's frustrating that I can't put that look into words, that I can't put his frustration into words. His suffering. His rage. And all he can do is stand behind his plow and think, "Well, maybe my son will blow up that American base tomorrow." There were times when I just wanted to get off the truck and go into a Vietnamese house and put my arms around them and cry to show them that I understood what was going on, what we were doing to them. It's really a heartbreaking experience.

The thing that had the greatest effect on me over there was being involved in this accident where the guy who was killed was my best friend. We were getting on the choppers for a combat assault, and I got tangled in some of my equipment when we had to change choppers at the last minute, and my gun went off, killing my best buddy. This really tore me up but I had to stop and think, am I going to spend the rest of my life feeling guilty for my friend's death? 'Cause I realized that in a war situation lots of men die in accidents. I'd seen ten guys wounded and one killed in my own company from accidents. But of course the army covers them over. The army knew this guy was my best friend and yet they were going to court-martial me for this. Weapons are always loaded on combat assault, yet the army said they weren't supposed to be and I was to blame 'cause mine was.

The army was pushing me over this accident. They brought me in from the field to await the court-martial, and, for the first time, I could get around more and see more and I was talking with more people and reading more and thinking more. Like when you're in the field all you're thinking about is, oh shit, is it gonna rain tonight? am I gonna be able to make cocoa? But when you get back in the rear you can think about the war—and you can think about the army 'cause then it's not a case of the army being the only thing you've got. Then I read a book on Vietnam, this guy's father sent it, *Our Own Worst Enemy*, by William Lederer. So I let all this stuff soak in. I had bunker guard and I'd just sit there all day and think. I'd smoke grass and I'd think. I still wasn't actively antiwar, but I came to the point where I realized I couldn't really shoot any more Vietnamese. Because it was their country and from what I could see the people would have been better off if we just left. As for the argument that all these people who helped us would be slaughtered by the North Vietnamese . . . if that's true, we'll just have to create communities in America to take care of these people—I think McGovern said that too.

Anyway, they postponed the court-martial and they eventually sent me back up to this fire support base. By this time everyone thought I was a communist and I got all these jobs like cleaning piss tubes. This super ass-kisser E-6 would give me a real hard time, yelling at me all the time, and finally I said, look, did it ever occur to you that maybe, just maybe, you don't have a complete right over my life because of that rank of yours; did that ever occur to you? He didn't answer me; he took me to another sergeant, and that sergeant started hassling me, and I started saying things like, you are the enemy of what America stands for, I mean you are the enemy as far as I'm concerned. When I came in the army . . . the reason I allowed myself to be drafted, the reason I didn't go to Canada, was because I thought I'd be fighting people like you, totalitarians, and his only remark—he just stared at me—was, "I bet you were on welfare when you were a civilian."

Another thing that pushed me over: our battalion had a siren on this fire support base and every time a company would kill a "VC"—which could mean civilian—the siren would go *eeeaaaooouuu*, like a police siren, and somebody would run out from the command post, usually the sergeant major, and he'd announce whose kill it was and shout, "Charlie company, Charlie company," and everyone would go, "Yea Charlie company!" And we had a board there, the *body count board* and they had Alpha, Bravo, Charlie, Delta, headquarters company and combat support company listed and had January, February, March and so on, and it had how many kills these companies had. I mean this shit was *sick*. Guys would be given three-day passes to Vung Tau if they could confirm a direct kill. I was enraged. When the siren would go off my friends and I would start screaming, *"Yea! Yea! Yea!, we killed some more of those stinking, fucking slant-eyes,"* as loud as we could just to put down the officers. The officers knew we were putting them down. They told us we were communists.

Another incident: I was sleeping inside the bunker one night and there was a guy on the bunker roof, a soul brother, and he had been in an accident in the States and his mind was really in bad shape, he had really severe headaches and stuff; you could see he wasn't functioning normally and that's why he wasn't in the field even though his training was that of an infantry-man. He was at this firebase where I was; he wasn't supposed to be around anything dangerous because he couldn't handle it. So this night he was on bunker guard, and they told him to throw a frag [grenade] and he dropped it, and he wasn't really conscious enough to jump off the bunker, and it went off and, like, for two days he was a vegetable, and then he died. I carried him out to the chopper pad. The guy was trying to breathe but his lungs were just destroyed. I could hear this faraway moan from way down inside him. I thought that maybe some part of his consciousness was awake and was moaning—it made me so sick I can't think about it now. This shit kept building in me and building in me, and I could trace it all back to the draft 'cause I knew that if we didn't have the draft we wouldn't have this insane shit. I really needed all this, the death of my best friend, my battalion fucking me over for exercising my rights, this guy dying and everything just to push me over. By this time I was so against the army that no matter what they did to me I didn't care anymore.

So all this shit was just building and one night I was on bunker guard and we were supposed to be throwing frags over the side of the hill on H&I [harassment and interdiction fire] and this sergeant came along and told me to throw a frag and I said no, and he said "Why?" and I said 'cause I might hurt somebody and he says, "Well, that's what you're supposed to be doing it for." I said, well, I think it's wrong; I don't think we should kill these people. He said, "Well, if you won't throw a frag, then fire a magazine—" He didn't really realize what I was saying—and I said, no, I'm not going to do it. So he went and got a captain who I thought was a lieutenant 'cause he never wore a shirt though I knew he was an officer 'cause he played the aristocracy thing, and he came over to me and said, "I'll give you a direct order to throw that frag," and I said no. We went through that three times, and each time I said no. I said, look pal, we can stay here all night and all you're going to do is beat me to death with second chances. This isn't what I'm looking for 'cause I'm not going to do it, so why don't you just bug off. So he took me to the base commander who came running out of his bunker and said, "Do you know to whom you're speaking," and I said, well, I don't know his name; I just know he's a lieutenant. He says, "That's Captain Johnson." I says, look man, I resign from the army; I am no longer in the army. I'd always thought that it's chickenshit to fight the army on little stuff—I decided that if I ever do it it's gonna be a complete thing. So these two captains just bitched and bitched and bitched. "If you're no longer in the army, if you're not going to defend this position, I'm going to put you outside the wire," he said, and I just laughed at him and said, what do you think I am, a sixth grader? If you do something like that, they'll court-martial you. I know you're not going to put me outside the wire; I know you're bullshitting. I was like speeding, in the true sense of the word speeding, you know, a chemical reaction; I was so scared, I was really afraid of going to jail. I was really afraid of the army when I said all this; I thought a great lightning bolt was going to hit me like I was on Mt. Sinai or something. You could trace all this back to the Army-Jaycee-America-Strong-Father-Figure-Judaeo-Christian-Roman-Catholic-Cruel-God syndrome. But I kept telling myself you've got nothing to fear but fear itself, the old cliché, but it really fit in that situation. "Well, we're gonna tell the lieutenant colonel tomorrow and you're gonna go to jail for fifty years." Then afterwards one of the captains came up to me and said, "Do you know that there are only something like 40,000 people who are going to make it to heaven? You're out now!" Then he starts quoting all this shit from the Bible and how it relates to communism and stuff. This was really freaky; here I am 12,000 miles away from home, and I'm in the grips of a madman.

They didn't call me in after I refused to fight; I was, like, isolated. So I went to see the lieutenant colonel and walked right into his command post and said, "Sir, I have a personal problem." This about gives a colonel an orgasm; they go, wow! I can help this grubby enlisted man with his personal problem, this whole paternal thing; it's nauseating to live under that. So he says, "Come on outside, *son*." I can still hear that "son." He said, "What is it." I said, "Sir, I'm not going to shoot anybody anymore. I'm through with the war." Then I walked away and thought, well, all hell's gonna break loose now 'cause I've resigned from the army. I was considered like a hero around the company 'cause I'd done this thing, but I didn't do it to sound big, showing off and stuff. Now the army was the ultimate evil in my mind, and I was going to go all the way to say no to it. In fact, they were more evil in my eyes than they ever could have been objectively. But in my mind they *were* the ultimate evil. The next day I woke up and nobody said anything. They were afraid that I was going to write *Newsweek* again.

I thought I was going to get crucified and nothing happened. I mean soul brothers would come over and shake my hand and congratulate me, but no officer would ever say anything. If they saw me, they'd turn away. I think it was because they have this ego-support thing, this rank, and when they run into someone who just laughs at them, it destroys them, it just destroys that whole false thing that they've built up and they can't accept it. It happened time and time again, where nobody gave me an order and I'd say, no man, you're nothing to me. That was it. They'd leave. And when I got court-martialed for the accident, the only charge they added on was the original one when I refused to throw the grenade. One time my battalion came down with this conscientious objector application and wanted me to fill it out 'cause it looks so bad to have a guy around who's refusing to fight. I said no, and the sergeant said, "Why," and I said, 'Cause I'm not a pacifist. I'd kill you if I thought it would help end this war and the oppression of the draft. I said I wasn't a CO. I'd fight to end the draft. That's all you have to do and the U.S. couldn't fight any more wars.

So there I was in the rear again. They sent me to Lai Khe to await my court-martial. It was like a holiday, man; I didn't have to do anything, and guys would say there goes that guy that never has to do anything. One of my friends was also in the rear and we'd rap together every night. There were always cold sodas for the heads and for the juice freaks [beer drinkers] there was always cold beer. So we'd smoke a little grass and talk. It was nice. In the 1st Division—we were a pretty grassy division—I'd say in the rear at least sixty percent were really heavy smokers and about eighty percent were trying it now and then. And even the juice freaks, while they didn't trust it, would try it at least once. But there were guys like me and my friends who smoked it every day, day in and day out, when we were in the rear. I mean I was stoned at my court-martial. I don't drink myself, 'cause I can't control alcohol—if I get drunk I lose control. But with marijuana, no matter how stoned I was, I could always bring myself down; I was always in control. Every morning we'd take a truck or something and go down to Di An, and we'd party all day, go around, entertain ourselves, go to the USO, eat a steak, and we'd talk to the Vietnamese. Then at night we'd be going to the movie at Lai Khe and guys would say, "Where were you today," and we'd say, oh, down at Di An. "Do you go to Di An everyday?" and I'd say, yeah, I'm commuting. Another thing we used to do is hop on the choppers with a medical folder or something and go down to Long Binh. Wow! Di An is nice, but to a GI, to an infantryman, Long Binh is *Paris*. Really it was a ball; it was a release 'cause I'd been uptight for so long. So like I was really happy. I had stood up to the army and was getting away with it. I really encouraged guys to say fuck it, get out of the field, refuse, drop out of the army.

For over a month I just vacationed. At Long Binh I went to LBJ [Long Binh Jail] and took pictures of it to send to my wife 'cause I thought I was going to jail and I thought it would be nice if she had some pictures of where I was. My lawyers were pressing for this correctional barracks at Leavenworth. I was trying to keep cool about it. And then my court-martial came. That was really a weird scene. When you walk into the courtroom, there's this American flag which covers one whole wall and it looks like it's about eighty feet long—in reality it just takes up this one wall. When you walk in there, you're overcome, why resist? You realize that all of America is on the side of that judge sitting up there. It makes you want to fling yourself down to the mercy of the courtroom. A pretty smart bastard who put that flag up there. I had this prowar lawyer who was for the draft, a real idiot, the Jaycee son-of-a-bitch. He was so establishment; even the tone of his voice was a cliché.

The court-martial system is unconstitutional, as we all know. Like in that book by Fred Gardner, he points out that it is possible to have only three enlisted men, and then they can be E-7 and E-8 sergeants—this is not a jury of your peers. If you're trying an E-4 why not have a jury of all E-4s. Well, because it wouldn't work. It would work if you didn't have a draft, though, because your E-4s would be pro-army; they would have pride in their units and so forth. Anyway, mine was a special court-martial where they either have three officers or one judge. I had one judge. They dropped the charge about the accident. Then they brought up the charge of refusing to throw the frag, refusing to fire up at the artillery base. Everyone told me I'd be going to jail on that. My lawyer called my first sergeant as a witness, who really wasn't a bad guy, and he testified that I was a good trooper out in the field, really a credit to the unit. He went on and on about what a great soldier I was. That I had always been ammo bearer, a shitty job, and I always did it and never complained—actually, I liked it because there was no harassment if you're doing that and I'd empty out half the ammo and put in cigarettes and writing paper and books and it would keep it all dry in the monsoon. Most guys didn't like it so the sergeant thought I was great for doing it. Well, that got me off; that saved my ass. I got a 150-dollar fine, a formal reprimand and a two-grade bust. The sergeant was Puerto Rican and they're really great guys, even if they *are* lifers, they're *real people*. He was the kind of guy who joined the army 'cause he didn't have any other livelihood.

Then Major Kelly came around and said, "*Get Riehle to the field*. Either two things are going to happen: he's going to go to the field and show that he's copping out because he's going to go out there and shoot those Vietnamese 'cause he wants to go home, or else he's *not* going to go to the field and we'll put the fucker in jail." Well, my unit had only seven days before it was to be picked up and taken back to Di An to get processed home—we were part of the withdrawal. So I did the only thing I could do, I went to the field but didn't load my weapon. I showed the lifers that I didn't have my weapon loaded and they'd say, "Riehle, you don't have your weapon loaded!" And I said, "Why should I have my weapon loaded, I wouldn't shoot anybody anyway?" Then they'd leave me alone. I didn't feel too bad about it either since we had an overstrength company and we weren't in a bad area for the last seven days. I mean I wasn't hurting the rest of the company by not having my weapon loaded. We were pretty sure we weren't going to run into VC, in fact we were so sure that we were all stoned every day we were out there—we were so stoned we were walking into trees. *We were going home.*

I had written my parents and they wrote back and my father said that it was the saddest moment of his life when his son was refusing to fight. When I got home my father thought I had been in the hands of the communists 'cause I was using these clichés like imperialism. But the U.S. *is* an imperialist in Vietnam. I thought my father would be the one to understand, but he didn't. He could not see that what I'd done in Vietnam was because I thought it was right. My parents thought I was crazy. What was really bad about coming home was seeing so many kids getting busted for such an inconsequential thing as marijuana—I mean after using it as an everyday thing, half the *army* using it, and then you get home and one kid gets caught with a speck and they put him away for two years. My father knew that something had happened to me in Vietnam; I'd changed radically. One night he was watching TV and my younger brother comes in and says, "Guess what, Dad's just watching a show on Vietnam and they mentioned that all these guys are smoking marijuana and he turned around and said, 'Do you think Jim's smoked marijuana over there?' " My mother knew that I did and she told him yes, I did, and he said, "That's probably why he's crazy." I tried to bring it up with him, I thought he'd have to open up his mind for this, but he didn't; he just said, "Well, when you go to pot, you go to pot." Really frustrating.

You want to know something really freaky? My father and I were arguing one day about Vietnam, like I had been there and he hadn't, but he knew all about it from *National Review*. Finally, I said, look, it's people like you who are going to be the cause of the revolution. And, I said, the way you are right now, I couldn't fight for you, I'd have to fight for the revolution. It's your kind of thinking that almost got me killed in Vietnam. Then he said, "Maybe you should have been, rather than lose your soul."

Another time we were watching some demonstrations on TV and he said, "What they ought to do is take all these kids and beat 'em with sticks." And I said, wow! that's really a Christian thing to say! And he said, "Well, Christ wasn't a revolutionary," and I said, are you shitting me? Why do you think he was crucified?

I was really frustrated that *Newsweek* didn't print my letter in the stateside edition. These were the people I was trying to reach, to tell people that here are six combat infantrymen who don't have any spirit, who don't want to be there, who know the war is wrong. And like most GIs get back from Vietnam and they forget; they don't say anything; they say, well, it's over, I can forget about it. And that's one of the reasons I deserted, right there, I didn't want to be part of that. I had to make my commitment. I had to make people stop and think, "Well, why the hell did he desert with only 137 days left?" This isn't one of those cases where people could say, "Oh, he deserted 'cause he couldn't get along with the army, or he's deserting 'cause he's a coward." Well, I got along with the army for twenty months and I spent ten months of it in combat. Throughout my whole tour in the army I had thought about deserting. Right at the end I was asking myself, are you army? have you been army all the time? do they really have your mind? To prove they didn't, I decided I'd leave. And I thought, maybe I'm a slave to that two-cars-in-the-garage promise I have when I get out of the army. I had a good job waiting for me, a good future in finance, and I thought, maybe I've done all that bullshit; I've helped the army; I've played their fucking game because I was a slave to my future. There was of course an element of parental rebellion in my deserting. But it wasn't so much that I was rebelling against people or a thing, but that I was rebelling against the person that I had been conditioned to be.

When I got back, I had it made for stateside duty. I had a good job at Fort Knox near home. My wife would come and see me every weekend. If I could have been a force for change at Fort Knox I would have stayed. But I didn't see what I could do; I was isolated as far as good people were concerned. I was at this reception center with lifers, and I didn't have time to talk much to the new guys, though I told a lot of them what to expect and how to shovel it back on the army. I'd tell guys they'd have to put up with a lot of crap, though, 'cause they'd made their mistake when they came in instead of going to Canada. One day I took these leaflets from FTA [*Fun, Travel and Adventure*, a GI paper; the acronym means "fuck the army" to a GI] which I got at the Fort Knox coffeehouse, and I put them in their barracks. When I got transferred from the reception center to an infantry unit at Fort Knox there wasn't anyone with whom I could relate. There was no one there I could share any thoughts with, talk about something I'd read. This caused my frustrations to build. What really got me when I got home was all the enlisted men I found. Enlisted men everywhere, lifers everywhere, and officers. There were more officers in one infantry company at Fort Knox than in my whole battalion in Vietnam. And they all thought Vietnam was great. That we should be there. I said, fuck you guys, if you guys are really talking about what brave fighting men you are and that we should be in Vietnam, why aren't you in Vietnam? If it's really such a great war, why aren't you there? Why is it all draftees who are fighting? This really got to me. The only way I felt I could show my ultimate contempt for the whole thing, the army, the war, what I had become, was to pack up, take my wife, and say goodbye. But, still, I didn't.

And then I read the book by Gardner on the Presidio Trials—bought it at the PX!—and that put me back into my Vietnam rage. At last I said, I've got to finally do something and it has to be drastic; it's got to hit people, to make a few people question this whole military thing. Even if it just lets a small piece of doubt come into their mind to chip away at the paranoia, the whole thing they have about the military. Then the Cambodian thing hit me. And I was still thinking about my friends in Vietnam. I got a letter from a friend in the 9th Division who went into Cambodia with a mechanized unit and the things he wrote me were so typical, like "The juice freaks are going crazy. When we go through a village and they see something that hasn't been damaged, they'll go out of their way to destroy it. Like they'll run over motorbikes, put them under the tracks." So here we are in Cambodia, a supposedly neutral country, and what do we do? We walk right in and shoot the shit out of the place. I know what the people think about the great machine coming into their country. And I know that the army doesn't care about civilians, that all they care about is pleasing Nixon by keeping the GI casualty rate down, and if that means shooting up everything and everybody in sight they do it. And then there was Kent State which was *complete* insanity. How did this happen? And the lifers thought it was the kids' fault!—even though no guardsmen were even treated for scratches—that the kids were running and were shot in the back and the side. OK, all this hit me and was working in my mind going around and around. Then I remembered reading where Lindy Blake (was it?) of the Presidio 27, got landed immigrant status in Canada after he escaped from the Presidio stockade and that they couldn't deport him. I always thought they could bring you back; the army said they could. Then I read the article in *Newsweek* by Stewart Alsop, about all the Americans in Canada—40,000!—and I thought this was really outasight. I realized that I could get landed; I had a wife, money, a car and could play the "big straight." So I mentioned this to my wife. I said, just because I've been a stooge for the establishment for twenty months, why twenty-four? That doesn't make it better. And she said, "You're right." I said, why haven't I deserted before? So I can live in America? So I can join the peace movement?—is that relevant? Am I using that as a cop-out so I can get out and get a job and forget about Vietnam? So then we just left, drove up to Windsor, came to Toronto, went to TADP, and they told me what I needed to know about finding a job and applying for immigrant status, and then they sent me over to the ADC and they sent me to the Dundas Street hostel and gave us a room for a dollar a night.

Deep down I believe the U.S. will get better, but it only will happen when people start saying no to insanity. I hope by my deserting that I can get more people in my realm, people who know me, to be open to those people who are working to change things. I hope I'm that weakness in the train of thought they've built up, I hope I'm that one thing they can't explain. If I can be that thing, and if they're intellectually honest, then they'll change. I hope by giving up on America that it will scare a few people. And it really pains me because I think the U.S. is a good place to live, that all this stuff right now is merely growing pains for the country. I compare myself to someone who was wounded in the war and who can no longer take an active part in American society. Let's say that in the struggle for change I did my part, but I can't share in the results, not for a while at least, perhaps never. But then Canada isn't a hardship. I'm not standing here at the border crying.

When I got to Toronto I asked where are the slums? And someone said, "You're living in them." I mean, Dundas and Spadina? Slums? It's nice! I look forward to being a Canadian citizen. I want to have a family and bring up a kid where he doesn't have to worry about a draft, where if he says he's against war, people don't look at him strange.

NINE

The First Priority Is Life

Paul Petrie, twenty-four, is an obvious Libra—he is personable, well-balanced and emotionally stable. His short, curly brown hair and aquiline nose reveal his French ancestry while his downeaster deliberateness can be traced to Old Town, Maine, where he grew up. Petrie rose from a bleak and difficult childhood that bordered on poverty and earned a fellowship to the University of Maine. He did postgraduate work at the University of Connecticut, made straight A's, was made a member of the honorary Phi Kappa Phi, and received a master's degree in sociology. With the cancellation of graduate student deferments, he was drafted out of a Ph.D. program.

Petrie was drafted into the U.S. Marine Corps (the marines have required a levy to help fill their ranks throughout this war) and after a very short time on Parris Island he realized that it was more than he had bargained for—he had resigned himself to the army but the marines were something else entirely. On leave, he visited Montreal to see if deserters were safe in Canada, and if they were, planned to continue with basic training and return to Canada when he received orders for Vietnam. Instead, he liked what he found in Canada and stayed and has never been back to the United States.

In Montreal he entered McGill and continued with his Ph.D. work, assisting in several courses on the side. But his primary interest lay with his fellow deserters. He worked with the Deserters' Committee as treasurer from June 1969 to January 1970 and was largely responsible for gathering financial support from the liberal segment of the peace movement in the U.S. and the National and Canadian Councils of Churches, and for helping to build the ADC into a competent aid organization. Following this exhausting period of activism, he left for British Columbia with a girlfriend and retired to South Pender Island in the Straights of Georgia for six months where they lived in a small cabin, chopped their own wood, hauled their water and planted vegetables in the spring. In the primordial solitude of their gulf island idyll he worked on his Ph.D. thesis. Returning to Vancouver in the summer he married his girl, found work with a research project at the University of British Columbia, and planned a family.

Below Paul Petrie talks about the military and about America, about Canada and the war resisters here, about "the revolution," and about life, and he expresses thoughts shared by perhaps the majority of the American exiles in Canada.

I received an induction notice in 1967 when I graduated from the University of Connecticut. I appealed for a conscientious objector classification, which was turned down, and that took about a year. And I appealed that and my attempt for an appeal was turned down. I didn't get an appeal. So they drafted me—out of school while I was in a Ph.D. program. For me at the time, the big question that I'd thought about for these two years—I talked about it with antiwar groups in the States; I was involved in the antiwar movement and demonstrations—was the possibility of dodging the draft. I was trying by legal means not to go in the army; I spent two years doing that. I couldn't get out on any medical grounds. So I hustled down to the Boston Resistance program and asked what was going on in Canada, what were the legal problems of getting into Canada and staying in Canada and they said, well, our preference right now is not to see people go to Canada, but to maybe consider getting drafted in the army and organize from within. They were trying to get everyone out on legal deferments if possible, and they weren't encouraging draft dodging at that particular time. What they were really pushing; what they really wanted me to do, was to refuse induction and go to jail, and I said I'd consider that. I considered that for six months, but then I thought, well, it's a choice between refusing induction and going to jail, or going to jail once I was in the army when I got orders for Vietnam. Finally, it was almost as if I accepted that fate; I was going to go in the army, refuse orders, and go to jail. I had taken Canada out of my mind by that time. I thought that for political reasons it would be smarter to go in the army, attempt to get a CO classification while I was in the army—and maybe not even go to jail; I had that dream of not going to jail while I was in the army, of possibly avoiding it, of spending two years in the army and somehow skipping the whole Vietnam trip. At that time my only objection to being a U.S. citizen was what was happening in Vietnam—there were no other problems that I could see. This was the only inconsistency I saw in America. All of my thinking revolved around that; how do I get out of this dilemma? how do I stay in America and still come to terms with this inconsistency? So I let myself be drafted, and decided if it came to going to Vietnam I'd go to jail. That was my initial decision. Until induction day when I was drafted into the marines.

On induction day I was chosen randomly. I would put "randomly" in quotes because that morning when we were going through the line the recruiting sergeant was reading off names and when he came to my name he said, "Have you joined any political organizations lately Petrie?"—apparently they had all your files there. I was picked "at random" among twenty-six guys to be drafted into the marines. That was a bit of a scarey thing—those two things connected. I don't think that was a coincidence. Anyway, I said what the hell, you said you were going into the service, maybe the marines is a heavier trip, but OK. So I got on the plane and flew down to South Carolina, Parris Island. We got off the plane in this really small airport outside of Parris Island and the minute we came into the airport terminal there was a young officer there waiting for us. Immediately he was barking orders at us and pacing up and down and screaming at people who were talking, and giving everybody shit. I thought Christ we're not even there yet! When we got to Parris Island at one o'clock in the morning, the drill instructor who greeted us when we got off the bus was probably ten times as ugly, ten times as profane, and ten times as inhuman as this officer who met us at the airport. It was almost as if they'd hit us with one of their nicest guys first so their ugliest guys would have a good impact. And he had a good impact. There were eighty-four guys getting off the two buses that we came in on and there were eighty-four guys really scared. The first flash that stands out in my mind when we got to the receiving depot at Parris Island was that he told us what attention was and he said we were at attention for the next eight weeks. Then without looking he picked up a sand bag and threw it right at a kid's face and knocked the kid over and cut his face up, and said "You weren't at attention you motherfucker." Without even looking. I was beginning to have real doubts about staying human in the marines from the outset.

They shaved the heads and there was a lot of pressure the first few days. What it was for me was probably one of the best seminars I've ever had on attitude, organization, and change. I'd had graduate seminars on that and graduate courses in psychology and sociology, but nowhere in an academic setting do you find what you would call a closed system; nowhere in the U.S. except maybe in the marines and prisons and mental hospitals do you have a situation where people have complete control, really complete control over what you're going to do next and how they're going to present you with a certain thing. And they take advantage of that in what I think is a fantastically effective way, and really inhumane way at the same time. I think they feel they have to be one to be the other. I don't necessarily think so. Anyway, the fear that they had instilled in people struck home the fifth day we were there when we were taking a battery of tests for thirteen hours, starting at five in the morning. And about four-thirty in the afternoon we were standing in line to speak to an officer who was going to tell us our scores which had been processed by then. Our drill instructor wasn't around for the first time; we were all standing there chatting, about nothing, about our mutual dumbfoundedness at what was going on, our disbelief of what was happening. And one kid lit up with a warm smile and said, "You know, this is the first time I've talked to anybody since I've been here." I said, wow! yeah, that's what's happening to all of us. A system geared to fear.

The thing that bothers me about marine training most is not that it's a rough time, that's something that everybody puts up with and comes out of somehow, but what these people are like after their four years in the marines. The keynote of being a marine is not to ask questions and not to consider alternatives to situations, but to follow orders. In a country that claims to operate on the exact opposite principle, they're really building a kind of person that's inadequate to handle democracy. But maybe that's what they're after, maybe they're after the person who isn't searching for different alternatives, who won't express themselves.

I won't make the analogy with the Nazi army . . . whether the methods are the same or not is hard to say because I just don't have that experience . . . but what I can say, what I do believe, is that the *end product* is the same. And I think it's because of the similar methods that are used. That was very saddening for me to discover. What I lost faith in, and it wasn't faith in the marines because I had no faith in the marines, was the U.S. People in the States were unwilling or unable to see what was going on. There's so much pride in the marines—but if that's what America professes to be proud of, then it's really time to reassess what we call pride. That was a big disillusioning thing. I'd never seriously considered coming to Canada until after I'd been in the military. Even then I had apprehensions about Canada. But more and more the marines built in me this even greater apprehension of four or five years in a marine brig. There was the promise by one staff sergeant who was lecturing on marine history—and this is interesting, for the first time in the marine's history, they were embarrassed because they had to draft people; for the first time in marine history there was a war unpopular enough, a cause unpopular enough that they had to draft people into the elite striking forces of the military—and so this marine sergeant was trying to come to terms with this embarrassment, like he expressed his embarrassment by pointing out that we who'd been drafted into the marines were the lowest scum of the lowest scum. We would all be grunts he told us. The only thing they were going to train us for was to kill *slopes*. "And I would guess," he said, "that out there among you are some so-called hippie communist antiwar Vietniks, but the loyalty of ninety-nine percent of the marines is with our goals all the way and any trouble that you try to cause will not be tolerated. Dissent, this is something the Marine Corps won't stand for; *you're liable to end up with a bullet in the back of the head.*" Guys caught that about the bullet in the back of the head, guys caught that.* He was talking about building a tight unit. They tell guys this as part of operating on the fear principle. They don't want to kill every potential dissenter, just kill a few as examples, leaving the threat over the heads of everyone else. Again, the long term consequences of this are what are really frightening.

He also told us that no marines ever deserted, desertion wasn't a Marine Corps phenomenon. It was, after all, a volunteer force.**

What the Marine Corps did for me was . . . it just forced questions. I said before that I was against the war and this was my main rebellion from American society—I was against the war. But a whole string of questions came up after that. I began to question the Presidency itself, the decisions Johnson had made. Things that I had heard in the past that hadn't really struck home were beginning to ring bells for me. One of the things that came back to my mind was the type of man Lyndon Johnson was—the thing that stands out in my mind, kind of a flash, was the 1964 Democratic Convention at Atlantic City when Johnson was a sure thing, renomination was a sure thing. Three things dominated that convention as far as I'm concerned: two pictures of LBJ forty feet high behind the speaker's podium, one to the right and one to the left. The third thing was Lyndon Johnson's ego. From there, just relating that to the war, I began to see the weakness of the man and the war. I'd been fooled by so many people supporting Johnson, I'd really been fooled by that, by the whole Democratic Party supporting Lyndon Johnson's war effort, except for the Eugene McCarthy boys who came out at the end, and then a faltering Robert Kennedy. It wasn't until 1969 that people were politically able to condemn the war. The whole credibility of the United States government system was being linked to the credibility of the Vietnam War. For the

*Marine deserters in Canada have reported that dissenting, morale-lowering marines in Vietnam have been eliminated during combat, from the rear, by special sharpshooter squads. A deserter who wishes to remain nameless says, "Why should I go around telling people this, no one would believe it anyway. But I can tell you that a lot of mothers got their sons' bodies back with a 7.62 U.S. calibre round in the back of the head."

**As many as one-quarter of the deserters in Canada are Marine Corps enlisted men, although the marines make up only one-twelfth of the U.S. Armed Forces.

first time, instead of just thinking about the war, I was thinking, how, *how* did this happen?

When I began to lose faith in the American ideal, so many things came into question after that: the initial repression of the Panthers, the so-called progress on the race issue, Nixon being elected, the Democratic Convention. In all my past understanding of government and history was the idea of progress, the liberal ideal that things keep getting better, inevitably keep getting better year after year. What I was beginning to realize was that things were getting worse. Like that was a big revelation to me; it's a cliché now, but at the time it wasn't. *Things were getting worse*, and when you realize that, you don't live on hope anymore. Then you begin to think and you begin to act. And it wasn't until I took this step that I was capable of acting against the U.S. government. Before that, I was almost going to submit, at a masochistic level, to going to jail, going to a marine brig instead of going to Vietnam because I still had faith. But when I started asking those questions, when I lost that faith in progress, saw that things were going in the opposite direction from what people were saying, it was then that I felt the need to act. It wasn't an obligation; it wasn't a justification; it was a real need. I was tired of this feeling of powerlessness.

I wasn't ready to go to jail after that. I wasn't ready to submit to their approved punishment for what I disagreed with. It was more a question of rebelling at that point. Then I came to Canada while on leave—to have a look around—and I ran into what was really a good thing, for me personally and for the expression of my ideas. There were two antiwar organizations in Montreal helping war resisters, and I found a community of war resisters. It really surprised me. These people working with the organization were receiving up to fifteen and twenty letters a day, guys asking how they could get to Canada, what it was like, saying they were planning to come. What I sensed that first morning in Montreal, was that there was a community of dissent that had formed within the army—like I had been into an antiwar community while I was at the university—but I found that there were people within the army who had gone as far as I had and also felt that same need to act. Now they were in Canada. That put a lot of things together for me.

The second day I was in Montreal I met a deserter who had been to Vietnam and who had fought in Vietnam and who had deserted after he had fought in Vietnam because of what was happening there. There are no better qualified persons to judge what is happening in Vietnam than the people who have fought there. Not too long after that I met another deserter who was a marine, a sergeant, and who was a veteran of Vietnam and who had six months to go before his discharge. These, to me, are the experts on Vietnam, and it was these people that I began to listen to. They have an awful lot more credibility than Lyndon Johnson or Richard Nixon or any secretary of state or "concerned" politician.

But I had been planning to go back and finish basic training in the marines as part of my own education if for nothing more. It seemed important for me to see that through because I felt I was finding out so much which my eyes had never seen; like Americans don't want to see that on television, what Marine Corps training is really like; I wouldn't have believed it on TV and would have said, "That's sensationalism." But hell, I was living sensationalism every waking hour of the day and in my dreams at night. If it's a distortion, then the Marine Corps is a distortion. If it's sensationalism, then the marines are sensational. I had only come up to see if Canada was safe for deserters because it wasn't clear to the people in Boston; I hadn't been planning on staying, but I was so impressed by what was going on in Montreal that I spent a couple of days, met the people in the resister community, and I saw more sanity in Montreal than I had seen in a long time. I was optimistic for the first time in a long time when I came to Montreal. It was a quick decision for me, but I decided to stay and do what work I could from Canada against the war.

For me the real potency in the act of deserting was that those people who were most directly affected by the war, those people central to the war effort, were saying no. This is a question of a person's total involvement, a total commitment, it is a question of your life—what are you giving your life up for? For those people who are directly involved with the war to reject it—and it's being rejected on a large scale—is beautiful, and that's what brought about my optimism. For me, what I mean by optimism is the capacity to act in some way, not to be disabled by despair. It was the idea that I could do something here linked with the recognition that it wasn't a meaningless act. It was important not just to act in any random and haphazard way, not just to dissipate frustration, but to act in a meaningful way. And when I found out that there were sixty thousand American war resisters in Canada then for me desertion was a meaningful act. That optimism provided me with a kind of starting point.

So for the next seven months I put as much time as I could into working with people in Canada. For the first time I was working out of optimism. I'm not trying to paint a beautiful picture of Canada itself; I'm trying to say something about my particular involvement at that time. When I had questioned what was happening in the States to the extent that it really began to lose credibility, and when I lost faith in that liberal vision of unending progress then I had that kind of general depression, like what can you do? In Canada there was a chance for me to do what I could, to remain free, to maintain some control over my future, not to be completely channeled, a chance to put my feelings out in the world rather than just have the dissent in my own head.

The other thing that impressed me in Canada was the closeness of people. First the closeness of the deserters, not a closeness for security, but a real, outright frankness—I've been in different universities for six years, and I met more *real people* who were deserters than I had known real people who were graduate students, believe it or not. My feeling toward fellow students documents what I think—I spent little, in fact no time with the graduate students at McGill; I spent all my time with the ADC. This was important for me to see—like, I was on the other end of the propaganda for a long time and I really believed that only a social fuck-up would go to Canada, desert the army and go to Canada. I really believed those things. I wouldn't always admit believing them, even to myself, but somehow I always had that apprehension. But the people here were fantastic. The people *are* fantastic. I feel a bond with these people here, a really strong thing. Partly because I really respect their courage to act. Guys come up under different circumstances and sometimes for different reasons—always for more than one reason—and you don't see too many going back. It's a question of people with a real conviction, a real need to act. I was really impressed with them as *alive* people, *intelligent* people, intelligence being different from education . . . When I was in the States I had two close friends who went to Vietnam, two really close friends. Like I was best man at both their weddings and they came back from Vietnam and they both . . . it was like they were trying to puke up what they experienced there and they kept trying to keep it down. I talked with them both about what they saw and what had happened, and they had both seen action, and they were both sick, and they were both somehow trying to say, "That's all over now." And there are people in the States who say that deserters are cowards . . . I guess it depends on what you mean by coward. I think there are an awful lot of real cowards in the States. People who have been involved in massacres, who have seen massacres and so on, and who were quiet. They were cowards to their responsibility to life.

The other thing that I was impressed with is the Canadian people themselves. Especially the French Canadian people. My exposure was originally with French Canadian people. I came to Montreal with no hair on my head at all. I was a shaved marine. It was a secret to nobody in Canada what I was or why I was there. And I really felt self-conscious and I didn't want to go on the subway. The first time I was out on the street a young French Canadian kid—English speaking—came up and said, "Are you from the States?" I said yeah, I'm a deserter, almost apologetically, and he said, "Well, congratulations!" and he stuck out his hand and shook my hand.

I think most Americans think deserters and draft dodgers come to Canada and then spend this life underground somehow, not only underground in terms of law in Canada, but underground in their own mind, the whole underground mentality of being persecuted and watched. I wouldn't say that I came to Canada as a hero or that Canadians saw me as a hero, but I would say that the Canadians that I knew had enough of an open mind so they respected what I did; they respected the fact that I acted. I found a really favorable response on the part of a lot of people.

It was a big blast to find the American Deserters' Committee office. A friend drove me up and we circled the block three times—this was at the Wolfe Street office—before we went in to see what it was like. And I went in and here were really friendly people, and I couldn't believe it; they were really open, they were calling up—they had a housing list of Canadian people—and they would just pick up the phone and say, "We have some new deserters in today and we're looking for a place for them to stay, do you think you could put one up for a few days." This whole thing amazed me, a complete *above*-ground, complete legality in Canada. At the same time, most Americans felt that you had to go to Sweden if you were a deserter. But, like, we were having open weekly meetings; guys were going out with Canadian girls; we were invited to parties; we had members of the press helping guys get landed. The whole thing was a bit too much for me. It was a reassessment of America by people other than myself. It's a funny thing, there's such a thing as reassessment from within the U.S. and there's such a thing as reassessment from without the States. It's a different evaluation. I think when I raised questions when I lived in the States I would make every attempt to apologize for what was happening, I was trying to find excuses for U.S. policies that I believed were morally wrong, but I was still trying to find an excuse. I don't think Canadians, for example, are into that. Canadians express their antiwar sentiment in a more rational fashion. They haven't reacted in a guilty fashion 'cause they haven't felt guilty. And their evaluation is an awful lot harsher than that of Americans who allow themselves the liberty of criticism. I found that that was a reassuring thing too; I felt less like an outcast every day I stayed here. And I was watching with my own eyes those letters coming in, new guys coming in to the office every day. The reality of that drove it all home in a very short time.

I had tended to be a hell of a lot more naive than someone in the marines with a working-class background. Partly because I was part of the system in a sense—I was going to be a university teacher, a professor, that whole deal— and I had that vested interest of defending what was going down, somehow trying to maintain an objective perspective, whatever that was. And I found that a lot of these deserters who came up had not been political before, but had been equipped to accept what they saw once they saw it. I had been what I had called sort of liberally political, and it was fairly hard for me to accept what I saw when I saw it. I would say a lot of these people are unchanneled. What happened to many deserters was that this was their first confrontation with channeling in America—I had been through it; I had been channeled in school; education is a kind of channeling system where your commitments become greater—these guys hadn't been channeled and their consciousness, their political consciousness, although less developed, was maybe more acute when it came to this confrontation with channeling. It took me awhile before I could see what was going on, but I think the other guys—and I'm not trying to make a generality because not all deserters are alike—saw more of a real confrontation with the system, with a system that they hadn't had that much faith in to begin with 'cause it had never given them that much.

I had a lot to lose in the decision that I made; I mean, I *thought* I had a lot to lose in that I believed very strongly in what I was doing: being in school, and then going to jail as a protest against the Vietnam War. Like I was going to go to Boston to burn my draft card that spring at a Spock rally with the consequent arrest and jail, but I had a talk with a friend the day before and I decided not to go. I came that close to going to jail. And if I had gone to jail, I think I would still be trying to justify what was happening in America like so many people today, desperately trying to justify . . . you know, they tried to justify bombing North Vietnam; today they're trying to justify Nixon's move into Cambodia. What are they going to try to justify tomorrow? How far do you go before you have to stop justifying insanity? Most of the guys in Canada I've met aren't trying to justify it, they've simply said no to it.

I started working with the organization and along with a number of deserters was involved in reorganizing the ADC so that we were able to house and feed and get the increasing number of people coming to Canada landed. The summer that I camē up there was a big influx of people, but it was a question of tripling and even exceeding that because Canada was now open to deserters, legally, as expressed in government policy, and the word was getting down to the people in the U.S. One of the things that I experienced during this work with the committee was seeing people who had lost faith in America but hadn't lost faith in democracy, or lost faith in what you might call participatory democracy, because the ADC was organized as a kind of forum for these people—it offered them a real opportunity to express themselves; it was a chance for them to become part of something as a real person which the army had denied them and which the U.S. was denying them more and more. This was part of my optimism. It stood out in my mind, just a small contrast, but it stood out as being worthwhile. These people were reaffirming their faith in man, in people, in themselves, while at the same time they were questioning their faith in a government, in a system, in a war, in a mentality. I think the weekly meetings and the steering committee meetings were really important for a lot of guys. We can look for alienation in Canada among Americans and we can see it—there are individual cases of alienation around every committee, and it's around the aid committees that you can see these people hanging around, hanging on—but I think the alienation that people in the States imagine and reporters come to Canada looking for is really out of touch with the reality. *Really* out of touch. I'll say this: I don't think guys up here are any more alienated than Canadian youth or than American youth within the U.S. What I'm saying is that if you're looking for a causal relationship between them being up here in another country and any alienation they may exhibit, it's spurious.

As for the way some writers judge us up here, I think Alsop's article in *Newsweek** revealed a lot more about him than it did about us in Canada. He came to Canada for three days and felt the guys in Canada were trying to justify being exiles by hating the U.S. Instead of seeing young Americans growing, freeing themselves, doing something positive for the first time in their lives perhaps, like working with the aid groups, he said they were all doing this, engaging in their criticism of the U.S., out of "a need to hate" as he called it. Well, I spent a year and a half here, and I don't find as much hate among Americans in Canada as I do among young people in the U.S. itself, partly because in the U.S. people are *more* frustrated by very real conditions than we are here. Somehow, he feels the exiles are hating a fantasy they've created themselves, to justify their act. At the same time—his major omission —he didn't consider at all *why* people might be up here, what kind of legitimate reasons they might be up here for; he didn't talk about the war in Vietnam. It was a shallow analysis. He's searching for a justification for his *own* position; he was almost reflecting his own insecurity of being part of the establishment. He shows his liberalism—he can never be a radical. We've made one political act, the act of desertion or dodging, but that's like a first step. Beyond that you do what you can. And you find all types of deserters and dodgers in Canada expressing their frustration, their unhappiness with the U.S., sometimes even their anger, a strongly felt anger, but I don't think I've seen hate. I think Alsop confused hate with anger. I see more of a positive thing.

My optimism in Canada is so much greater than it was in the States . . . there's just greater sanity in Canada. You hear Canadians talking more often about a standard of *life* rather than a standard of living—something they measure in terms of their humanness, not in terms of their pocketbook.

---

*Stewart Alsop, "The Need to Hate," *Newsweek*, July 27, 1970.

There's a real sensitivity to that, that I was becoming blunted to in the States. And I don't think I could regain that optimism if I returned to the U.S., if I could return, because I don't think America will ever be the same again. First of all, I don't think you can erase from the conscience of the American people the fact that they've been in Vietnam, and, second of all, inevitably, that they're going to have to face the fact that they've lost in Vietnam. And those are real scars, both of those, and they are scars that are going to take a long time to heal; they're going to take generations, and they'll never be really healed; there will always be a mark. Something else that bothers me . . . it takes a strange mentality to tolerate a war that's being tolerated like this, for so long. And I don't care what people say about being against the war: they're still tolerating it if they haven't acted in whatever way they could to do something about it; they're still tolerating it, and as long as they're paying taxes for it they're still supporting it. I really think the Vietnam War has emphasized a mentality whose seeds were already there. It's a mentality of intolerance; it's a mentality of racism; it's a mentality of destruction, whether it's destruction of life, destruction of the environment, or destruction of freedom. It's a destructive mentality. Coming to Canada has freed me of that—some. Coming to Canada was an attempt to get out of this, to rethink. It was not an attempt to get away from America. It wasn't an attempt to no longer be an American. It was an attempt for me to be first a real person and then to contribute what I could to America, to whatever I find myself a part of. Whatever I have to contribute now will be contributed to Canada because I plan to stay in Canada. I'm not waiting up here for some fantasized amnesty. I'm not working for an amnesty while I'm here; I'm really not interested in that.

What was happening to me when I was in the U.S. was that the system was geared so that my life was being lived for me; I was being channeled, whether it was an education that I was "choosing" or whether it was in the marines and being channeled to Vietnam. My life was being lived for me. I think the first thing that I can do, not the only thing, but the first thing, is to take that initiative and live my life first. This frees my frustration because I've seized that initiative and I've done what I could to *live* what I want to see America *be*. That to me is the first step.

Another thing I'm particularly concerned about is the quality of life that my family will have. I'm concerned with that level of living as much as I'm concerned with my nationality. If I hadn't deserted from the marines and I had a family in the States today, I would be doing what an awful lot of Americans are doing now, and that is considering moving my family to another part of the world. It's not like something is keeping me in Canada; it's like something is keeping me away from the U.S. It's not that the U.S. says I can't go back, it's that I don't necessarily want to go back. If I went back to the States now, I would have to go back as a revolutionary. And I don't have any delusions about carrying a gun back to the States. I refuse to make my life a reaction to what I see as a destructive mentality. I refuse to acquire a destructive mentality in destroying a destructive mentality. It's that whole trip of the athiest who feels a need to spit at the church everytime he walks by and is really no freer than the person who is inside praying. I can't stir up any hate; I can't get that in me. I don't "hate" the States for it's so easy for me to look back and see myself there; it's so easy for me to look back at the States and see myself trying to justify every mistake, like it's that close to home for me.

Now I have a Canadian wife and by the time this book comes out I'll have a Canadian family. And I'll take up Canadian citizenship. And the first thing I'll do is live a life-style that is real for me, and, to the extent that that life-style is impeded by whatever, then I'm engaged at that point in change, in social change, and precipitating social change in the way that I think is most effective; and I don't think that there's any one particular tactic that's necessarily the most effective. My whole feeling right now is that this idea of either change the individual or change the society—the political revolutionaries versus the cultural revolutionaries—is really the basis for the polarization that's taking place in the Left itself. If you ask me, "Do you change the individual?"—is that my way or do I go out and do the mass thing, the "political" thing—I would answer that those are not two different things; they are the *same*. Like, if a successful revolution is going to be made, it's not going to be made by one or the other. It has to include both. You can't just change the state first, as in the Soviet Union. Anyone who sees this as a dilemma is seeing differently out of each eye, it's a perceptual problem, not a dilemma.

The second thing that I feel, I guess you'd call it an internationalism, is that I have real problems with boundaries. Especially since I've been in Canada. I don't see what's happening in Canada as unconnected with the States, I see everything as intricately linked to what's happening in the States. So as far as the "movement" goes, or the "struggle" goes, or the "revolution" goes, I certainly have my own ideas for change, and I implement those in ways where I can be most effective. And that's not by carrying a gun into the States; it's not by destroying before re-creating. I can't spend my time looking down at the States impotently when there's so much to be done around me. There's such an opportunity in Canada to participate in life. For me that's the first priority, not to deal a death blow, but to participate in life.

TEN

Exiles

The winter and spring of 1969-1970 saw the largest flow ever of American war resisters into Canada. The majority were deserters, the lottery system and easier medical deferments having diminished the number of draft evaders. By mid-summer of 1970, however, there was a noticeable decline in the number of arrivals recorded by the various organizations. It would be inaccurate to judge the size of the influx entirely on reports of the exile aid groups for as information about Canadian immigration became easier to get in the U.S., fewer people were bothering to visit their offices. It was not uncommon to meet a deserter or draft dodger on the street who was immigrated, working, and happily settled in Canada and who had never heard of the local exile organizations. Also, the summer of 1970 found literally hundreds of thousands of youths on the highways seeing North America and hitchhiking to opposite ends of the continent; the shoulders of the Trans-Canada highway were home to many of the newest and youngest war exiles. Nevertheless, the aid groups did provide a gauge for measuring the flow. After each new crisis in the U.S.—the Pueblo affair, Nixon's candidacy, the Cambodia invasion—there had always been a surge of new arrivals the following week. So as the aid groups showed a decline in the number of arrivals by late 1970, it was undoubtedly true that fewer resisters were coming.

EXNET (Exile Network), an effective intergroup newsletter set up at the Pan Canada Conference of Deserters and Resisters and published weekly by a group in Toronto, gave a tally of available figures from the thirty-two exile groups. A study of these figures showed a definite decline from May. Montreal's two counseling groups reported that July was the slowest month in nearly a year with only 133 new arrivals. The total was broken down as follows: eleven Vietnam veterans, forty-three other deserters, fifteen dodgers with induction notices, twenty-four men with 1-A status but without induction notices, nine nondraftable men, twenty-seven women with war resisters, four independent women. Toronto was still receiving approximately 350-400 people a month, only a slight decline over the fall of 1969, though by late fall 1970 it was down to approximately two hundred. Vancouver's figures were the highest in Canada and a large increase over the number for the previous year. They were also receiving a large number of transients. Vancouver's increase, however, did not offset the general decline across Canada but it did point out two other phenomena: that more war resisters were heading for the hills and woods of British Columbia rather than to the eastern cities and that more West Coast youth were heading north rather than continuing to live in the L.A. or Berkley underground. Vancouver's figures for one week in July totalled ninety-nine persons: three Vietnam veterans, twenty-four other deserters, nine men with induction papers, forty-two 1-A's, fifteen nondraftable men, four women with war resisters, and three independent women.

One reason for the decline in the exodus could be attributable to the demoralization of the peace movement in the U.S. and, ironically, to the fact that the peace movement had previously been successful in preventing many antiwar youth from entering the army. At the same time the radical off-base GI movement which had funneled deserters out of the country had nearly collapsed while on-base organizing was meeting with more successes and gaining more adherents—meaning to many GIs who otherwise might have deserted that if they stayed in the army there was the chance they could help change things. Fewer men were being sent to Vietnam. One could *not* attribute the decline to the troop withdrawals from Vietnam, however. If anything, more Vietnam veterans were deserting than ever before. Partly because they found no heroes' welcome and now realized that what they'd seen in Vietnam *was* wrong, and partly because men who had served an agonizing solid year in combat (more than most GIs saw in World War II) were not being discharged upon their return like their predecessors in other wars but were being forced to readapt to the tight discipline of a stateside military base for their remaining six months. For many this was more than ingratitude, it was an insult. The lack of front-line discipline which existed in Vietnam during the closing stages of the ground war—companies of draftees deciding for themselves what they would or would not do and captains obeying the will of the men instead of the other way around—would not be tolerated by the NCOs and officers in the U.S. On most bases the Vietnam combat veteran was treated worse than a new recruit and so many left in disgust. Nonetheless, there were still fewer men coming into Canada. The original wave of deserters that had accompanied the dissemination of knowledge that Canada was safe was not followed by another surge, for the peace movement, or what was left of it, chose not to make desertion a popular issue. The total flow of deserters into Canada leveled off to between seventy-five and one hundred a week, almost half the weekly number for the previous year during which, from May 1969 to May 1970, six or seven thousand ex-servicemen crossed the border.

And so 1970, it seems, saw not only more American exile activity in Canada than in any other year, but it also marked the final phases of the five-year history of the war-induced exodus. This did not mean that the total immigration of Americans to Canada was diminishing. On the contrary, more U.S. émigrés—not war resisters—than ever before were crossing into Canada and the

Immigration Department figures for 1970 would show an increase over previous years. But there were fewer war resisters. Their story, however, was not over in 1970. Although they were casualties of war and would now pass into history along with the other 350,000 Vietnam War casualties, they were still alive and whole and free and planning a new life and so their story was really just beginning.

●

Jack Todd is an army deserter and a city reporter for the *Vancouver Sun.* He is 6'6'', with a long, sharply carved face, jet black hair and long sideburns; he dresses modishly, expensively for casual Vancouver. Like many exiles, he works for a conservative organization, yet he tends to identify more with disaffected youth and fellow exiles than with the establishment which employs him. A former editor of the *Daily Nebraskan* and president of the SDS chapter at the University of Nebraska, he says that the entire staff of the school newspaper and the president of the student body at that time now reside in Canada. In a page-long piece in the *Vancouver Sun* entitled, "The young men who can never go home," Todd wrote:

> The question is always asked in innocence, always framed in a voice of concern, always with a gently painful naiveté. Every Canadian I've met gets around to it sooner or later. "You can never go back, can you?" they ask ... The question pulls out images topsy-turvy, a mixed bag of memories good and bad: flashes of a tiny Nebraska town tucked away in the western badlands, of early years yearning for the uniform of an American soldier, of an Air Force Academy appointment declined, of fruitless protest marches and finally the induction notice and the brief fling with compromise in the U.S. Army. And underneath, the persistent refrain: "You can't go home again ..."
>
> Home—the U.S.—is now a jangled chaos, a great nation writhing in contradictions, groping for a solution through force or flowers. But it's still home, still a magnet whose force field cannot be ignored, even by the thousands of young men like myself who have chosen to reject it rather than participate in what we consider its greatest folly... [There] is a fear that most of us will carry into middle age, a fear born of being wanted for a crime we do not consider a crime. We will carry this, and the desire to go home just once, and the labels "draft dodger" and

"deserter" and we will always answer the innocent question: "You can never go home, can you?" We will make this our country and give it our skills and our commitments. History may judge us as cowards or heroes, but we are simply young men caught in a vortex of events whirling beyond our control. We had a choice—war, prison or exile—we made it, and we will make the best of it.

Making the best of it was not always easy. Perhaps only fifty percent did as well as Jack Todd. There was an alienation here, even if it amounted to nothing more than never being able to return home. For an American, having been raised in the belief that after America there was no place else to go, this was quite enough. There was not only the usual alienation shared by North American youth, there was the disorienting stress of being forced to live in an unfamiliar place to which one was not likely to have come under other conditions. Simply because of what being an American has always meant, Americans were not readily equipped for the task of readjusting to a new life in a new country. Especially if one was an unwilling immigrant, had chosen emigration as the best of bad alternatives. Unlike their alienated Canadian counterparts in the large cities, the young Americans in Canada were a long way from their families and they could not go home for a hearty Sunday night dinner or to borrow ten dollars. Being alienated within five miles of where one grew up, which is the story of young Canadians in Toronto or Montreal or Vancouver who seldom exchange their native city for another, is a very different thing from the experience of feeling alienated and being separated by an untraversable international border from friends, family, and all one's ever known. Sharing this common experience, exiles have tended in all too many cases to keep to their own community of war resisters; some American exiles have no Canadian friends at all.

Nevertheless, it could be argued that the alienation of the younger war resisters was in no way as serious as that which was suffered by unemployed youths in New York or Los Angeles. There is no violence in the air of the Canadian cities, no fear, the streets are safe for the people who are forced to spend a lot of time in them; the streets are friendly, people are warm, open, less uptight than in U.S. cities. If one is traveling, there are government-operated youth hostels in the summer; there are government-sponsored youth-aid agencies, and in comparison with the U.S. there is little to fear from police either in the cities or the country; visits to private physicians or hospitals are entirely without charge. In all, alienation in Canada can be more genteel.

By 1970 the most serious problem was jobs as Canada's unemployment rate was even higher than that in the U.S. (The colony always suffers first when things go bad in the mother country of the empire.) Applying for welfare was grounds for deportation so exiles suffered more than out-of-work Canadians if they were unable to find employment. But unemployment was not unique to Canada in these times. For the young anywhere in North America it was nothing less than a depression, though young people had a way of getting by and therefore were scarcely noticed. As long as one could get by, why work at a demeaning job? There would have been a terrible crisis, maybe even a revolution, if they all demanded work. (But they didn't. Abbie Hoffman had pointed out that there was no way the system could possibly provide jobs anyway for all the unemployed youth so the leaders should have been glad that so many people were volunteering for unemployment.)

In Canada, it was far more important for a newly arrived war resister to have a job *offer*, in order for him to become immigrated, than it was to have actual work. Occasionally people were hired by sympathetic employers but after they passed immigration they declined the job, preferring part-time work or not to work at all. Apartments were shared; collectives were formed; urban communes and cooperatives grew up, and living was as cheap as could be. Still, it was always terribly disturbing to meet a freshly arrived American, just out of college or the army, well-fed, healthy looking, and then see him on the streets three or six months later, drawn, colorless, perhaps even sickly. This was not the fault of his being a refugee particularly, but rather the fault of the international corporate empire and North America's brand of capitalism which can operate well, to the advantage of the corporate elite, only when one third of the population is continually disadvantaged, i.e., in debt, underpaid, or out of work. Following college or the army, the same young man would probably have been going hungry in the United States as well.

In Canada he may have been nutritionally hungry, losing weight, and experiencing serious deprivation, living in substandard rooms and so on—but his spirit was not hungry. It was consuming madly, glutting itself on *life, freedom*, and a new hope; its nourishment was a reaffirmation of faith. One young, unemployed resister in Toronto, who hadn't yet got enough money together to clothe himself against the approaching Canadian winter, said ebulliently, "I was reborn last night—it was a whole rebirth, metaphysically. I had made the break intellectually only. Now it came home—after twenty-two years of struggle, it's all over. I'm free." But people cannot live on the rejuvenation of the spirit alone. Alienation on a full stomach is better than alienation on an empty one. In April 1970, Naomi Wall of the Toronto Anti-Draft Programme told the federal government's Committee on Youth that U.S. exiles recently arrived in Toronto were finding it hard to get jobs and harder to get landed immigrant status. She said that in two months two exiles had committed suicide in Toronto and that the TADP was constantly having to bail out U.S. exiles charged with drug dealing, vagrancy, and such crimes as shoplifting. Many of the very young exiles were "starving on the streets" she stated and she made it clear to the committee that the arrival of many working-class deserters with very little education coupled with the deteriorating economic situation had created a near crisis for the exile community. Canada was no longer getting very many well-educated middle-class draft dodgers. She asked that U.S. refugees be granted landed-immigrant status on humanitarian grounds and pointed out that over forty percent of Canada's immigrants are admitted for humanitarian or family reasons.

To help alleviate these problems, some aid committees ran a job co-op for part-time or day work—"rent a deserter" services. Sympathetic people would call in for men to mow lawns, paint houses, clean out basements. Word spread by word of mouth and jobs multiplied. *EXNET* gave a weekly report on the job situation across Canada, listing where special skills were needed and so on. In Windsor, the UAW women's auxiliary, sponsored a job placement center for exiles staffed by three full-time people. The Toronto American Deserters' Committee during the spring and summer of 1970 provided effective job counseling with the help of twenty-six-year-old Richard Orlandini, AFL-CIO card holder and graduate of the University of Michigan with a B.A. in urban anthropology. He was working on his master's when he was drafted. Orlandini has counseled approximately four hundred deserters and has met "over fifteen hundred," and he was looked upon around the ADC as the "village elder." He talks about his job program and discusses deserters in general and the culture shock they encounter in Canada:

Initially when I came to Canada I wasn't going to do anything with the war resisters, I was going to get back into labor organizing. But you know, pangs of conscience. The first thing I ask a guy is if he belonged to a labor union. If it's an international brotherhood it usually carries over and he can get in here. The unions here in Canada have been more than receptive. We send some kids to the unions as unskilled laborers and they usually go out of their way for them. Some are really sympathetic. Some unions have set up apprenticeships for deserters—one electrical union in particular. In counseling the guys I always ask what the army taught 'em. I had one kid who repaired fork trucks in the army and I had no trouble getting him a job. Another kid, a deserter, said he was a paratrooper. I asked him if he really liked to jump out of airplanes and he said he did. So about six phone calls later we got him an appointment with Lands and Forests and they sent him out to Alberta where he's now a smoke-jumper. The army had taught him something. I got one guy a job repairing the helicopters that are used by the Toronto radio stations. He got his experience in Nam working on choppers.

I suppose it would be discouraging, though, if I knew exactly how many exiles were *not* working. Some, of course, don't want to work. But of those that do, some don't find work because they're American deserters—they *do* run into prejudice. Some companies will say, sorry, we don't hire Americans because we might be hiring a deserter or dodger. Like once I had this kid from Louisiana who had worked on off-shore oil rigs, he was a rig man, a good one. We got money together and sent him out to Calgary where there were a lot of rig jobs available but they wouldn't hire him 'cause they are all American firms. On the other hand, IBM hires plenty of exiles. No problem. Honeywell hires; they just hired a deserter as a scab. The ADC almost lost some good labor contracts because of that. A lot of my job is helping guys do things like make up a résumé, and you've got to tell the kid that the shoes have got to be polished, and the shirt has got to be ironed, the pants pressed, he's got to wear a tie. Fingernails must be clean. How important is the hair? For me it's biological, not metaphysical. It grows back . . . you get it cut for the job! You don't go there with long hair and hope to get a job.

Talking in real generalities, stereotypes, the average U.S. Army deserter that I see—I only see a certain type of course—has 11½ years of education, he's unskilled. He's drafted or he enlists, gets in there and runs into the—not the political hassle—but a moral and a disciplinary thing and for the first time he sees that despite the American dream he's treated as shit. More than likely he'll go to Vietnam. With most of the deserters I don't think it's a situation of being conscientiously opposed to the Vietnam War, but it's not being able or willing to take the kind of shit the army puts out. It's not like World War II where the people saw the troops off and welcomed them home, where everyone participated in the war; and the guy knows his country isn't threatened by the sweeping red peril—he knows no Vietnamese is going to come over and rape his sister. So they don't have the same motivation that they had in the World War II. Today kids, white and black, from the slums go into the army because it's the only way out of their situation. And this makes a lot of difference in discipline and army morale all the way down. The black kid out of the slums was reading Malcolm X in high school. They've learned early not to put up with the white man's horseshit. And it's the same with the Puerto Rican, the Mexican-American, and white kid from the slums and then they get into the army and they say, why should I have to take orders from this hillbilly; a kid out of New York has to take orders from some rinky-dink ROTC lieutenant from the University of Tennessee or Oklahoma. That creates *more* dissension. Now some of this rubs off all along the line, all through the army, and you get dissent. Meanwhile, resistance against illegitimate authority is part of our time and naturally this infects the army. And then of course Vietnam has gone on too long for the average kid who was maybe thirteen or fourteen when it started.

Today's deserter is different from those in other wars because not all that many desert from the battle front as men did in Europe. Very few people are really under fire in today's army. Most of your deserters split from the States, about ninety percent. They're more against the army than the war. Again, the shit that they take today isn't that much different from what they took in 1942. It's the same amount of shit coming down on you and a person can accept an awful lot of it if he believes in what he's doing, but he's not going to accept any shit from anybody when he says, what the hell do I care about Vietnam? His tolerance level is a lot lower because he doesn't believe in it. More than that, there is no better model in the U.S. to teach a guy class structure. He's got to obey this lieutenant because he's been to college at Wombat University. "Fuck the Army," they say.

One of the big things that affected the desertion rate is that for the first time the American kid who's read history books and listened to his teachers tell him all about the great American presidents found out that a president actually lied to 'em. That's shattering for a young kid. They always thought everyone was telling them the truth but then Johnson came along and they saw that wasn't the case. And then there was My Lai and that had a lot to do with it.

And so the kid comes to Canada, and he can't put his fingers on it but there are real subtle differences that hit him when he crosses the border. At first it's just like another American city. But eventually, within a week, he starts to notice small, subtle things that *are* different. For one thing, he doesn't get the constant American bullshit over the radio. He'll go through culture shock, an inability to cope with a new cultural situation, depression will set in. There is an inability to talk to the "natives"—being in this situation, Canadians. It's hard to relate to others, even your own peers. Withdrawal will become apparent. The U.S. Army deserter has a dual problem: one, he's going from one country to another, he's left Yankee culture under which he grew up; and in addition he just left *military* culture. He's dehumanized to a degree, moving from a military style of life to a civilian style of life, and, for the guy who gets out of the army without deserting, that transition is made very easy for him; his parents say, OK Johnny, you're out, you've done your thing for God and country; we're gonna give you a vacation. The deserter gets out, leaves the military for civilian life, comes to Toronto, and, no matter where his head is at, the first people he meets are street people, long-haired, hippie, freak radicals and that's a pretty heavy trip for him. Then he goes to the organizations, and they say here's what you gotta do: you gotta do this, this, and this to get in. Nobody's patting him on the head. Nobody's saying he should take a vacation. Nobody helps his transition from military life. He goes and stays with a middle-class Canadian family on the housing list and they tell us he seems lazy, sleeps late, has little motivation. Eventually guys get out of this, if they don't go back—some do go back—and it takes about six months to a year to straighten out.

I'll exert more effort than usual in trying to help a kid who's thinking of going back. I know one kid who deserted from Fort Leonard Wood, got caught hitchhiking across Illinois, got picked up and taken back to the stockade, jumped the stockade, deserted again, got to Michigan, got caught, sent back, deserted again, got to Canada finally, was in Canada two weeks, decided he needed money, went to Detroit to get a job, worked three weeks in construction, went to cash his paycheck in a bar, was nineteen years old. When he came out of the bar he ran into a cop who asked him what he was doing in a bar, said he wasn't supposed to be in there—you can kill in America at eighteen but you can't have a beer—ran an all points on him, and he ended up back at Leonard Wood. He deserted again and is here now, doing very well. Working for IBM.

By bringing more guys to Canada, we're showing guys in the army that if he raises shit and talks other guys into raising shit, then he has a viable alternative other than sitting in a federal penitentiary for fifteen years. When the heat is too strong, you split to Canada. But if we didn't induce others to come first, then he'd have no way of knowing. In other words, the *threat* of desertion, which is a serious threat to any army, is meaningless without the *reality* of desertion; there *are* guys here, maybe ten thousand of them. So the word spreads and the army can't paint the johns fast enough. Thinking about FTAing?* Here's the number in Toronto. It's written on the inside of the john. By inducing desertion, we're supporting dissent by keeping Canada open as a viable alternative. I mean you can't expect that many guys to dissent with the threat of jail hanging over them. I really don't think that it's that much of an issue that we're taking dissenters out of the army. I do know one thing, and I've been in enough jails in the South in the civil rights days, that a man is a nonfunctioning entity in a jail as far as I'm concerned. You can't do fuck-all in a jail unless you're into being a martyr, and I'm not into martyrdom. You can't do anything in jail except sit there and rot. You *can* do something in Canada—a lot do.

●

Dr. Carl Kline is an American self-exile who left the United States four years ago, symbolically on the International Day of Protest, April 15, 1967. Giving up a successful psychiatric career in Wisconsin which included a lucrative private practice and the directorship of the Child Guidance Clinic in Wausau, Dr. Kline and his wife Caroline and their two draft-age sons moved to Canada. Their sons had made their own decisions not to serve; Dr. Kline's reason for leaving was objection to the war itself. As early as 1965 he made it clear that he would not pay income taxes to a government which used napalm and antipersonnel bombs on small

*See page 305.

children in Asia and made militarists of children at home. "We began to see that the children in the United States are all growing up in a vast and different kind of ghetto: *the military ghetto.* This ghetto hems in and holds captive all of our children. It is vastly more destructive to children than any slum living can be." The government seized his assets to recoup unpaid taxes. Dr. Kline resigned from Rotary and left the Wausau Club and their country club, and he and Caroline devoted all their time to peace organizations. His experience as a navy psychiatrist in World War II and his later work with children had demonstrated to him what America's violence-dominated society could do to people. "In my psychiatric practice I had been hearing more and more children voicing fears of being annihilated by a nuclear bomb. Their drawings were dominated by mushroom clouds, air force bombers, and battleships. Children were saying to their parents, and to me, 'I don't want to grow up because then I'll have to go into the army and kill people.' " The Klines soon found their phone was tapped and that friends were calling them communists. They knew they had to leave and they sold their house. Government agents immediately paid a visit and under the threat of confiscation, forced Dr. Kline to pay one year's advance taxes on his estimated income for the following year. Now in Vancouver, he is director of orthopsychiatric services at the Children's Aid Society and Assistant Professor of Psychiatry at the University of British Columbia. Caroline does volunteer work for the Committee to Aid War Objectors.

Dr. Kline naturally became interested in the war resisters, their reasons for leaving, their adjustment to a new life in Canada. Along with Katherine Rider of Children's Aid, he studied a sample group of thirty military refusers and their wives for a report entitled, "The Young American Expatriates in Canada: Alienated or Self-defined," which he read before the American Orthopsychiatric Association convention in San Francisco.

Of the thirty men, twenty were draft resisters, ten were deserters and sixteen were married. The average subject was white,

Anglo-Saxon, Protestant, from a middle-class background, and college educated. His history was "singularly free of evidence of psychiatric illness or characterlogical disturbance . . . family stability appeared to be a characteristic." The fathers of seventy-five percent of the men had served in World War II. In the majority of the men's families, religion played a significant role. Few were pacifists; some said they would fight for Canada if it were attacked. Eighteen men stated that their families were conservative Republicans. Kline writes, "We were impressed by the attractiveness, the openness, the idealism, and the maturity of these young men and women who so readily agreed to discuss their recent experiences and life histories with us." Kline stabilized his sample by ruling out transients and unlanded deserters or draft dodgers. "The disadvantage to this limitation" says the report, "is that it excluded the men who could not garner the points to become landed, but who nevertheless stayed on illegally and the men who chose to ignore the system and not become landed. These men, in general, experience far greater adjustment difficulties in Canada, tending to be angry and bitter with society in general; they fit the definition of being truly alienated." Dr. Kline later explained in his office at Children's Aid that he feels this alienated group nevertheless shows healthy signs of throwing off at least their personal alienation if not their social alienation.

> A lot of them *are* hung-up; the confusion, disorientation, and paranoia they experience the first several months here are serious problems. They are frightened, defensive, angry, but I've talked with a lot of these men, and it is apparent that, given their particular situation, these are all normal behavior patterns, not psychosomatic abnormalities. What one must realize is that they have taken a positive first step toward removing the obstacles of oppression which they were faced with. That can only be called a *healthy* thing. While I believe the incidence of real misfits is very low, there *are* many emotionally unstable types among them. But I've found most exhibit a high degree of emotional maturity with which they face their very difficult problems. These are all very sane individuals.

As for the men in the study, the report discusses the growing awareness of the state of affairs in America which the men experienced and the increased disillusionment caused by the credibility gap, "a term which they rejected as a euphemism for government lies." The report traces the doubt, anxiety, bewilderment, and anger experienced by the subjects and the difficult struggle for self-respect, self-definition, and personal integrity that ultimately required the refusal of military service. Several individual decisions of a purely moral nature were reported: "One young man who had decided to go to jail, rather than to war, reported for his preinduction physical and was classified 4-F because of a hernia. For three months he felt completely disoriented. 'To continue with my draft resistance work, urging other men to go to jail, seemed very armchair, so I came to Canada.' " A serviceman who was antiwar yet not forced to fight, being permanently assigned to teach in a language school in the U.S., felt it took more courage to desert than to stay in a plush assignment for the duration. He said, "On the day they locked up Captain Levy, I hopped on the bus." Another young man was an A student at a top-ranking university but he felt he was hiding out in his 2-S classification. He left school, mailed his draft card with a "letter of resignation" to Selective Service, and took a last tour of the U.S. on a thirty-day Greyhound pass before heading to Canada. A Vietnam veteran "who had entered the service with strongly conflicting feelings" discovered that "it was wrong for him to have participated. When he realized that in just four months he would be an 'honorably discharged veteran of the Vietnam War' he decided he could not wear that label for the rest of his life." He deserted and made his way to Canada.

The report states that most of the men saw the war as "one major symptom of a decaying society," and proceeds to outline the reasons which the subjects gave for rejecting a role in the war:

1. They view participation in the Vietnam War as immoral; they said that they would feel ashamed to have to admit to their children that they had participated.
2. Having been raised to cherish autonomy, self-direction, and individual responsibility, they reject authoritarianism and question the motives underlying the U.S. use of power.

3. They see the Vietnamese, and other people, as human beings and don't buy the Madison Avenue techniques of dehumanizing them . . . they see much of this as racist propaganda.
4. They perceive war in the nuclear age as barbaric and stupid.
5. They condemn the U.S. value system and argue that today's society is not worth saving.

As for alternatives, the study points out that all of the subjects had been aware of

the various manipulative modes of avoiding the draft. They knew about the phony problems, the psychiatric letter, the felony conviction, and the divinity school registration . . . In general they expressed an unwillingness to sacrifice self-respect by dishonest maneuvering . . . Going to prison as an alternative was variously viewed as "buckling under in another way," as pointless self-sacrifice or as an act of self-destruction . . . One young man confessed that in view of the present political trend in the U.S., he feared that he might never be released from prison if he went to jail . . . Wives often influenced their husbands against going to jail.

The report stresses the important role women played in these men's lives by providing encouragement, support and stability.

The report mentions the "emotionally charged experience" of crossing the border and that it was "usually characterized by feelings of profound relief and joy." It says there was an "uneasy curiosity" among the subjects about other military refusers in Canada. "Would they be the misfits and 'freaks' commonly represented by the news media? As they met their fellow exiles, they invariably were relieved and reassured. Friendships among them developed easily and proved stabilizing and supportive. Only a few isolated themselves from other Americans, doing so as part of their total rejection of everything American and embracing all Canadians." Only one of the thirty expressed a desire to return to the U.S. and live.

The Kline-Rider report concludes that "In all instances the result of their actions in coming to Canada was increased self-respect, greater confidence in problem-solving ability and restored belief that their lives were again in their hands." Addressing itself to alienation in the summary it says:

> Fromm defines alienation as "a mode of experience in which the person experiences himself as an alien." He emphasizes that the alienated person is out of touch with himself. These young people appeared to believe that they had come to Canada to avoid experiencing themselves as alien. They equated emigration with ego-preservation. To them, cooperation with Selective Service meant dehumanization and sacrifice of self-hood . . . They are certainly young men who trust their own decisions and are guided by them much more than by decisions of the culture or the group. They saw the parenting generation as trapped, rigid, and unresponsive . . . Although they were not conquered and subdued by their society, neither were they able to influence its attitudes significantly. In this very liberal sense, they were alienated from their society, but not from themselves.

The report regards the men's experiences as "important developmental milestones . . . as an opportunity to exercise autonomy in the face of a mammoth authoritarian system, and as a chance to open up opportunities for identification with a new country and people. The effective way in which these young people have handled a major life crisis appears to us to indicate a level of mature emotional functioning which is often aspired to but seldom attained."

●

There are not many black war resisters in Canada. A very rough estimate would be five hundred to a less-likely thousand. Draft dodgers, whatever the race, are largely middle-class, and the black middle class is disproportionately small in America. Youth of the black middle class were less likely to reject their families' newly-won economic franchise; in most cases they would choose to carry it on. They had more to lose by dodging the draft. There are not more deserters because being black and being a military deserter in North America has not been proven to be all that much better than being in Vietnam—save for the front lines. Nevertheless, in Toronto in the spring of 1970, a group of black resisters got together to assist the increasing number of black deserters and dodgers who were coming to Canada—the deserters, especially, faced real problems. The Black Refugee Organization (BRO) offered a more personal form of assistance and counseling, by black people, than the TADP could provide. BRO was not recruiting, however (as Eldridge Cleaver was, encouraging black GIs to desert and make their way to Algiers). Jim Russell, of BRO, said on a CBC television interview, "Canada is a reasonably sane country, not altogether, but saner than some I could mention. But it's not that easy for blacks in Canada so I would say to brothers on the other side of the border to stay there if it is at all possible—do what you can to resist there."

Eusi Ndugu, a draft resister who traded in his slave name when he traded in his country, wrote in *AMEX* that he felt black youth *should* be told about Canada, that blacks in Canada could at least spread the word via black student unions and community groups about Canada as a last resort while encouraging men to resist the military and the war. "I arrived in Canada the last part of November 1969 and felt like a beautiful black crow who had escaped from the bullet of a farmer. Ever since I was a child in Mississippi I had heard that a certain portion of my race had escaped brutal treatment by following the North Star to Canada. I am a twentieth century run-away slave—I ran away from an oppressive and racist country. I feel that more young black men would come to Canada to evade the draft if they only knew more about other black draft dodgers and deserters who had succeeded in becoming landed immigrants." He concluded, "To you black people who refuse to fight for the U.S., I will be glad to offer a helping hand in any form necessary to help you leave the country."

E. J. Fletcher is a draft resister from Cleveland, Ohio, who worked with BRO for a short time. As he is from the middle class, his story corresponds to that of many white resisters. Awareness came through the antiwar movement; there was lots of reading about the war which led to reading Fanon, Carmichael, Marx—"I read Marx and began to see the war issue and the race issue as very related, not unrelated as I had thought." Militancy increased; the failure of liberal projects gave way to despair and alienation and the necessity of having to make a choice: whether or not to devote oneself to radical action. For Fletcher, caught in a post-college period of disorientation, the decision was influenced by a notice from Uncle Sam. Canada seemed the only answer. After three and one-half years at Western Reserve and Cleveland State where he majored in chemistry, Fletcher immigrated in March 1969 and found a job in the microbiology lab of the Princess Elizabeth Hospital in Toronto. His fiancée came up several weeks later and they were married—she discontinued work on a Ph.D. in French at the University of Chicago in order to join him in Canada. From his experience in the Toronto black community, to which most blacks eventually gravitate, Fletcher comments:

> The dodger tends to come from a middle-class upbringing most of the time. On the other hand, the deserter is from a poor class economically, educationally. It's nothing to meet a black deserter with only a tenth-grade education, it's very common. I've encountered more black deserters recently than dodgers. As for why there aren't more blacks up here: The history of the army is that, although it's just as racist as the rest of the society, it was a place a man could go, get three squares a day with no hangups. And I think it's still the case for a number of guys. For many young blacks there is still no opportunity open for them outside in the real world. Thirty percent of the army in Vietnam is black. Also, I think information of the alternatives, what's open to you, is much more available to whites, especially white middle-class college kids who've been through the whole Vietnam peacenik trip, the same trip that I went through more or less. Black kids don't have the same access to information.

As a black, Fletcher's reaction to Canada is understandably very different from that which whites experience. He would much rather be back in the U.S. On the other hand, Canada has opened him to somewhat of an international perspective from which to view the black world. Black Canadians are as likely to be from Trinidad or Ghana or Zambia as they are to be descended from the first travelers on the underground railroad. Fletcher sees the goals of black Africa ("The United States of Africa") as being as important as the American black struggle and he views the latter as more of a *black* revolution than an American revolution. He has not found an identity in Canada, however, and therefore is thinking very seriously of perhaps one day moving to Africa when he and his wife have saved enough money. "Guinea and Tanzania —those are the two I'm really thinking of right now." Below, Fletcher relates his feelings about being a black American exile in Canada:

At first, when I got immigrated, I felt like it was a new start, new country, different people—a very average response for someone who's not that aware yet. I liked Toronto—maybe because it was spring. Lots of girls out. Physically, the way people were dressed and so on, it appeared that this was a freer sort of city than Cleveland. When I first came up it seemed girls were wearing their skirts about three to five inches shorter than they were in Cleveland. Canada was a new experience. Most of the people I was around were white because I didn't know any blacks. I even found myself getting into a new type music, the Hendrix style music, white music really. I was looking at Toronto as a completely different sort of thing, sort of like overlooking the racism that was here. What it boiled down to was that I was really kidding myself. Once I made the statement, Johnny Winter sings the blues better than any black man ever sang the blues. And that, like, hit me. That knocked me over. All of a sudden my attitudes about the people here, the music, changed. I realized I knew nothing about the black people here. All I knew was that there were a lot of white people here. So I found the black people. At the same time I more or less found myself.

At first, in other words, the city looked good, but there was always this coldness. When I first came I think I was hoping it would be a nonracist society. In fact, I was willing to give people here the benefit of the doubt. One of the things I did find was that I was able to get into more white people's heads, than in the States. I can find out how they're really feeling by talking with them, rapping with them, and just letting them disrobe themselves, letting them come out. Here you can get it out in the open. And I think that's what makes you aware of your identity, of who you are. It seems the identification with the English and the identification with Europe—the whole Anglo-Saxon thing here—forces you to pretty much relate to your blackness. Also, I think anyone who's away from home is going to make a more conscious effort to find themselves and find an identity. That's the case with a lot of the white draft dodgers I know.

Being in Canada forces me to seek out my true identity. Being in Canada makes you very aware of your blackness. Mainly because you're in the midst of whiteness. But I think it's an experience in the sense that

I think you really find out what racism is all about. Canada, in a sense, is actually more racist because it is more white. The black man in the States has had such a profound effect on that country that in fact there are many institutions, the music, the foundations of jazz and blues for instance, which are for the most part black, and so even though the black man sees all this racism in the States, he can also see his own society, a black community, his own culture. But up here it's very different in that there are *no* black institutions. It's like the white kids up here. When they think of blues they don't think of B.B. King or Otis Redding, what they think of is Johnny Winter, The Blues Project. Now and then I'll buy some Miracles' albums, some Temptations' albums, even the Supremes and I listen to them and I'll get—what's the word?—nostalgia.

I started doing some really deep thinking, and it's brought me to the point where I've become—I'm no longer an *American*. I would call myself an Afro-American, I would call myself a *man*, a human, one for humanity ultimately. Being an Afro-American is a *fact*, and it is also a tool, a device, a means by which a black man can attain a sort of society that we can all relate to. The thing about race that I've formalized is that a black person is black of necessity in that he has to be concerned with being black whereas a white person should forget about being white and should really be a *person*. A black has to be black first, know that he's black, be proud that he's black, learn what it means to be black and *then*, then he can begin to worry about how to be a person.

I would never advise a black person to come to Canada because they would have to undergo all these frustrations about identity here, the one thing that's common to all black dodgers and deserters no matter what their background. Even if a guy goes through the sort of Baldwin or Hendrix or even Richie Havens trip, it's not easy to relate here. But if you don't have any other choice, you don't have any other choice.

I'm very pessimistic about the U.S. 'cause I see the Right and the Left really getting farther apart, and I see the Right, which is really in control of things, doing everything possible to maintain its power and to more or less let the Left think that they're doing something. They let the Left have certain victories, but the Right, through its press, is managing a sort of anesthetizing effect on the people, playing down the poverty, violent outbreaks and so forth. One advantage of being outside the U.S. is that you're away from the American press. That's one of the differences between the U.S. and Canada. It seems the press is more open here, whereas the press in the States has its hands cuffed. You just get a feeling that you're not getting all the news when you live in the U.S.* Like with

*Case in point: Peter Arnett's A.P. reports on wanton destruction by American units in Cambodia, including severe looting of villages, was censored by A.P.'s president who declared it was not in the American people's interest to read such things at that time. The international wires, however, could not be censored and Canadians were able to read news reports denied to the American people.

attitudes on, say, Red China, the press here is a lot more open than it is in the States. Even though I'm pessimistic, I would go back if I could because I would like to help influence things to move another way.

My family came up to visit us. They've just been really beautiful through the whole thing. Like with the FBI. The FBI trip was kind of strange because my parents are very friendly, warm people. So the FBI man comes to the door and says, "We'd like some information about your son," and they say, "all right, come in," and I guess that kind of freaked out the FBI men 'cause usually, especially in the black area, they get a rough time. He says to my father, "Why don't you try and talk your son into coming back and we'll go easy on him," and Father says, "Well, that's up to him, but we'll pass on the message." Then the FBI man said, "We'll talk to the neighbors and keep an eye on the place." My folks felt paranoiac about that but then the guy came around some more and afterward was a bit more open and friendly and said, "Look, as long as your son's up there, we can't go and get him, so you better tell him to stay up there."

●

The first national exile conference since the beginning of the exodus was held in Montreal in the spring of 1970. The Pan-Canada Conference of Deserters and Resisters was hosted not by the established draft resister groups, nor by visiting radical groups, but by U.S. Armed Forces deserters. The American Deserters' Committee brought nearly a hundred American radicals and exile activists together for a three-day "convention" in a Montreal community center auditorium. The exile organizations exchanged information, coordinated activities, and discussed mutual problems which Americans face everywhere in Canada, and for the first time exile activists from across the country discovered they shared similar feelings and came to an agreement on the desirability, limits, and modes of political action. They discussed with the U.S. delegates the practical problems of draft resistance, the GI movement, desertion, and the underground railroad. Complimentary tactics were worked out between U.S. movement groups and exile organizations. For the first time, the American movement was recognizing the exiles, and the exiles were throwing off their traditionally cautious "nonpolitical" stance. Essentially, the conference, which few people thought would really take place, was one of those rare times when all of the Left, from liberals to

Marxist-Leninists, manages to come together for honest and sensitive political communication and a searching-out of new directions. Rhetoric, invective, and corrosive arguing were absent; the two-page conference agenda was followed to the letter.

Carl Oglesby, New Left theoretician and editor of *New Left Review*, made it clear that he believed "it is the overriding political responsibility of the American exiles to guarantee the integrity of American refugee access to Canada." The overwhelmingly articulate Oglesby continued, "you must keep the pipeline open. It is the obligation of the American community in Canada to make the option of Canada a reality for now and in the future. You must prepare the Canadian consciousness to face a new exodus. South of the border there is a great likelihood of a fascist closing of the fist and people will need to get out. There will be a surge to Canada as great as that of the war resisters." Understanding that the war resisters in Canada had to exist within the legal framework of landed immigrant status and not as political exiles in a revolutionary country such as Cleaver in Algeria, writer-activist Fred Gardner said, "We're hoping you can pull off a discretionary politics with a sense of etiquette. As American exiles, you must become visible in some way that isn't offensive to Canadians. Nothing could serve the U.S. government's purposes better than for you to remain inconspicuous. Richard Nixon certainly doesn't want the moral pressure of 50,000 or even 100,000 young exiles weighing on the national conscience."

A few weeks before, Gardner had written in *Hard Times*, an influential radical newsletter, that the peace movement in the U.S. had to reassess the existence of the exile community in light of the massive desertion rate and, at the same time, reassess desertion, something which the movement had never really supported yet which was a *fait accompli*. "Judging from the history of how armies fail," he wrote, "it appears that disintegration, not dissent, may characterize the final crisis. There has never been an army that fell apart through the exercise of civil liberties; but there have been some big ones cracked by mass desertion. As a tactic, desertion has the under-rated virtue of simplicity . . . Any glib son-of-a-bitch can express a noble motive; but few people act so directly against the war as the soldier who refuses to take part. It is snotty of American radicals to put them down as escapists. Escape from oppression is a political act; not the highest form of struggle, obviously, but political just the same . . . desertion and dissent are two aspects of the same movement and reinforce one another." He proposed that the U.S. movement organize parents and friends of exiles as a counterpoise to the political pressure of the Air Force POWs' wives. He had suggested a national campaign to make "the physical and moral presence of thousands of American exiles felt within this country."

Tom Hayden, still recuperating from the Conspiracy Trial, also stressed the need to generate visibility: "Anyone either in Canada or the U.S.—Americans or Canadians—who doesn't want to do this is a collaborator with imperialism. It is important to us in the U.S. that you politicize your movement here. First, you must continue to make it clear to people in the States that you are here, and here in huge numbers, and then you must insist publicly that all political exiles should be allowed to come home, that you intend to return by whatever means necessary." At the conference Hayden encouraged more political action directed against the U.S. from Canada, and suggested that exile groups form ties with Cleaver. However, he insisted that Canada be viewed only as a temporary sanctuary. Tactically, this may be sound, but this thinking does not recognize the exiles, perhaps half of the total, who have no intention of ever returning to the U.S. and who are not even thinking about it yet, whose exile is nonetheless a political phenomenon. Deserters, especially, have performed an important political act, yet for many of them it would be psychologically devastating not to take Canada seriously, to continually think about going home "by whatever means necessary." While it may be good theory to talk about "politicizing" exiles to the point where they voluntarily give up their cushy sanctuary and return to "join the struggle," it may be asking too much. An exile's "first step" in crossing the border is very often the beginning of a revolutionary consciousness to be sure, but not necessarily in a political sense. They are not all Eldridge Cleavers . . . and anyway, at this writing, Cleaver is still in Algeria.

While the exiled and nonexiled Americans were nearly unanimous in their desire to strike at the heart of the beast, which was the United States, Canadians at the conference disagreed in no small way. Dimitri Roussopoulos, spokesman for Canada's Extra-Parliamentary Opposition, or New Left, appealed to the exiles to engage intensely in Canadian affairs, but within the context of established Canadian groups. The most unpopular man at the conference was a Liberal Party member of Parliament who sat through most of the three-day parley and finally, on the third day, got up to say, "If you're going to live here, but only be concerned about the country you left, then go back, the struggle is there for you, not here. I don't want you to use our soil as a base for your anti-American views and actions." This man, who had led the fight in the commons for the right of deserters to legally enter Canada, had to be listened to even if no one liked what he said. If the main obligation of the exiles was to keep the border open then this M.P. and his friends were the men who would help them do it. It was a serious mistake among American radicals in Canada to regard men like this as suspect and devious, to neither trust them nor work with them. There were more radical members of Parliament who supported the exiles, members of the New Democratic Party, but the NDP was a minority party and could accomplish very little by comparison. It remained to be seen whether or not there would be "a discretionary politics."

Perhaps it was a good thing that the ruling-party M.P. had left for Parliament Hill before the telegram of greeting and fraternal support from the Vietnamese National Liberation Front was read to the convocation and the tape from Daniel Berrigan was played in which he urged people to join him in the underground.

Following the Montreal meeting the exile aid groups across Canada instituted the policy of discouraging draft resisters from immigrating to Canada if they didn't have to, and henceforth gave first priority to deserters. Deserters who were interested would be offered political counseling. It appeared that the aid groups were deciding for themselves who would get help and who wouldn't, that they would decide who could come to Canada; but this was not really the case since the groups schooled themselves in draft counseling, an extra burden when immigration counseling alone was difficult, and by doing draft counseling they could tell a young man what his immediate options were in the U.S. and perhaps help him find a way out without having to permanently leave the country. This left more room in the immigration program for deserters. In Montreal, the ADC took it a step further. They not only immigrated men, but attempted to politically educate as many deserters as possible. Unfortunately, it became dogma for the ADC to inform deserters that Canada was merely a sanctuary and that they would receive little help if they planned on making it their new home forever. Needless to say, this turned off a lot of newly arrived deserters and the ADC popularity in the exile community began to slip. There were hundreds of deserters who were simply a long way from this state of political consciousness and all they wanted was a place to sleep, some food, help with immigration, a job, and a new start. People were becoming disenchanted with all the political rhetoric. One counselor said, "The reason I work for the ADC is not to stop the war machine—taking men out of the war machine isn't going to stop it—but simply to help save as many people as we can." The Montreal Council moved out of the ADC offices, opened a new office, and continued counseling on the basis of need and not ideology. A hostel and job-counseling program called the American Refugee Service was formed in the fall of 1970 while the ADC "central committee," a salaried staff of four including a French-speaking deserter who had lived underground in France for three years while learning all the bombastic rhetoric of the French Left, opened a new office under the name, American Exiles Counseling Center. The new exile in Montreal now had a wide choice.

Clearly, the situation had changed by the summer of 1970 from what it had been five years before. Draft resisters coming to Montreal with the intention of immigrating were now being counseled by army *deserters*. Deserters were explaining to them that if they simply left the country without fighting the draft in a substantive way, or without joining the army first and sewing seeds of dissent the only result of their act would be that a black or poor white or Puerto Rican would simply go in their place. The deserter was educating the draft dodger! Not a few draft resisters walked out of the ADC office on Boulevard St. Laurent wondering just what the hell was going on. Some immigrated anyway and tried to forget that they ever heard about the American Deserters' Committee. Yet some went back to join the army and resist and then desert while others went back to resist the draft in the courts, or to be inducted and then refuse to step forward at the induction center, an act which really threw a wrench into the works. (Few people were ever arrested doing this. A court had to indict them first.)

●

Public discussion in Canada about Americans engaging in exile political action was originally sparked, not by the Montreal conference and the radical proposals discussed there (the conference was closed to the press), but by a demonstration in Toronto on May 9, 1970. In response to America's invasion of Cambodia and the deaths at Kent State, the Vietnam Mobilization Committee in Toronto swung into gear and organized one of the largest anti-Vietnam War demonstrations ever held in Canada. The tensions of those early May days in 1970 were as evident in Canada as in the U.S. and the march of five thousand people, ending at the U.S. consulate, got out of hand. There were ninety-three arrests, four times the number at the huge rally in Washington, D.C. Fifteen of those arrested were American exiles and soon the demonstration and the accompanying violence, normally foreign to Canada, were blamed on Americans. In a speech Mayor William Dennison mentioned in an offhand way that "a serious Toronto problem is hippies and deserters." In another speech he said, "draft dodgers and military deserters should leave their pet hates at home ... Toronto will not allow newcomers to start a war here to protest a war that their country is engaged in." From Ottawa, Conservative Party leader Robert Stanfield, Trudeau's opposition, was prompted to comment: "Young Americans should not try to form a sort of government in exile ... if they consider Canada nothing more than a base from which to attack their own government and if they insist on importing methods of dissent that may or may not be appropriate elsewhere, but certainly not here, then we must reluctantly conclude that they have little to add to Canadian society." The *Globe and Mail* sided with exiles, however, asking the mayor to substantiate his claims. On May 20, Red White & Black (RW&B), an exile group formed in 1970,* the ADC, and TADP called a press conference in the Town Hall of the St. Lawrence Center to answer the mayor's allegations that Americans were responsible for the May 9 violence. John Wenthe of the TADP said, "We deny any alleged association of TADP in the organization of the demonstration." Red White & Black said, "We do not believe that any significant number of Americans have been involved in political violence here, either as instigators or participants. We think we would know about it if it were true. We ask the mayor to substantiate or particularize his statements of yesterday." Paul Copeland, a lawyer for the exiles, pointed out that the Vietnam Mobilization Committee was a Canadian group. On May 25, Mayor Dennison met with representatives of Red White & Black, the American Deserters' Committee and the Toronto Anti-Draft Programme in an attempt to iron out differences. On May 26, the mayor announced that "the ringleaders of the May ninth march unfortunately were Canadians ... and 85 percent of their followers were Canadian too."

At the same time, American exiles were receiving criticism from another quarter: the Left. Robin Mathews, an English pro-

*See Chapter 11.

fessor at Ottawa's Carlton University and long-time supporter of dodgers and deserters, began speaking out publicly on a new theme, "Draft dodgers as American imperialists." Along with the Montreal Conference and the controversy in Toronto, Mathews' comments produced a deep introspection in the exile community. Mathews wrote in a liberal magazine called *Canadian Dimension:*

> . . . Canada has a "moral obligation" to U.S. political dissidents. It had a moral obligation, and recognized it, to the Hungarian and Czechoslovakian dispossessed. The obligation, however, was to provide [the Americans] with a sanctuary, not to hand the country to them. But at the present time, as we all know, Canada is not threatened massively, or even slightly, by the imperialism of Hungary or Czechoslovakia. And so the claim that our obligation to U.S. citizens is "the same" as it was to Hungarians and Czechoslovakians is simplistic, sentimental nonsense. For the U.S. exile in Canada is different politically, socially, culturally and individually from any other exile we could conceivably harbour, because of the immense effect of U.S. imperialism in Canada, because of his own conditioning before he comes here. It has been estimated that there are between sixty and seventy thousand U.S. dodgers and deserters in Canada. A very large proportion are, understandably, passionately involved with U.S. issues; they tend to turn any discussion among groups in Canada to the morality or immorality of U.S. internal policy . . . many are blindly ignorant of the Canadian fact. A draft dodger declared for his Canadian audience [in a recent magazine article] that the American dream is dead in New York but "we" hope to keep it alive in Toronto!

Mathews pointed out many examples of how draft dodgers have contributed to the colonialization of Canada which unfortunately were all too true. American war resisters in Canada were sometimes American imperialists, not because they were imperialists but because they were American. He was distressed, also, at the Americans' proclivity to distrust the Canadian government as they distrusted their own, i.e.: "U.S. residents and Canadian organizers alike talk about the Minister of Immigration and his work as if he is an enemy. Strange. Especially strange when there is no doubt that under like conditions of unemployment and threat of political and economic domination no U.S. government would even consider allowing a like proportion of aliens to cross its boundaries." And so there was a lot to think about.

But perhaps, in the end, there wasn't really such a huge disagreement among exiles, American radicals, and liberal Canadians as to what was acceptable political behavior for the war resisters. The *Toronto Star*, Canada's largest newspaper, in a lead editorial in August entitled, "Memo to Dodgers" explained what it thought American exiles should be doing. The editorial was prompted by misreading an *AMEX* editorial in which editor Pietlock, shortly after the Montreal conference, had searched for worthy political goals for exiles, other than returning to the U.S. as revolutionaries, and had stated: ". . . as the U.S. is the oldest and closest enemy of Canada, perhaps it is our role to lead the fight, physically, against the U.S. from our exile." Although Pietlock had not made his point clearly, a more careful reading of the editorial would have shown that Pietlock was merely saying exiles should, perhaps, *join* the Canadian fight against American domination of Canada since fighting American imperialism abroad, as the Vietnamese were doing (in their case, violently), is as radical as fighting it within "the heart of the beast"—even though Tom Hayden hadn't seen it that way. (Americans had taken over 500 Canadian firms in 1968-1969.) The *Toronto Star* rejoined: "The first thing for American exiles to understand is that Canada is not a country that regards itself as an enemy of the U.S., or vice-versa . . ." but then continued with, "Canada is trying now to avoid becoming an economic and cultural colony of the United States. To the extent that this entails *fighting the U.S.* [italics mine] the weapons will be diplomacy and legislation and dollars of Canadians trying to buy control of our country's economy. Canadians are struggling to define their identity and to forge an independent future." America may not be Canada's enemy, but Canada will soon be an American enemy when the Canadians begin to succeed with what the *Toronto Star* advocates, which is economic independence and Canadian control of resources. The editorial continued with the astute warning: "We don't want here the kind of confrontation politics that led to Kent State and the bitter, insane factionalism that has all but destroyed the American

Left and polarized that country. We remind our American exiles that the political life in their own country is the reason most of them left it. And what may seem to them like provincialism in Canadian life is the reason why they have been able to find sanctuary here." Then the editorial urged the new arrivals to make the solving of Canada's problems their new cause ... yet for Pietlock and the exiles, Canada's chief problem is *the United States*. "We hope they will do this for their own sakes as well as ours. Bad things can happen to emigré groups. The situation in the homeland changes but they are not able to keep up with it. They become isolated and sad. They are cut off from the political life in their former country and they have no roots in their new country ... Those who want to work peacefully for a strong and independent Canada are welcome. Those who want to fight the U.S. came to the wrong country ..."

Somehow, I can't see any difference between working for a strong and independent Canada and fighting the U.S. In the sense that there is no difference, and accepting the modifier *peaceful* for either case, the majority of the American war resisters in Canada will be fighting the United States for a long time to come. Aside from whether or not the individual resister chooses to return or to become a citizen of Canada, he does *not* wish to see Canada become a further victim of U.S. economic and cultural imperialism. If Canada, in the years ahead, becomes pronouncedly more "anti-American," it will be, in part, because the United States has sent Canada 50,000-100,000 young anti-Americans who know the nature of the beast.

ELEVEN

The North Country Fair

After you've been in Canada awhile you begin to marvel at all the war resisters you casually meet. They are everywhere. While writing this book, I became a census taker, asking every young person I suspected of being an American exile if, in fact, he was. A lot were. Every week in Montreal I meet several more. I'm buying some record albums at Phantasmagoria record shop, and the clerk is a deserter; we talk, someone joins the conversation, he is a dodger. While buying a poster at Eaton's photo department I hear the clerk apologize to a customer for not being able to speak French; English Montrealers either speak French or they don't say anything. I ask the clerk if he is an American. He is a draft dodger from Florida, just graduated from the University of Florida. His father gave him enough money to get to Montreal, and he found work right away. He has never seen snow and he can't wait for the Quebec winter. I tell him he'll be thinking of Florida about mid-January. A kid is living in his Volkswagen camper parked on the square in front of our house. I find out he is a draft dodger. He lives in his van for two months, looking for work, and no one bothers him, and finally he gets a job as a probation officer for the city of Montreal. One day, walking through Old Montreal with a deserter who's doing some photography we pass by a boistrous group of youths whose American swagger gives them away. We hear them talking about the army and comparing Canada to the U.S.; they are all deserters and I have never seen any of them before. I go to lunch with my photographer friend and his brother and his wife who've driven up from New Haven to see him. The brother and his wife seem to believe that Ross is the only U.S. Army deserter in Canada until we step out of the restaurant and a young man in a coat and tie approaches us and asks if we know where Place du Canada is. He is an army deserter on his way to a job interview. While traveling across the country in preparation for this book, we find Americans everywhere. The clerk in the Toronto bookstore is a draft resister; his Brooklyn accent tips me off. One evening I'm walking down Toronto's Yonge Street and a tall, well-built, crew-cut man in his mid-twenties approaches me, shakes my hand, and says, "Hi, I saw you on the David Susskind Show [which had been taped in Montreal] when I was in Chicago. I just got here, three years marines, two years Nam. I've had it." I write out the phone number of the ADC and hand it to him. In the West, the only hitchhikers we pick up happen to be a dodger and his girl who are scouting for land to buy in British Columbia. His *thing* is hydroponics, growing plants without soil, and he and twelve fellow exiles including several University of Toronto faculty members are moving to northern British Columbia to build a "city" of geodesic domes. He says they already have fifty thousand vegetable plants growing under glass in Ontario. Together, they've pooled one-hundred-thousand dollars with which to set up their frontier city. He has just completed his pilot's license so he can fly the group in to whatever site they finally select. He is hitchhiking in order to save money for "the big move." In Banff National Park we camp for a few days at the Lake Louise Campground and camped next to us is a draft resister and his wife. His inlaws, from Cincinnati, are camped alongside, having driven out to British Columbia to visit them. He is sitting by the campfire reading the works of Lenin under a Coleman lantern. In Vancouver one afternoon, walking along East Georgia Street, I see a long-haired youth getting frisked by police who are carefully looking through his papers and his pockets. I go up and ask him what the trouble was and he says, "They're just looking for dope. I'm used to it." I made a remark about the police and he says, "It's not so bad up here in Canada." I ask him if he's American. "Yeah, but I don't think I will be much longer. I'm thinking of moving here."

The Vancouver Committee to Aid American War Objectors fills a huge, long, barn-like room behind an old storefront on East Georgia Street near Vancouver's Chinatown. Old cars and multi-colored Volkswagen mini-buses come and go out front bearing license plates from as far away as Florida, Pennsylvania, New Mexico, and New York. The inside is a museum piece for the antiwar movement, a masterpiece of revolutionary decor. Counters are piled high with GI papers and underground papers and political tracts. There are maps of Vietnam, North and South, maps of British Columbia, maps of Canada, maps of Vancouver. There is a large American flag with skulls and crossbones in the star field, and next to it is the *Life* magazine cover for the story, "One Week's Dead," and the photographs of 242 young Americans killed in Vietnam. A large poster says in bold black letters, "Dear Mom and Dad—your silence is killing me, in Southeast Asia, on campus, in the streets." There are huge photographs of Ho Chi Minh and Bertrand Russell and Lenin. There are "End Canada's Complicity in Vietnam" and "Don't Eat U.S. Grapes" posters and there is a poster of the most famous and terrible American war photograph ever taken, in living color: a pile of dead Vietnamese civilians lying in the road at My Lai 4. It asks, "And babies?" and answers, "And babies."

A twenty-foot long bulletin board is divided into "jobs," "housing," "rides," "messages," "for sale," and is a collage of notices. A square of old stuffed sofas makes a reading room and across from it is a glass counter displaying local crafts called Peace Work which are for sale. There is a coffee corner with fresh coffee brewing in a big urn; there is a "free store" which is really a big pile of used clothes beneath a sign saying "help yourself." There are counters and tables and desks and chairs and typewriters all arranged in a fashion that creates six counseling booths which are full of people having Canada explained to them by trained counselors. There are six counselors presently on duty. Altogether I count twenty-four people in the office at this moment. Canadian staff member Peter Burton answers the phone every three minutes or so while deserter Peter Maly surveys the scene with tired eyes—he has counseled for a year and a half and has about had it. He comes in late now. A straight and serious young man is typing out a job application form for a resister. He is paid by the Unitarian Church to do job counseling while the other staffers draw their salaries from the Committee. Fund raising is the responsibility of the Co-ordinating Council for American War Refugees. A pretty staff member from Montreal is greeting newcomers and American self-exile, Mike Carley, is seated in a counseling booth with a young couple who are bringing a new baby to Canada with them. Carley is a graduate student at the University of British Columbia in city planning. He is very freaky with long, ratty, black hair and dungaree jacket and pants. He lends an aura of respectability to the office for the many West Coast freaks who come in and feel uneasy in the presence of the more straight looking radicals.

Amid the cacophany I am talking to a deserter and asking him how he found out about Canada. "I saw a copy of the *Police Gazette* in the PX," he says, "and there was a big article on deserters in Canada and it said they were here legally. Before, our captain had told us, 'And don't think any of you guys can go to Canada 'cause the FBI and the RCMP work closely together and they'll turn you over to us as soon as you cross the border. Whether you've been gone one hour or one year, we'll get you for desertion.' " He was awaiting his final counseling before being assigned a driver to take him to the border for immigration. A neatly dressed youth who had just returned from the border comes in to tell everyone of his successful immigration. "I'm in!"

he says. Another youth sits quietly, pensively, awaiting counseling, and he tells me his story. He had been ordered to Vietnam five times and had gone AWOL five times. A friend in the military police warned him of the army's plans for the sixth try. He was to be put aboard the plane in handcuffs with two armed escorts who would release him when he "set foot on Vietnamese soil."* "Now my parents are going to support me here, let me go to school at UBC. They've come a long way. The first time I refused to go to Vietnam, they thought I was a communist."

In the late afternoon a very unusual looking draft dodger walks in. He is unusual looking because he doesn't look like the usual draft dodger. His name is Ely and he has very short, greased black hair, and is dressed in the clean and neat J.C. Penny weekend casuals of the American workingman. He is from Oakland, California, but he would not be out of place in a bus depot in Alabama. He sure was out of place here. I am positive he is a deserter or at least an agent of some kind. He tells me he is a draft dodger, but draft dodgers are all middle-class bohemians with moderate-to-long hair and a tendentiously déclassé look about them. He is twenty and has worked two years in a plastics factory operating an injection molding machine. It strikes me that he could well be the very first American workingman to dodge the draft. I ask him where he got the idea to avoid military service and he says, "I have a brother in Vietnam who wrote and told me that stuff like My Lai is an everyday thing over there. He said 'Split, man; don't come over.' And I've got friends who've told me about seeing Vietnamese POWs get thrown out of helicopters, you know. Mainly, I just want to get out. In the States you get stopped by police on the streets every day; they run computer checks on you; you can't even walk in the streets in America. It's really a fucked-up place, I don't want to live there anymore." I ask if the men he works with agree with him. "Not on everything, though the

*This is a common occurrence. I have talked with several GIs in Canada who were taken to Vietnam in handcuffs.

younger guys do. They all think I'm right about the draft, that I should go to Canada." He shows me a letter of support from his family in which his mother asks people to help him. He says he's already found work in a plastics concern in Vancouver. I'm thinking there must be another reason that he's come to Canada. Young workers do not dodge the draft; it is too lonely and difficult a decision to make outside the bounds of the college environment. I press further and he mentions his oldest brother. He tells me about him—the name rings a bell. Ely's brother is Nesrey Dean Sood, of the Presidio 27, who was sentenced to fifteen years at the mutiny trials. If anyone knew why he was dodging the draft, Ely Sood did. He gets up to go, and I wish him well.

The office is still crowded. It has been crowded all day. I remark on that and Peter Burton informs me it is a slow day. Standing shyly to one side are two freaks looking like they just arrived. There are freaks in Montreal but West Coast freaks are something else again—they are not to be surpassed. They're almost scarey but a look into their eyes reveals two very young and very warm and very peaceful individuals. "Deserters or dodgers?" someone asks. "Neither," they say softly. "Far-out!" comes the reply. I ask why they've come to Canada then, and their answer is one that the men who rule America would do well to contemplate: "Just getting out, just can't handle it anymore." We are exiles, they are émigrés—we are all refugees from an oppressive country.

Peter Burton runs down some statistics for me. "We're getting seventy-five to a hundred new people a week. We're landing about eight to fifteen. You can see the backlog. Two out of four of the deserters we're getting now have college degrees. The most important thing though, is that thirty to forty percent of the people we've gotten this summer are neither dodgers *nor* deserters. They're just people leaving America. It's amazing. And they're all really well-educated. We're getting the brain drain again." Giving credence to Burton's statement is a hippie-looking family talking with a counselor. He is twenty-eight, has never been drafted, and holds a Ph.D. in water resources. They have three children, the tiniest is in the woman's arms. The counselor doesn't spend much time with them since with their credentials immigration is as good as automatic. It occurs to me that this office may never close down. It might take a new name one day as fewer "war objectors" come—something like, "Vancouver Committee to Aid American Refugees"—but it will continue to do a steady business long after the war is over.

That evening there is an article in the *Vancouver Sun* under the headline "Voyageurs Seek a New Land" about a busload of American youths heading to northern British Columbia from New Mexico. No one in the bus was avoiding military service. The article said, "As if reenacting the western movements of the mid-nineteenth century, the young Americans, including one girl, were on their way to the Peace River country in search of a place to settle away from their turbulent and congested homeland." They hoped to be settled before the first snowfall. They were equipped with a ton of food, a generator, an arc welding set, and a propane stove, and intended to live in the bus until they were able to build cabins. They planned to become farmers and craftsmen. Then I recalled all the truck and van loads of Americans we'd seen on the Trans-Canada highway while driving from Montreal—right out of a Steinbeck epic. I would talk to them, ask if they were exiles and half the time they were not. "We're just leaving, it's got nothing to do with the draft," said a man from Washington, D.C., who, along with a couple in a second van, was headed for the Canadian West. The driver of a truckload of California hippies, none of whom were war resisters, told me on the North Shore of Lake Superior that they were getting as far away from California as they could. "We're on our way to settle in Nova Scotia." Further underscoring this phenomenon is an article in *Life* magazine, the same week we are in Vancouver, titled, "An Indiana Family Leaves the U.S. for Keeps." It says, "More and more Americans are emigrating to Canada." The story is about Charles and

Jean Argast who had moved to Vancouver with their ten children. They said they no longer felt comfortable in Indiana. America: love it or leave it.

●

The physical beauty of western British Columbia is incomparable—what is left of it after thirty years of unrestrained lumbering, mining, and real-estate developing; magnificent, glaciated peaks stand majestically above clear shimmering bays and fjords; thick fir forests reach steeply down to the sea. American youths are attracted to Vancouver and Vancouver Island by the moderate climate. It seldom snows in the city, and commune dwellers on the inland coast and on the island find that winter is not a hardship and that vegetables can be planted in early March and harvested in late May. The political climate is not so moderate. It approximates that of the U.S. West Coast more than the rest of Canada, yet it is really uniquely British Columbian. An almost indecipherable brand of conservatism coexists remarkably well with the New Democratic Party socialists, more of whom have been elected to Parliament from B.C. than from any other province. Several mayors are in the NDP. But an ugly polarization arrived in B.C. in the summer of 1970 as the city government attempted to repress youth, both transient and local, and Vancouver police and "hordes of hippies" had a slam-bang riot at English Bay. By its very numbers, youth may be getting the upper hand in the greater Vancouver area, and real-estate developer-politicians like Vancouver mayor Tom Campbell, who makes U.S. mayors like, say, Sam Yorty, look like models of enlightenment, began to react. The mayor made inflamatory speeches against "hippies, yippies, and draft dodgers," blaming B.C.'s troubles on American radicals. When the federal government was setting up free hostels in local armories across Canada to aid transient Canadian youth, Mayor Campbell opposed the use of Vancouver's armory for this purpose. After he was overruled he explained, "I was concerned that a military establishment was becoming a draft dodger, deserter, and hippie haven." All summer the youth responded to the mayor's stubborn obstructionism and provocations by continually staging mass rallies in front of city hall.

In contrast to Vancouver is the city of Burnaby, Vancouver's largest suburb, which has for mayor a calm, reasonable and intelligent NDP member. Mayor Robert Prittie describes himself as a "moderate socialist." He is in his late fifties yet he staunchly defends youth. He also strongly supports the Canadian policy of admitting draft dodgers and deserters. He was in the Royal Canadian Air Force for six years, but he says, "If I were a young American today I would come to Canada rather than fight in Vietnam. Neither would I go to prison or become a CO." At one time he housed several U.S. Armed Forces deserters until they were able to get landed and find work. "The neighbors asked a few questions," he recalls, "but there was really no objection. Most people I know generally sympathize." Mayor Prittie had recently taken an unpopular stand on youth's behalf and he told me about it in his pleasant office in the Burnaby Municipal Building. "The Vancouver Liberation Front and the Maoists held a rather large demonstration in front of the Oacalla Provincial Prison which is located in Burnaby. They were demanding the release of drug offenders. The crowd broke through a fence into the prison parking lot, but they didn't enter the prison itself. The press called it an invasion. The police wanted to begin arresting people at that moment, but I asked the police not to, unless the demonstrators attempted to enter the prison. There were no arrests." Then he read me some mail from several of Burnaby's 126,000 citizens asking why there were no arrests. One person wrote, "Has Burnaby become a haven for American lawbreakers?"

The talk of American radicals, draft dodgers and deserters being behind the Vancouver demonstrations had become a recurring theme that summer. It is, of course, an insult to young Canadians who are militant enough all by themselves. It is also nonsense because American activists—the real "instigators"—

choose to stay in the U.S. and fight. Few would feel imperialistically ordained to help lead the struggle elsewhere. Naturally, American exiles do show up at demonstrations, but they are not leading them. If every last American exile were shipped out of Canada, the movement in Vancouver, in any Canadian city for that matter, would not be affected at all. Mayor Prittie informed me that he had just been at an *in camera* meeting of all the greater Vancouver municipal mayors which had been called in the wake of the recent "violence"—hardly violent at all by American standards. The discussion had been dominated by talk of what to do about all the . . . here goes again . . . "hippies, yippies, and draft dodgers," in Mayor Campbell's immortal words. Several mayors raised the question of immigration and one-third of them wanted to draft a letter there and then to Immigration Minister Mac-Eachen in Ottawa demanding that the permanent admission of young Americans to Canada be strictly curtailed. The letter was not written, thanks in part to Robert Prittie.

●

The sign in the CRYPT building in Winnipeg says, "Yankee Dodgers and Deserters, Welcome to Canada—Don't crash at office, see someone at desk. You better dig it here, you're stuck!" CRYPT stands for Committee Representing Youth Problems Today, a group which provides free medical services, crisis care, legal counseling, and food and accommodations to both local and transient youth. The organization, which is entirely run by youth, is a provincially recognized social agency. The government pays the salaries of the twelve-member staff which includes three American exiles. Winnipeg was the first city in North America to provide a free youth clinic and transient hostel and CRYPT has been the model for many other similar programs. The Winnipeg Committee to Assist War Objectors rents an office in the CRYPT building for one dollar a month and employs Canadian Selwin Burrows as a full-time counselor. Burrows was formerly the youth organizer for the New Democratic Party, the ruling party in

Manitoba. "Did you know the government of Manitoba is the only socialist government in North America?" Burrows asks. He gave up his job to work with American war immigrants.

It is a warm evening on the Manitoba plains and the sky is an ethereal blue, the kind of sky and the kind of blue that people in the Eastern cities never see. Dozens of young people with bedrolls and knapsacks are waiting outside CRYPT for the bus which will take them to the hostels for the night. Some of these travelers are American; some of them discover Burrows's office; many decide to immigrate in Winnipeg rather than at the end of the line in whichever direction across Canada they are headed. It is relatively easy to immigrate in Winnipeg. The Committee to Assist War Objectors also sees a number of Americans who come directly north from the middle border, Minnesota, Wisconsin, the Dakotas. If you've grown up in North Dakota, Winnipeg looks like Paris— it's the nearest large city and in the past two years it has attracted more war resisters than anyone would have guessed. Burrows tells me, "Last week we had eleven dodgers and deserters on one day. Normally it's three or four a day, fifteen to twenty a week. We're landing all of them. We counseled about 325 war resisters after we opened last year. This summer we've counseled about three hundred guys already." Burrows explains that many young people are coming to Winnipeg expressly to get away from the alienation of the large cities. "A lot of kids just want to get away from it all. After opposing the war and seeing confrontation in the U.S., they want to forget protest and politics and violence and so they come here." A typical case was David, a draft resister from New Jersey, and his wife Nancy, who were camped in a big green tent in Burrows's backyard. The tent was a wedding present. They had tried Toronto, but the congestion and pollution and radical politics of the Toronto Anti-Draft Programme had turned them off. "We came out of the TADP office after this guy had laid this heavy political indoctrination thing on us and there was a parking ticket on our truck. That was too much; we just looked at each other, hopped in, and didn't stop driving until we got to Winnipeg." They had just found teaching jobs in a tiny plains community west of the city. David is a very conventional, young American. Appearances suggest that he would fit quite well among the Young Republicans at Ohio University, attending business administration classes and living in a fraternity. He may very well represent the majority of the American war resisters in Canada. At any rate, one thing is certain: they are a very happy couple and he isn't going to kill or be killed in Indochina.

Seventeen hundred miles east of Winnipeg on the Trans-Canada Highway is Ottawa, the capital. Like Winnipeg, Ottawa has been attracting more and more American refugees, at least seven hundred so far. Ottawa has the dignified air of a national capital yet retains the warmth of a small town. Few draft resisters have come to Ottawa; it is mostly deserters who are settling there. In the spring, several deserters put out a newsletter called *Ambush*, which they mailed to U.S. bases and movement groups. Social life during the summer and fall revolved around an exile coffeehouse managed by two young Canadian folk singers. It was operated on a grant from the Mennonite Church of Canada, providing a place where deserters, girlfriends, and Canadian youth could congregate three or four evenings a week. During the day it serves as an exile reception center and reading room. Bob Lanning runs a job-counseling service at the coffeehouse when he isn't working on his religion degree at Carlton University. The army wouldn't honor his religious beliefs and he served three months in the stockade at Fort Sam Houston before deserting. "I used to go to the chaplain," he explains, "and he'd get out the Bible and open it to Romans 13: 'Let every person be subject to the governing authorities. For there is no authority except from God, and those that exist have been instituted by God. Therefore, he who resists the authorities resists God . . .' " He got the same story from three different chaplains—it's right there in the Bible. Lanning resisted the will of God anyway and came to Ottawa with his wife and decided the best service he could perform would be to help other men resist as well.

I am surprised to find so many deserters here. I buy a copy of the *East Village Other* on the downtown mall and the street vendor is . . . a deserter. Another youth is selling a rock music magazine which he produces with a little help from his friends. He is a deserter. While there are a number of older, somewhat established deserters here, most of the exiles in Ottawa are very young— eighteen, nineteen, and twenty—having been referred to AID by other exile groups and American counseling centers. Quiet, unpressured Ottawa seems to be a good place for them, a place where they can "get their heads together" and not fall into the wretched, drug-saturated street culture of Montreal and Toronto. Waiting for their internal immigration appointments this summer is a whole roominghouse full of these very young war resisters. The roominghouse is located across the Ottawa River—and across from Ottawa—in Hull, Quebec, which has a little-used immigration office and a sympathetic immigration officer. To immigrate through the Hull office, it is necessary to have a Hull address and so deserters began taking rooms at 106 Eddy Street, a European-style *pension* run by a French immigrant named Christian. The young, modish yet fatherly Christian liked deserters and now won't rent to anyone else if a deserter is waiting for a room. Clean rooms and linen and use of a large, bright kitchen goes for nine dollars a week and there is a waiting list. Twenty-one war resisters are living here now. Christian fixed up a comfortable commons room with sofas, card tables and a large TV on the wall—a deserter den!—as he realized these men needed a place to call home for several months while they looked for work and waited to immigrate.

The place has the air of a mid-western fraternity house. The men *look* like mid-western fraternity men. Guys are wearing sweatshirts and cut-offs and surfboard T-shirts and tennis shoes and there are the usual posters everywhere and bulletin boards by the telephone and guitars in the corners and the guy who always sleeps till one makes his bleary-eyed way to the shower with a towel around his waist. It could have *been* a fraternity house except that it was much too clean. There are only two draft dodgers in the house, I am informed, a young Argentine immigrant to the U.S. who was drafted and an eighteen-year-old from Chicago who had burned his draft card while he was still in high school. Vic, a deserter, is sitting at the kitchen table reading Jerry Rubin's *Do It!* and across from him Stan, another deserter, is writing a letter. Vic is the archetypal kid next door, with pleasant eyes and an honest face. He tells me, "We've got three Vietnam vets, one guy who deserted from marine OCS [Officer's Candidate School], one lifer who split, and an air force deserter. Most of the other guys split from stateside bases." I ask Vic about himself:

After two years of college I dropped out and applied for CO but my draft board turned it down. So I got drafted and my parents pressured me into going in. I said, all right, until I get orders for Nam. I applied for CO again, but the army kept turning me down. I found most guys who were in the army went along 'cause they considered army service as paying your dues. I talked with a lot of guys in my company at Fort Leonard Wood and told them they were stupid if they went to Vietnam. I told 'em I wasn't going. So then I got orders for Nam, and I went home and told my folks that I wasn't going and they took it fairly well. My dad was a major in the army in World War II, but he said he doesn't blame me for not wanting to go to Vietnam—he doesn't like the war. My mother was against me deserting at first but then I said, "Do you want me to go to Vietnam and get killed?" "No," she said, "and I don't want you to go to Canada either." Finally she started folding my clothes. What helped was that a friend of mine had just gotten out of the hospital—he'd been wounded in Nam—and he came limping in one day on crutches with his shattered leg and we all said, "Wow! man, what happened?" "Mortar shell," he said. I said, wow! not me, I couldn't see that happening to me, not for this war.

The kitchen starts filling up. Guys are coming to listen, to talk, to fix themselves sandwiches. Some people are coming home from work. Two men bring in several huge shopping bags of food. Soon there are about fifteen people in the kitchen talking to the writer who was enjoying listening to their stories. There is much laughter. One man recalls the previous evening in the commons room when they had all been sitting around trying to remember army acronyms and what they stood for. "It was really funny," he says, "all those names. Those army people have got to be psycho."

There seem to be a number of Southerners among them. Stan, writing his letter home, is from South Carolina and he says that he knew when he went in the air force that something was wrong with this war, but he couldn't associate it directly with his assignment. "Then I started reading about the war. I subscribed to *OM* and wrote to Roger Priest who puts it out and he wrote me some letters. Then I decided I wouldn't go to Taiwan where I was to work on the planes that would bomb Vietnam. I read in *OM* about Canada and started thinking. Then, on leave, I saw *Hair* in New York and I couldn't come down for about three hours afterwards. That night I decided to desert." The musical *Hair* might be passé, even bourgeois entertainment in New York, but it would probably be banned as subversive in Charleston, Stan's hometown. It helped subvert Stan. People start talking about the movement, the Chicago Eight, the Chicago Fifteen, Daniel Berrigan, William Kunstler, Lee Weiner, the pros and cons of various U.S. draft resistance groups, and draft board offices that had recently been blown up—discussion of the latter eliciting much laughter and lots of "right on's!" We talk about drugs and they tell me the police have been in once but they just stood around, talked, and left. "They asked us if we had any drugs," one of them says, "and it's true, we don't. Not in here." A deserter tells his story about being medevac-ed out of Vietnam and flown to Japan for over-use of amphetamines. "I had a bleeding ulcer from speed, wow! I'll never do that again, but it *did* get me out of Nam. I deserted in Japan." Frank, an extraordinarily articulate hippie type, the only longhair in the place, reminisces about Vietnam and cracks everyone up. "We weren't on the lines in Vietnam so they wouldn't give our group any weapons—they knew we all hated the officers and NCOs. It's a good thing I wasn't in the infantry 'cause if any captain had said charge that hill I'd have shot him. Once in a while we'd break into the weapons room at our compound at Nha Trang and take out a gun. The sergeants would really get worried—they'd lock their doors at night. They didn't sleep well until they found it. When I got back from the Nam, I started organizing and turned my whole battalion into a hornet's nest." The army had threatened him with another tour in Vietnam if he didn't quit his antiwar work and so he left.

There was a beautiful camaraderie here. The men respected one another no matter what their backgrounds, age, personality. There was no phoniness, which definitely set 106 Eddy Street apart from the analagous fraternity; there was warmth and kindness and cooperation. There was a greater morale here than I had ever seen on the front lines in Vietnam—they were sharing not in the fear and horror of battle, but in the experience of becoming new men. These men *are* in a fraternity, I think to myself on the way back to Ottawa, a brotherhood of consciousness and conscience.

●

A lot of kids don't find a 106 Eddy Street in Canada. Some are almost without hope when they find they don't qualify for immigration, cannot work legally, and must remain underground. And some do go back, further complicating their young lives. Going back usually means six months in an army stockade which can destroy even the strongest-willed. The time does not count off from army duty, meaning that after the stockade the pattern is repeated again: the man deserts, but this time something has been taken away from him; he is cynical, angry, bitter.

While thinking about these young men, the story of John, an eighteen-year-old deserter, comes to mind. John has a benign, boyish face and a slightly overweight body that has not quite lost its baby fat. His nickname describes him: Lumpy. He graduated from a well-known private boy's school in the East and was subsequently drafted. He said he had been "into drugs" for three years at school and was dealing. As far as drugs go, the army was simply a continuation of high school. "Out of the two hundred guys in my company, only four drank," he had told me. "We had some really strange people in my company." When his company went to Vietnam, the men were glad, for it meant cheap grass. He was assigned to a combat helicopter battalion in the highlands and could watch air strikes from his bunker.

> We used to all come running out of our bunkers when we heard the Phantoms. It meant napalm. When you're stoned, napalm is beautiful. Guys would come scrambling out and watch the big fire-bursts with really wide eyes and say, "Wow! napalm!" I used to volunteer for door gunner and I'd always go up stoned 'cause the tracers were really beautiful when you're stoned. On my second mission the guy sitting next to me suddenly had his head blown away. It went all over the inside of the chopper, all over the pilots, the plexiglass, into the propwash and all over me; he just sat there hanging out of the chopper with no head. I was so upset I had to kill something, so I shot a water buffalo. Some guys really love to kill but I couldn't kill anyone; I just shot a water buffalo.

Lumpy had been wounded and sent to Fort Benning, Georgia. Later, on leave, he had been picked up in Savannah for possession of three grams of marijuana. In Vietnam, marijuana had become so commonplace that afterwards he, like most soldiers, didn't think anything at all about carrying it around. He spent six weeks in jail. "The Savannah county jail, more than the army, turned me against the United States," he had explained. "You wouldn't believe what it's like!" While being turned over to military authorities he had escaped on foot and borrowed money for a bus ticket to Canada. At nineteen he was a Vietnam combat veteran, a fugitive felon on a drug-abuse charge, a military deserter, and an American exile. Now he is a prisoner because a minister and a lawyer and a colonel wrote him and said to come home, that his drug charge would be dropped and that he would only get two or three weeks in the stockade for desertion. The last I heard, via a smuggled note from the stockade, he had received something like six months for desertion and the Savannah prosecutor had *not* dropped the drug charge so he faced that when the army was through with him. He said he was going to get back to Canada somehow. But he didn't know that his drug charge would prevent him from becoming a landed immigrant.

The young Southerners, especially, have it difficult when they find their nineteen-fifties world shattered by their experiences in the New Action Army. They have to learn so much so quickly and some like Steve Argo go to extremes to do it. Steve, known as "Tex," went from high school into the Marine Corps football team. As he tells his story:

> I was born and raised in a small town in northeastern Texas where I was quite successfully indoctrinated into the system because I had no idea of anything but what they told me. Now I feel I've been lied to, I've been cheated, I feel like my mind has been exploited. I feel that the U.S. is raising a generation of psychopaths. I deserted 'cause I got orders to Vietnam and it was the final realization that I was finally going to go over and kill people . . . I won't kill my brothers and sisters.

Now, it is hard to find a Marine Corps football player beneath the shaggy hair, long beard, gentle eyes, and homemade clothes. Tex describes himself as a professional hippie and recently made his way across Canada and back without money and only a leather shoulder bag and bandana-tied bundle holding his few possessions. He is in Montreal now, looking for a way to get to India to study the Bhagavad-Gita in the mountains somewhere. And there are Southerners like Mike who are learning that the world is not what they'd been told it was in Birmingham, Alabama, that majors and colonels weren't really Southern Gentlemen, but men bent on advancing their careers by pitting young Americans against "communists." He was managing a Seven-Eleven store in Birmingham when he was drafted. After a year he deserted. "They tear you down into a Zombie, then they build you back up again in their image. I couldn't take the loss of identity." He moved his wife and children to Canada. Gerald, another Southerner from Columbus, Georgia, expresses the changes he underwent. He had hoped for an appointment to West Point but didn't get it so he enlisted.

> I was made a platoon leader and an acting sergeant, a high school graduate bossing around all these M.A.s and Ph.D.s. It seemed ridiculous. I started talking to these guys who'd been to college, and started reading, and meeting some of these antiwar people around Fort Jackson, went to the coffeehouse there. If a girl I met, who had worked in the peace

movement in San Francisco, hadn't started me asking questions, I probably would never have listened to these antiwar people or done any reading. I was the outstanding trainee at Fort Jackson, but I asked my CO if I could be a chaplain's assistant. They gave me hell. Then they gave me hell when I put a poster of Joan Baez on my wall. It built up and I finally knew I had to leave. I'm glad I deserted now. If I hadn't, I'd probably have been an ultra-fascist type by the time I got out of the army. I mean I could see signs of it in me. I'd have hated hippies and longhairs and Negroes and anyone with ideas different from mine. Probably I'd have been big in the Klan, like my uncles.

For some young men, then, the metamorphosis forced on them by the changing times and particularly by the Vietnam War was, in the end, a good thing. Some men were crushed by these bad times, and then saved; others were awakened by the times, and then crushed. Many of this generation were born anew and many of this generation perished. The future waits upon the final tally.

●

In the early spring of 1970, the American exile community in Toronto began to revolve around a new group called Red White & Black which took over the offices of the Union of American Exiles. RW&B was formed to help ease the pain of exile, aid disaffected young Americans, and help integrate American youth into the Canadian community.

Where the Union of American Exiles had stressed politics and the antiwar movement, RW&B devoted its energies to "community development." Ted Stiener, a twenty-two-year-old draft resister from Kansas City who balances an ingenuously youthful élan with an intense seriousness, founded RW&B along with several other resisters and their wives and a middle-aged radical named Judith Merril. Miss Merril, the science fiction writer and anthologist, explains why she and her daughter, who married a deserter, left the United States: "I had to make a choice between becoming an active revolutionary and leaving the country." Miss Merril feels that in Canada she can be active and remain nonviolent and she sees Red White & Black as representing the "community of the dislocated" which in Toronto is not only young American exiles, but Canadian youth as well. "I've heard too much bullshit rhetoric for the past thirty years," she says. "I'm only interested in things I can do." In a RW&B newsletter she had written, "Not just draft dodgers, and deserters, but a broad spectrum of political, creative, and religious refugees are coming to Canada today in search of the old American dream of civil and ethical freedom, away from the American nightmare which is perpetuating the war in Indochina, supporting dictatorships in other countries, and persecuting dissenters at home—exploiting the resources of other countries and destroying the resources of its own." She says of the exile community:

> Here we can offer a lesson in rehabilitating a country when the U.S. establishment falls. You can build in Canada. You can't build in the U.S. and destroy at the same time. Those who are doing the destroying— which is probably necessary and inevitable—will be changed by the experience of destroying the monolith. The U.S. revolutionaries will have to establish a monolith to deal with the monolith—they could lose the concept of the society they were trying to build. Perhaps in Canada we *can* build the alternate society.

By late summer, RW&B was closing its St. George Street offices and, along with the Whole Earth Family, opening "The Hall," a Canadian-American community center. The Hall, formerly a community center for Finnish immigrants, has a large hall and a stage situated above a *cave*-type coffeehouse. At The Hall is the "community switchboard," a youth information center, a free store, a free kitchen, a day-care center, a twenty-four-hour reception center for American refugees sponsored by the antidraft and deserters' committees, yoga classes, French and Canadian affairs classes for new Canadians, sewing, art, dance and drama classes, the Free Music School and on *ad infinitum*. As The Hall formed a base in the larger Canadian youth community, Red White & Black phased out its separate functions, and American exile activists were being channeled through a group located at The Hall called the Committee to Aid Refugees from Militarism (CARM). Same people, new name, Red White & Black having carried too much of an American connotation, that of exiled American (Red White & . . .) anarchists (Black). (Anarchy may be the ideological foundation of the alternate-culture, but it always gets a bad press.)

With American exiles becoming more and more prominent in community affairs in Toronto, it was necessary from time to time for the exiles to defend themselves against the usual allegations of conspiracy and subversion. In one of the most comprehensive statements to be written about the American exile community in Canada, an issue of the Red White & Black newsletter in the spring had explained:

> We have taken it upon ourselves to speak on behalf of a loose community for whom we hold no formal brief, but whose composition, moods, attitudes, and behaviour we know very well . . . 1. The large majority of new American immigrants to Canada are here precisely because we were unable to subscribe to the violence of *either* the U.S. government (abroad or at home) *or* of the militant opposition groups within the States . . . we are as a group strongly opposed to violence of any sort. 2. We are even more keenly aware than most Canadians of the difference in political atmosphere and personal liberty in Canada and the U.S. We have experienced the disasters of violent polarization at first hand and we value, to the extreme, the opportunities which still exist in Canada for peaceful social evolution through the ordinary political processes and public channels of communication. 3. Most of us are keenly conscious, ethically, of our situation as guests of the Canadian people. All of us are conscious, practically, of our status as immigrants, not-yet-citizens on the sufferance of the Canadian government. 4. As Americans we feel we have one special function to serve as Canadians: That is, to remind other Canadians of the dangers of pursuing the course the U.S. has followed, and to help foster the growth of a healthy new Canadian nationalism which will throw off American economic and cultural domination (of the Left as well as the Right), put an end to Canadian complicity in the war in Indochina, and reject the American patterns of violence and anti-communication which we have already rejected as individuals.

It was hard to say how many Canadians that statement would reach. But there was little question that a new film about draft dodgers playing during the summer at eight theaters in Montreal and Toronto would reach several hundred thousand. The film is *Explosion.* I am reading the big ads for it in the papers: "DRAFT DODGERS WHO FLEE TO CANADA, today's generation, living by their own code! Strung-out, hung up, hassled by the establishment! Filmed in Vancouver—where it's happening *today*!" Or, on the theater marquees in downtown Montreal and Toronto: "The establishment calls them 'DRAFT DODGERS'—They're Angry, Defiant, and one of them is ready to EXPLODE." The "young filmmakers" who had produced *Explosion* had received a quarter-million-dollar grant from the Canadian Film Development Corporation to make a sensationalist skin and violence picture which equated draft resisters with psychotics and criminals.

●

A draft resister writes his impressions of Toronto in the *Toronto Star* and says, "Toronto, I was happy to find, was a combination of American well-being and a beautiful sense of Canadian tranquility and peace. I remember being surprised when I first saw it. The city wasn't filthy, de-humanized, spiritually decadent, threatened by crime, or filled with street rats." In another article, a deserter's wife is quoted: "About the third night we were here, we asked a fellow in our roominghouse where we could go for a walk. He said, 'It depends on how athletic you are.' We said, 'No, no, where is it safe to go for a walk?' He said, 'What are you talking about? You can go for a walk anywhere!' What a novel, delightful idea that was!" She added, "Detroit is almost completely gray. Toronto is so colorful. The people are friendly, and they're much more fashionably dressed; you see men in bright shirts and wide ties whereas downtown Detroit is a sea of blue and black suits. The architecture is much more pleasing to the eye, and the parks are beautiful."

There is a difference between the U.S. and Canada, the exiles were learning, and this discovery forced thousands of young Americans to take a very hard look at America. They would, armed with the knowledge that the American Way isn't always the best way, be a force for change if they were allowed to return—if they *would* return, if anyone would let them return. Many war resisters, for example, were stunned when they learned that Detroit, with a population only eight times that of its sister city of

Windsor, Ontario, reported 244 times as many homicides in 1969. (Officials reported there were 488 murders in Detroit compared with only two in Windsor.) Americans are surprised to learn they can get around easily in Toronto (as well as Montreal and Vancouver) without a car; public transportation is quick, clean, safe, and it goes everywhere. *AMEX*, in a spring issue, revealed a "fascinating story of how mild Canadian socialism has made a fool of reckless U.S. capitalism." The story is why Toronto has the largest fleet of streetcars in North America. The first American reaction to these streetcars (Toronto also has a subway system which, like the masterpiece of public transportation in Montreal, *Le Métro*, runs almost without noise) is that they are old fashioned. We Americans are well-conditioned to denounce anything we don't have as "old fashioned." Americans in Toronto, however, quickly find that streetcars are a delight. They're smooth, quiet, cheap, efficient, run exactly on schedule, and don't emit noxious fumes. "Why did U.S. cities get rid of all theirs," *AMEX* asked? Reportedly, according to *AMEX* research, during the 1950s many medium-sized cities had their transit companies bought up by a syndicate known as North American Transportation Enterprises (that's *free* enterprise) which is owned by rubber and oil interests. "NTE was formed as an outlet for their products, not to provide cheap efficient service to the public." Bus systems were installed; GM sold buses to nearly every U.S. city. Not counting repairs and vehicle costs, it costs twelve cents a mile to operate a diesel bus, six cents a mile to operate a trolleybus, and three cents a mile to operate a trolley. The city of Toronto bought its trolley rolling stock from Cincinnati, Cleveland, Birmingham, and Kansas City and despite its age it is expected to last until 1990. Diesel buses last ten years. Again, the American taxpayers lose. It will be hard to convince a lot of draft resisters who have lived in Toronto to ever return to America and see their taxes go for inefficient, smelly buses . . . or Lockheed C-5A jet transports.

The newly arrived exile rides the noiseless and clean Yonge Street subway to the end of the line, and there he finds the

Toronto Anti-Draft Programme office tucked away in the basement of an office building. Its four rooms are so cluttered with desks and typewriters and telephones and materials that new arrivals are asked to wait in the hall, the walls of which are covered with messages and information. He reads this stuff while he waits. If it's one of those busy days with forty or fifty new arrivals he waits a very long time. Maybe he's told to come back tomorrow. If he gets in he is assigned preliminary counseling along with five or six others. Final immigration counseling is private. I am sitting in on a welcoming session. There are three couples: a young and uneasy deserter and his girlfriend from Florida; a twenty-year-old gas station attendant from southern Ohio and his wife—his lottery number assured him a good view of the war and he is going to resist the draft—and an older draft resister and his wife from New York City. John Lyss, a draft resister finishing his Canadian law degree at the University of Toronto and working forty hours a week for the TADP, is counseling. He is asking if everyone is absolutely sure he is ready to come to Canada, explaining that it is a very final decision. He asks who has thought of transferring induction to Oakland, refusing to step forward, and delaying his indictment for approximately three years (thanks to a huge backlog in the Bay Area). "It will give you time to finish your studies, get some money together, or learn some skills—jobs are harder to get here than there." The New Yorker seems interested; he hadn't known about this. Lyss asks them:

> Have you considered applying for CO? It takes about a year for the decision to come down. And if you should happen to get it—few do—then you simply forget to show up for alternate service. We don't know of any prosecutions yet for failing to do alternate service. It really screws them up. They don't know what to do . . . don't just escape the war yourself, help stop it. We're only saying you can make something of your antiwar act if you want to. You can actually do the system more harm, without causing yourself any inconvenience, by staying in the U.S.

Turning to the deserter he says, "Of course I don't mean you." The draft resister from Ohio listens quietly and then asks, "How do we immigrate?" Lyss makes an appointment for immigration counseling. The New Yorker asks about Oakland and the CO thing.

At another session there is a couple in their mid-twenties from Maryland. She is pregnant. There are two draft resisters, students from Eastern colleges, and several men up for the weekend to look around. There are also two deserters who have just escaped from the Fort Riley stockade. During the session their story comes out since everyone wants to hear it. One had gone AWOL for several days because he couldn't get emergency leave when his grandfather died. The other one had returned from a year in Korea which, he said, "wasn't so bad 'cause I stayed stoned all the time." When he returned to Fort Riley he couldn't take the stateside discipline: "I lost my identity, I didn't know who I was anymore. I went AWOL, deserted really, and joined a commune in California for a while. I was caught after two and a half years underground. I'm really sorry I had to leave the U.S. All I want to do is be able to live and walk around and breathe." Ken, who had gone AWOL and to his grandfather's funeral, later returning to the base, was beaten by three guards the first day in the stockade. Attempting to resist, he was sent to "the box" for fourteen days and fed nothing but lettuce. He says he saw guards beat a man to death in the box: "He escaped twice. When they brought him back the second time they beat him so hard that he died on 'em." Lyss asks if they have any money. They don't have much. He tells them to go down to the ADC who will house them for free. The wife of the draft resister from Maryland slips them a twenty dollar bill as they leave.

Across the hall in another office draft resister Dick Burrows, a tall, handsome, full-bearded Texan is talking to two Dutch girls who are representing an international peace organization which is in touch with people in Japan who are trying to get a group of twenty-two deserters to Canada since their hideout has been discovered. He is alternately talking on the phone to the Vancouver Committee and asking the girls questions. God knows how it will ever work out. In the main office a girl is mailing out *Anti-Draft Manuals*. She says they are receiving about forty to sixty pieces of mail a day from the U.S. Meanwhile, the hallway is still crowded.

Downtown at the American Deserters' Committee on Huntley Street it's a similar scene. Since February the ADC has been headquartered in a three-story brick house which provides accommodation for the staff collective on the upper floors and office space below. In the front room deserters are reading and playing cards; an urn of coffee brews in the corner. A man is receiving final counseling in the meeting room and is looking for a proper pair of shoes to go through immigration with; all he has are tennis shoes with holes in them. The chairs and old stuffed sofa in the office are full of people asking about Canada. Some had come directly from the U.S. to the ADC and others had been sent down from the TADP for housing. A staff member is on the phone to the Wellesley Street cooperative looking for a room. Out on the front porch a deserter sits quietly. He asks me what I know about the job situation here and if I know of a cheap place to stay—he and his wife and two small children are staying at the Holiday Inn. He says he has to get immigrated quickly because he has a family to support. He worked in an army hospital in Chicago and had been busted on a fake marijuana charge, he said, after he had attempted to pass out antiwar leaflets to the staff. He was awaiting court-martial when Nixon invaded Cambodia. "I think Cambodia, and then Kent State—I'm from Ohio, not far from Kent—that did it. I could finally see what that country was all about."

A car with Alabama plates pulls up in front of the ADC house. You don't see many Alabama cars in Canada. Carlos gets out, along with a friend, another deserter. I had known Carlos in Montreal and had not seen him all summer. I was afraid he had gone back since he received about two phone calls a week from Birmingham imploring him to return—the we-know-general-so-and-so-and-he-can-get-you-off kind of phone call. Uncles, cousins, friends, his mother, and grandfather had called and Carlos wasn't so sure anymore that he should stay. A twenty-year-old Southern boy with short hair, a long accent, and no money, no clothes, and no skills doesn't stand much of a chance in Canada and he was beginning to realize that. But he hadn't returned. Now, here he was in Toronto looking for work and here was his mother and grandfather from Alabama; they had driven all the way up to bring him some clothes, some money, and to see how he was getting along. His mother had been a campaign worker for George Wallace. "She really freaked out when she saw the ADC office," he informs me, "you know, the pictures of Ho Chi Minh and all. I thought they were going to take me back." Somehow, he had convinced his mother that what he was doing was the right thing for him.

He had been drafted and during basic training he had read Lennie Bruce, Joan Baez, and Eldridge Cleaver, in that order, and he soon began to identify with the counter-culture. He started asking questions and he perceived that the army didn't have any answers. In the spring, he spent a weekend pass at the Ellipse in Washington and joined the demonstration against the Cambodia invasion and the Kent massacre. "I was into nonviolence," he had said, "so my friends and I sat around the Washington Monument and got stoned and drunk and stayed peaceful. Then the pigs came and gassed us while we were just sitting there and they beat on heads and chased everyone away. I was really pissed. I mean I had been *peaceful*. I hadn't run off with the militants. And I got my head beat. I decided right there that I'd had enough. I tore up my military ID cards, my friends drove me out to the airport, gave me seventy-five dollars, all they had, and I got a plane for Canada." Carlos had a good friend with him with whom he was going to share an apartment. He introduces me to John, from Albany, Georgia, a handsome kid with an earnest look about him, very polite. John tells me about his escape from the Fort Riley stockade—another one—and says he was underground for fourteen months. "I ran over two fences with another guy; we hitched into town and got jobs right away. I've really been lucky. I didn't have to resort to crime while I was underground, I always got jobs. But all this running was gettin' to me. One day I saw an article in the *Los Angeles Free Press* about deserters in Canada and learned I could come here and be free." Carlos is talking to his mother now. Then his grandfather gets out of the car and puts his hand on Carlos' shoulder. They get back in, Carlos waves, and the green Oldsmobile from Alabama heads slowly down the street.

Jim, a deserter from Massachusetts who left the army when he received orders for Vietnam, is manager of the Wellesley Street cooperative hostel. He and his wife share the ground floor apartment with another couple—it's cramped but nicely fixed up, freshly painted and clean. They live on a modest salary from the deserters' committee. The co-op is self-sustaining as men pay one dollar a night for lodging; there are eighteen deserters living here presently and Jim shows me the rooms. It too looks like a fraternity house minus the books and expensive stereo sets; it's all very clean. I could imagine how grateful new arrivals must be when they find this place. There are kitchens on all three floors and the men cook communally. Through his day-work job program, Jim manages to find most of the men in the house enough work to pay their rent and buy food. There is a fair turnover; men stay until they get landed and are then encouraged to move out, but some want to stay and turn Wellesley into a permanent commune. Jim goes back to painting the halls when I leave. He says his parents are coming for a visit next week.

Across town, on Dundas Street, is another large Victorian house rented by the ADC. Eventually, it is hoped, it will be as well-managed as Wellesley, but for the present it serves as a hostel for men without money, though those who do have it are encouraged to contribute the customary dollar per night. There are about twenty-two deserters staying at the Dundas hostel and they had recently elected a manager, a tall, husky deserter with a university degree named Big John. The mood of the Dundas house was markedly different from the other hostels I'd visited. Here were men with much less of a chance of really making it in Canada, people with no skills, education, money, and so on. Building the necessary sense of community, without which collective living fails, was obviously more difficult here. At the same time, all kinds of people seemed to be getting along. There were four couples in the house, eight deserters including four Vietnam veterans, several draft resisters, and a baby. I am informed by Paul, a UCLA graduate in theater arts who had just secured a good job with a well-established Toronto theater group, that one of the Vietnam vets is a speed freak and they are really worried about him. Although the people with the most problems were the deserters without high school diplomas, it was a middle-class college graduate—a deserter —who had attempted suicide two weeks before. He had slashed his upper arms with a butcher knife from the kitchen and bled all over his third-floor room before leaping to the sidewalk below, severely fracturing his skull. He remains in critical condition, I am told, but at least his parents had come to see him. The guys had found two letters in his room, one from his girlfriend saying unless he turned himself in to the authorities, she would have nothing more to do with him, and one from his parents disowning him and calling him a communist and a coward. When the police were given the letters, one of them said to the guys in the house, "How can anyone write a thing like that?"*

●

The person responsible for the housing cooperatives in Toronto is Tony Wagner, a twenty-one-year-old deserter who had enlisted after leaving Cornell following his sophomore year. Wagner, who bears a modest resemblance to the rock singer Country Joe MacDonald—the same gentle eyes—is an Austrian who immigrated to the U.S. with his family when he was eleven. His father is a research chemist in New Jersey.

*Author's note: After brain surgery and several months of intensive care, the young man was taken back to the U.S. by his parents who turned him over to the army. He was sent to the stockade and put in solitary confinement to await a court-martial for desertion. He was let out of solitary after several weeks of peace movement pressure channeled through Senator Goodell's office. He is reported to be suffering permanent brain damage, yet the army still will not discharge him.

I was just going to go into the army and get it over with, and sort of ignore Vietnam. I was being trained as a supply sergeant, part of a machine, a desk job. I grew up near Mauthausen [Nazi extermination camp] and it made me think about the role of the desk clerk. The army in Vietnam has one function, to destroy a people and a country, and I was part of that, what I was doing was not much different from those desk jobs that many Austrians did during the war for the camps, and later denied guilt. I eventually told my CO that I wasn't going to train anymore. Then I heard about Canada. I went to Washington from Fort Lee and flew to Toronto. We flew over the Pentagon. It was sort of sad, leaving a lot of things behind, my new country for ten years—but the last image I had of the U.S. was the Pentagon and the congested highways around it.

In Toronto Wagner had seen a problem and offered a solution. He suggested the ADC provide more than counseling, rely less on placing deserters in private homes, and instead, set up communal houses where men could work out their various problems together. At the same time, he believed, collective living helps to instill a new set of values, values which are the cornerstone of the counter-culture, group consciousness, sharing and so on, and this is exactly what deserters needed, not offices and organizations and meetings and political rhetoric. Having seen a lot of the latter, I find myself agreeing with Tony as he talks:

About half the people we see at ADC are problem cases. The army takes the uneducated, the poor, people who've been in some sort of trouble, and, as these people begin to become aware, many desert of course. But you see so many problems you actually become afraid of them because you know you cannot really help them. The co-ops, on the other hand, are in a position to absorb a great many problems. The idea is to build a stable community of American exiles, and the co-op is a stepping stone to a more independent existence for deserters and dodgers. It is an experience, and the benefits that they derived from communal living can be passed on. A lot of the more political people don't see this as important; they are in a hurry to change things; they say we are all doomed if there isn't a revolution in the U.S. very soon. They think exiles must be made more political so they can play a political role as exiles against the United States. I don't agree. People are coming here for a *personal* revolution, to make a revolution in their own lives. The cooperative living they find here, or go through for a period, is part of this, it is a cultural thing, not political. The willingness of young people to share property and so on is the hope for the future, and this is a cultural change. I think the cultural revolution will eventually bring new values into the national consciousness, in every country. I'm not so pessimistic about the next few years in the U.S. as some of the more political people I know because I don't think the impact of this new culture has really been felt yet. We're maybe only in the beginning of the cultural revolution—the values are already recognizable but do not predominate. They will be predominant in perhaps ten years. And eventually there will have to be a merger between the great number of young people, this new society, and the political system. Right now there is really a society within a society.

Despite Wagner's optimism, working with the immediate problems creates a less sanguine outlook:

It's psychologically very self-destructive to be involved in this for a very long time. These people come to you and you feel responsible; you have to do something, but your resources are very limited, no money. What do you do when you have these people with no money and you have to feed them? But there are the bright spots, like when someone whom you thought would never get landed gets landed and then they get a good job.

Wagner is enrolled in drama at the University of Toronto. When classes begin in the fall, he intends to phase himself out of the ADC.

Urban communes were originally brought to Toronto by draft resisters. In 1966-1967, a half-dozen of them sprung up, partly out of need, partly because the war exiles involved had been doing the same thing in the U.S. Presently, in a Chinese district in downtown Toronto, there is an alternate-culture community of American exiles which centers around a "liberation tribal store" called the Yellow Ford Truck; Ragnarokr, a leather shop; the Baldwin Street Gallery; the Whole Earth Family's Fourth World Grain Store; and the 167th Street General Store. They have nothing to do at all with Toronto's famous Yorkville which has gone the way of Greenwich Village with teeny-bopper speed freaks, weekend hippies, and hip-capitalist boutiques. The "community" on Baldwin Street is entirely different: a group of cooperatively-owned and collectively-run businesses which sustain a large group of people dedicated to the communal experiment. Phil Mullins met Pat and Jim Wilson at the John Street draft-dodger hostel in

1968 and following a period when they were all active with the Union of American Exiles, the three of them formed the nucleus of a commune and opened a craft shop which they named after the commune's yellow Ford truck. Mullins, from Gainsville, Florida, says, "We were interested in jobs, running a hostel and so on at the UAE, but nothing happened but meetings, meetings, meetings. We had all been through that before in the Southern Organizing Committee. A lot of us here came out of that. We opened the Yellow Ford Truck and another group from the commune eventually opened the Ragnarokr. We're really not interested in politics anymore."

At the Yellow Ford Truck Pat Wilson, who came to Canada for a new start with her draft-resisting husband, talks about the past in her easy South Carolina accent:

> I was into civil rights first, back in the early sixties, then went through the whole college anti-Vietnam thing. Then I went to New York and worked for a couple of years with the Young Socialist Alliance, you know, *analyzing* everything, meeting and discussing all night long; it seems like all we ever did was talk. Then I went with the Motherfuckers and we were doing a lot of trashing, a lot of violent stuff. Finally it all got to be a drag. I could see we could kill ourselves analyzing, kill ourselves trashing, and it wasn't going to change things. We had really thought it *would*, you know, like the revolution was around the corner. But that's just not where it's at. You've got to learn to *live.*

Pat and Jim along with another couple from Berkeley, self-exiles, alternate the operation of their shop with running a farm they just bought in northern Ontario called Morning Glory. The idea is to get away from the city; they do their craft work in the country and sell it on Baldwin Street. More Americans are coming, they say, to join Morning Glory. The Americans come and they bring their alternate culture and alternate economy with them. Three draft resisters had recently helped put together The Whole Earth Family commune and store. Among the young craftsmen I meet is an army deserter, a candlemaker, who is wearing a Frisbee on his waist in a purple velvet case. He tells me he had been the best shot in his company, "but I traded in my M-16 for a Frisbee."

TWELVE

Going Home and Other Problems

The American exiles have gained a new perception. Living outside the borders of the United States has provided an opportunity to see their homeland in a new light. It is not a roseate view from afar. Getting out of the trees and seeing the whole forest also permits one to see the forest fires burning in the distance, burning brighter every moment and coming nearer. If one does not incur a total sense of hopelessness about his country, expecting it to burn before it changes, then one at least makes the inevitable comparisons between his own lot in his new country and the lot of his former countrymen, and, in either case, the desire to return home is thereby diminished. Now that they have nothing more to lose, they can accept the realities about the United States; they are not defending a false premise, nor a vested interest, nor a "promising" future, and so they can afford the critical perception which informs them that America is a sinking ship. They are not interested in riding it under, but they are interested from their land-view in who gets saved and who goes down, as some would return one day to join their comrades in the salvage.

They would all return right now—granted they *could*—to help build a new nation if they thought there were possibilities for nation-building and the promise of a real future, but by the time there is, if ever, the majority of the exiles will have made new commitments to building a life and a nation where they find themselves. It may be ten or twenty years before the fires have cooled enough to permit reconstruction in their homeland; they can build in Canada now as we have seen. Others, a small group, who would like to get on with the revolution, or the destruction, or the repression, or whatever, will not wait; they will return . . . they will take themselves to a thousand Finland Stations and join the call to arms, or they will return with the ardor and hope of Che to the Bolivian hideouts of the Adirondacks and Sierra Nevadas. God help them. Still others, I suppose the saddest of the lot, will simply remain exiles, calling themselves that for years to come, watching, thinking, writing, waiting, remaining unalterably *American* to the end. God help us.

Of immediate concern: A campaign to secure humane asylum in Canada for U.S. deserters was under way by late 1970. The Committee to Assist Refugees from Militarism was preparing briefs to be presented to the government which outlined the problems deserters faced in Canada. The exile groups were asking that U.S. Armed Forces deserters be treated as refugees from oppression in the same manner that Czechs, Hungarians, and Greeks had been. At the same time, immigration policies were under government review as immigrants, mostly Europeans, were entering Canada illegally and taking advantage of immigration law (it was clearly stated that deserters and dodgers were not part of this problem). With a change in the immigration laws and an elimination of the appeals process, there was a chance that people who failed to gain landed immigrant status would have the opportunity to request humane asylum. There was little chance that all military deserters would ever be granted asylum en masse, but it was a possibility that a deserter who did not qualify for immigration, yet who could prove that he would face incarceration and inhuman treatment if he were returned to the U.S., would be granted permission to stay.

This would end a great deal of hypocrisy on the part of many Canadians who liked to believe that Canada's liberal policies toward U.S. exiles were exclusively a generous manifestation of goodwill and humane concern, or even proof of their government's displeasure with America's war in Asia. There was certainly a fair measure of goodwill and antiwar sentiment in the friendly reception the exiles have received, but goodwill is not represented in government policy. The exiles' right to enter Canada is based solely on the Immigration Act which both conservative and liberal Canadians have taken great pains to make sure is administered without discrimination. Within the law there has been little discrimination, almost none in fact and this deserves praise, but the law itself is extremely discriminatory. It discriminates against the poor, the uneducated, the unskilled. It is far from America's "give me your poor, your huddled masses" immigration policy. Immigrants to the U.S. who are finally admitted are not chosen on the basis of America's skilled-manpower requirements. Uneducated and unskilled people are regularly admitted to the U.S. This has been true in Canada, but only when unskilled manpower has been needed. It has not been applied to U.S. residents. Only skilled or educated Americans—including all the war resisters to arrive between 1965 and 1971—have ever been legally admitted to Canada on a permanent basis.

The nature of the Canadian immigration policies is embodied in the name of the department which administers them: The Department of Manpower and Immigration. This was formed in 1967 during a reorganization of the immigration department which included adopting the point system to determine who qualified for immigration. The point system reduced prejudice in the system and therefore actually aided the exiles who were coming then; by a fair application of the point system it has been possible for thousands of military deserters to be admitted. But, also, by a fair application of the point system perhaps as many as five or ten thousand young draft resisters and men who deserted with the belief that they could live in Canada have not qualified for immigration. It is their fate that is at stake in the campaign for asylum.

In their essay, "The Exploitation of Youth: U.S. Draft, Canadian Immigration, and Manpower Channeling," Rick Ayers and Melody Killian point out that, "when unskilled labour was needed to man the railways and early factories, Canada accepted runaway slaves from the U.S. . . . when professional and technical workers are needed, Canada accepts middle-class draft dodgers. Canada seeks to import already trained personnel to compensate for her lack of educational facilities." Statistics show that engineers, physicians, physical scientists, and architects who have immigrated to Canada make up more than half the total graduated from Canadian universities. And so, with these policies, the deserter suffers. If Canadian unemployment rises, the point system will be adjusted accordingly to exclude lower-category skills and jobs and the deserters will be among the first to feel the crunch, yet Canadian liberals will pride themselves on Canada's humane concern for them. There is little concern for them if they must look forward to spending the rest of their life in the Canadian underground.

Quoting Ayers and Killian, "These are the people really caught by the totalitarianism of the continental youth-channeling system; they don't have the right class background to keep out of the army or to get into Canada . . . No one should be forced to leave sanctuary in Canada because he does not measure up to the impersonal and bureaucratic requirement of the Immigration Act. No one should be turned over to military authorities by Canadians. No one should be deported from Canada to face a stockade or a battle in Vietnam. Equality under the immigration law for deserters is not enough. Only asylum for deserters will end Canada's complicity in enforcing repressive American law."

The American exiles are not denying Canada the right to decide who can immigrate to Canada—every nation has that right; few in today's world can afford to open their borders as they did fifty years ago. And whatever one says about the discriminatory nature of the immigration policies, they are perhaps necessary if Canada is to exist independently of the giant to the south: Canada must carefully control its economy by using those few means still at its disposal, one of which is immigration. All the American exiles are asking is that the Canadian government reconsider the plight of U.S. military deserters and draft resisters who do not qualify under these laws for permanent residence in Canada yet who feel a need to leave the United States rather than fight in a lost war or go to prison, and that the government treat them as it has treated the thousands of other refugees from all over the world which Canada has hitherto generously admitted.

As for other problems, one of them was the War Measures Act, which was invoked in October 1970, in response to the kidnappings of labor minister Pierre LaPorte and British trade commissioner James Cross by the Front de Libération du Quebec. First, it should be made clear that the War Measures Act was in no way used against American exiles or their organizations. Several deserters were arrested in Quebec, not because they were deserters, but because they were at the wrong place at the wrong time. Bill Mullen of the Montreal Council was held for five hours, briefly questioned, and released; he was picked up for the length of his hair, not because he worked for the Montreal Council. In Toronto, Christopher Ewing, a deserter employed as a social worker, was arrested because he had been a demolitions expert in Vietnam and had had the misfortune of making "the wrong kind of friends" in Montreal where he lived before moving to Toronto. His lawyer, Paul Copeland, immediately started *habeas corpus* proceedings in the Ontario Supreme Court to have his detention ruled illegal. It was the first action in a Canadian court to attack the War Measures Act. Ewing was released after eighteen hours and his story appeared on the front pages in Toronto and Montreal while the press remained strangely silent about the 453 Canadian citizens arrested in Quebec. Although it is true that the ADC in Montreal felt threatened and closed its doors under the advice of an attorney, it soon reopened and the office was never raided. But, in a clear-cut

case of police abuse of the emergency law, a deserter who operated a news distribution company called Polis Germinations had
his stock, which included the *Village Voice*, confiscated and he
was threatened with deportation if he tried to distribute papers
such as the *Georgia Straight*, the *Los Angeles Free Press*, the *East
Village Other*, *Rat*, *Harbinger*, and so on to Montreal newsstands.
The emergency powers did not include dictates for either this kind
of censorship or for deportation, yet the police did the former and
threatened the latter. There were, however, no actual deportations
of American exiles under the War Measures Act.

The War Measures Act did have two unfortunate effects, aside
from scaring hell out of young Americans who neither expected
such a thing in Canada nor could accept that a Western government would so lightly suspend all civil liberties for six months: It
has served to discredit Prime Minister Trudeau among exiles whose
previous estimation of the man bordered on adulation, and it has
opened the government of Canada to the same suspicion and
contempt with which young people, both in Canada and the U.S.,
view the American government. The invocation of the Act forced
a political alienation on youth and intellectuals in a country where
it appeared that that would not happen. Secondly, while the
possibility still exists that Canada will, in its unique, quiet way,
manage social change peacefully in the coming decades—and that
is the hope the American exiles are relying on—there is now also
that chance, and a very real *opportunity* as provided by the severe
Public Order Act which replaced the War Measures Act, that the
government of Canada will respond to the need for equity in the
social order by locking up its critics at five o'clock in the morning
as it did in Quebec—in short, adopting police-state tactics, not as
some local police forces in the U.S. do, but as legal, national
policy. Fortunately, the Canadian government should have no
need to ever again employ these terrifying powers with which it
has invested itself; but then *need* may be interpreted differently.
The mayor of Vancouver already said publicly that he "needed"
the act in his province to deal with hippies and draft dodgers.

Should Canada elect a prime minister whose sympathies match those of British Columbia's premier or Vancouver's mayor (Trudeau's definitely do not) . . . that could be the end of freedom in Canada and exiles might find themselves getting homesick for the bad ol' U.S.A.

In 1970, while homesickness did not characterize how most war resisters felt about the U.S., there was often the desire to return briefly for a visit with friends or family; there were camping trips, secret rendezvous, treks to demonstrations, visits to movement groups. Many exiles returned for the May 9 protest of the Cambodian invasion in Washington; many went down for the huge moratorium gatherings of 1969. It was fairly easy to drive across the border providing the car was relatively new and the hair was not too long. (I have returned a number of times, for the Woodstock Music Festival, to see friends in Boston, to drive through New Hampshire in autumn.) *AMEX* carried articles on "how to do it" and the "odds of getting caught." The Toronto paper, *Guerilla*, however, warned that people doing this were occasionally being apprehended, most commonly by flying in. When flying to the U.S. from Canada, one goes through U.S. immigration at the Canadian airport. One Canadian writer at JFK Airport witnessed a draft dodger being picked up who had cleared immigration in Ontario. The U.S. inspector had submitted the young man's name to a master list in Washington and then phoned JFK when it was learned that he had been indicted for draft evasion. Deserters took the risk less often, especially after a Pentagon directive over the signature of Deputy Secretary David Packard ordering special computerized files to be kept on all U.S. deserters including those in Canada and other countries. The Pentagon had also asked Congress to increase the reward for a civilian apprehending a deserter above the existing bounty of $25 plus expenses. All military desertions were hereafter to be linked with the FBI's computerized National Crime Center so that police in the smallest communities could quickly check out any young man they picked up. The directive ordered the establishment of a Deserter Information Point in each branch of the military and also required that reports be sent to the Assistant Secretary of Defense on each deserter "known to have gone to a foreign country for the apparent or stated purpose of protesting U.S. policies or engaging in subversive acts." The RCMP has access to the files of the FBI's National Crime Information Center, but this fact does not change anything for deserters in Canada, excepting of course police abuse or a change in Canadian government policy toward deserters. The people for whom this new crackdown was an absolute terror were the tens of thousands of young men hiding out from the armed forces in the U.S.

Fewer people were running the border following the 1969 shooting of a deserter who attempted to enter the U.S. from Quebec, was discovered, pulled a gun and wounded a border guard, then tried to run back toward Canada. The border patrol called his death suicide and the *New York Times* recorded it as such. His friends in Montreal said he was definitely not suicide-prone, though he was foolish enough to carry a gun and attempt to visit the U.S. New York State police tracked him down a half mile or so from the U.S. Customs shed in the direction of Canada. No one could explain why he would run for his freedom and commit suicide at the same time. Following this incident, all U.S. border guards east of the Great Lakes were issued weapons along the "friendly, undefended border." The Canadians were infuriated. The Americans explained there were dangerous drug dealers who cross at these points. Another reason to think twice about making needless forays into the motherland was Operation Intercept which, in effect, continues to be conducted along the Canadian border. Canadians, whose Liberal Party (Trudeau's party) recently voted at its annual convention in favor of government control and distribution of marijuana and hashish, were not pleased with the treatment they were receiving at the border as the American customs officers relentlessly searched their cars in their war on grass and hash. Two buses with 107 young people and their chaperones on board were detained for five hours when they attempted to attend the Woodstock Music Festival in 1969. One bus was kept sealed in 100-degree heat for more than five hours. Everyone was stripped, one by one, girls to bras and panties; clothing, baggage, and the buses were searched, and three people were arrested for possession of marijuana. A forty-seven-year-old female chaperone for the young group, an immigrant to Canada from Austria, was also stripped. She said later, "The way we were shoved around I thought I was back in the war again with the Nazis. I never want to see the U.S.A. again." The buses were forced to return to Canada. Only the Canadian papers reported the outrage. Learning of incidents such as these, fewer exiles dared to travel south. Unless, as *AMEX* put it, "you know someone with a remote farm that straddles the border."

In 1968, two exiles, David Schwartz and Raymond Zimmerman, in widely reported cases, returned to the U.S. to face prosecution and jail after personally deciding that remaining in Canada was not a valid antiwar statement. Some men, perhaps more than anyone likes to admit, returned out of sheer frustration and despair after a few months in Canada, hoping either to take their cases to court or, in the case of deserters, to receive court-martials for extended AWOLs by returning voluntarily. As militancy among the exiles increased, other men returned to join the underground because they felt they could not be politically effective any longer in Canada. Still others made brief incursions to engage in open political activities—the ADC of Montreal sent several deserter-delegates to the Revolutionary People's Constitutional Convention in Philadelphia. The militants were encouraged to think about going back by Tom Hayden who had exhorted them to "let the world know that you are going to return by whatever means necessary." Hayden had succeeded in making a certain extreme radical segment of Americans in Montreal and Toronto feel guilty about remaining in exile while "your brothers and sisters are dying down there."

For the most part, however, nearly all the exiles are resigned to remaining in Canada, if not for life, at least for a decade or two.

Few are optimistic enough to believe that a government which bases its existence on militarism and the nurturing of the corporate state which feeds that militarism is going to drop charges against people who refused to obey its military recruitment laws in the face of war. If President Nixon is not going to be the first U.S. president to lose a war, neither is he going to be the president who grants an amnesty to several hundred thousand people (in Canada, in the U.S., around the world) who have refused to fight the war he has decided not to lose. Nevertheless, a great many people in the U.S. have been talking seriously of the possibility of an amnesty for the war refugees.

In 1968 Senator McCarthy mentioned several times during his campaign that he favored a "kind of amnesty" for dodgers who've fled to Canada. In August 1968, seven protestant bishops signed a Clergy and Laymen statement urging amnesty for those who have fled or been jailed. In December 1968, several hundred people made a Christmas trip to Allenwood Federal Prison in Pennsylvania to hold a "celebration of conscience" for twenty-seven prisoners and to back appeals to President Johnson for a Christmas amnesty for those in prison or exile. In January 1969, *Avant Garde* magazine wrote in a straightforward editorial:

> By now only the believers in the myth of military "victory" and the mad dogs in our midst are not united in the hope that the Vietnam War will soon be ended. The pursuit of peace has suddenly become the official policy of our government. And yet America's martyrs to peace, thousands of protesters and draft resisters, men and boys whose crime has been that of saying "no" to a national moral disaster, are being prosecuted, jailed, and driven into foreign exile with unparalleled ferocity. These are America's political prisoners.

The magazine called for an "Amnesty now . . . for the exiles who fled in their dismay at a homeland that appeared to them to have gone mad, to have deserted *them*. Let us waive the unjust law and bring them back, if they will have us."

In February 1969, William Sloan Coffin and a delegation from Clergy and Laymen met with Henry Kissinger to ask for a postwar amnesty for those in jail or "self-exile" for refusal to be drafted or to fight in Vietnam. Needless to say, the administration was not swayed. Discussing Coffin's draft resistance speeches and his meeting with Kissinger, Tom Wicker in the *New York Times* wrote convincingly on the possibility and political propriety of amnesty. Wicker's reasonableness, however, has not been shown to be in any way matched by reason on any level in the White House, to which the column is directed. It is talking to the air, but it is good talk anyway:

> For how long can and should a nation punish political dissenters? . . . At first glance amnesty might appear politically difficult for President Nixon, even after a settlement of the war; yet it would represent the kind of magnanimity that enlightened nations often pursue and usually boast of. Practically speaking, an amnesty would provide a bridge between him and the younger generation as would almost no other step.
>
> Is a permanent band of American exiles to be left reproachfully in Canada or Sweden? Or, as these exiles drift back one by one over the years, are the divisions and animosities of the Vietnam era to be kept alive by repeated prosecutions and jailing for offenses long past? Even the contention that amnesty would foster great disrespect for the conscription law runs afoul of Mr. Nixon's own criticism of that law and his repeated pledges to abolish it and provide a volunteer army.
>
> It is not true that amnestied youths will have paid no price. To stand on moral grounds against the general view is never easy—physical exile is a haunting personal situation; and the fact that amnesty for draft resisters is so controversial a matter suggests that all too many who choose exile on an issue of conscience will find no real end to it when they return to the society that bred them.

Wicker assumes the United States is still an "enlightened" nation. He also recognizes that amnesty is an improbable issue before a "settlement of the war." That was over two years ago. Today, as I write this, U.S. fighter-bombers are laying waste to the outskirts of Phnom Penh after destroying nearly half the villages of once lovely Cambodia. B-52s are flying heavier raids than ever before over Indochina. What settlement of the war was Wicker optimistically alluding to in 1969? (I fully expect to see Tom Wicker in exile before any of us are found legally returning home. He will be welcome.)

Also in February 1969, Senator Edward Kennedy presented a bill to revise the Selective Service laws and the final paragraph called for an amnesty study "to determine the appropriateness of granting amnesty in the near future to those registrants presently outside the United States who are liable for prosecution." The bill was defeated, and with it went the proposed study. In an interview Senator Kennedy noted that "many times in our history we have, as a nation, been magnanimous enough to grant amnesty." Two particular cases were Washington's amnesty to the farmers who staged the Whiskey Rebellion and Andrew Johnson's 1868 amnesty for Southerners. Mentioning these precedents, Dr. John Swomley, of the Methodist St. Paul School of Theology, asked in a speech, "If presidents could grant amnesty for the more serious offense of armed insurrection, why should amnesty be withheld from men who were apparently motivated by humanitarian opposition to war?" That's what the resisters would like to know.

In April 1969, Representative Edward Koch of Manhattan introduced H.R. 10501, a bill which would enlarge the definition of conscientious objector to include conscientious opposition to military service in a particular war. Retroactive clauses allowed for people awaiting prosecution for draft evasion and those already convicted who have left the country to return and refile under the new law for conscientious objection to the Vietnam War. Another clause allowed men already inducted into the armed forces and men who had deserted to be temporarily exempt from combatant duties or punishment resulting from refusing such duties while they applied for discharge under the new definition of conscientious objection. As it related to the exiles, Koch's proposed legislation was dubbed "the second chance bill." It was academic for the exiles to discuss whether or not they would return to take advantage of the law if it were passed for there was no chance it would be. I would hazard, however, that only a small minority would reopen their CO cases—others would take advantage of the restraining order on prosecutions to return for a visit—but it was doubtful many exiles were ready to take a second chance—with all the psychological havoc that entailed—with a system which had already denied them a first chance, a system they have no reason to trust. Neither could the thousands who left the country entirely on moral grounds be expected to compromise their stand against the war by crawling back to legally take advantage of one more loophole which would still favor the rich, the educated, the articulate. Few were ready to return to pay homage to a system with which they had once refused to cooperate and so the bill had little realistic bearing on the exiles' situation. The bill, in fact, which in succeeding months prompted much serious discussion, had little bearing on reality at all: Curtis Tarr, director of Selective Service, in a letter to Koch which was read into the *Congressional Record* in September 1969, stated unequivocally, ". . . I have concluded that the Selective Service System could not carry out its mission of insuring the maintenance of adequate armed forces if the law were to recognize selective objection [to a particular war]." At the same time, there was no conceivable way that Congress would consider a bill that would debilitate the draft system and at the same time allow hundreds of thousands of men to refuse combat or be discharged from the armed forces simply because they objected to the Vietnam War. This sort of opposition to the war by congressional "critics" seemed to exiles little better than absurd. A year and a half later Representative Koch's bill was still in committee.

In what was nonetheless a sincere attempt to have a first-hand look at the exile community in Canada, Representative Koch at the end of the year traveled to Toronto, Montreal, and Ottawa to meet with delegations of war resisters, becoming the first elected American official to do so. He was, at this time, more directly concerned with the issue of amnesty and whether the men in Canada warranted it or wanted it. At a New Year's Day 1970 press conference in New York Koch reported on his visit:

America has always welcomed immigrants from abroad who have fled religious and political persecution . . . now paradoxically America drives out its own young men and women of conscience—it is a shame and a disgrace. They should be welcomed back neither as heroes nor as criminals, but as young men who are doing their best to uphold the finest traditions of this country. It is time this country woke up to the fact that there are at least 45,000 young Americans and as many as 60,000 who, since 1965, have already emigrated to Canada and that thousands more are likely to follow. Amnesty surely should be considered and discussed by Americans—for our sakes as well as theirs—for what the Vietnam War has done to these young men and what it has forced them to do.

All Koch got for his honest appeal to American integrity was a mountain of abusive mail denouncing him and calling the exiles cowards, scum, and yellow-bellies who have no right to ever come back to America.

As Ed Koch was surprised to learn during his visit, there has been little discussion of amnesty in the exile community. Amnesty is viewed by most as an issue designed to assuage liberal guilt—"We will not be lackeys of liberal guilt," goes the cry—and salve for the consciences of liberals who were silent as the war was being expanded and exiles were making their decisions not to go. The ex-students among the exiles can recall such well-known liberals as McGeorge Bundy and Roger Hillsman arguing in favor of the war at teach-ins that had been called in protest. They knew what the war would lead to; they warned of the mounting casualties and what opening a land war on the Asian continent could mean. All along they were right, and they find it difficult now to respect the liberals who have only just discovered how right they were; or, if those leaders knew earlier that the war was wrong, they have certainly lost the exiles' respect for not throwing their weight against it before it was too late. The exiles did what they could; these liberals did nothing or made excuses. With few exceptions the exiles now see themselves, along with millions of people in the Third World, as victims of policies instituted by what is now little better than a criminal government. They are being forced to defend their responsibility as citizens to refuse to participate in murder. A government which legalizes murder as America has in Vietnam cannot be considered a legally constituted authority under the precepts of international law. Recognizing the United

States' own Nuremberg principle establishing individual responsibility in the face of a nation's criminal activities, the exiles have, as responsible citizens, refused to participate in their nation's crimes. They feel it is not for them to ask for clemency from the government which perpetrates those crimes. The men of that government have forfeited their right to judge others; now they must be judged. Amnesty assumes otherwise; it is the government's term, implying pardon for a wrongful act, a word which seeks to rectify mistakes of men whom the Left no longer considers to be legitimate authorities. Should these men be concerned with amnesty, it is a concern of their own making and it arouses no enthusiasm among the Americans in Canada.

There is no intention among the exiles of disparaging the efforts of those well-meaning people who have attempted to secure their return. They would welcome any such activity on their behalf although they may choose to define these earnest efforts in different terms, as not being fundamental to the *real* problem which is the criminality of the present government in the United States of America. For the exiles, to campaign for amnesty on that government's terms or give credence to such a campaign in the U.S. which, to quote an *AMEX* editorial, "like other liberal issues, asks for sympathy and trustworthiness from a viciously heavy-handed and conniving regime," would only dilute their manifest opposition to that government and its war. Their protest expresses much more than yearning for a speedy return and a safe niche in the American nightmare; it is a demand for radical change and an end to a system which sustains itself by rape, brigandage, and killing. *It is for the exiles to continually remind America who the real criminals are and not to spend their time hoping the criminals will forgive them.* Criminal may be a harsh word, but I don't know what else to call the men who are guilty of perpetuating poverty in a wealthy nation, plundering resources at home and abroad, and murdering over a million Vietnamese people. And what else but criminals are the men who are directly responsible for the wounding, disabling, or death of 350,000 American soldiers?

Dr. Don Burke, a resident surgeon in Montreal and a U.S.

Army deserter, writing in *Antithesis*, a magazine of the ADC, makes the point clearly:

> Our exile is a price we must be prepared to pay for allowing ourselves to be moved by sensitivities and insight, like those whose sensitivities and insight led them into opposition to the Nazi regime, of whom it would have been absurd to expect them to ask for forgiveness or even amnesty. For this would have meant that their opposition to the regime was wrong and the actions and politics of the regime were ultimately moral and therefore it had the right to dispense forgiveness or amnesty. Instead, they had to appeal to and wait for the powers which then represented freedom and liberation to indemnify them as victims of a criminal system. Today, as victims of U.S. criminal activity, we have the right not to ask forgiveness or amnesty but to demand full restoration of our civil rights as U.S. citizens and punitive action against those people whose political decisions have destroyed a nation, brutalized its people, and driven so many of us from its repressive and inhuman institutions into exile.

The exiles can never be entirely compensated, any more than the soldier who has lost a leg in Vietnam can expect to get it back, but, if their exile has influenced more people to resist conscription and resist within the military, activity which in the past five years has indisputedly brought changes in those institutions, then they have done some good and their sacrifice has not been without result. Like the wounded soldier, the exile is a casualty of war. Together, they can only hope that the war they either fought or opposed has at least forced a second look at the American system and has wrought change which, in the end, will be for the good.

There will be continued discussion, both in the U.S. and in Canada, concerning the future of the war resisters. The issue—amnesty in liberal terms, *repatriation* in the exiles' terms—should not be weakened by the fact that many of the exiles do not immediately wish to return to the United States. The question, really, is not whether or not they *want* to go back—that is a personal decision—but whether or not anyone, or any government, has the right to *prevent* them from returning when they have done nothing, in light of the Vietnam war, which can remotely be called a crime.

They have the inalienable right to return.